Oneida
Community

The Breakup, 1876-1881

A YORK STATE BOOK

Oneida Community

The Breakup, 1876-1881

Constance Noyes Robertson

SYRACUSE UNIVERSITY PRESS / 1972

HX
656
.O 5
R63

Library of Congress Cataloging in Publication Data

Robertson, Constance (Noyes)
  Oneida Community: the breakup, 1876–1881.
  xv, 327   *24 cm*
  (A York State book)
  Bibliography: p. *317 - 320.*
  1. Oneida Community.   *I. t*
  HX656.O5R63   335'.9'74764   72-38405
  ISBN 0-8156-0086-0

Manufactured in the United States of America

*To my sister Barbara
with all my love*

CONSTANCE NOYES ROBERTSON, granddaughter of John Humphrey Noyes, has lived most of her life in the Oneida area and has known many members of the old Community. Both her parents belonged to the Oneida Community generation called Stirpicults, and her father, Pierrepont B. Noyes, played an important part in reanimating the joint-stock company that succeeded the old Community, now the modern silversmiths, Oneida Limited. Mrs. Robertson is the author of nine published novels, including a book club selection, *Firebell in the Night,* and the companion to the present volume, *Oneida Community: An Autobiography, 1848–1876.*

Contents

Illustrations

Preface

As a third-generation product of the Oneida Community, I have heard the history of the old Community, from its founding in Putney, Vermont, to its maturity and later years in central New York, ever since I can remember. In a companion volume, *Oneida Community: An Autobiography, 1851–1876,* I discussed the beginning and middle years of the longest-lived and most successful of the mid-nineteenth-century attempts to create utopian communities. I felt it was the story of a happy people, led by my paternal grandfather, John Humphrey Noyes. The present story is not a happy one, but must be told to complete the history of the Oneida Community.

The various factors leading to the breakup of the Oneida Community on January 1, 1881, have never been examined in detail before. Based on extensive collections of private letters and documents, the present volume offers my own view of the causes of this tragic debacle. Many and often opposing theories have been promulgated by students and even by friends and descendants of the Oneida Community. Some of these theories seem superficial or biased or both. Some would appear to mistake the symptom for the disease. No simple solution to so complex a problem is convincing.

The only remaining evidence at this date must be found in the members' own writing, as published by themselves, or in the few precious surviving documents, private papers, diaries, and letters written during the crucial period. Critical examination of these accounts, testing them against each other, may, one can only hope, bring to light at least the main strands in this tangle; might, with enormous good luck, unravel it.

Besides the usual list of printed books and pamphlets published by and about the Oneida Community, all of which I have read and most of which I possess, I have been incredibly fortunate, first in the generosity of friends who have lent me family papers and diaries of the greatest interest, and secondly in what I can only describe as a windfall.

As has been stated elsewhere, the great mass—all, it was supposed at the time—of the archives of the old Community were destroyed after the death of Mr. George W. Noyes, in whose possession they had been for many years. In these archives were private papers, letters, journals of the Evening Meetings at both Oneida and Wallingford, minutes of the meetings of the council and certain of the committees and boards, as well as papers addressed to the Community by John Humphrey Noyes and other members and other miscellaneous material.

This was the material, it seems certain, which Mr. George Noyes intended to use in the third volume of his projected history of the Oneida Community, the first two volumes of which covered the religious experience of John Humphrey Noyes and the Putney Community. For this purpose he had selected material out of the archives, and either he, himself, or possibly a friend or one of his daughters, copied it by typewriter. It actually amounts to 798 foolscap pages, single-spaced; a veritable gold mine of irreplaceable documentation.

Mr. George Noyes's work on volume three was begun and carried, in rough draft, from the early days of the Community, January 22, 1855, to January 1878. After Mr. George Noyes's death, this manuscript was lent to his close friend and contemporary, Mr. Stephen R. Leonard, himself a descendant and a devoted student of the Community, who sorted and categorized the manuscripts, pasted some of the typed sheets together, and finally arranged them in a strong green binder, under appropriate headings. Since in the manuscript the story goes only as far as the end of the administration of Theodore Noyes and the return to power of his father in January 1878, Mr. Leonard, to complete the story, inserted in the book 145 pages of the typed material, carrying the account from June 28, 1880, to September 30, 1880. The hiatus of more than two years—from January 1878 to June 1880—remains a blank.

Or would have remained a blank except for what I have called my windfall. How it happened, why it happened, I have no idea. What I do know is that a year or two before his death, my father, Pierrepont Noyes, former president of Oneida Limited, asked me one day to take over two boxes of papers—he did not explain or describe them and I apparently did not ask him to—which he wanted me to have, to keep safe. I did so, stowing them rather carelessly under the eaves in my attic until around 1967 I came upon them, opened the boxes, and started reading their contents.

At first, because I had never paid especial attention to Community history, I did not understand them. What were these papers? How did they come there? Then I remembered my father's giving them to me, but I still could not imagine how he got them. As the only possible source of information, I appealed to my cousins, the daughters of George Noyes—Charlotte Noyes Sewall and Imogen Noyes Stone—who read them. They could not specifically identify them, but thought they must have been a part of their father's material. But that had all been destroyed. How did *my* father come by this treasure trove? No one living can tell me for certain.

It is proveable that the last 145 pages in Uncle George's green binder are identical with the last 145 pages of my collection of carbon copies. There are also other identifications of documents, letters, and so on, with material in several of the diaries I have been lent. There can be no doubt of the authenticity of these papers. It is merely the miraculous manner of their appearance that staggers the imagination. For convenience of reference, I have called them the PBN Papers, as distinguished from the G. W. Noyes Manuscript, but it is almost a certainty that they all came from the same source —the Oneida Community archives.

Of the diaries and journals which have been an invaluable source for this book, I must cite first the journal of Mr. Francis Wayland-Smith lent me most kindly by Prudence Wayland-Smith. It is the most lucid, well-written, and well-arranged diary of any I have seen, and, since he was intimately involved in the so-called political struggles going on during the years treated here, I have quoted from it extensively. The diaries of Tirzah C. Miller lent me by Imogen Noyes Stone are excellent, especially for the feminine version of O.C. history at that time. The diary of Cornelia J. Worden (later the wife of Francis Wayland-Smith), also lent by Prudence Wayland-Smith, is excellent, spare, and factual. The diaries, in several volumes, of my paternal grandmother, Harriet M. Worden, which belong to my sister, Barbara Noyes Smith, are a mine of information for the several years she kept them, and the half-dozen

quaint little notebooks written by Julia Ackley, my great-grand-
mother, which were left to me, tell largely of comings and goings
since for years her job was to receive and entertain "nice company."
There are, however, occasional tart little remarks I would not have
missed. The unpublished autobiography written in her late years by
Jessie C. Kinsley, the property of her granddaughter Jane Kinsley
Rich, is as charming as she was and in many ways informative.

Beyond these diaries, I have the O.C. *Register* for 1849, 1864,
1869, 1879, by different hands; The *Wallingford Journal,* January
2, 1880, to May 31, 1880; a diary that was kept at the "Brooklyn
School," 1849–50. I have also—not mine but in my keeping—at
least a dozen folders of miscellaneous material, letters, articles,
notes, and so on dating from the early days to twenty years after the
close of the Oneida Community, some of great interest, and all the
property of the O.C. Historical Committee.

I have had access also, through the kindness of my cousin,
Adele Noyes Davies, to copies of letters from Dr. Theodore R.
Noyes to Dr. Anita Newcomb McGee, written in 1891 and 1892;
other correspondence from Dr. McGee to J. B. Herrick; and a copy
of her article, "An Experiment in Human Stirpiculture," from the
*Proceedings of the American Association for the Advancement of
Science,* XL (1891); also a copy of the article, "A Gynecological
Study of the Oneida Community," by Dr. Ely van de Warker from
The Journal of Obstetrics, August 1884.

I am indebted to my cousins, Helen Noyes Wood and Albert
Kinsley Noyes, for permission to quote from "A History of the
Oneida Community, Limited," written by their father, Holton V.
Noyes, unpublished. It is particularly valuable as being the only account, in detail, of the history of the Oneida Community, Limited,
from its beginning. I must in this connection cite *A Goodly Heritage*
(New York: Rinehart, 1958), by my father, Pierrepont B. Noyes,
as giving from his own characteristic point of view the flavor of the
early years of "joint stock." Another family book from which I have
quoted here is *The Days of My Youth,* by my mother, Corinna
Ackley Noyes, privately published in 1960 when she was eighty-
eight years old and telling, from another viewpoint, the experiences
of a child at the breakup.

The other titles cited include my own collection of O.C. pamphlets, papers, and books, as well as some modern publications and all periodicals predating or published during the years of the Oneida Community.

It should be understood that beginning with Chapter 1 through Chapter 3, all quotations not otherwise identified are from the George W. Noyes Manuscript. From Chapter 4 to the end of the book, all quotations not otherwise identified are from what I have called the PBN Papers. All other sources are specified as letters, diaries, and journals, which, unfortunately, are privately owned and not available to researchers. A number of quotations from newspapers are dated only as they appeared in the *American Socialist.*

I should like to give especial thanks to certain persons who have spent generously of time and thought in the making of this book: to my sister, Barbara Noyes Smith; to my nephew, Pierrepont Geoffrey Noyes; to my cousins, Imogen Noyes Stone and Charlotte Noyes Sewall; to my friends, Helen Dick Davis and Winifred Halsted. I thank Rupert Smith for the skillful making of pictures, Nora Anthony and Virginia Rann for hours of Xeroxing and miles of typing, and Marie Magliocca for help in a hundred ways. I am as always indebted to the Oneida Community Historical Committee for material borrowed. Finally, I should like to thank my brother, Pierrepont T. Noyes, for his enthusiastic backing of this project, and my husband, Miles Robertson, for his patient endurance of a writing wife.

Autumn 1971   CONSTANCE NOYES ROBERTSON

Oneida
Community

The Breakup, 1876-1881

The Sea of Faith
Was once, too, at the full, and round earth's shore
Lay like the folds of a bright girdle furled.
But now I only hear
Its melancholy, long, withdrawing roar,
Retreating, to the breath
Of the night wind, down the vast edges drear
And naked shingles of the world.

MATTHEW ARNOLD, *Dover Beach*

Prologue

For nearly thirty years the members of the Oneida Community lived secluded, dedicated, and, by their own testimony, happy lives. They had unwavering faith in their own somewhat heterodox religion and in their leader, John Humphrey Noyes, whom they believed to be inspired by God. They practiced a social theory, Complex Marriage, which they held to be completely justified by their religious credo. They worked very hard and devoted not only their lives but all their worldly possessions to this cause. They put into actual practice the only experiment in human eugenics that has ever been tried. They lived together peacefully and lovingly. Quarreling, unkind behavior of any kind at any age was sure to bring down criticism upon the offender and hence was almost unheard of. Hurt feelings, jealousy, grudges were recognized as nothing but the offsprings of egotism. They called themselves Perfectionists or Bible Communists.

The history of the Oneida Community begins and, in some sense, ends with its founder, John Humphrey Noyes. A Vermonter, son of a well-to-do congressman and a conservative, Noyes graduated from Dartmouth. Then, after his conversion by one of the numerous popular evangelists of the period, in 1831, he left the practice of law, turned to the theological schools, first at Andover and later at Yale, where he was licensed to preach as a Congregational minister in 1833. But during all these years of training he had, as his father warned him, been in rebellion against authority. When he announced his new doctrine of Salvation from Sin, his father said, "That is heresy. They will whip you in."

"Never," young John replied. "Never will I accept any doctrine that does not commend itself to my mind and conscience."

1

The next year and for a dozen years to come he was to learn the penalties for such heresy. In 1834 he announced from the pulpit of the Free Church of New Haven, Connecticut, his text: "He that committeeth sin is of the devil." The effect was electrical. Word spread through the seminary and the town: "Noyes says he is perfect!" and immediately, "Noyes is crazy!" In response to the attacks of friend and foe alike, he replied, "I do not pretend to be perfect in externals. I claim only purity of heart and the answer of a good conscience toward God." Within weeks he was notified that his license to preach had been rescinded and he was asked to leave the seminary.

This confession of sinlessness was made on February 20, 1834, a date always celebrated in the Oneida Community as "The High Tide of the Spirit." From this time onward the next several years were a kind of Valley of Humiliation for the young convert. Cut off from his college, his church, and his family, dropped by many of his erstwhile friends and adherents, he wandered, often on foot and without money, up and down New England, New York, and New Jersey, preaching, exhorting, spreading his new faith. Two ventures in publishing, *The Perfectionist* in 1834 and *The Witness* in 1837, were short lived.

In 1837 a letter written by Noyes to a friend and not intended for publication was printed in a new paper entitled *The Battle-Axe and Weapons of War* and called forth almost as much furor as his earlier announcement. Noyes's new theory adumbrated in this letter advocated neither a plurality of wives nor a community of wives but a nullity of wives: "When the will of God is done on earth as it is in heaven there will be no marriage. Exclusiveness, jealousy, quarrelling have no place in the marriage supper of the Lamb. In a holy community, there is no more reason why sexual intercourse should be restrained by law, than why eating and drinking should be—and there is as little occasion for shame in the one case as in the other."

As Mark Holloway wrote in *Heavens on Earth* (p. 183):

Since Noyes had made his unlawful system of sexual intercourse depend upon membership in a holy community, the next step was obviously to found one. In 1834 Noyes had returned to his parental home at Putney, Vermont. Here he began to give Bible classes and to convert his family to his views. Here he married, in 1838, Harriet

Holton, granddaughter of a lieutenant-governor of the state, and began to publish *The Witness* which was written, composed, type-set, printed and mailed by the family.

In 1840 the Putney Association came into being—as a purely religious body, thus described in *The Witness:*

"Our establishment exists in the midst of an ordinary village. A few families of the same religious faith, without any formal scheme of written laws, have agreed to regard themselves as one family, and their relations to one another are regulated as far as possible by this idea. The special object of the association is to support the publication of the gospel of salvation from sin. Formal community of property is not regarded by us as obligatory on principle but as expedient with reference to our present circumstances and objects. We are attempting no scientific experiments in political economy nor in social science. Our highest ambition is to be able to preach Christ and to act out as far as possible the family spirit of the gospel. When we find a better way than our present plan to attain these objects we shall freely change our mode of living."

In 1844 the group formally adopted communism, both of property and of family living and association, based on Noyes's *Battle-Axe* letter theory of Complex Marriage and regulated by his newly formulated ideas of what he called Male Continence—birth control —both of which were adopted by the Putney Community in 1846. These radical departures from the worldly norm were too much for their orthodox neighbors in the Vermont village. Noyes was indicted for adultery and on the advice of his lawyer brother-in-law, Larkin G. Mead, left the village and state. The other members bided their time until the next spring when, in March 1848, Noyes moved the whole group to a new setting he had purchased in Oneida Reserve, an area in upstate New York where a handful of his early converts had already begun a tiny commune. Here, in a farmhouse, a few outbuildings, a log hut, and a sawmill, was the true beginning of the Oneida Community.

In the first *Annual Report* which they published, January 1, 1849, they wrote:

The Oneida Association is located in a secluded valley on the Oneida Creek, in the towns of Lennox and Vernon and the counties of Madison and Oneida, in the State of New York, three miles south of Oneida Depot which is the half-way station between Utica and Syracuse. The lands of the Association are part of the territory reserved till recently to the Oneida Indians. The domain, consisting of 160 acres lying on both sides of the Creek is mostly alluvial soil of good quality. It includes an excellent water privilege which is now occupied by a saw mill and other lumber machinery and affords abundance of power for a grist-mill, machine shop and other works already projected by the Association.

On the first of January the whole number of persons connected with the Association was *eighty-seven*. Adults (over fifteen) fifty-eight; children (under fifteen) twenty-nine.

The professions of the male members are as follows, viz.: four are farmers; two are carpenters and machinists; two are cabinetmakers; two are blacksmiths; two are millers; two have been schoolteachers; two were bred to the ministry; one is a printer; one is a wagon-maker; one is a gun-smith; one a lead-pipe-maker; one has been a merchant and publishing agent. Some of the members are conversant with several other professions such as those of editors, architects, harnessmakers, masons, etc., etc.

The invitation to resettle in this new location came about after a convention at the tiny hamlet of Lairdsville, New York, where a man named Jonathan Burt, who owned a sawmill property at Oneida Reserve, together with three other families—the Ackleys, the Nashes, and the Hatches—had commenced a partial association on November 26, 1847.

In the latter part of January following, Burt and his associates invited J. H. Noyes by letter to visit Oneida. The *First Annual Report* recorded it:

The invitation was accepted and the result of the negotiation which ensued was that on the 1st of February the present Association was commenced by a full union between J. H. Noyes and J. Burt, and a transfer of $500.00 of U.S. Stock by J. H. Noyes to the stock of the new union. Purchases of land were immediately commenced and the whole of the present domain was soon secured, having two comfortable houses, besides Burt's. . . . In the course of the spring and summer, all the refugees from Putney, in all, seventeen members of the original Association, with their children, were reunited at Oneida.

Thus the Putney Association died and rose again. In the resurrection at Oneida the Association entered upon a period of growth. The Association has been enlarged to its present number by accessions of new members and families. Its first and strongest reinforcements came from the central counties of the state of New York. Subsequently it received a valuable colony from Northern Vermont and later still, was joined by a delegation from Massachusetts.

The original accommodations of the Association, consisting of two ordinary dwelling houses and two small cabins, were put to full occupation in the course of the year; but their capacity, with the help of ingenuity and good will proved to be almost indefinitely elastic, and sufficed (with the addition of a rough board shanty erected early for the dormitories of the young men) until more liberal quarters could be prepared.

THE ERECTION OF THE MANSION HOUSE

With a saw-mill at command, and all the timber necessary on the domain, and with a goodly number of carpenters and joiners in the Association, this undertaking was carried through pleasantly and successfully. The whole of the work except the plastering was done within the Association. All hands, whenever free from other necessary occupations, were merrily busy on the house. Even the women joined the sport and the lathing was mostly the work of their hands. Many valuable lessons in regard to gregarious and attractive industry were learned in this operation. The house was ready for occupation before the advent of winter, and gave the Association seasonable and ample relief from short quarters.

In connection with this main enterprise, the Association worked its farm successfully and kept the saw-mill and other lumber machinery in operation. It did not undertake or expect, however, by these or other labors, to meet the expenses of the year, but looked mainly to the capital coming in with its members and to the subsidies of its friends for subsistence and the means of building, regarding this first year as properly and necessarily one of preparation and outlay. The opportunities and prospects of the Association for profitable business, in lumbering and several kinds of manufacturing already commenced or contemplated, are very good, and it is not unreasonable to expect that after the present season of necessary preparation, it will become a self-supporting institution.

Previous to the completion of the Mansion House, no special classification was attempted in the arrangement of the households. However, when the Mansion House came to be occupied, the following classification took place. The best of the ordinary houses was converted into a nursery and all the children between the ages of two and twelve (seventeen in number) with the necessary housekeepers and teachers were established there, by themselves. The other principal dwelling house was also converted into a nursery and given up to the infants (six in number) with their nurses and housekeepers. This arrangement proved to be very favorable to the comfort and goodbreeding of the children, and at the same time saved the main household of the Association from much noise and confusion. The women serving as attendants of the children for short periods only and in rotation, found the business not a burden but a pleasure.

The meals of the Association at the Mansion House were served at one table, extending through the dining room and were alike for all, not differing materially in quality from the meals of respectable households in ordinary life.

Early in the summer, in consequence of some speculation on the subject of women's dress, some of the leading women of the Association took the liberty to dress themselves in short gowns or frocks with pantaloons (the fashion common among children) and the advantages of the change soon became so manifest that others followed the example, till frocks and pantaloons became the prevailing fashion in the Association. Another new fashion broke out among the women. The ordinary practice of leaving the hair to grow indefinitely and laboring upon it by the hour daily, merely for the sake of winding it up into a ball and sticking it on the top or back of the head, had become burdensome and distasteful. There was a general feeling in the Association that any fashion which required women to devote considerable time to hair-dressing is a degradation and a nuisance. Accordingly some of the bolder women cut off their hair and started the fashion which soon prevailed throughout the Association and was generally acknowledged to be an improvement of appearance as well as a saving of labor.

After the concentration in the Mansion House, a gathering in the spacious parlor after supper became a matter of course every evening. At the ringing of the bell all came together and immediately the roll of the Association was called, not for the purpose of ascertaining the presence or absence of the members (as all were free in this respect) but in order to give each member an opportunity and invitation to present any reflections, expressions of experience, proposals in relation to business, exhortations or any other matter of general interest that might be on the mind waiting for vent. Systematic provision, however, was made for a series of exercises suitable for occupying that part of the evening which remained after roll-call. Monday evening was devoted to readings in the parlor from the public papers; Tuesday evening to lectures by J. H. Noyes on the social theory; Wednesday evening to instructions and exercises in phonography; Thursday evening to the practice of music; Friday evening to dancing; Saturday evening to readings from Perfectionist publications; Sunday evening to lectures and conversation on the Bible.

The Association, though it has no formal creed, is firmly and unanimously attached to the Bible, as the text-book of the Spirit of Truth; to Jesus Christ, as the eternal Son of God; to the apostles and the Primitive Church as the exponents of the everlasting gospel. Its belief is that the second advent of Christ took place at the period of the destruction of Jerusalem; that at that time there was a primary resurrection and judgment in the spiritual world; that the final kingdom of God then began in the heavens; that the manifestation of that kingdom in the visible world is now approaching; that its approach is ushering in the second and final resurrection and judgment; that a church on earth is now rising to meet that approaching kingdom in the heavens and to become its duplicate and representative; that inspiration or open communication with God and the heavens, involving perfect holiness, is the element of connection between the church on earth and the church in the heavens and the power by which the kingdom of God is to be established and reign in the world.

A system of *mutual criticism* has been relied on for regulating character and stimulating improvement. This system was instituted by the Putney Association during the period of its most rapid advancement in spiritual life and was introduced to some extent at Oneida but the number of members was so large that it was found necessary to change the mode of proceeding in order to make it lively and effective. Instead of subjecting volunteers for criticism to the scrutiny of the assembly, the Association appointed four of its most spiritual and discerning judges to criticize in course all the members. The testimony of one of the members was, "The effect of criticism on me has stirred up an ambition and energy for improvement and increased my love and confidence in those I have received it from."

One of John Humphrey Noyes's most original concepts was what he called the Law of Fellowship, ascending or descending. Ascending Fellowship was the association between persons so that the drawing of the fellowship was upward, from the less spiritually minded to the more devout; Descending Fellowship was a drawing of the fellowship downward. It was possible for an individual to realize when he had reached the point where it was safe for him to indulge in Descending Fellowship. Even the children were instructed in this matter and were frequently criticized for too much "horizontal fellowship" which they found could lead to trouble.

The *Second Annual Report* was published on February 20, 1850. At this time they announced that their whole number of members was 172. They had enlarged their domain to a total of 218 acres and had erected a new children's house, a building for a store, and two added wings on the original Mansion House—total cost: $4,400. They calculated that for the past year the cost of board for all members including the children was $.45 per week for each individual. The cost of clothing, $10.50 per individual per year. "In association," they wrote, "where a spirit of love and accommodation rules, much saving and convenience in the article of clothing may be secured by exchanges. Thus a dozen garments, as overcoats, cloaks, etc., suitable for going abroad are found sufficient to accommodate the whole Community."

It was true, they admitted, that the Association had not for the past year supported itself by its own production. That it had *nearly* preserved its capital was a fact that gave them entire satisfaction with the past and full confidence in the future. That labor had become attractive there, they said, was a fixed fact in their experience:

> The repugnance universally connected with labor in the world is not repugnance to *action,* purely considered. That, of itself, is natural to man, wholly congenial to his constitution and taste. It is the goading demon of necessity which imposes labor as a condition of *"getting a living"* that makes it revolting to the soul. Here we have been enabled to rise above this feeling of necessity. The practice of doing work "by storm," or in what is more commonly called a "bee," in which men, women and children engage, has been found very popular and effective. It may be employed in a great variety of operations, especially of outdoor business, and always contributes to enliven and animate the most uninteresting details of work.

The *Third Annual Report,* published February 20, 1851, announced an increase of thirty-three members during the past year, bringing the number up to 205, of which three were born in the Association. There had been one death and one member expelled. Of the living members there were sixty-nine adult male members, sixty-six adult females, twenty youth of both sexes, and fifty children under ten years of age. At this time there were thirteen members living in the Brooklyn commune, including those engaged on the sloop; five at Newark, New Jersey; and eight at a new commune on a farm at Manlius, New York.

During the winter of 1850–51 a Connecticut couple, Mr. and Mrs. Henry Allen, became converted to Community ideas and donated their farm of more than two hundred acres at Wallingford to Community use. Mary Cragin, a much beloved member, was sent there in the spring of 1851 to start a school for the children and even the older members of the new colony. Its buildings were, as Robert Allerton Parker wrote in *A Yankee Saint,* "comparatively rustic. Its small wooden buildings, without ornament inside or out, were 'without modern conveniences—even without a door bell. Here our hall is a plain unshapely room and for music we have only a parlor organ and some singing girls.' The Wallingford Community was, by train, only a half-hour distant from New Haven and Yale and was used in the sixties and seventies as headquarters for the young men from the Community who were sent to the University."

Here they developed a factory for making silk thread, as they did at Oneida, and it was here that the spoon-making business was begun. The *Circular,* their paper which succeeded the *Spiritual Magazine,* was edited and printed here for four years, from 1864 to 1868, and book binding was also one of their industries. Perhaps its main value to the Community was as a resort, a change for the members. A small cottage was bought at nearby Short Beach, on the Sound, and was called Cozicot, a favorite vacation place in summer, corresponding to Joppa, the cottage on Oneida Lake for the Oneida group. The Wallingford property remained in the possession of the Oneida Community as long as it existed and passed to the ownership of the joint stock company after the breakup.

Aside from minor additions and improvements to the main Community dwelling, the Mansion House, the main improvement of that year was the erection of a large and very substantial building for mechanical purposes, on the ground formerly occupied by the Indian sawmill. It embraced, they said, a sawmill, a shingle machine, a flouring mill, machine shop, and mechanics' shop for wagonmakers and carpenters, with appropriate machinery. They hoped to use the attic for a printing office and to "secure the advantage of water-power in working the power press." The estimated value of the new buildings was $5,850. They also reported spending $2,089.61 for the purchase of fifty-five acres of valuable land which increased the domain to 271 acres.

"Motives of *policy,* as well as good taste and the habits of the community life, invite our efforts in the direction of making our domain a *garden,* rather than what is usually understood by the term *farm.*" However, the keeping of cattle and hogs, they remarked rather scornfully, was less prosperous than any other department "which accords with our idea of a perfect life and the destiny to which we are called. It is not in the line of our ambitions or attractions to make a main business of waiting on animals."

But what was more important than any other accomplishment of the past year was the developing of a satisfactory "theory of the *organization* of *trades.*" They wrote in the *Third Annual Report:* "The ideal to which we are committed—perfect unity—demands not only the organization of individuals into the community spirit, through subordination of one to another, but it requires a similar organization in everything; and primarily in the department of labor. Say that industry has everywhere a common object, which is getting a living; this common object, instead of tending to real organization, is precisely and necessarily calculated to produce the distraction which we see. Instead of proving a bond of union and order, it is the genius of endless confusion."

Printing, the Communists declared, was "the art which stands nearest related to mind and spirit." In this aspect it took precedence of agriculture and all other trades. "We propose then," they wrote, "that the publication of truth shall be our central business object around which all other industrial interests shall organize. We do not look to have introduced among us any system of agriculture or manufactures as a *leading* interest; but are content to fill the position of *producers of the truth.*"

As late as September 1853, in the *Circular,* under the heading "Programme of the Millennium," they name horticulture as the "leading business for subsistence," and this announcement continued to appear on their front page until December 5, 1854. From that date until January 25, 1855, there occurred a hiatus in their publication owing, as they explained, to the removal of their printing plant from what they called the Brooklyn Commune to Oneida, "an interval of removal, confusion, rest and commencing reorganization," after which they promised to bring out an improved paper, once weekly instead of the ambitious tri-weekly of the year before, but one "improved by the education experienced in the Brooklyn campaign and with a broader basis and greater momentum." Their new masthead, under the heading Business Directory, advertised nursery fruit trees, rustic furniture, seats, tables, arbors, steel traps, sewing silk, traveling bags, an assortment of our own manufacture, palm-leaf hats, milling, job printing and designing, and wood engraving. All these at Oneida, while the Newark Commune offered printing presses, jewelers' tools, and machinists' lathes; the Putney Commune advertised gardening, nursery, milling; and the Wallingford Commune announced fruit and market gardening, milling, and traveling bags, according to the *Circular,* January 25, 1855. No mention anywhere of horticulture as a leading business for subsistence.

In a financial history of the Oneida Community, published in the *Circular* for January 9, 1865, they admitted that, although strongly advised to do so by an enthusiastic admirer, they did not take an annual inventory—nor actually adopt any accurate system of bookkeeping—until 1857. During that period of nine years they had established and then, from motives of economy, abandoned, five or six branch communes, and by 1857—a year of bank failures and tight money—they had reduced their holdings to the large community at Oneida and a smaller one at Wallingford, Connecticut. Nevertheless, they confessed, in the *Circular,* January 9, 1865, that "between the years 1848 and 1857, the Associated Communities sunk, in round numbers $40,000.00." "But," they added, it was "invested in our own Education, which is like sinking an oil well— expensive at first but lucrative afterwards, *if you strike oil.*"

Fortunately, they did "strike oil." During the succeeding eight years, from 1857 to 1865, their net earnings amounted to $154,998.62. Fifteen years later, by the end of 1880, their total worth was a half-million dollars. In 1864 they employed an average of one hundred persons not Community members. In 1868 they reduced their chief industries to four: steel traps, sewing silk, preserved fruits and vegetables, and the manufacture of bags of various kinds, with brief forays into such sidelines as silk ribbon, mop handles, and strawberry boxes. The tableware business was started in 1877.

After several unpleasant experiences with lawsuits or threats of such, the leading men of the Community realized that they must have effective legal protection from these attacks. They consulted Ward Hunt, a respected lawyer in Utica, who helped them to change their original constitution to a "Constitution of the Four." Under this new constitution, all Community property was transferred to four "property owners"—a committee consisting of John H. Noyes, Erastus Hamilton, William H. Woolworth, and Charles Otis Kellogg. It was specifically stated that this arrangement was merely one of convenience and that every member still had equal ownership of the Community's assets. By this method they placed themselves beyond the possibility of blackmail or extortion. To the end of the Oneida Community its property remained legally in the possession of the Four, until it was formally transferred to the joint-stock company known as Oneida Community, Limited.

In the course of time it was inevitable that there should be occasional bad years when economy and tight belts were the watchwords; business slumps in the country affected them as it did other businesses. But they survived and in general prospered, and, through bad times and good, they never abandoned their "central business object"—the publication of truth. The *Circular* was published from 1851 to April 1876, to be followed by the *American Socialist*, 1876–79. For parts of three years they published a tiny paper, intended only for themselves, called variously the *O.C. Daily* and the *Daily Journal*, briefly in 1863 and again in 1867 and 1868. The last issue of their final publication, the *American Socialist*, appeared in December 1879. The next year, although the main businesses were kept running, the Oneida Community, as such, practically ceased to exist, and its members were absorbed in the painful business of preparing to enter what they had always called "the World."

Names mentioned in the chapters to follow are of persons who played parts in the events of the breakup important enough to deserve particular introduction to the reader. Although John Humphrey Noyes moved to Niagara Falls, Canada, in 1879 and still continued to influence Community life as its leader in spirit, various individuals, by various means, tried to rechart the Community's direction. Chief among these were James W. Towner, a comparative newcomer to the Community. His "right bower" and a member from the earliest days was William A. Hinds, a man highly intelligent and of a subtle mind. These two, together with Mr. Henry W. Burnham, an ex-Millerite, an ex-Congregational minister, and a member from the early Vermont days, with a considerable following of relatives and friends, comprised the so-called Townerite party in the final struggle for control of the Community.

On the other side, Mr. Erastus Hamilton acted as Mr. Noyes's viceregent after his departure; he was a religious man, deeply devoted to Community principles, but not a strong leader.

At his side were Albert Kinsley and his eldest son, Myron, George Campbell, one of the early New Jersey converts, Homer and Alfred Barron, Vermont born, and George Miller, a nephew of JHN. These, together with a majority of the members of the Community, formed what came to be called the Loyalists. The political contest of the last years was further complicated by what was called the Third party, consisting of Theodore Noyes, son of the founder, and Francis Wayland-Smith and Edwin Burnham, young intellectuals and independent thinkers who opposed the Townerites and were personally attached to John Humphrey Noyes but in this crisis advocated conversion of the Community into a joint-stock company.

Since from the beginning women's roles in the management of the Community had been important and respected, those mentioned most frequently hereafter are Ann Hobart, for a time the leading "Mother" of the Community; Harriet Skinner, sister of JHN and a fighter with a mind of masculine strength, a keen intuition, and a gift of lively expression; and Augusta Towner, née Hamilton, described by one member as "proud and haughty," but certainly aggressive and combative in the contest that followed. Tirzah and Helen Miller, nieces of JHN, were his devoted adherents; Harriet Worden was in the anomalous position of being devoted to Mr. Noyes while at the same time being a friend to Mr. Towner, which left her, at the end, between wind and water, as the saying goes, bereft of all support.

With their background, their lifelong habit of harmony and unity, the dissension, hard feelings, recriminations, the division into opposing parties which darkened those last years were not only painful but actually shocking to all the members of the Community, whichever party they espoused. When, in 1879, after more than three years of growing discord and virtually leaderless, they abandoned their social theory and retreated to marriage "after the fashion of the world," even communism of property was untenable. They spent most of the next year, 1880, in working out the best and fairest plan for dissolving the old bonds and providing for the support and safety of the men, women, and children who had for so many years been Oneida Communists. The businesses and other properties were transformed into a joint-stock company under the title of Oneida Community, Limited, and Bible Communism was at an end.

When any seemingly thriving institution suddenly is seen to fail, the beholders, be they well-wishers or enemies, naturally try to account for the failure. It was because of this, say some; or because of that, say others. If it is an event of enough importance or is strange enough to warrant even a small place in history, it and the debate concerning it will continue, and perhaps no one will ever discover the true inwardness of what happened. But this is fairly certain: no one thing was the cause of it.

In so common a happening as a divorce, the breakup of a single marriage, the odds must be a hundred to one against a single simple cause for the parting. In the case of the dissolution of the Oneida Community, where there was not a single but a complex marriage, where there was not the usual small family unit but a family unit of nearly three hundred persons, the odds against a single, simple cause of its breakup must be astronomical. And add to the incredibly complicated web of human relations existing there the almost equally complicated structure of its business organization and you have a riddle to daunt a modern Oedipus.

The answer to this riddle must be a multiple cause, a weaving together of a number of strands, each one originally separate and in itself powerless to bring about the final disaster, but together of irresistible effect. To understand this effect it will be necessary to trace each of these strands back as nearly as possible to its first appearance in the fabric of the Community; to study it from its harmless beginning to its fatal end. And because the Community fabric was composed of human beings, it will be necessary to deal with persons and personalities. The story will not be a happy one.

Although these strands may be named separately, in the actual event, of course, they were almost inextricably intermingled. However, for the purpose of this book they must be recognized clearly for what they were.

First and perhaps most important was the dominant influence of John Humphrey Noyes—his many-faceted intelligence, his magnetism, the intuitive wisdom with which he dealt with the human problems bound to arise in a community of two or three hundred persons, the warmth of his outgoing nature, in short, the truly indescribable gift of natural leadership. While he was in his prime, which lasted well into his fifties, he was a kind of embodiment of security to his followers; his faith was unquestionably their faith, his wishes were their will, they believed that they prospered because of his "luck," by which he meant his inspiration from Christ and Saint Paul. When age and infirmity, in the form of deafness and a throat ailment which largely prevented his public speaking, to some degree lessened his effectiveness, his hold over his flock weakened, as it was bound to do. But as long as he lived, at Oneida and even after his retirement to Niagara Falls, a majority of his followers remained loyal to him. Those who disagreed with him formed an opposition party. This division between the Noyesites and the anti-Noyesites was a major strand in the multiple cause of the final disaster.

Probably second in importance, Complex Marriage, the Community's name for their social system of each married to all instead of the world's system of monogamy, was a feature which had been eagerly subscribed to for twenty-five years but which became in the end one of the most serious disputes between the dissident parties. In the Community the practice of this unique system was regulated by a strict discipline during all its successful and harmonious years, but toward the end it became the subject of a bitter struggle for control between the old regime and the new party which wanted new freedom and new rules.

The original point at issue between the opposing parties was the Community's lifelong rule that in order to avoid unwanted propagation which it could not afford, it was better for the young of both sexes to associate sexually with persons already initiated into the practice of Male Continence. According to the doctrine of Ascending Fellowship, it was deemed important also that the young should associate with persons with superior experience and character which, of course, meant those of both sexes, older than themselves. Mr. Noyes, as the leader both religiously and secularly, was naturally the acme of Ascending Fellowship, and thus he, and certain of his central members, undertook this responsibility.

Although there was some talk of legal action, actually there was never any such attack upon the Community. The opposition party, led principally by James Towner and William Hinds, had other grievances; they complained of Mr. Noyes's autocratic government of the Community, called for a freer system of Complex Marriage, and demanded more voice in the management of the businesses. What began as a personal complaint finally took shape as a budding revolution which, in the end, in spite of a majority of loyal members representing the old way of life, succeeded in overthrowing the Oneida Community.

It should perhaps be noted here that the frequent use of the phrases "social theory" or "social practices" which occur in all the Community material is, as Theodore Noyes wrote to Dr. Anita Newcomb McGee in 1892, "a localism—confined to the Community. It arose in the early days, as an euphemism, I suppose, for the word *sexual* before the word *social* was used so much in its economic sense as nowadays."

John Humphrey Noyes's son, Dr. Theodore Noyes, wrote of it many years after the end of the Community, in a letter to a fellow physician:

In opposing your view that the monogamic instinct was a chief factor in overthrowing complex marriage I said that the quarrel was one over government, but qualified the statement by adding "especially in the conduct of the system of complex marriage which was peculiarly his [JHN's] own, where his hand was always on the helm." To get at it, you must realize that the government of the Community was *by* complex marriage. Much has been said about mutual criticism and in itself it certainly was a very powerful force in favor of law and order, but all moral government, no matter how benign, in the end has to look to penalties for its enforcement. The power of regulating the sexual relations of the members, inherent in the family at large and by common consent delegated to Father and his subordinates, constituted by far the most effectual means of government. Father possessed in a remarkable degree the faculty of convincing people that the use of this arbitrary power was exercised for their own good, and for many years there was very little dissatisfaction and no envy of his prerogative. Of course I do not pretend to say that this was the only inducement to good conduct; for the obligations of religion had a very high place in the Community, and even in the line of penalties these were the same as exist in all business organizations and armies, viz., degradation from position for misconduct and promotion for good behavior. But for the close relations of complex marriage the power of an arbiter, to bind and unloose, is an absolute essential, at least in the present average moral development of human nature.

Another strand of the greatest difficulty in this tangled web was the practice of what the Community called Stirpiculture, or race culture, equivalent to what is known nowadays as eugenics or genetics. This had been an ambition of the Community since its inception but owing to their poverty it had been impossible to put into practice. The *Circular,* January 23, 1858, stated: "The subject of bearing and rearing children, though second to none in interest, has been for various considerations postponed until we should arrive at it in the due order of things. Childbearing, when it is undertaken, should be a voluntary affair, one in which the choice of the mother, and the sympathy of all good influences should concur. Our principles accord to woman a just and righteous freedom in this particular, and however strange such an idea may seem now, the time cannot be distant when any other idea or practice will be scorned as essential barbarism."

By 1869 they had become sufficiently prosperous so that a committee was appointed to study the matter and then to approve certain matings between more than four score young people who had volunteered to take part in the project. By 1879, sixty-two children had been born under this system before changes in the control and structure of the Community necessitated the closing of the only controlled experiment in selective breeding of human beings ever tried. The idea was enthusiastically welcomed by the whole Community at first, but in the uneasy political climate of the last years it, too, became a bone of contention and must be listed as one cause of the final struggle.

A fourth and not necessarily less important strand was the only major psychological error in a career of successfully radical innovations. The error was a very human one. After four still-births, the only living child of the marriage of John Noyes and his wife, Harriet, was a son, Theodore. Although it was against Noyes's own theory of Special Love, it must seem to any biographer reviewing Noyes's career that his feeling for this first-born son was a partiality which he did not recognize but which he never got over. Considering this, how very human it was that this father should try, over and over again, to make this son his successor. He was wise enough to realize, as he said to the Community in May 1877, that "a father has the right to give his property to his son, irrespective of that son's character. I do not claim that right. I have renounced it and pledged myself to the Community that I will never commit its government to an unbeliever or to one who is in any way unfit to be its leader."

After his four years at Yale, Theodore was an avowed unbeliever. For this reason he had left the Community in 1873 and only returned on the proviso that he consider himself in training which he hoped would eventually result in reconversion to the religion of his father and the Community. A year and a half later, when his father again nominated him as leader of the Community, Theodore said in a letter of thanks, "I can honestly say that faith which realizes the substance of things hoped for is the trait which commands my highest respect." He also said that it was his ambition to unite science and religion in the true proportions, but beyond this the records never show that he publicly or privately confessed to a true conversion to a belief in God, Christ, or Salvation from Sin. In this sense, Theodore's apostasy and his father's persistence in placing him at the head of the Community form a broad stripe in the twisted pattern of the Community's final web.

As a sort of footnote to the ill-starred reign of Theodore as leader of the Community must be listed his unfortunate conjunction with Ann Hobart. She was the young woman, attractive and intelligent, who had worked with Theodore as a medium in his spiritualistic investigation. After his apotheosis as leader in 1877, she, although never appointed as such by Mr. Noyes or the Community elders, became the "Mother" of the Community. For various reasons, the combined rule of Theodore and Ann came under criticism by the majority of the Community and finally by John Humphrey Noyes. The uncomfortable situation ended in a severe criticism of Ann and her confession and retirement, after which she left the Community. It also ended Theodore's final attempt at leadership.

Another strand, difficult either to date or document exactly, was the fact that even before the "Great Discussion"—which was Theodore's first formal rejection as leader of the Community—a spirit of unrest had been abroad in the Community, vague at first but finally polarized in the leadership of a few men into an opposition party. At this time, 1875, a group had formed under the leadership of a recent joiner who had made his presence felt at first as a religious man and a follower of JHN and later as his fiercest opponent and who finally carried with him a fair number of the Community members as his partisans. This man, James Towner, came from a free love community at Berlin Heights in Ohio, in 1874, and had been variously a minister, a soldier, a lawyer, and a judge. He was a powerful and rather romantic personality, and his presence in these troubled waters created a turbulence difficult and finally impossible to quell.

Two other probable influences are described by Theodore Noyes in a letter written in 1892:

There were two things which tended to lessen Father's influence in religious thought which had grown up in the Community in its later years and which had some secondary bearing as leading up to the change. But he had introduced them both himself in the hope of bettering his position and, so far as I know, neither had much bearing on Complex Marriage. In the first place there were some of the younger generation who tended to what is now called Agnosticism or Scientific Materialism. As a corrective to this Father proposed an experimental study of "mesmerism" and "spiritualism"; I, myself, undertook an extensive course of reading in this line and traversed the whole matter experimentally and visited all the prominent mediums of the country. The result was somewhat different from Father's anticipation for, while the materialists were somewhat liberalized by their investigation, some of his oldest religious disciples, who had never questioned his inspirations, turned spiritualist and found independent sources of spiritual communion. They, however, remained loyal to him in temporal and social affairs, with one or two exceptions, and did not join in the opposition which led to dissolution. So this did not contribute much to the change directly, but it led to new habits of independent thought and made it easy to introduce the second anomaly, revivalism.

After this spiritualistic excursion, Father betook himself to another method of propagating the faith, which had never been before resorted to among us. The Community was the outcome of religious revivals, but its methods of religious exercise were not of this kind, and developed very little excitement. He was too wise to let in religious sensationalism but turned the religious current in the direction of self-improvement by criticism and organic obedience. At the time I speak of, there were, among the new members some who had been strong and successful revivalists; and in the freedom brought about by the investigation of spiritualism they began to practice their art. Father, who had himself come out of a fiery revival in his youth, encouraged this, thinking it might strengthen the religious tendency and his own influence, but he found that the revivalists were beginning to arrogate to themselves the position of leaders to his discredit, and he called a halt. This caused much dissatisfaction among the revivalists and was a powerful force in the quarrel which subsequently arose.

What must be designated as a strand in the fabric, one widely publicized and therefore much better known by the general public outside the Community than any internal difficulties, was a concerted attack by the local clergy. This was not the first time that these worthies had mounted such an assault, but hitherto the Community had serenely ignored and taken no harm from them. This time the clerical forces were better organized under the leadership of an old enemy, Professor Mears of Hamilton College, and of Bishop Huntington of the Diocese of Central New York, and so violent were their threats of "blotting out" the Oneida Community as an intolerable moral strain on the fair name of New York State that it was assumed by most contemporary observers and some later writers that this was the cause of the breakup of the Community. Actually, aside from a threat of indictment against John Humphrey Noyes, never legally implemented, it was largely sound and fury, signifying nothing.

It has been suggested that another strand in the final tangle of Community affairs was the increased involvement in the management of the several businesses of the Community which may have been a divisive factor in the last years. J. H. Noyes, in a communication addressed to the Community on June 26, 1879, wrote: "As communism of property was the prominent characteristic of the state produced by the Pentecostal afflatus, so it was the prominent characteristic of our Community afflatus in all the early and prosperous stages of our growth. Without intending to accuse any person or party, I think I may say without danger of dissent in the Community, that we have departed from this blessed state. Is not this fact sufficient to account for all our troubles, and for the danger of dissolution which is upon us?" Whether or not he was right, it is certainly true that the emphasis if not in their publications, at least in most of the journals and private papers of this period, is upon the personnel of the various business committees and councils and the various problems, legal and commercial, of the businesses.

The last strand was perhaps the most cogent of them all. In our modern argot, it is called the generation gap. Between the years of the early 1830s, when John Humphrey Noyes had his first great commission to convert the world to Salvation from Sin, and the late 1870s, when the first seeds of dissolution began to germinate, was a gap of nearly forty years, longer than the usual generation and a period which saw a tremendous change in intellectual climate. The 1830s were an era of great revivals, of boiling religious excitement. Religion was the new thing, the thrilling new word to the young as well as to their elders. A hundred thousand converts were made in one state in one season. A score of splinter theologies developed and new groups assembled. Noyes's conversion was only one of thousands, but his interpretation of his new belief was his own, an original concept of salvation at a moment when the common cry was, "What shall we do to be saved?" The group of men and women who gathered under his banner were almost all young people, in their twenties or early thirties; they were enthusiastic converts who embraced Noyes's brand of theology and his later introduction of communism with eager arms, willing to stake their lives and their futures on this very radical venture.

During the next forty years the climate changed. The young men of the second generation, especially those whom the Community had sent to be educated at Yale and Columbia, discovered that the new word for them in the 1860s and '70s was *science,* and some of them returned to the Community as convinced agnostics. It shows both the liberality and the flexibility of Noyes's mind that when he encountered these new ideas he welcomed them—at first. He read Darwin and Mendel and Galton. He was interested in geology and hereditary patterns in genetics and was willing to concede that not all of the Old Testament account of the creation must be taken at the foot of the letter. But he never budged an inch in his belief in God and Jesus Christ or from his belief in his own inspiration regarding them. This was the real rift in the lute; one that, try as they might—and most of the Oneida Communists were men of good will, however they differed in dogma—was never mended. The dissolution of the Oneida Community was the final result.

1

The Great Discussion

As early as the mid-1860s, when the *Circular* printing office had been moved to the Wallingford Commune, Noyes showed interest in the advances of science. "We should aim," he said, "to become thoroughly reliable oracles in matters of science. Genius must have freedom. We should seek to clear ourselves of everything but inspiration." He urged his people to meet attacks on the letter of the Bible "not by crouching down in a spirit of fear but by going way beyond and being more liberal and confident than the scientific people themselves."

In adding this new ambition, however, Noyes had not abated a whit in his original religious fervor or his ambition for the enlargement of his communistic enterprise. In December 1866 he said: "The opening and promise before our young people is to be heads of communities. They must prepare to be spiritual fathers and mothers before they are natural fathers and mothers. The demand for communism is going to be enormous. I should not think it strange if within two years we should be scattered to the four winds, except for a skeleton organization here, and that changing all the time." A handbook for the information of inquirers was published. New branches were established in New York City, at Willow Place near the new factory at Oneida, and at New Haven, for the residence of the several young students then at Yale.

The year from August 1866 to August 1867 has been called by George Wallingford Noyes the culminating year of the experiment —a year of unprecedented prosperity. There had never been a year when the internal condition of the Community was more sound and satisfactory. There were no seceders; earnest expressions of unity with Noyes were not confined to the older generation of members but were heartily echoed by the young, particularly Noyes's son, Theodore.

As G. W. Noyes has written in an unpublished manuscript:

22

In the summer of 1865, at the age of 24, Theodore had come into close religious sympathy with his father, and, as he possessed in a high degree the intellectual and moral qualities of leadership, he was, in August 1866, generally acknowledged as leader of the rising generation. This was a great relief and satisfaction to Noyes, who was now 55 years old and naturally wished to feel that the work he had undertaken was not dependent on his life alone.

In January 1867, during a vacation at Yale, Theodore went to Oneida and started a powerful revival among the young folks. This was followed, at Noyes' suggestion, by a series of daily "Noon Meetings," open to all and lasting throughout the summer, in which the hearts of young and old were drawn together and the religious life of the entire Community was powerfully quickened.

In a statement to the Community on August 8, 1867, Theodore expressed his own position, and doubtless that of many others in the following words: "I have had lately an unusual sense of the magnitude of our movement. I want to throw away every consideration except that of being a transparent medium of the inspiration that God has brought upon the earth. I think I can say with perfect sincerity that I don't want and won't have any independence of this movement, of which Father is the center. I shall look with a jealous eye upon anything that turns me from it. In a certain sense I desire to be servile in my adhesion to it."

In a conversation with his father at about this time, Theodore was asked if he had any difficulty in his mind about the Bible. He replied that he had no difficulty that he allowed to influence him in regard to present faith. "I find that I allow myself," he said, "before I know it, to put a rather freer construction on the first part of the Old Testament than some folks do."

This was, perhaps, his first admission of a breach in his "adhesion" to his father's inspiration. John Humphrey Noyes answered it with the intuitive sympathy that was one of his unique talents: "*I* put a pretty free construction on that, myself. I take the ground that the account of creation may be, if you please, an invention, a fable, a poem, and yet be inspired and convey substantial truth. In fact, I do not know but Mother Goose's Melodies are inspired. God provides such things for children. Perhaps in the times of the Old Testament the world was not in a condition to appreciate anything better than that account of creation. That account places God supreme over matter, which is the beginning of all truth. I wonder if anybody is going to be stumbled by what I said tonight. I think the time has come for us to pitch into the freest discussions about the Bible, among ourselves; and we shall come out with a tighter grasp of the Bible than we ever had."

It seems extraordinary that Noyes could have taken up so liberal a view of biblical history and at the same time so furiously inveigh against what he called "this infernal Boston literature," by which he meant German rationalism stemming from Goethe. Carlyle, Bayard Taylor, and the Boston writers were, he said, trying to "import that old, second-hand stuff" into America. They were "intellectual, literary folks with feeble hearts. A brain that is subordinate to the heart ultimately becomes stronger than these heartless brains."

It was this "infernal Boston influence" that was particularly affecting certain of the younger men, particularly a brilliant young man named Daniel Bailey who, in spite of being crippled by an accident in early life, had become something of a leader in thought among the rising young intellectuals of the Community. In 1866 Bailey had been criticized for "getting into too much sympathy with German poetry and German thought." Since he was a chair-bound paraplegic and could take part in no active work, he devoted himself to short-hand reporting, journalizing, and writing for the *Circular,* but his ideas, German or not but certainly what was called Positivist, gained so much favor in a certain group that the leaders of the Community began to feel that his influence caused "darkness and hardness in certain individuals." It was not, they thought, a scientific influence but rather a "narcotic one, dulling the spiritual sense."

One young man, Joseph Skinner, the son of Harriet Noyes Skinner, JHN's sister, was a special follower of Bailey's. He was a nephew of Noyes, just graduated from Yale and, in 1869, on his return to the Community, was put in charge of the newly organized Community Academy. At this time both he and Bailey were warned to be "careful about meddling with German literature and introducing it." For some time after this, the progress of German rationalism appeared to be checked in the Community.

However, in a letter written by Bailey to JHN on January 1, 1871, he related that three years before, Theodore Noyes had entered his room suddenly and "poured out a passionate criticism of me for attempting to supplant him in the hearts of the young people, over whom he had been made leader." This Bailey denied and, he wrote, supposed he had succeeded in convincing Theodore until, a year and a half later, Theodore renewed the old charge, especially in regard to Bailey's influence over Joseph Skinner. This also Bailey denied, and in this letter he requested that Mr. Noyes would make it possible financially for him and his mother, who cared for him, to retire to some other part of the country as a permanent home.

After this charge Theodore was appointed to deal with Daniel. In his report to the Evening Meeting, February 19, 1871, he said that instead of the brief and passionate outburst Daniel had described in his letter, there had been a two- or three-hour conversation, in which Bailey had said that Theodore had accused him of *trying* to take his place. Instead of that, Theodore reported, "I accused him of *taking* my place." When Theodore was appointed editor of the paper he had found two of the young girls who worked on it "so bound up in slavery to Bailey's opinion they dared not say their souls were their own, about Bailey's articles." It was to break this connection that he had attacked Bailey.

According to Theodore, during that conversation Daniel had said, "Now that I have got my mouth open, I shall never shut it." There were many things in the administration of the Community which he considered foolish, if not hurtful. He had said in an unguarded moment that several years ago he had had come over him what he would call "a crust of heathenism." He distinctly repudiated now and forever the idea of anyone leading him. Theodore had replied that he considered Daniel an infidel, "not in a mere technical sense, but because in making distinctions between us and Goethe, he looked only at externals." As to the claim regarding which Bailey had written Mr. Noyes, he hoped for $10,000 but expected less. However, if it was refused, Bailey said he would feel morally justified in writing against the Community.

The next evening Theodore was able to report that Daniel had receded from his plan of going away, agreed to continue to accept a home in the Community, would submit to Community discipline, and would do his best to work into vital harmony with the Community. He had spoken and written, he said, under the influence of passion but had already said the worst he could say or feel, in fact stronger than he really felt. Theodore believed that they could trust to time and kindness to make him over. Notwithstanding his resolve, a year later Daniel Bailey left the Community.

Before the Bailey affair irrupted, it had not appeared that Mr. Noyes's liberal attitude toward science had weakened the faith or loyalty of the young people. In 1870 he had said that the experiment of sending the twelve young men to college, though a bold one, was proving entirely safe. Only a week before the Bailey letter was written, the *Circular* for January 2, 1871, had carried the following statement: "The Community enters upon the new year with bright hope. With improved buildings, better industrial arrangements, an increasing demand for our manufactures, good schools and educational facilities, daily evening meetings, a better state of internal harmony than ever before existed, unshaken confidence in our leader, faith ever growing in God's protecting care, we give ourselves anew to the glorious cause to which we have been called, of establishing a society in which Christ shall reign supreme."

Just a week later, after Theodore's report in the meeting had stirred things up, the Community was compelled to shift from the offensive to the defensive position. The immediate cause now was the discovery that Joseph Skinner was in much the same state of mind as Daniel. Presently it became apparent that now even Theodore, though to a lesser degree, was affected. By October, Theodore appeared to be gaining a victory over his troubles, but Joseph was laboring under a cloud. "A concerted effort," G. W. Noyes wrote, "for the relief of Joseph was now made." Exactly what form this effort took is not stated, but it is probable that not only his mother and his uncle but his other Noyes relatives and the rest of the so-called Central Members labored with him. In the end he wrote to the Community:

> It is known to you that for a good while I have been in a hard unbelieving state, making myself and those around me unhappy. I have not been single-minded, but on the contrary, a large share of my attention has been toward the world. This led recently to a quarrel with my mother, and I finally wrote her a letter, saying, in substance, that if she would not change her position with regard to me, I wanted to leave the Community. Within the last day or two I have been enabled to see that the course I have been following leads to darkness

and misery, and cannot lead to anything else. I have seen its selfish-ness, cruelty and foolishness; and that throughout my life, selfishness and egotism have been my chief motives. Unselfish impulses have been rare, and unselfish actions rarer. My greatest desire now is to be saved from selfishness and my old life and to begin a new life of devotion to God and the cause in which Mr. Noyes is engaged. I feel that in my own strength I am weak, but I have faith that God will help me to keep a resolution to serve him with my whole heart. I shall be thank-ful for any criticism or discipline that will bring me to Christ and make me soft-hearted. Feeling that Wallingford, by its nearness to New Haven, is a place of temptation to me, I have asked to return to Oneida with Theodore. There I shall pray for and expect a new experience.

Yours sincerely and devotedly,
Joseph

This communication was read aloud to the Community in the Evening Meeting by Mr. Noyes who was still somewhat dubious about the situation. He had heard from Joseph's mother, his sister Harriet Skinner, and from Ann Bailey, Daniel's sister who was at this time Theodore's first assistant, that, "so far as Joseph's intellect and testimony are concerned, he continues in a quarrel with the Community." Noyes wrote, "He is a skeptic in religious matters and is free to acknowledge that he has no particular confidence in me. I do not see any way to discharge my duty to him but to accept his invitation and to criticize him."

Whether or not this criticism was administered, there is no record. In the *Circular* of the next week, January 8, 1872, Joseph Skinner's name was listed as bookkeeper for the coming year, pre-sumably at Oneida, but in spite of this, he left the Community on April 10 of that year. In a paper announcing his departure, Mr. Noyes wrote: "In consequence of abandoning himself to science and to Daniel Bailey, Joseph had become substantially a Positivist. The unbelieving spirit over him gave way more or less at times but re-turned, and finally could not live in the atmosphere of the Commu-nity."

But this was not the end—or the worst—of it. A year later, on April 14, 1873, Noyes's niece, Tirzah Miller, wrote in her diary:

I have been a little "off" now for several days, brooding over those doubts and fears which seem to come upon us. This morning he

(Mr. Noyes) called me to his room and began to probe my very soul. I longed to tell him all and yet shrank from giving him pain. At last I said, "Does Theodore feel just as he used to? He does not seem as he did at Wallingford or Willow Place. I have not had a word to say to him and yet I can't help feeling as though he were troubled by some of these temptations which are depressing me." At the mention of Theodore's name Mr. Noyes leaned forward in his chair, his arms folded, his eyes flashing and his brows quivering with an almost alarming expression. After a moment he broke in on me with the greatest emphasis: "I have long had this same doubt about Theodore. You go straight down to the office and charge him with all you have said."

I found Theodore alone in the inside office and reported to him what had passed between his father and myself, ending with his last remark. An expression of the most intense relief crossed Theodore's face. He drew a long breath and straightened back his shoulders like one eager for an affray in which he would not have taken the initiative. He said he was glad he could throw off the cloak he had been wearing and unburden himself. I was shocked and confounded by his revelations, his unbelief in existing institutions having carried him so much farther than I had gone. I went back to tell his father what he had said. He had a good deal to say in reply and as neither wished to meet the other face to face, I passed back and forth between them steadily from noon to 7 o'clock in the evening. One remark of Theodore's gave me considerable pain although I did not really believe what he predicted. He said that the Community would inevitably go to pieces before many years and that when the catastrophe occurred he meant to be on hand to see that justice was done. He did not look upon the prospect as one of unmitigated evil, but on the contrary seemed to have little regret about it.

This extraordinary dialogue by messenger continued for three days, after which Theodore submitted to a criticism by committee, but to no avail. On July 3, 1873, Mr. Noyes read a paper to the Community assembled in the Evening Meeting:

> The Community all know what Theodore's state has been for some time. A few days ago he proposed to go away, but I persuaded him to wait until Charles Cragin came home. I wanted to bring to bear all the influences I could to help him, but I thought if Charles did not have any influence upon him, I should have to give him up into the hands of God. My purpose has been from the beginning, if he did not experience some change, to let him go away; but I did not tell him so, and he thought I was not going to give my consent to his going at all. He did not intend to go against my will. Yesterday I found that Charles Cragin had not helped him any and thereupon I prepared for

his going away. This morning he was in a good deal of perturbation, and I told him that I would not prevent him from going away, that he might be free to go or stay. He was soft, apparently, and broken down, but there was no change in his theories. He immediately concluded to go, and presented me with a receipt in full for $50.00. I told him, if he considered this a final secession he should take the full amount, $100, but if he considered this only an excursion with the expectation that he might return, it would be proper to take $50, or any other sum that he chose, and the door would be open to him. He chose the latter course, and only took the $50. The last thing I said to him was that I hoped he would come back. His reply was that no one could wish he could be changed more than he, but unless he could be changed it would probably be a permanent separation.

Two days later Theodore wrote his mother from New York. He did not "see any way to compromise my beliefs," but the tone of the letter is patently homesick. "Home and the love of friends," he wrote, "are the best things we can have," and this feeling came between him and all schemes for self-advancement. He says wistfully, "I wish some way might be devised by which we could get along together. I wish it were possible to live with you and enjoy a reasonable degree of freedom in thinking and doing."

Although this letter touched his father so deeply that the *O.C. Journal* noted that he "wept like a child," still, in the main matter of dispute he was adamant. In the paper he read in the Evening Meeting he said of Theodore: "His good sense will show him that I cannot essentially change the habits of the Community to accommodate his case, nor allow his belief to change the belief of those over whom I am placed. What further liberty I can give him, consistently with my duty to the Community, I do not see." And he added with a tragic simplicity: "I can truly say that my sorrow for him, especially since his letter came, has been wonderful to me and at times almost overwhelming." His first-born, his son, dearer perhaps than any other child he had; perhaps dearer than any other person in his life: "O my son Absalom, my son, my son."

Theodore's reply, written two days later, came to the conclusion that the ties he had formed in the Community were too sacred and strong to permit him to find happiness in any isolated career. He was, he wrote, apart from religious belief, a communist and must always remain so. He offered his father a choice of four courses by which he could rejoin the Community: first, to profess a belief in Christianity and act a part; second, to obtain a true conversion to Christianity and a belief in immortality, which did not then seem possible but which might occur later; third, to return and consider himself under treatment for a disordered condition of mind and await results; and the fourth course, which he preferred, was to assume that he was a confirmed unbeliever but be allowed to live in the Community, partake of its social life, take part in whatever occupation his father thought best, but "both parties to avoid controversy." He so definitely preferred this course that he went so far as to urge the idea of a nonsectarian community which would extend its benefits to unbelievers and leave the religious to their consciences. This, he added, might "save the coming generation to the Community, for they *will think*."

This proposition his father rejected vigorously. It contradicted the beliefs of his heart and the theory of his understanding of the essentials of communism and stultified the labors of his life: "I can have no hope of the unity which is essential to Communism without agreement in religion. To introduce the beginning of an infidel party in the Community would be simply to kill the Community. If we cannot save the coming generation without this, we must let them go."

He did not withdraw his invitation to Theodore to return, but it must be understood that this invitation was "based unalterably on my hope that you will be converted. If it were not for that hope, I should a thousand times prefer that you stay away." He offered, however, a fifth course, which he advised; this was not to confess what he did not believe but "to come with an honest wish and purpose *now* to go through the change which you admit is possible in the future and which is an inexorable necessity if you are ever really to rejoin the Community." This letter was delivered in person by Mr. Herrick. That night he and Theodore took the train for Oneida, arriving the morning of July 15.

Three days later Theodore penned a communication to the Community. He desired to reenter the Community. He recognized that the Community could not tolerate a nonreligious state, and consequently he desired to concede all he could to make a satisfactory union and to that end would accept their views "as a solution of what, to my mind, appears to be insoluble." This he could do with a clear conscience since he had no hypothesis of his own to conflict with those of the Community. He hoped to achieve faith, desired criticism, and would accept any occupation assigned to him. He desired "for the present, to avoid argumentative thought, pro or con, if possible." This communication, when read in the Evening Meeting, was received with cheers, and the vote for his reinstatement was approved, "after which the hearts of all beat more freely."

Although father and son were alike in some ways—a first-class mind with a strongly philosophical bent, a talent for organization in practical matters, and an active imagination—they also differed in many ways. John Humphrey Noyes did not have red hair and a prognathous jaw for nothing; he was by preference and belief a man of peace, but he was also capable of being a fighter, as he had proved during the long years of his early struggles. Theodore was, as he wrote many years later, like his mother, a natural recluse. He could be obstinate and stand fast on a point in which he believed for a time, but, as in this case, ultimately he capitulated.

It is not and never has been an easy lot to be the child of a genius. Overshadowed from the first by the greater man, Theodore chose to challenge the one vulnerable point in his armor. For all his passionate conviction, John Humphrey Noyes could not prove, by scientific fact, that his religious belief was right and Theodore's scientific skepticism was wrong. In this first sharp contest of wills, Theodore had yielded and agreed to try to believe. In this emergency, his father's agile, rationalizing brain came up with a possible solution.

Modern spiritualism had sprung into popular life after the so-called Rochester Rappings and the apotheosis of the Fox sisters. It was claimed that these two young girls, Margaret and Catherine Fox, were mediums, communicating with the spirit world by a system of rappings which was called the Spiritual Telegraph. This phenomenon, first exhibited at the little town of Hydesville, near Rochester, New York, caused a tremendous furor at the time, and self-proclaimed mediums sprang up throughout the country. In the early numbers of the *Circular* Noyes had denounced it and rejected it for himself and the members of the Community as, he noted on December 7, 1851, "rappings from Hades, a disorder brought on not only by credulity but by infidelity." After the death of the beloved and venerated Mary Cragin in the sinking of the sloop *Rebecca Ford,* in 1851, there was some temptation among the bereaved to adopt the new craze and try to communicate with her. This Noyes forbade. Hades, he said, was the "sphere of the miscellaneous dead" and was therefore "Descending Fellowship." This defined his position in regard to the rappings, and for more than twenty years the Community held aloof from spiritualism.

Now, however, it appeared to Noyes as a possible weapon against Theodore's apostasy. With the aim of opposing spiritualism to positivism, he authorized Theodore to undertake a thorough investigation of the subject in the hope that it would bring him back to a belief in immortality and the possibility of spirit communication. Theodore, with his natural scientific bent, took this up with enthusiasm. He developed a half-dozen homegrown mediums from among the Community members; a special meeting room was arranged in the Mansion House attic, seances were held, and finally he and a companion visited some of the most celebrated mediums in the outside world.

A year later, in August 1874, after earnest study and investigation, Theodore reported to the Community family that he had made "substantial progress toward rehabilitation." He now accepted the phenomenon of spiritualism as sufficient evidence of immortality. He had, he said, "a great yearning toward something better and higher, and earnestly desired a nearer union with Christ." He believed that he and his father were both guided by an intelligence higher than either, one which would eventually lead them into perfect unity.

Noyes interpreted this in his own way. Theodore was "swept out of our reach by an awful wave of Positivism but God provided the return wave of Spiritualism to bring him back to our faith. If my estimate is correct, he is going to be far more effectually joined to me in my work than he would have been without this experience."

Theodore's conclusions were stated in a paper to the Community in March 1875:

I think there is conclusive evidence of the existence of a spiritual world, inhabited by spiritual beings. I think it extremely probable that these beings have lived as men and women in this world. The question of spirit identity I do not think fully settled, but our continued existence in the spiritual world seems to me a fact, and furnishes a satisfactory ground for action. I think I *believe* it as fully as anyone in the Community.

I think improvement must be possible there as well as here. Consequently, there must be individuals so far advanced in goodness that they fill any conception we can form of God. How far they can affect us, and what their limitations are, I do not know; but I believe they can help us in many ways and I pray to them often with sincere desires for assistance. I think in this sense I am spiritually minded.

Considering the fact that Theodore Noyes was the accepted and elected leader of the Oneida Community only for the seven months from May 1877 to January 1878, it might seem that the attention devoted to his career is excessive. Actually, in or out of office, his effect upon the course of the Community, because of his effect upon his father, was out of proportion to his weight as a personality. He was highly intelligent, he was competent as an administrator in certain positions, but he was neither as strong nor as able as his father. He could be obstinate where his father would have won his point by being flexible. He could rule only by being what the Community called "legal"—that is, by instituting laws and insisting upon obedience where his father was so confident of his powers that he could govern almost without laws or penalties. He thought of himself as a psychologist, but he could be completely beguiled and ruled by a woman he believed himself to understand and dominate. He insisted that he must be free to think and act for himself, but twice, in 1873 and again in 1878, he left the Community with the declared intention of seeking his fortune in the world, and twice, within no more than a month or two, he returned and asked to be readmitted to the Community.

None of this would have been important except as it affected John Humphrey Noyes and the Community. It has already been said that as a father, John Noyes could not abandon the dream that Theodore should succeed him as leader of the Community. The situation was understood and discussed by the members for years, ever since the young man had returned from college. It was obvious that ultimately someone would have to follow their first leader, and Theodore's first efforts at management in 1869 as a financial adviser were very promising. His introduction of certain economies and efficiencies was praised, and he continued in this position for three years. It may have been that at this time he tried to assume too much authority. However it was, in 1872 his father resumed the reins, reorganized the businesses, and Theodore, after a brief nervous breakdown, retired from the lists as a possible successor, taking a subordinate position which he held for the next two years.

In 1875, at the suggestion of one of the young men, John Humphrey Noyes again proposed to the Community that Theodore become the leader of the Community. After a somewhat heated discussion in the Evening Meeting this suggestion was rejected, and Theodore joined his father at Wallingford where he served as a sort of deputy to the older man. A new harmony appeared to develop between them, and when Theodore was sent to Oneida to straighten out an organizational difficulty, he was cordially received. Again the next year, to settle an altercation between Wallingford and Oneida, Theodore proposed that the two communities combine so far as possible, both for the sake of economy and of pacification. This idea delighted Mr. Noyes who thereupon once more urged the Community to accept Theodore as his successor. This, at length, it did, and in May 1877, Theodore Richards Noyes succeeded John Humphrey Noyes as leader of the Oneida Community.

His short term of office and the complication of events that followed led, perhaps by foreseeable steps, to the final debacle and the end of the Community. For this reason, in following the strand in the Community fabric which represents the career of Theodore Noyes, both in relation to his father and to the Community as a whole, it is necessary to recapitulate by a few years.

The financial report for the year 1867, as reported in the *Circular,* January 20, 1868, called the results of the year satisfactory but admitted that the lack of ready money during the greater part of the year had made their position a difficult one. Although at the beginning of the year they were nearly free from debt, by fall, when the various businesses needed capital preparatory to the fall sales, their liabilities exceeded their cash assets by $59,000. This strain upon their resources, they wrote, caused them much serious study and the adoption of certain conclusions "whereby we trust we shall be able to clear our affairs from some of the annoyances that have beset them in the past."

Under the pressure of orders, they confessed, "the tendency to add a few improvements here and there, whereby the cost of production may be lessened, was almost irresistible." There was "a problem of continence in money investment," and they "made a stern resolve to forego all expense not absolutely necessary." They had learned the misery of borrowing money. "We have made our 'out,' " they wrote, "and now we are going to get 'back.' "

In an Evening Meeting in March 1868, Theodore was spoken of "as one qualified to take the lead in finances and develop a true policy for the Community. The nomination was received with expressions of satisfaction. It was thought Theodore was well qualified to fill such an office." He was first appointed chairman of the committee for the disposal of dead property. Then, by request, Theodore "unfolded some of the workings of his mind on the financial question. So far as he has matured any plan, it is to look the books over and learn how the different businesses 'have run' for the past four or five years; how much capital each has required and put the whole thing in black and white."

Spring was the usual time of year for the organization of the Community's businesses, and it may be that Theodore's hand was shown in certain changes made in this year. First, so to arrange the businesses that times of extraordinary pressure from orders should find them provided with a larger stock of goods on hand than heretofore. The fruit business was moved to the old mill in place of the bag business which had not been doing well lately and was gradually closing out. In May the Community closed its office in New York City, retaining only a room on Broadway with a desk and bed for the use of their agents when in the city. The *Circular,* with its staff and printing office, was moved back to Oneida. The financial report for the year 1869 showed an increase of nearly $60,000. The Community owed not a dollar and had invested $20,000 of surplus cash in U.S. bonds. After this success, Theodore was retained at the head of the finances until 1872.

As might have been expected, with the easing of the financial stringency of the previous year, expansion was resumed. A new farm was added to the domain at Willow Place; a factory and water privileges were bought at Wallingford; and the construction of a dam commenced for the purpose of enlarging the silk and publishing businesses there. The fruit business, which had been suspended for a year, was revived and the New York Office reopened. Even more interesting to the family, a new brick wing to the Mansion House was built, and the old wooden building was demolished, except for one smaller portion which was moved away and fitted up for a seminary for the children.

Another period of expansion, and John Humphrey Noyes, made cautious by experience, urged that the new young management "come about" on the tack of economy, while the latter, headed by Theodore, pushed for further enlargement. There was a clash of wills and a temporary adjustment was reached, but during the ensuing year occasions of dissatisfaction steadily accumulated. As G. W. Noyes wrote: "The Business Board no longer held its sessions. Theodore appointed all the heads of departments and they came to him separately for consultation. The Community had little chance to review or even to know what was going on. Young men occupied nearly all the important positions. There was a good deal of talk about "putting the older generation on the shelf" and running the businesses on a moneymaking basis.

Finally, in January 1872, the whole business administration came up for discussion and Noyes expressed himself thus: "We must have more spirituality in our business. Theodore is tempted to rely too much upon ability and financial machinery and does not appreciate the tremendous importance of inspiration. I see more and more the necessity of a Business Board that will meet every week and help us control one another. I should want counsel from the heads of departments every chance I could get. If Theodore feels able to guide the whole thing himself, he is a greater man than I am. I think he will break down if he attempts it. Let us throw all these things open to the daylight. Let all departments offer themselves for criticism, and have no irritability about it. Let us not consider the business arrangements settled, but let the Community discuss them and be free to alter them. I ask the privilege to look them all over myself, and see what I want done. I began my career with the principle, "Seek first the kingdom of God and his righteousness and all other things shall be added unto you"; and I had rather have all our departments of business stop than go along on any other principle than that.

This discussion was followed by a reorganization of business. While it was in progress, Theodore had a nervous breakdown and went to a sanitarium in Dansville to recuperate. On his return four months later, his attention was occupied by other matters and he did not for several years reenter the ranks of business.

It would seem, from the timing of these events, that Theodore's breakdown was less the effect of overwork than of his defeat by his father and the older men of the Community. It seems equally possible that the "other matters" which occupied him after his recovery may have been the study of positivism and the companionship of the intransigent Daniel Bailey. However it was, after his brief rebellion and secession—based only, it then appeared, on his repudiation of Community perfectionism in favor of agnosticism—on his return no mention was ever made of a disappointment in his career as a manager of the businesses.

During the next two years there is no record extant of his holding any official position except sharing with Dr. George Cragin the post of physician to the Community and his membership in the committee on stirpiculture. It was also during this period that he became absorbed in his study of spiritualism in the course of which he and a companion, frequently Francis Wayland-Smith, traveled to Vermont and other New England centers to observe the performances of various celebrated mediums. It is possible, too, that although he is said to have recovered from his nervous difficulty during his stay at Dr. Jackson's Water Cure at Dansville, New York, his health may not have been altogether restored. Wayland-Smith notes in his journal that "he was at that time very corpulent and somewhat inclined to apoplexy. At Dansville he became converted to unbolted wheat flour and on his return he introduced that and the two-meal-a-day system at O.C."

However this may have been, it was not until the spring of 1875 that Theodore underwent another confrontation with the Community. Its immediate cause was no act or attitude of his but lay in a curious concatenation of events which at first did not touch him. It had happened that in September of the year before, 1874, Charlotte Noyes Miller, JHN's younger sister, died. For twenty years she had been the official adviser to the younger class of Community women, a very important post. After her death, Ann Sophia Bailey (later known as Ann Hobart) took her place. Ann, like her brother Daniel, was highly intelligent and highly ambitious, and among her other gifts she was supposed to be a "sensitive" or medium, and as such she had worked closely with Theodore Noyes in his investigation of spiritualism.

When, in early January 1875, Mr. Noyes went to Wallingford for a long stay, he appointed William H. Woolworth as "Father" of the Community in his place. This man of fifty, although a sincere follower of his leader, was no disciplinarian. The position was onerous to him, especialy as it dealt with the affairs of the younger generation, and occasionally, when Ann applied to him for help in some problem, he begged to be excused. Carrying this heavy responsibility alone was, apparently, too much for Ann, and finally she appealed to Harriet Noyes Skinner, the "Mother" of the Oneida group, and to Frank Wayland-Smith for relief. Both sympathized with her difficulty and in a letter dated March 1, 1875, Wayland-Smith wrote JHN suggesting that he appoint Theodore to Mr. Woolworth's position while he, JHN, remained the over-all leader, able to assist with his counsel.

This suggestion must have pleased Noyes, but he was too cautious to take such a radical step without the concurrence of the whole Community. He replied to the suggestion: "The fact that you have confidence in Theodore is a strong testimony in his favor with me. But Theodore's course in the past has been so divergent from mine and from that of the Community, and is still so far doubtful, that discussions and explanations seem to be absolutely necessary before he can take the place in the heart of the Community, which he ought to have to be its leader. All that I can do is to consider your proposition in order as a nomination, and proceed to ascertain whether the Community will accept it."

The diary of a Community woman, Harriet Worden, in an entry dated March 10, 1875, described the situation: "This has been an eventful week. The subject of Theodore's leadership is still under discussion. There are two very decided opinions in the Community on the matter. A good many blamed Frank for taking the responsibility of writing Mr. Noyes about it. There are some people here who do not recognize that Frank, as well as the rest of the young people, are no longer children. I do not feel so sanguine as he seems to that Theodore is fitted for the place, although I am more favorably impressed with this plan than any other yet mentioned. Still, there is something in me that recoils at the idea of putting a man in for leader who has not found God."

On March 21 she returned to the subject: "The past week has been pregnant with thought and talk on the part of everyone. The discussion as to leadership became a very exciting one—one party representing the legal element in the Community—the religious, conservative, and, I may say, bigoted—and the other, religious too, but free, open and liberal in its views. William made some cruel statements really accusing some of wire-pulling and underhanded operations in regard to getting Theodore into office. The next evening he was obliged to retract this—as he had founded his statements on a false report. The discussion was then taken up by the other side—those in favor of Theodore—and closed."

Two days were allowed for reflection and the discussion itself occupied six evenings. This prolonged debate that the Community, which loved to name things, always referred to as the Great Discussion, offered reasons as various as the persons who gave them for refusing the nomination—from the religious, that Theodore was agnostic; from the old, that he was too young; from the ambitious, the objection that a son's following his father was the establishment of a dynasty; from the extreme loyalists, that Theodore was not sufficiently united with his father. In short that the Community did not welcome him as a leader.

Theodore made a formal reply to this criticism:

> The present agitation of my candidature as leader of the Community was uninvited by me. I have no desire to put myself forward unless it can come without strife. I sincerely think a fanatical tendency in some of the members needs the antidote of my tendencies of mind, and I am quite confident that I could sympathize with the struggles which many of our children go through, in a way which would improve the handling of them. But of course I could not help as leader without kindness and charity on the part of those who have more definite views. This would seem like a concession to the Devil, and I am well content to wait until I am wanted by all hands. There is one thing greater than my love of unity: that is my love of truth. But the cases are rare where these must conflict, and happily this is one in which there is

no occasion for wrangling. The Community certainly need fear nothing from my ambition. I am not too humble to say I cannot do a thing when I think I can, but I certainly grasp at nothing but a place in the hearts of the whole Community.

As the nomination of Dr. Noyes was considered withdrawn, a feeling was expressed that this discussion had better be closed. The question was raised as to what should be done to provide a helper for Ann. William Hinds, H. W. Burnham, and others thought that Mr. Woolworth, if surrounded and sustained by the Community and relieved of his business responsibilities, would feel his commission renewed, and give satisfactory service as in times past. A motion was made requesting him to continue as Father of the family for the present, and was passed unanimously. The meeting closed with an apparent good feeling all around.

2

JHN's Retirement

In June 1875, three months after the Great Discussion, Theodore wrote to his father: "The Community most needs spirituality, that is, a life from the interior. This is what I am most ambitious to do: to tend the growth of my spirit. If we could find some common ground of action, I should be glad to be working for spirituality in the Community more actively than I do." Shortly after this, hoping perhaps to find this common ground, he went to Wallingford to be in closer contact with his father who was then battling strongly with the "fever-and-ague principality" which was epidemic among the members of the Wallingford group.

For a number of years the health of the members of the Wallingford Commune had been an increasing problem. G. W. Noyes wrote:

> Sickness became general in a wide belt around Wallingford and was diagnosed as malaria. Seventeen members of the Wallingford Community (about half the family) were stricken at once. The situation was so bad that on the 18th of September, 1871, Noyes put the seven worst sufferers, "the refuse lot" they were called, aboard cars for Oneida, assuming charge of the party himself.
>
> [Three years later] the fever-and-ague situation at Wallingford dragged along with little if any improvement, and there was increasing difficulty in keeping the Wallingford Community manned. Many of the sick ones used quinine and "German drops" freely, although, as a member remarked, it was a little repugnant to Community ideas. At last, in the summer of 1874, the question of abandoning the Wallingford branch came up for serious discussion. After various arguments had been brought forward on both sides, Noyes addressed to the Community a paper on the subject: "My feeling was that we *must* get rid of the fever and ague; and on the other hand that we *cannot* leave Wallingford immediately and that we ought not to leave it at all. Has the battle finally gone against us? Have we exhausted the virtue of our old standard medicine, criticism? As I hate the ague, so I hate to retreat before it. I am willing to notify God

41

that we cannot stand the ague at Wallingford beyond this season: that we will do our best in the light of faith we have, and if he gives us strength to make an end of it before next winter, we will gladly go on with the great enterprise begun at Wallingford; but otherwise we shall have to quit."

This view of the matter was greeted with laughter and cheers and the little Community girded itself for a continuation of the fight. A short time before winter the attention of the Community was directed to the Turkish Bath which was just then coming into vogue, and Theodore was sent to New York to investigate it. His report was favorable and a small experimental Turkish Bath was installed. Noyes soon saw in this a new and more hopeful weapon against fever and ague. "In our battle against diphtheria," he said, "we used criticism and ice. Why not now use criticism and the Turkish Bath?" The idea seemed reasonable and a strong detachment of men and women was appointed to carry it out.

The war was waged not only in the Community but in the surrounding neighborhood and bulletins were published in handbills and in the columns of the *Circular*. Many surprising cures of outsiders were reported and in September 1875, four years from the time when the "refuse lot" was shipped to Oneida, the statement was made that there was not a single case of fever and ague in the Wallingford Community.

After his arrival at Wallingford, in December 1875, Theodore began cooperating heartily with his father. They agreed in all important matters of policy and especialy in Mr. Noyes's firmly held idea that the true object of business was not money-making but education. A new harmony and appreciation of each other was growing between them, and when a letter from Oneida urged that Theodore come there to meet an important visitor, and asked also for his and his father's advice on a proposed change of organization in the business, Mr. Noyes decided to send Theodore to O.C. With him he sent a message: "As to plans of business, I have no hesitation in giving Theodore *carte blanche* to act for me. I have entire confidence that his views are substantially in accordance with mine, and that he is heartily devoted to the Community interest. At the same time, I do not send him to dictate arrangements. The best way is to have a meeting for consultation and free expression. Then, if there is divergence of view, let him report to me. I hope his visit will be an occasion of new harmony."

Two months later Theodore addressed to the Community what was, in some sense, an apology for his past intransigence. In his single aim to "cultivate a sensitive conscience," he realized that he had given offense. His only excuse he said was that, from the character of his mind, it was necessary to strip himself down to bare positivism in order to make a beginning of perfect sincerity. Having secured his, he hoped to carry it through all the heights of belief between this world and heaven.

How much this placated his erstwhile critics cannot be known, but at an Evening Meeting on December 5, 1875, Frank Wayland-Smith quoted Theodore as saying that his father hoped that the Community would invite him to take a more general control of the business: "He did not want to crowd us into that course unless we saw that it was the best. If we put Mr. Noyes into that place, he wants Theodore to help him."

When the question was thrown open to the meeting, there was a surprising unanimity in the comments. Mr. Woolworth, the Father *pro tem* of the Community at Oneida, said rather sadly that "when the Committee first met, there was no heart to go on and arrange our business in the old way. We felt that a crisis had come and that we were called to put our business into Mr. Noyes's hands, to be reorganized as he might choose." After that, everyone was disposed to agree: to offer the business to Mr. Noyes and make him free to use any instrument he pleased. Even Mr. Freeman, William Hinds, and Mr. Towner, three men who had been the most vigorous opponents of Theodore during the Great Discussion, now confessed their confidence in him. The question was put to vote, and the ayes were unanimous.

Mr. Woolworth wrote to Mr. Noyes: We have had a good time with Theodore and I think the whole Community hails the dawn of a better day. There are many signs that the spirit of unity is developing."

During the next year and a half, from December 1875 to May 1877, the Community was led by a dual regime, with Theodore as his father's agent or helper in the management of the business and the affairs of the Community. JHN was still the active responsible head, with Theodore as his chief minister.

One subject, always dear to Noyes's heart, was a possible change in the character of the *Circular* whose subscription list had dwindled to only eight hundred names, nearly all of whom were on the free list. Frank Wayland-Smith, who had been very active on the paper, urged that something be done to increase the circulation, possibly by changing the character of its content and certainly by charging a reasonable fee for subscription.

Although he could not give up forever his dream of a free daily paper, Mr. Noyes was practical enough to agree that it was not feasible at that time and was pleased with the idea of succeeding the *Circular* with a new weekly to be called the *American Socialist:* "Communism is really the true sphere of a free paper, and so far as we print for people beyond that sphere we may as well put their selfishness under tax for the benefit of communism. It seems to me that our paper has kept open doors to tramps until it is overrun with them. While we keep communism among ourselves, we have to buy and sell with the world; and if we make our entire institution self-supporting in this way, there is no reason why we should not make our paper self-supporting in the same way."

The last published number of the *Oneida Circular,* March 9, 1876, carried a *Prospectus* in large type announcing "a New Weekly Paper Devoted to Socialism, to be printed on a large quarto sheet of eight pages and mailed to subscribers at $2.00 per annum. The aim of this Journal will be to make a faithful public record of facts relating to the progress of socialism everywhere, and to offer to Socialists of all kinds a liberal medium of exchange and discussion. John H. Noyes, editor, W. A. Hinds, assistant editor, F. Wayland-Smith, business manager." They hoped to be able, they wrote in this hail and farewell editorial, "with the experience both of failure and success which has now accumulated, to solve the question which has for so long been the despair of theorists—how to form communities that shall be sure of permanence and success."

Hopeful words but perhaps not partaking of the famous "luck" which JHN claimed had accompanied him as a gift from his relation to Christ and the Primitive Church. The first difficulty that arose involved some of the young men. The general question of government by deputy which was Theodore's role in the present dual regime, was not always acceptable to some of the men over whom he was placed. G. W. Noyes wrote this account of it:

Theodore, acting for his father who thought that some of the businessmen made trips abroad to the detriment of their spiritual character, undertook to obtain data as to the amount of traveling needed, but met with a rebuff from one of the superintendents. A short time after this, while Theodore was still at O.C., Noyes sent E. H. Hamilton to act as father of the O.C. family and this same superintendent raised a protest, saying that Hamilton did not recognize anything as true inspiration which differed from his own and that he doubted if Hamilton would get ten votes in his favor. Theodore took up the proffered gage:

"Let us not cant about inspiration when we simply want our own way. You and the other young people have repeatedly expressed unlimited confidence in Father, and if you are not hypocrites you will take what he thinks best for you and stand to it like a man. I agree with Father that what is wanted at O.C. at present is less disorganized liberty which drifts toward secularism in business and social relations, and more of the sturdy moral sense which aims at setting spiritual education uppermost.

"You and others of the second generation have quite misunderstood my attitude about liberty if you think I want a slack administration in which everyone can do just what he has a mind to. When those of the young men who have bright faculties drift away from spirituality, shirking the struggle we must undergo to purify our souls, and take refuge in the excitements of business, I think we are lucky to have some left of the sterner sort, who make a serious study of ethical and spiritual problems, and if I have any voice, they shall have a large place. The Community is ruined when it tucks its philosophers and spiritually minded off in a corner and gives its heart to money-making."

The young man addressed in this letter, somewhat chastened, resigned his superintendency and went to Wallingford, "to separate himself from the temptations of the world and seek a new spiritual experience." Possibly roused by this affair, Mr. Noyes took this opportunity to make another move toward settling the vexed point which had agitated the Community for more than a year. The question of the successorship was still hanging fire. Noyes wrote:

Let us not think of debate as a permanent condition. A debate is good for nothing except as it leads to a conclusion. Some practical conclusion should now come and we should go about our business. It will be remembered that, when there seemed to be no end to the discussion about the location of the new house, all parties finally concluded to leave the decision to me, and the result was a decision that satisfied all. Now I ask the Community to consider whether that is not the proper way to terminate all important controversies that occur among us. I see no other way except the old one of the Phalanxes, which was to fight it out and break up.

The great question, secretly or openly labored on in all our dissensions, certainly since a year ago last winter, has been whether Theodore is to be the leader of the second generation. There are two parties on this question, each of which holds its opinion quite as earnestly as parties have ever done on previous questions. Can you not trust me in this, as you have trusted me before? Am I not more likely than any of you to understand the merits of the question at issue and the awful responsibility I am under to find and do the will of God? I am free to say that I think you declare *me* unworthy to be your leader, so long as you think I cannot be trusted to decide the question that has now come to the end of debate and awaits decision. What shall we do? Is the Community to end the controversy in the old way or shall we go on in secret strife to dissolution?

Mr. Hamilton, perhaps doubtful of its reception, hesitated for some weeks before presenting this letter to the Evening Meeting, for approval or rejection. When he finally did, nearly everyone voted in the affirmative, although there were two or three notable exceptions. Community discipline held, however, and the objectors were finally brought into agreement with the rest of the family.

What happened next would seem an unlikely cause for discord, especially in a group brought up on revivalism, steeped in biblical lore, and dedicated to religion. It happened that, in November 1876, George Miller, Mr. Noyes's nephew, came on to the O.C. from Wallingford and delivered a series of lectures on the Bible. This inspired the formation of Bible classes led by Mr. Henry Burnham and Mrs. Candace Bushnell, both old revival hands, and suddenly the Oneida family was stirred by a revival more powerful than any it had experienced in years. At first Mr. Noyes, who had come to Oneida in December 1876, encouraged it as did other of the Central Members, but as it progressed some of the more zealous began to criticize the Wallingford family for infidelity and worldliness. It was felt that the Wallingford group, under the leadership of Theodore and Ann, had not seconded the mother commune in piety but had entered on a gay and secular course.

The G. W. Noyes manuscript reported:

Upon this, George Miller, who had returned to Wallingford, wrote to Oneida, criticizing the leaders of the revival (which his lectures had possibly suggested) for narrowness and legality. Mr. Hamilton replied [February 17, 1877], defending the revival and deprecating the growing irritation between Oneida and Wallingford. A month later Mr. Noyes became convinced that the revival was being conducted in a disorganizing spirit and that the time had come to call a halt. Accordingly, on April 3 George Miller, who had come from Wallingford for that purpose, addressed the Oneida family in the Evening Meeting; he believed that the Community was dependent on the revival spirit for existence, but it would be best to discontinue the Bible classes in the form they had assumed: the history of the Community had been a succession of such changes: it had always been characteristic of Mr. Noyes to see the proper time to change and by so doing he had been able to secure the profit of any given course without falling into the dangers to which it was liable. The result of the meeting was that the Bible classes were obediently though rather reluctantly dropped.

Taking advantage of this conflict between Oneida and Wallingford, Theodore made a proposal to combine, as they had done in 1855; to gather the majority of the members at Oneida, dismiss as many as possible of the hired help, thereby developing home industry and perfecting the organization. A letter which he wrote to Ann Hobart at this time has a critical cast and a reaching for power which might have surprised his father: "I am convinced that unless we do this we shall have no peace. The Community here are perpetuating the same narrowness which has given us all our trouble and if we do not take hold now to conquer them, we shall never do it. Then, in a few years, we can live together again in such a happy family as W.C. has been."

John Humphrey Noyes seized upon this plan with enthusiasm: "If we can get all hearts interested in gathering together here, it will be a conversion of the whole family. As it is now, the Community is divided up into cliques that have but little to do with each other. However heretical Theodore may be thought by some, this idea of seeking unity and sacrificing financial considerations is orthodox to the core. He really proposes not a four-day but a four-year 'protracted meeting'! The old revivalists certainly ought to favor that. I go for it heartily and I guess the family will."

This view of the matter promulgated in the Evening Meeting

was greeted by clapping of hands and stamping of feet, and during the months of May and June 1877 the plan of concentration at Oneida was carried out.

Riding this wave of happy unanimity, on May 17, 1877, John Humphrey Noyes returned more powerful than ever to his dearest project, in a proclamation to the family:

> In this last stage of my labor I find myself in front of the last problem of Community-building, which is the *problem of successorship; how to carry a Community through the change from one generation to another.* I must work out this problem, or leave my work unfinished and even in danger of coming to naught. The Community did not form itself by getting together and choosing a president. I was the president from the beginning, called not by vote of the members but by the will of God, and as such I formed the Community. That relation between me and the Community has remained through its entire history. There has never been a time when I did not claim the prerogative of criticism and final decision over the whole Community and over every member of it: and there has never been a time when the Community as a whole did not concede me that prerogative. We have had free discussions, but these discussions on the one hand have been proposed and granted by me, and on the other hand have been brought to a close by me, and the final decision has been referred to me as judge after the debate.
>
> On these grounds I claim that I have a certain right to dispose of the government of the Community. But now let us see what I do *not* claim. A father has the right to give his property to his son irrespective of that son's character. I do not claim that right. I have renounced it, and pledged myself solemnly to the Community that I will not commit its government to an unbeliever or one who is in any way unfit to be its leader. I claim only the right to choose the *fit* man to be my successor. If the fit man proves to be my son, so much the better. But his being my son does not entitle him to my place, but only his fitness.
>
> To show the real ground of my choice, I must go back in history to Theodore's original nomination. He was nominated and the nomination was warmly accepted many years ago. He was at that time, I may say without fear of contradiction, our most promising young man, not only for business ability and intellectuality but for spirituality. This nomination should be regarded not as an actual installation but as the commencement of training. In the course of the training Theodore had gone through great changes of theory and experience; such changes as at one time seemed to disqualify him for leadership. But these changes did not necessarily invalidate his nomination, because his actual lead-

ership was future, and other changes fitting him for leadership might come before his training ended. Such changes have come. He now believes in the spiritual world, in Providence and in inspiration, and I have evidence that he is inspired by the same control that has carried me through my career. Difficult as it may be to reconcile all minds to my choice, I must say that I see no other person in the Community or out of it, who would be chosen by so many or so good a class of persons as he.

It seems necessary on many accounts that the question of successor-ship should be settled now. I am providentially disabled, so that I must perforce resign many of the duties of a leader to others. I can still help by counsel, and I am in the best condition I ever was for conducting the paper. My present calling then is to transfer my leader-ship and devote myself to reporting what I have done. It is evident that the unsettled state of the Community for the last few years has been caused in great measure by the unsettled state of this question of leadership, and confusion will continue until my choice is made known and accepted. I therefore designate Theodore R. Noyes as my successor.

What else he said was reassuring to the doubters, soothing to the angry, encouraging to his supporters; that Theodore had been a successful manager of the business—but that now he intended to develop "home industry, hygienic habits, and above all to sub-ordinate money-making to spiritual interests." Noyes urged them to cooperate with any changes the new leader might make and to "take hold with patriotic zeal in counsel and action."

In a letter of thanks to the Community for approving his elec-tion, Theodore said, on May 18, 1877: "I think we can all take hold in unity for the pursuit of truth in the great circle which embraces Spiritualism, Christianity, Communism, stirpiculture and science of every kind. It has been my ambition to unite science and religion in the true proportions and I think in the practical discipline of Com-munity life we shall be able to do it. I hope also that the fathers and mothers of the Community will find themselves more and more honored, instead of being laid upon the shelf."

The Great Discussion appeared finally to have come to an end.

3

Theodore and Ann

The strand perhaps most readily recognized, most commonly plucked out of the tangled skein of the Community's final misfortunes is the ageing and the retirement of its leader, John Humphrey Noyes. On May 24, 1877, the *American Socialist* announced, as though it were spreading glad tidings, that "the Editor-in-Chief of this paper has the pleasure of announcing that he has resigned the Presidency of the Oneida Community and will be free henceforth to devote himself wholly to editorial labor. J. H. Noyes parts with the Community to which he has given thirty years of his life, in entire harmony, leaving his son, Dr. Theodore Richards Noyes, to be henceforth its responsible head."

Naturally this almost casual announcement of so momentous a change caused a great outcry in the press, both local and distant. Some applauded the move and explained it "on the two-fold supposition that Noyes has entire confidence that the Community will continue its career of peace and prosperity independent of his personal leading and that he considers his function as editor of a journal devoted to the general cause of socialism more important than the management of any community."

The *Utica Herald,* June 7, 1877, attributing all of the Community's success to the genius of its founder, doubted that it could survive without him. The New York *Daily Graphic,* on June 14, hinted that the younger generation at Oneida had outgrown the religion of the founder and took a cautious view of its future. The *Springfield Republican,* also on June 14, thought Mr. Noyes's retirement an event as well worth notice as the abdication of a monarch and suggested that whatever his present claims, he would remain as the power behind the throne as long as he lived.

The editor of the *American Socialist,* June 24, 1877, returned a mild ansver to these diatribes: "In commenting on the extraordinary career of the Oneida Community, the newspapers all lay great

50

stress on the assertion that its success in business and its internal harmony are due to the personal characteristics of its founder. Without such a leader, they say, it would soon come to an end or be greatly modified. Nobody believes more thoroughly than ourselves in the prime importance of good leaders. But we differ from the croakers in this, that we believe that plenty of good leaders will be ready and available when the time becomes ripe."

The most amusing reply to all these speculations came from the pen of the subject, himself, in the *American Socialist* for June 7, 1877: "While admiring the insight and liberality of the writer, the founder aforesaid begs leave to say that he cannot think the whole story of the Community's success is told in that article. However flattering it may be to his 'personality' to have his 'authority' and 'shrewdness' represented as the 'sole secret' of the success in question, truth compels him to say that in his opinion the result is due to a great complexity of cooperating causes. If any one of these factors had failed—and they certainly were not secured by the authority or shrewdness of the founder—the Oneida Community would have failed and been forgotten long ago."

Despite the gentle deprecations of the editors of the *American Socialist* and the more explicit rebuttal of Mr. Noyes, the press and possibly some of the public maintained its role as prophet of doom for the Oneida Community. Inside the Community itself there had been signs and portents which the percipient must have observed.

At the time of the election of Theodore Noyes as the new leader of the Community, the *American Socialist* wrote optimistically on May 31 that the change marked an important era in the history of the Oneida Community: "It takes effect at a time when the Community is in great internal harmony and free from external persecution." The drive for concentration which Theodore had proposed in the spring was going forward rapidly at Oneida and during the last of June more than forty members of the Wallingford group arrived at Oneida where they were warmly welcomed. Some twenty persons were left at Wallingford as a sort of skeleton staff to be on hand "to wait for something to turn up." The fortunate "something" did turn up almost immediately in the form of a proposal by Theodore that they begin the manufacture of spoons at Wallingford, a plan which was enthusiastically approved and put into effect with Charles Cragin in charge.

But that was all the good luck they had for some time. When he took office, Theodore, as his father had approved, chose his own cabinet and, for his female helper, in the role of Mother of the Community, Ann Hobart, a young woman of the Community of whom Frank Wayland-Smith wrote in his journal an admiring description:

One could not understand the situation of the Community at this time without some acquaintance with Miss Ann S. Hobart. Ann was born the daughter of Seba and Jane Bailey, a family of hard-working people who lived in one of the western states. She had for brothers and sisters Daniel, Zerah, and Israel Bailey and Maria, Virtue, and Lily. The last two were, however, half-sisters. Her father died when she was a little girl. As Ann grew up in the Community she was known as a bright, quick-witted attractive girl. She had a beautiful complexion, with rosy cheeks, blue eyes and curling hair. As she became a woman she forged ahead of her mates into a position of responsibility. At length she had a child by Joseph Skinner, Mr. Noyes's nephew, and this connection brought her a good deal of trouble, besides which, her brother Daniel became discontented and left the Community, taking their mother with him. Her brothers Zerah and Israel had previously left, and her sister Maria had died. Added to these bereavements, her half-sister Virtue had also died. Then her only relative remaining in the Community was Lily, her half-sister. The anti-communistic spirit shown by her family determined Ann and Lily to change their names from Bailey to Hobart, which was their mother's maiden name.

At the time Dr. Noyes began to investigate Spiritualism, Miss Ann Hobart developed very readily as a writing medium, and it transpired that she had some clairvoyant powers. From that time on an intimate acquaintance existed between Dr. Noyes and Miss Ann, so that when the Doctor was chosen as Mr. Noyes's successor in the leadership, he associated Ann with himself as "mother" of the O.C.—a position for which she is particularly qualified. Earnest, sincere, and truthful, very clear-headed and very kind-hearted, at thirty years of age she is the strongest woman we have. Her influence is felt everywhere, even on the Doctor. Perhaps it is felt on him most of all. He lacks the intuitive faculties which she possesses in an unusual degree. He thoroughly realizes his need of her advice and support and, as I view the situation, I consider that if his administration shall prove a success, it will be largely due to her admirable qualities of head and heart.

Even at first, not all the members of the Community agreed with this eulogy. One young woman, a niece of Mr. Noyes, whose case of Special Love had been punished by what she felt were Ann's machinations in driving her lover out of the Community, threatened to leave herself rather than submit to Ann's rule, until she was pacified by Theodore and John Humphrey Noyes. Shortly after this, Harriet Noyes Skinner, Mr. Noyes's sister, had a brush with the young woman who had been appointed to take her place. In this difficulty she appealed to her brother to "sit down with her and get her straightened, if possible, about Ann."

Mr. Noyes sent for Ann and had a long frank talk with her regarding her relations with the older woman who had, until now, been the general woman-superintendent. Ann said she was sorry, but that was not enough for Mr. Noyes: "I judge that a spirit was upon all of W.C. [where Ann and Theodore were then living] which pushed for great changes without much care about the method of transfer from the old officers to the new. The old officers were not going to be pushed out and left in disrespect." Ann received this criticism very meekly and they agreed that the real difficulty lay in a want of sufficient communication with Mr. Noyes. His advice to Ann now was to distrust her own judgment on account of distance and the temptations that had been besetting all of them, to which Ann agreed.

This episode occurred in May, but for all their good intentions, matters did not run smoothly. In July Theodore had several strenuous talks with the Community at the Evening Meeting. Those whose duty it was to distribute jobs to the various members were having a hard time, he said. Many were public-spirited but others were refusing to do as they were asked. He also said—which came strangely from one who had made himself known as an individualist—that this seemed to be one of the faults of individualism into which the Community had fallen lately. He objected "to the spirit which says, 'I will' or 'I won't,' " which was anything but the spirit of brotherly love. It was subversive and made him "feel utterly powerless."

In order to counter this rebellious spirit Theodore set on foot a method of keeping statistics in order to find out how much work the members did: "There are some among us who suffer from what is no more than laziness. I do not feel like mincing the matter at all.

Talk is good for something but deeds are a great deal better. If we can get a revival of old-fashioned faithfulness in the use of our time, the financial problem will be easy; but if we go on in our luxurious habits, it is going to be a serious thing in a year or two."

A few days later he was obliged to remind them that all money, whether gained by individual exertions or in any other way, belonged to the Community. He said, "we do not want the Community to be divided into rich and poor. We may find it best occasionally to take account of things that people call their own, and reduce all to a common level. All income, whether of cash or other property, should be turned into the Community treasury before it can be passed to the individual."

A week later, another embranglement occurred, this time on the subject of the proposed plan in regard to the children's clothes. Hitherto, each mother had been responsible for the care and sometimes the making of her children's clothes. Under Theodore's new organization, one person, in this case Mr. Towner, was put in charge of providing clothes for all the Children's Department wardrobe and now he complained that the mothers were loath to give up their individual care of their children's clothes and allow the Community's Children's Department to take their places.

Dr. Noyes defended his lieutenant quite warmly: "I want it distinctly understood that I am back of this committee. I am willing to be charitable but when I hear remarks which show that persons do it simply because they have to and take back everything they can, it is trying to the soul. Those of us who have the burden to bear have to make these things a matter of conscience."

William Hinds went even further: "After the talk the other evening about appropriations, I heard grumbling remarks on the part of individuals who feared that their freedom would be curtailed. It makes it very hard indeed for those who undertake to foster Community spirit to have this back-water pressure."

This was an area in which there had been a good deal of contention. Theodore met the challenge with force:

> I don't pretend to be such a lover of children as some are, but I do pretend that my general course with them would be as likely to turn out good and healthy men and women as that of the tenderest mother.

When I take this attitude I am subjected to the accusation of not understanding a mother's feelings and it makes my labors a great deal heavier. It is obvious that the most sensible women need the strength of men in governing children. If the Community, in passing from the old to the new form of society, fails to furnish the masculine element, the true order of things will be reversed. Those of us who wish to be happy in communism will have to get rid of the idea that communism can be carried on without interfering with individual liberty. This is a fact, not because I or anybody else says so but because the logic of events proves it to be so. We might as well make up our minds to it, first as last.

An even more delicate and difficult subject came up for discussion presently. This was what they called sexual organization. Dr. Noyes, as he said earlier in another connection, did not feel like mincing words: "People seem to have fallen into the way more or less of taking care of themselves. I judge there is some Shakerism among us: but according to my idea of a Community there should be a good deal of life in that direction, all of it thoroughly organized and tending to elevation and refinement."

One of the men asked him what kind of organization he would like. He was not prepared to be definite:

We had a plan at W.C. that operated very well, but whether it would operate well here, I cannot say. We shall have to experiment some. There was a regulation so that those in control knew what was going on. That was practically the case when the Community first went into complex marriage. Father and others associated with him knew pretty much all that was going on. For a great many years it was considered of primary importance to have the invitations given by responsible women. Now that custom has, to quite an extent, passed away and such matters are often arranged with personal friends. How far any definite organization is desirable I will not attempt to say without more experience. My general feeling in regard to labor, spending money, and pleasure of all kinds, especially sexual pleasure, is that the great regulator of all of them is *walking in the light*.

Ann, in a ladies' meeting, made things more definite. After some consultation with his elders, she told the women, Theodore thought it best to try, at least for a time, the system they had had at Wallingford. There, Theodore had said that if he were to be held responsible, he wanted to know what was going on so as to act intelligently, and from that time until they came to Oneida. written reports were handed to him every Sunday. He was not a curious man, but as leader and also as a physician he thought he ought to know. Some of the young women might have injured their health by not being supervised; some had been injured spiritually, and there were others not in the Community current. Beyond this, he thought there had been some departure from the original spirit of the Community in these matters, and it would have a purifying effect if all such things were done in the light.

The plan proposed was to have the invitations to sexual intimacy given in the usual way through an intermediary, but if there was any doubt in the minds of those asked to deliver the invitations as to the propriety of the visit, they were to consult certain of the older women whose names were given. All women carrying invitations were to report to these women who would keep a record to be given to Dr. Noyes. "Theodore," Ann said, "does not want this tried unless there is entire willingness about it but knows no better way to keep track of things." General approbation was expressed by the ladies attending.

A more general criticism of the state of things in the Community was the subject of a meeting several months later. In October Theodore said in Evening Meeting that he had felt quite nervous all summer about their contact with the world, and the matter was taken up by a number of the members. For example, the girls were allowed to be off by themselves at the Fruit House until Ann got nervous about it and made a change. It was also thought that the contact with horses and hired people had been a bad school for those engaged in it. Further, some of the boys were getting quite well acquainted with the diningroom girls and it was noticed that a number of the young people seemed to hold attendance of the Evening Meetings lightly. Another more serious fault was the state that criticism had fallen into. There was little disposition on the part of the members to offer themselves for criticism. Theodore suggested that unless there was some earnestness on the part of people offering themselves for criticism, they would have to start a system by which everyone would come under criticism by routine.

Other minor matters such as an unsatisfactory state of things at recent picnics by excursionists and too much interest and attendance at the Oneida Fair were mentioned, but a more serious note was what was termed a "terrible spirit of irreverence on the part of some of the young folks, especially the class of larger boys." They did not have an earnest spirit of self-improvement, were not filled with the keen ambition for education which would enable them to be "tight toward the world." They had too much spare time and were not careful in the disposal of it. They would be happier as a family, Ann said, if they did not care for the ways and fashions of the world. When the Community got old enough so that all the relatives of the members were inside, they would be better than they were now.

What the G. W. Noyes Manuscript called the "Three-Cornered Interview" also occurred at Oneida in October when Ann Hobart went to Father Noyes and charged that Frank Wayland-Smith had a bad motive in urging that the *Circular* be superseded by the *American Socialist*. The reason, she alleged, was not to improve the Community paper but to free himself from an unwelcome associate on the earlier paper. She further alleged that this had caused Theodore much suffering. Noyes called Frank into the room to answer the charge which he immediately declared to be untrue, and further declared that it was Ann who was false to the Community ambition to have a high-class press, had shown no interest in the paper, and had persuaded Theodore to share her feeling about it. Upon this, Ann became extremely angry and denounced Theodore as being false to Community beliefs, especially Male Continence. Frank defended Theodore valiantly and "threw all of Ann's charges back upon herself."

Dissatisfaction with Ann, whether by Noyes or the Community in general, seemed to be spreading from this time. It was claimed that she interfered between lovers, to her own advantage, so that the gentlemen involved "lent a more willing ear to her own proposals." The G. W. Noyes Manuscript says that "Ann was at this time laying her nets for complete control over Theodore and for this reason contrived stratagems which would interfere with any other social connections he might have."

Astounding and preposterous as it would seem, "a rumor was spread through the Community that Theodore and Ann were planning to establish themselves with a few favorites in a villa overlooking the Hudson River. They were to have a palatial yacht in which they could make long trips, and they would govern the Community by means of administrative reports, rescripts and regulations. Another rumor had it that they were to build a fine house at Lewis Point, on Oneida Lake, and run the Community from there."

As was bound to happen with an intelligence as sensitive to emotional climate as JHN's, by late fall 1877 he had begun to pay attention to this situation. In early December he wrote about Ann's case that her recent sickness had been brought about by her ambition which drove her to do more than her strength allowed; "that she had concealed her infirmities when she should have made them known and submitted to be disabled and displaced by them; that she had taken responsibilities about Theodore's course which did not belong to her and which only oppressed him." A faithful criticism, he was convinced, was what she needed.

So concerned was he that on December 29 he wrote to Theodore about the matter. It was necessary to apprise him of certain facts involving his relation to Ann which might affect the general confidence in him as a leader of the Community. The situation was this:

> As far back as about the 20th of October, she voluntarily disclosed to at least four leading persons here, including myself, a state of things between you and her which, if accepted as true, would go to destroy confidence in you. I did not accept her representation at par, but stuck to my confidence in you and sealed my lips and advised that other person to do so. But on discovering later that Ann had approached others as she did me, and that in connection with late events there was a tendency in the Community to criticism of Ann and her relation to you, I have been compelled to open the case more or less to leading members and give my views of it. Unavoidably Ann's communications have penetrated the Community even beyond the small circle that has open knowledge of them and I assure you that there is a growing uneasiness here which will in the end lead to public discussion.

An urgent request by his father that Theodore come to Oneida immediately was answered on December 30, 1877, by a telegram evidently advising that Ann was very ill and asking for help from Oneida. His father replied by sending "a strong delegation qualified to give spiritual help as well as service in nursing." In the letter which followed the next day, Mr. Noyes went even further in his criticism of Ann: "The truth is that there has long been much dissatisfaction here with Ann, and since it has begun to be known that you were dissatisfied with her and that I did not support her nor accept her accusations against you, and since events have indicated the probability of her permanent disablement, these thoughts have more and more found vent. I think she ought to resign. By voluntarily withdrawing from the attempt to be the leading mother of the Community she may easily allay any present agitation and subside into a quiet position as a good humble woman in ordinary membership." He was, he admitted in a postscript, "suffering some from the return upon me of old responsibilities and the necessity of talk."

The next document is a criticism of Ann Hobart by John Humphrey Noyes, on January 4, 1878. In this he made clear the course by which Ann had assumed the female leadership of the Community. JHN had never nominated Ann for this position but had accepted her as being Theodore's choice until that day in October when she had come to him with charges against Theodore, "the first impression of which went to destroy my entire confidence in him; and I cannot doubt that her intention was to produce that impression, so far at least as to induce me to interfere and help her to establish her authority over him."

The criticism went on to detail Ann's allegations against Theodore including the surprising remark that in the course of her disputes with Theodore he had told her that his connection with her was the greatest misfortune of his life. At this time Mr. Noyes did not commit himself, although, he said, he was "ready, like Job, to rend my garments and sit down in ashes." However, he decided not to judge his son by Ann's testimony but to wait at least for a representation from Theodore's side.

For almost two months there was no word from either Theodore or Ann. "I waited long and struggled hard to evade the logic of the facts," the criticism continues. "That logic, as often as I confronted it, declared inexorably that I must either give up my confidence in Theodore or my confidence in Ann. I had to proceed to the conclusion that she herself had destroyed, by her attack on him, her only title to leadership and to the confidence of the Community. It is important to observe," he says in conclusion, "that the only practical point toward which I have moved has been to get Ann to resign. I have not asked Theodore to displace her. I have not judged her final character. I have not thought of interrupting her continuance in the Community or her hold on our love and care. But I have acted on the belief that she is disqualified for being the leading mother of the Community, first, by her disagreements with Theodore, which have been long-continued and well-known to many, and secondly by her bad state of health which has actually taken her out of office already and which she herself attributes in great measure to the mental strain caused by her discord with Theodore."

The only witness called upon to testify in this criticism was a young woman who had been a staunch admirer of Ann's but confessed that she had been pained by the disagreements between Ann and Theodore which she had witnessed at Wallingford and "wondered that such discord existed between persons in their position, when all the time they were the most intimate and dependent of friends."

"She made a good deal of fun of his doctoring and really talked very disrespectfully of him. I can scarcely remember an instance of his beating her in their discussions. He had to defer to her judgment, for she is very strong in argument and always convinces you that she is right." Mr. Noyes concluded the criticism by saying he thought that Theodore would be a greater man when left to his own judgment.

Four days later, on January 8, Theodore answered this criticism in a long letter in defense of Ann. His history of his relationship with her went back to 1873 when he had begun the study of spiritualism with Ann as his special medium. "She showed the characteristics of a medium in the highest degree of anyone I ever sat with, and unavoidably she has the excellencies and defects of that class of persons to a marked degree." These characteristics, he went on to say, were mental and spiritual phenomena quite at variance with those shown by non-mediums. The chief one and the one that gave rise to most others was inconsistency; "in their likes and dislikes, their feelings and tendencies of thought, mediums are variable and capricious," a trait which he attributed to their mind-reading power which makes a medium think and feel as their most intimate associates feel."

It seems that there was a very delicate point of theology involved:

> As we went on to seances and began to have communications from spirits, gradually a spirit manifested itself who made objections to certain [Community] doctrines advanced in meetings. Here the first mistake was made. That spirit, instead of being a familiar of Ann's and indicating her state of spirit, was really connected with me. I had no objection to his presence: his talk was nearly identical with my own thoughts. When Ann was in the ordinary state she held her spirit aloof from mine; but when she came under control, the utterances of this spirit were the evidence of her involuntary rapport with me. Some who were jealous for Community doctrine criticized her for being the medium of this spirit when she could not help it so long as she was so much with me.

There were other sources of difficulty which he recounted: a misunderstanding when Father Noyes had asked Ann to sit for the control of the Primitive Church and she refused; her relations with another man and woman who, Theodore said, were "non-magnetizers" who always had a peculiar effect on mediums so that "the dreadful cramp of conscience" which finally drove Ann to the exposure of himself was due to her rapport with those legal moralists.

There was nothing to be gained, he wrote, by separating him from such a friend as Ann. Her true place, he believed, was as a link between himself and his father, whom he urged to draw out Ann's love for him so that, "instead of using her as a lever with which to work on each other, he and his father could send messages of peace and concord across her."

JHN was not persuaded by this appeal. In a letter to the family on January 11, 1878 he made an answer: "It will be noticed that Theodore and I have exactly opposite theories about the relation between him and Ann. He sticks to it that he has psychologized her from first to last, and I hold that she has psychologized him from first to last and is the cause not only of the late unprincipled conduct which she complains of in him but of his whole departure from the faith of the Community."

His argument went back to the revival of 1863 when Theodore was a religious enthusiast and Ann was his prize convert: "The great question of his history is, what took place at or near this time

which switched him off to his later course of unbelief and irreverence? My answer is that in the early revival a spiritual junction was
formed between him and Ann in which he thought he captured
her, when, in fact, she captured him; and that he has been her
prisoner ever since."

There was one other point which the members of the Community should be able to recognize: the Bailey spirit. It could be per-
ceived in Ann's physical structure as well as her mental makeup;
she had been distributing the spirit of her father. Even her brother
Daniel, "though a bad man, was a shrewd observer of character,"
and he had said to the Community of Ann: "You will find her
out; she has got her eye on being the head of the Community."
That, said JHN, is the Bailey spirit—*diatrephiasis*.

In this extraordinary passage two typical Community locutions
should perhaps be explained. *Psychologized,* as Mr. Noyes used it
here, meant apparently something between a kind of psychiatric
understanding and perhaps even hypnosis. It certainly contains the
idea of influence and even control of one person by another, as when
Theodore claims to have "psychologized" Ann in her rapport with
him, while his father believed that, on the contrary, Ann had so
far dominated him as to cause his departure from the faith of the
Community. Secondly, Ann's ambition, as predicted by her brother
Daniel, was to be the head of the Community. This, Mr. Noyes
said, using another familiar Community phrase, was "the Bailey
spirit—*diatrephiasis.*" This last was a word JHN had invented some
years before to describe "the preeminence mania, or the Who-shall-
be-greatest mania." "This enlargement of the *ego,*" he wrote in the
Circular, February 25, 1867, "is the most constant symptom of
virulent mania."

The end of the chapter was a long and astonishingly frank
confession by Ann. She had been, she said, cruel, heartless, ill-
natured in her dealings with her lovers:

> All through my life I have had this heartless cruel way of being very
> affectionate and demonstrative toward people at one time and at
> another indifferent, with apparently no cause for the change. I have
> not only made the men themselves suffer, but sometimes their friends.
> There has been that in me that was willing to absorb the attention of
> men, careless as to whether it took them away from other friends or

not. Though I have *said* I wanted them to love others, in my spirit
I have been selfish and uncommunistic.

Most of all I have had this cruel spirit toward Theodore. I made
him suffer terribly and then I would feel impatient and as if I was the
one who was abused. I have abused Theodore in a great many ways,
domineering over him about his own personal affairs. There has been
that in me that knew, if we had any disagreement, that he would come
to me and make up, and I have often held out until he did it; and
then instead of being softened by his better example, it only hardened
me and made me tyrannize over him the more. I have held on to him
when I believe he would have been glad to get free.

The final sweeping-up of the pieces is described in Frank
Wayland-Smith's journal, dated January 14, 1878:

Since my last entry there has been a complete overturn in the leadership of the Oneida Community. The events of the last month have
been tragic and saddening. Mr. Noyes instituted a very thorough examination of Ann Hobart's career. He found that Dr. Noyes had, in
his six months of leadership, departed from old Community ideas in
such a way as to largely undermine confidence in him, and Mr. Noyes
adopted the theory that Ann had psychologized him. Dr. Noyes would
not accept this hypothesis or admit that he had been going wrong.
This led to sharp collisions between him and his father and ended in
Dr. Noyes resigning the leadership, his father accepting the resignation. At length Ann Hobart broke down and confessed that she had
been wrong and that Mr. Noyes's judgment of her was correct.

After Theodore resigned his position as leader, Mr. Noyes had
Judge Towner draw up a paper in the form of a will, signed and sealed
and duly witnessed, providing that in case Mr. Noyes should die before Theodore should be restored to Community faith and to his position as leader, a committee of thirty-five persons whom he named
should take charge of the Community and make such provisions in regard to leadership, etc., as seemed to them wisest.

A vague reference has been made to Dr. Noyes's perversion from
the faith of his father. I will briefly state here the ground he holds, as
nearly as I can understand him, my opinions being formed from what
he has said to me. Theodore does not believe in the divinity of Christ.
He thinks Christ was a medium of some good and powerful spirit, but
he was only a man and not the son of God, as he claimed to be; i.e.,
he was not divine as to his origin more than other men. He believes
in the doctrine of evolution implicitly, and will not undertake to define
the Creator or First Cause. He has read the works of all the leading
German materialists and become considerably impregnated with their

ideas and modes of thought. While leader for the past six months his endeavor has been to secularize the Community and subordinate religion. He has, himself, taken little or no part in the religious exercises of the family, such as the Confession of Christ, expressions of faith, etc., and although Ann *has* taken part in these matters, it is not generally believed that she helped him to be more religious.

4

JHN Resumes Command

The year 1878, having opened with a grand climax in the resignation of Theodore, fell into a rather melancholy anticlimactic humdrum. No news was good. Charles Cragin, the brilliant and irresistible young man who was a romantic hero to the whole class of Community girls, died suddenly at Wallingford of a combination of overwork and too much quinine in that malaria-haunted spot. After his death, letters and a diary disclosed that his real love had been the beautiful Edith Waters who was herself dying of tuberculosis in a sanatarium at nearby Verona Springs. One woman's diary notes that "we *all* feel very sad. Emily and Marian are full of grief and Lily is almost frenzied. Belle probably feels very bad and Leonora, Edith and Jessie etc. are all very sorrowful."

A male member's journal gives a more objective account of the affair. "Certain disclosures convinced Mr. Noyes that Ann, Dr. Noyes, and Charles had formed a 'ring' and laid unwise plans. It was found that a class of girls from 16 to 20 years of age had been captivated by Charles and drawn away from true Community principles. The news of his death made them frantic. They had idolized him and, as afterwards transpired, he had persuaded them, one and all, that each was his particular favorite. So they vied with each other in mourning him until their conduct became the subject of a sharp criticism by Mr. Noyes."

By the first of February JHN had fully resumed the practical leadership of the Community. He appointed Erastus Hamilton, James Towner, and Martin Kinsley as his assistants in the management of the businesses and announced that in the future his officers should be subject to periodical criticisms by the family. Myron Kinsley was appointed to take Charles Cragin's place in the management of the spoon business at Wallingford. This new enterprise, however, was found to be in such a bad state that at first Noyes proposed they sell out all their property at Wallingford and concentrate their energies at Oneida. Fortunately this was not carried out.

The Theodore-Ann situation still hung fire—Theodore at Oneida, Ann at Wallingford. Father and son had been on very distant terms, but on January 25 a "good letter" from Theodore to his father was read in the meeting, as recorded in C. J. Worden's diary: "He says he desires to come into unity with his father and will for that end either write for the *Socialist* or go to Joppa with him or even lounge in his room. Anything to promote unity."

Whether or not this had the desired effect is not stated, but it is certain that JHN had taken the helm again in no uncertain way. In that same meeting he brought forward a proposition that they should sell their resort cottage at Short Beach, on Long Island Sound, which they had named Cozicot. He also suggested that the Community stop propagation. Unfortunately there is no record of the response to these suggestions. The next night, evidently by his decree, it was announced that there was to be no more "timekeeping," by which one must assume was meant the rule for weekly reports of "social" connections which Dr. Noyes and Ann had inaugurated. A new children's committee of six was appointed.

It seems evident that the Community's financial situation was worrying Mr. Noyes. The proposal to sell the Wallingford property was not voted, although Theodore, who was considered the financial expert, estimated that the property, minus the house and home lot, was worth $67,000 which was, conveniently, the exact amount of the Community's debt incurred during his administration. Other means must be found, and within the next fortnight Mr. Noyes called a meeting in which he discoursed on economy in general and especially exhorted the members to economize in dress and food, advising everyone to "save all they could, make all they could, and sell all they could." Later each member received a printed slip with the following question on it: "First, can you get along comfortably until March 1st, 1879, without any appropriation? Second, if not, how much will be sufficient until that time? Third, how much of your appropriation are you willing to supply by selling watches, jewelry, or other articles in your possession?" C. J. Worden, one diarist who recorded this questionnaire, answered flatly that she needed $11 and would like as much as $17.75, and added that she had nothing to sell. The final piece of economy she recorded without comment: that the New York office was to be closed for a while.

She also noted in early March that "Mr. Noyes's mind is full of projects for making money during the coming summer by entertaining visitors. I guess it will be an eventful time. He intends to give daily concerts and have the children on the stage, and besides this he is going to have the outdoor brass band play twice every day and the military band for marching and an organization to play for dances. He has invited everyone to make any suggestions that occur to them and that will make a success of the thing." Sober and burdened he may have been, but not for long. Here were the old resilience, the old buoyancy, optimism, and ingenuity.

Another journalist noted that "Mr. Noyes has conceived the idea of making an unusual effort to entertain visitors the coming summer. The Rev. Joseph Cook of Boston is preaching or lecturing on the subject of marriage, family relations etc., and denounces the O.C. Bishop Huntington, of Syracuse, also denounces the O.C. in a pastoral address and both call for legislation to suppress us. The newspapers comment more or less and altogether there is abundant evidence that we are likely to have a heavy run of visitors. Mr. Noyes thinks we ought to do our best to entertain them and at the same time make some money out of them, so he is planning a heavy musical season."

He had also arranged to have the Bible classes started again under the instruction of Mr. Towner and Mr. Henry Burnham and "to push for a revival." Theodore, it was noted, was very sober and did not attend meetings. He kept to his room mostly and argued with his father by writing and through a third person. In the midst of this new activity, mourning for the adored Charles had more or less subsided when another period of agitation occurred.

It was known that Ann Hobart was becoming very restive at Wallingford, but it came as a complete surprise to Oneida when it was known that she had written to Joseph Skinner, JHN's nephew, then living in New Haven, asking him to come and see her. This, of course, was entirely against the Community's rule against associating with outsiders, and later Ann was "under conviction" and confessed her act. There was much traveling back and forth. Joseph urged her to marry him. She refused, then changed her mind, and the final clap of thunder for Oneida was the announcement they had run away to New Haven and got married.

This was naturally extremely painful for Theodore. As Frank Wayland-Smith noted in his journal:

> He upbraided his father with having driven Ann out of the Community and they had some very bitter altercations. From that time, Theodore rapidly turned from his father and on the 22nd of March proposed to leave the Community, taking one of the young women with him as his wife. He did not intend to entirely separate from the O.C. but only to live outside and do business for us, still being regarded as a member. Mr. Noyes would not agree to that. Theodore tried various suggestions but as they were all opposed, he finally left the Community, alone, for the second time, on Friday, March 29, 1878, at noon. His plan was ostensibly to be gone only a month to try life in the world but he told me only an hour before he left that if he could succeed in maintaining himself, he should never return.

This was now the situation. Dr. Noyes and Ann Hobart, who six months before had been in unlimited power as an acting administration over the two communities of Oneida and Wallingford, had now both left the society and gone out into the world. It was learned later that Theodore had gone into partnership with Abel Easton, an ex-Oneidaite, who was running a Turkish Bath in New York City. For this purpose Theodore withdrew from the Community the $3,500 trust fund which had been left him by a Vermont relative. It appeared that his last connection with the Oneida Community had been severed.

Perhaps to distract his mind from what must have been a severe emotional blow, John Humphrey Noyes found a new interest in spiritualism which he had heretofore approved only as a diversion for Theodore. Now he took it up with enthusiasm, held daily seances in his room, and announced in the Evening Meeting that he considered himself a medium, and neither a preacher nor a writer. He did discuss the perpetuity of the Community and said that its insurance depended upon the fulfillment of his mission to unite heaven and earth. At least one member recorded this meeting as "grand."

In June there was talk of more members seceding. Arthur Towner and Augusta Hamilton who had already left, sent word that they had married, although later they repented and wanted to return and be readmitted to the Community. A most surprising letter was received from Theodore asking the privilege of coming to Oneida to write an article for his father. He said that it was very hot in the city but that was not his object in leaving. He arrived on July 5 in an apparently chastened mood, but by the next day, in a talk with Frank Wayland-Smith, he broached the subject of leadership.

As Frank recorded it: "He evidently intends to make some arrangement with his father which will allow of his returning as leader. Strange situation! Think of an outsider coolly calculating whether he will return and be king over 300 people, the same people meanwhile awaiting the decision without a word of protest! This shows J. H. Noyes's control of men." Three weeks later he noted that "Dr. Theodore Noyes is still here on a visit. He and his father seem to have arrived at a tolerably fair understanding, but in the Community at large there is a strong prejudice against his being leader again."

After many long discussions between father and son, on August 4 in Evening Meeting Mr. Noyes presented a proposition to readmit Theodore to membership in the O.C. Mr. Noyes made some prefatory remarks in the course of which he repeated what he had previously said, that he should never again appoint Theodore leader in any formal, arbitrary way but that whatever influence he acquired must come by faith and good works; that in this respect he should be on precisely the same footing as any other member. A vote was taken on the proposition and Theodore was unanimously accepted as a member.

The next ill-wind that troubled the Community waters was a blast by the New York *Times* on August 8, 1878, so scurrilous and sensational that it was copied widely in various local papers and gave rise to the rumor, based on its statements, that the Community was about to dissolve. Its headline was "Oneida's Queer People; Trouble in the Community of Socialists. Withdrawal of Members and Abandonment of the Sub-community in Connecticut—Why Brethren Secede Without Causing Commotion—Dissenters from the Views of Noyes, the Founder."

The article itself, the first of three appearing on three successive days, was replete with whole-cloth inventions. It reported that "Mr. Abiel Kingsley, one of the original founders of the Community, withdrew some time ago, the Community paying him $10,000 in cash for his share. I am informed that one of the withdrawing parties—a woman—was paid $500 in gold, although the contract upon entering the Community specifically waives legal action for recovery." The reporter, who may have been Francis Gerry Fairfield, admits that John Humphrey Noyes and William Hinds and other older members were "somewhat reticent, but the younger Noyes, the physician, discussed the subject very frankly, and unreservedly," from which he learned that deeper causes than the mere discontent of a few restless members have been actively at work. "Of the younger members, many of them are extremely skeptical of the apostolical claims of Mr. Noyes and the value of his revelations. Among the skeptics is young Noyes, himself, who has become the leader of a strong party." He also adds that "the elder Noyes is growing somewhat infirm and his personal influence, once so potent, is on the wane."

The next article, on August 9, opened with a pathetic scene: "As the carriage turned the corner and the entrance gate came into view, I saw a withered figure bend over an open rose and kiss it with a pathetic tenderness, like a mother kissing her baby." This was sad enough but the rest of the description must have drawn tears from his readers: "The woman could not have been less than 45 years of age. Her face was pale and somewhat haggard and there were dark shadows beneath her eyes. Her hair was short. She wore a faded calico skirt cut like a camisole. It descended but a trifle below the knees. Turkish trousers completed the costume. It was a sorry and ridiculous figure, only that little tenderness of kissing the rose lent a species of pathos to the uncomliest outfit that a woman in the full possession of her senses ever put on."

The Community did not dignify that piece of fustion with a denial; no one, they assumed, would believe such arrant nonsense. They were greatly amused, however, by one fatal slip made by the *Times* reporter. In describing the Evening Meeting he wrote, "A grand piano ornaments the stage and the verse you will hear as often as any other is from Etienne Cabet's 'Song of the Socialists.'

> Travaillers de la grand cause
> Soyons fiers de notre destin;
> L'egoiste seul se repose,
> Travaillons pour le genre humain.

"It spoils the effect of this," the *American Socialist,* August 29, 1878, said drolly, "to record the fact that no song with this refrain was ever sung in the Community Hall at Oneida and that the *Times* correspondent heard no singing whatever during his hour's sojourn at the Community. Where, then, did he get this fine refrain, and how did he come to copy it into his description of the O.C.? Well, while he was here he wisely invested sixty cents in a copy of Hinds's *American Communities,* which, besides giving an account of the Oneida and Wallingford Communities, describes the other successful Communistic societies of the United States; and in its description of the Icarian Community occurs the passage which the *Times* at once applied to the O.C."

The only allegation in the *Times* articles which the Community denounced as "deliberate slander" was from the last of the series, published on August 10: "The other night at one of their evening meetings where all questions of Community policy are discussed, it was gravely proposed to expose the children, at regular intervals, to scarlet fever and diphtheria-infection, in order to test their vitality and secure an experimental illustration of the Darwinian hypothesis of the survival of the fittest. It was urged that under the existing conditions children unfit for survival are encouraged to grow up, and that the ultimate result must be a larger percentage of adult invalids than is desirable. The question was not settled but remains to be talked over again."

The *American Socialist,* August 21, explained how this piece of vicious slander was put together:

It was distilled from two innocent passages in a pamphlet lately issued from our press, entitled *Report on the Health of Children in the Oneida Community, by T. R. Noyes, M.D.* That pamphlet was put into the hands of the *Times* reporter during his visit to the O.C., and the fact that the above item has absolutely no semblance to truth except what it gets from the following passages in that pamphlet, makes it certain that it was thus distilled.

First extract: "The Community children have been (whether desirably or not) secluded from measles, whooping-cough, scarlet fever, and the mumps. It is a question admitting a good deal of argument whether it is best to seclude children from the measles and whooping-cough. In favor of seclusion it may be urged that these diseases are known to check the growth of children, if not followed by more serious consequences; while against it is the strong point that grown people suffer much more during an attack than children. The propriety of exposing the children in detachments and at suitable times of year, to measles and whooping-cough has been discussed in the Community, but nothing has yet been done" (*Report,* page 4).

Second extract: "When we consider the suffering and labor entailed on women in bearing and nursing the 30% of children born which die under ten years of age in the United States, and all the untold agony of disappointed affection, to say nothing of the waste of time, food, and clothing to the commonwealth, we may be pardoned a little pride in showing a state where this wasted suffering is almost wholly avoided.

"We must not be blind, however, to a defect which lurks in this, as in all other attempts of civilization to save lives which would be lost under rougher conditions. In proportion as sanitary science saves weakly lives and throws protection around tender shoots which otherwise would yield to the storm—in this proportion science must grapple with the increased diseases of adolescence and middle life—diseases which tend to invalidism rather than death. The abolition of natural selection, by doing away with the vicissitudes which the strong alone can survive in childhood, must certainly lower the tone of adult health, unless artificial selection takes its place. Our social state admits of the application of intelligent artificial selection, and therefore can ultimately, we believe, overcome this, as all other defects" (Report, Page 8).

The *American Socialist* on August 22 explicitly refuted the *Times* article:

In these passages we easily identify the elements out of which the *Times* item was concocted; the alleged discussion appears in the first, and the alleged reason for it in the second; these two elements are brought together in the item, though they are four pages apart and have nothing whatever to do with one another. The simple truth of the whole matter is this:

First, the entire idea of any discussion at all in our public meeting, "the other night" or at any other time, on the question of exposing our children to infectious diseases is pure sensational fiction. No such debate was ever held.

In the second place, there was never any talk, public or private, about exposing the children, as the *Times* reporter maliciously alleges, to *scarlet-fever* and *diphtheria* or any other such deadly diseases, but only to measles and whooping-cough, which are comparatively harmless, and which are generally supposed to be unavoidable. The application of what is said in the pamphlet about measles and whooping-cough, to scarlet-fever and diphtheria, was manifestly made with deliberate malignity of purpose.

Thirdly, the motive alleged by the Reporter, viz., "to test the vitality of the children and secure an experimental illustration of the Darwinian hypothesis of the survival of the fittest," is wholly imaginary, as is the pretended debate on the subject. The only motive of the individuals who talked about exposing the children to measles and whooping-cough was to save them from having those diseases at unsuitable times and in dangerous forms—all of which is manifest from the language of the pamphlet.

Finally, the reference to the Darwinian hypothesis of the survival of the fittest in the pamphlet stands in connection with statistics and observations which show that *in the Community family of 57 children under ten years of age there has not been a single death in eight years,* and that we take "a little pride" in this fact instead of talking about providing against it, as the *Times* man insinuates.

And now to show what the author of this slander intended to effect by it, and how he succeeded, we select from the *Syracuse Daily Courier* [August 12, 1878] the following preface to the venomous item from the *Times:*

"A letter to the *New York Times* describing the state of affairs at Oneida Community, tells the following monstrous proposition made by the members of the Community, *to kill off their sickly children.*" The *Times* item and so the slander in its most virulent form commences its tour round the world.

In accounting for the success of the Community for the past thirty years, the *Times* claimed to have discovered the great secret which had hitherto eluded all other investigators, i.e., their system of Mutual Criticism:

The Community have weekly meetings for abusing one another which they enjoy to their hearts' content. But only one member can be abused or criticized at a time, and he must sit silent, biding his time of revenge, which comes after a while, as all have to take turns as subjects of criticism. But as there are a great many to be criticized, it is a long time before any who have been abused in this way can get even with all his critics—so long, in fact, that when it comes he is liable to have to undergo another course of criticism. And so, no matter how much any of them might wish to leave the Community, he was always determined to stay until he could give each one of his critics as heavy blows as he himself had received. This was the real tie that held the Community together. They lived on in order to "get square" with their fellows at some future meeting for "social criticism" that Noyes should have recognized the fact that he could bind his followers together by the bond of mutual hate, stamps him as a man of real, if perverted, genius.

It was heartening to the folks at Oneida that a number of other newspapers sprang to their defense; the most notable, the *New York World,* in a long and admiring article which painted a pretty if not always accurate picture of the Community and which claimed that it "exemplified a perfect system." Local papers—in Utica, Syracuse, Fulton, Elmira, Madison, and others—wrote, almost unanimously, that the members of the Community were "truly a Christian people, their purposes are honest and just beyond cavil or doubt."

For themselves, the Community, in the *American Socialist* for August 15, 1878, was almost too euphoric:

> There is no serious dissension in the Oneida Community. We have not had a greater number of withdrawals the past year than in some other years of our history. Of those who have left, only one was a prominent member, and he did not wish to have his withdrawal considered as a final separation, and has already come back to the Community. There is not a growing party in the Community opposed to its social or religious views. There has not been so great a degree of harmony in the Community for years as at the present time; and though the hard times have depressed some of our businesses, our leading branches of manufacture are fairly prosperous, and a new business, recently started at Wallingford, promises to give us an important additional revenue.

For a time reporters from near and far flocked to Oneida and created quite a stir, but the excitement subsided and the Community went back to its old ways. The enthusiasm for education which had burned so brightly in earlier days seemed about to flare up again, and Theodore Noyes was appointed to superintend the education of the young people. Since it was still summer, the usual excursions flocked to visit the Community. At first, after the newspaper stories, not so many tourists appeared—only fifty one day, because of the rumors of chaos—but later as many as six hundred at a time, which brought in a welcome $600 for the treasury. Two of the most notable seceders, Arthur and Augusta Towner, returned, and after pleading hard, were readmitted as members. Another pair talked of leaving. Mr. Noyes proposed a family fast for a week from all stimulants such as tea, coffee, cider, beer, meat, and cards. His object, said one diarist, was to "promote unity by a state of prayer and earnestness." Theodore, who had been ailing with jaundice, recovered and petitioned his father to be allowed to start a business in making malleable iron, using the old foundry on the Wilson property near the Willow Place factory. There was some objection to undertaking a new enterprise at this time, and the matter was put over to the first of the year. The new north wing of the Mansion House was nearly finished, and some of the members were already moving into the rooms on the first three floors. An analysis of the circulation of the *American Socialist* showed that it had dropped to 524, which was discouraging, and an editorial to be printed after the New Year, on January 30, 1879, gave notice that unless the paper became self-supporting by December 31, 1879, it would be discontinued. An observer would say, wrote one diarist, that things had never gone so smoothly before.

5

Crusade of the Clergy

The events of the first six months of 1879 should really be scored in a kind of counterpoint, recorded, as it were, on two levels, the ground-bass being the stated or unstated dissension going on in the Community itself; the antiphon being the outside movement against them, which came to be known in the newspapers as the Crusade of the Clergy.

The first notes were sounded in the treble in the form of an article in the Utica *Daily Observer*, December 13, 1878, announcing that a convention would meet on Friday, February 14, 1879, "to consider the Oneida Community and make a more decided expression in regard to it." Invitations to this convention were sent to churches throughout New York State, and this invitation, referred to as The Call, was supposed to be kept a secret by all who received it. Unfortunately, "some enterprising members of the press of Syracuse," learning that a meeting was to be held and that a circular had been sent out, visited Chancellor Haven of Syracuse University a few nights previous to the assembly and "were graciously granted an interview and a copy of The Call." This, however, did not placate the press which was, throughout the Crusade, unforgiving. They had been barred from attending the convention, and from that time on they berated and made fun of the embattled clergy and championed the Oneida Community.

At the Community, Mr. Noyes was unconcerned. He had suspected that this might happen, since whenever there was a stir-up about the Mormons there was usually one soon after about the O.C. This time, he was sure that Dr. Mears, of Hamilton College, was at the back of it and probably wrote all the unpleasant remarks in the papers, as he had in 1874, when his address to the Presbyterian Synod had contained so many unintentionally flattering references to the O.C. that some of the newspapers had considered the whole thing greatly in its favor.

76

The report of November 1874, whose style would seem to identify its author as Dr. Mears, said of the Oneida Community, "by their thrift, their industry, their activity, they have vastly improved not only the large farm which they occupy but the neighborhood generally has risen in prosperity. Land is more valuable. The poor have employment. The Community does good work and has an excellent business reputation. A number of newspaper articles, with a single known exception, were more complimentary to the Community than to the Synod itself."

The *Circular* remarked demurely on November 23: "This fact need not discourage the Synod. If they will industriously attend to their own business for 27 years and do good work, as they say we have done, they also may earn an excellent reputation and draw complimentary notices from the press. There is room for all of us."

It was remarked in the Evening Meeting on February 12, 1879, that the most that Mears and his confreres could expect to accomplish by this latest attack was to work on public opinion through their ministers so as to bring some legislation against the Community.

Noyes appointed William Hinds, who was assistant editor of the *American Socialist,* to attend the convention as a reporter. It was understood that this convention was to be a union of Episcopalians, Presbyterians, and Methodists. It was the Community's opinion that there would be an attempt to bring about some legislation against it.

The Call read as follows:

Syracuse, New York
January 23, 1879

Dear Sir:

The great wrong done to society by the institution known as the Oneida Community from its deadly opposition to the principles of Christian morality appears to demand some united counsel and action on the part of teachers of the Gospel and defendants of public and domestic virtue in this part of the country.

After some informal consultation we, the undersigned, are encouraged to write you to attend a preliminary meeting at Syracuse, in the University Building, on Friday, the 14th day of February, at 2:30 o'clock, P.M.

Will you kindly inform the Rev. A. F. Beard, Syracuse, whether
you may be expected to be present:

John W. Mears	A. Huntington
A. F. Beard	E. O. Haven
E. G. Thurber	

On February 13, the day before the convention was to be held,
the *Utica Observer* uttered a warning: "Zeal without knowledge is
sometimes dangerous." They said of John Noyes that there was
nothing in his long life to indicate that he was either a hypocrite
or a knave, and they concluded ominously that it might be well for
the Syracuse gathering to know that "the people at the towns in
which the Community is located are inclined to defend it from
assault."

The *Utica Herald* also cautioned them against attempting to use
legal means: "The most careful scrutiny has failed to construct a
case which would bring either the individuals or the Community
within reach of the courts." The *Albany Evening Times,* on February 12, started off with a terrific blast: "A telegram published yesterday announced that a movement was on foot to dislodge the
nest of unclean birds known as the Oneida Community." Later it
modified its language: "Its social system is only to be named with
horror and disgust; yet the visitor sees nothing either to alarm or to
annoy him in the least. One sees and hears as little to shock decorum
as he would at a Presbyterian prayer-meeting."

Both the *New York Herald* and the *Syracuse Daily Standard*
sent reporters to Oneida and both interviewed William Hinds, who
answered questions freely and refused to be alarmed:

Whatever comes out of this, we await the issue with calmness. But in
our opinion it is all nonsense for this conference or any other body
of persons to think of breaking up the Oneida Community. We have
been settled in our present location for 30 years, and have built up
large business interests. We certainly have some rights in the matter
and among these rights is that of living as we do in a combined household; there is nothing wrong that can be made out of that. When these
people talk about breaking us up it looks like a conspiracy to injure
us, and it is certainly the kind of talk a Christian body should not
indulge in. If we break any existing laws, we are amenable to their
just penalties, and if any new laws are made they can only affect our

John Humphrey Noyes, founder of the Oneida Community; photo probably around 1870. By 1876, controversies over his leadership of the Community had coalesced into three main groups: the Noyesites, loyal to JHN; the anti-Noyesites or Townerites, led by James W. Towner; and the Third party, whose members advocated converting the Community into a joint-stock company.

Harriet Holton Noyes ("Mother Noyes") was born in Vermont. In 1838, "on Community principles," she married JHN and began with him the Putney Association and later the O.C. She was deeply religious, unselfish, loving, and loved by all.

Harriet Noyes Skinner, JHN's sister, was converted by him in 1836. An original member of the Putney Association and a prominent writer in all O.C. publications, she was a vigorous defender and adherent of her brother.

Left: George Cragin, Sr., born in Massachusetts, was a staunch supporter of JHN. As a young man in New York he published the *Advocate of Moral Reform* until he was converted by JHN in 1839. He joined the Putney Association in 1840. *Below left:* George E. Cragin, M.D., son of George, Sr., grew up in the O.C. and graduated from Yale. Despite this worldly experience, he remained loyal to JHN. *Below right:* Charles Cragin, son of George, Sr., also grew up in the O.C. and graduated from Yale as an engineer. He was responsible for the beginning of the O.C. silverware business.

Mansion House,
prior to 1870.

Entrance and east front of Mansion House, early 1870s.

Road-mending bee. A typical Community measure for easing boring or time-consuming tasks, bees were held less frequently during the late 1870s.

Oneida Community family on north lawn, 1863.

Theodore L. Pitt, originally a Perfectionist from New Jersey, joined the O.C. in 1853. He was a devoted Noyesite and went with JHN to Canada in 1879.

Sewall Newhouse, a pioneer blacksmith in the backwoods of Oneida County, joined the O.C. in 1848. He invented the steel trap which the Community later developed and manufactured.

Picnic at the Cascades, about fifteen miles from Oneida at Stockbridge Falls.

Summer House, 1866, a popular gathering spot for the O.C. family.

Albert Kinsley, a convert to JHN's writings whose loyalty never wavered, brought his family from Fletcher, Vermont, to Oneida in 1848.

Martin E. Kinsley, elder son of Albert Kinsley, was one of the responsible managers of the O.C. businesses. He later joined James W. Towner in the anti-Noyesite party.

Myron H. Kinsley, younger son of Albert Kinsley, left the O.C. for a time but returned to be JHN's "strong right arm" in the final years.

William H. Woolworth, a convert from
Massachusetts, joined the O.C. in 1849.
A much respected member who served as
surrogate "Father" at Oneida when JHN
was away, he was one of the four trustees
for the Community.

Erastus Hapgood Hamilton, a deeply religious man devoted to O.C. principles, acted as JHN's viceregent.

Charles Otis Kellogg came to the O.C. as a youth in 1849. He was loyal to JHN and was named one of the four trustees for the Community.

South garden, tended by
O.C. women.

Oneida Community Orchestra, showing the wide range
of musical instruments played. JHN is eighth from
right; Francis Wayland-Smith is eighth from left.

Community women in their famous short dresses and long pantalets.

The O.C family on lawn and garden of south side of Mansion House, before 1878.

Above left: Henry Allen, originally from Wallingford, Connecticut, gave his Wallingford farm to the O.C. when he and his wife joined. A branch commune was established there in 1851. *Above right:* Henry G. Allen, son of Henry Allen, was a devoted Noyesite who remained in the O.C. through the breakup and was for many years a director of the new company. *Right:* George Allen, younger son of Henry Allen, was an O.C. "peddler," here showing a spool of silk thread which was one of the Community's many manufactures.

p left: A few members of the family in the Quadrangle, before 1878. *Top right:* mily group on east lawn of Mansion House, 1870s. *Bottom left:* A few family mbers in the south garden. *Bottom right:* Front porch of Mansion House and veway, with garden back center, prior to 1870.

Theodore Richards Noyes, M.D., born in 1841, only son of John Humphrey and Harriet Holton Noyes, led the Third party. Much vigorous discussion in the O.C. concerned Theodore's succession to JHN, who wanted his son to lead the Community. Theodore, however, could not reconcile himself to his father's religious principles.

Ann Sophronia Bailey, known in the O.C. as Ann Hobart, was a brilliant and attractive young woman who joined the Community with her family in 1859. During Theodore Noyes's period as leader, she became the dominant power, was much resented, and finally left the Community at the age of thirty-two and married Joseph Skinner.

conduct as individuals; they cannot touch the question of our existence as an organized body; communism of property and living in combined households can never be made crimes.

In the Evening Meeting on February 14, the day of the conference, Mr. Burnham, who had also been in Syracuse, reported that there had been fifty clergymen present; that Mr. Hinds, with other reporters, was refused admittance; that Mr. Hinds had taken a room at the Vanderbilt Hotel and was writing for the Syracuse papers, both of which had promised to publish anything he wrote. Two days later Mr. Hinds returned to make a report to the family. At first he had some difficulty in finding a suitable person to distribute the copies of the *Socialist* which he had brought for that purpose but that, on calling on the editor of the *Standard,* he was met cordially and furnished with a reliable person who would present a paper to each minister as he entered. Mr. Somers, the editor, had also said, "D--n it, what do they want to do? D--n it, why don't they mind their own business?" In spite of his profanity, Mr. Hinds thought him quite a nice man.

The *O.C. Journal,* February 16, 1879, reported the occasion:

At 2 P.M. Mr. Hinds went up in a hack with two other reporters (in good style) to the University, and as they entered saw 20 or 30 reading the paper in the vestibule, and laughing and talking. One said, "This is bearding the lion in his den." He said that Prof. Mears, who seemed to be the ruling spirit of the occasion, was dodging about with a black patch over one eye, presenting a very comical appearance. William, with the other reporters, took off their overcoats and called for a table. He said that in looking around just before the call to order, the scene that presented itself reminded him of the farce we have on our stage where the children come filing in with those great handkerchiefs before their faces: for there sat the crowd buried each behind his *Socialist,* eagerly perusing its pages.

Prof. Mears requested all persons not invited should leave the room. Mr. Flanagan, the reporter from the *Utica Herald,* walked around among them and told them they were making a great mistake to exclude the reporters, but go they had to, and did. Here Wm. spoke of the wonderful resource and cunning these reporters have on such occasions—that they make it their business to be prepared to find out in some way what they want to know in case they are barred out. Those who had graduated there at the University knew ways to hear what was going on in that room.

Mr. Noyes thought it very probable "that all the reporters were excluded in order to exclude Mr. Hinds and that if he had not gone up there, the ministers would not have offended the editors as they did."

A confidential letter was received by the Community from Charles B. Atwell, editor-in-chief of the *Syracusan,* a student publication, saying that "the late meeting in opposition to the Oneida Community has awakened an unusual interest among us, especially as the doors were closed against us," and requesting a short communication from Mr. Noyes representing his views on the subject. Mr. Noyes responded in a jocular letter in which he called their attention to the "vigor of the terms used in the convention—They are to be 'broken up,' to be 'extinguished,' to be 'suppressed,' to be 'eradicated,' to be 'wiped out,' to be 'stamped out,' to be 'demolished.' "

As had happened often before on occasions of unusual publicity, applications to join the Oneida Community began to pour in. The attitudes of both the public and the press were almost uniformly in their favor. A "brevity" in the *Buffalo Courier* said that they were "pained to hear that there was a movement on foot for the Oneida Community to suppress the clergy." Mr. Noyes said that he really thought they were stretching public opinion in this country into a more thoughtful state than it had ever been in before: "There is a chronic irritation going on between the press and the clergy and the press is constantly getting the better of the clergy. It is a very fine thing that in this struggle between the press and the clergy we have come up, not as patrons of the clerical system but of the newspaper system, so that we are in sympathy with the new that is coming up and thrusting out the old, with the growing instead of the decaying."

Mr. Hinds thought if they ceased publishing at the end of the year, it would be well to keep their materials in readiness, so that they could get out a paper at any time. Mr. Noyes replied that he had not the least idea that they would stop publishing, essentially. There were a great many ways in which they could go on; for instance, they could go on writing for other papers.

The secret of how the report of the proceedings of the Convention had leaked out was made known on February 15, 1879, by the

Utica Herald which noted that "upon the adjournment of the meeting, every reporter who had patiently waited outside in the hall was tendered verbatim an abstract report of the proceedings by from one to three of the clergymen who did not approve of their exclusion from the conference. Students representing the local press were among those permitted to remain and take notes and the result of their work was soon public among the press men."

The "verbatim abstract report" was nothing more interesting than that the first resolution offered by Professor Mears had read, "for the suppression of the Oneida Community," but upon Chancellor Haven's suggestion that the Community could not be suppressed the words "immoral practices" were inserted. Professor Mears then offered an amendment: "Resolved, that a committee be appointed to whom shall be committed all questions of fact and law relating to the Oneida Community, and of measures which ought to be adopted, and report at a future meeting which the committee will call." This amendment was adopted. A discussion ensued during which several of the reverend gentlemen grew quite heated, and the Reverend Smith of Oswego demanded that those present should take the bull by the horns and do something practical, as the evil complained of was apparent to all. The meeting then adjourned.

The reporter of the *Syracuse Courier* apparently had sharper hearing or a more efficient pipeline to the closed convention hall. His account on February 15 included several items which the others had missed:

> Professor Mears gave a brief sketch of the rise and progress of the Institution. He explained that in the Oneida Community men and women live together in a sort of concupiscence. No woman has a husband of her own and no man a wife. They declare that they live in the resurrection life in which they neither marry or are given in marriage. They are not allowed the right of choice. If they violate this rule and show any particular attachment for one another, they are criticized for so doing. Their institution is the outgrowth of vile passion. A person going through the Community sees nothing there to offend. All is secret. Our students who visit the place say that the men look passably well, but that the women have a dejected look, and how such women can be the mothers of an excellent stock of men is one of the problems which the students discuss.

Bishop Huntington agreed that it should be shown up in the

light: "There is an impure emanation from it. Young people go there and return with these impure thoughts and associations in their minds." Mr. Brownell, of Lyons, said that the least they could do would be to find a way to suppress this evil. Or, as Hercules said, "either find a way or make one."

Bishop Peck was more pacific. The evil was too deep-seated to be easily eradicated. The method of treatment must be moral and scriptural. If the Community stood alone without sympathy from the outside public and with less sagacious leaders, it might be overcome by a popular uprising. Hot-headed men would do them no good in this work. He moved that a committee be appointed to investigate questions of fact and law, and to report to this body at a subsequent meeting.

L. W. Hall, a prominent member of the Syracuse Bar, gave as his opinion that if they could get a moral sentiment aroused and public feeling turned against Oneida, they would not need legislation. He added that if a statute in regard to disorderly persons were to add the words "all persons living in concupiscence and adultery" were inserted, it would embrace everyone in the Oneida Community. Although some thought that it would die out of itself, he thought that legislation would speed it on its way. Mr. Smith of Oswego, always an activist, thought that much more decided action should be taken. He wished every man, woman, and child to understand that there was no doubt as to the immorality of the Oneida Community. He thought they should not be afraid to express themselves in unequivocal terms in regard to it. Dr. Fisk thought that Mr. Smith was laboring under a misapprehension.

After a good deal of discussion a committee was appointed— which included Professor Mears—and after the conference had been informed that somehow their secret announcement had got into the papers, it was decided to furnish the press with the resolutions and such other matter as they saw proper. It had been a mistake to eject the reporters. Chancellor Haven said they had nothing to be ashamed of. The convention was thereupon adjourned.

At the Evening Meeting at the O.C. on the Twentieth of February—"the day we celebrate"—several extracts, quite favorable, were read from different papers—from which it appeared that public opinion was being educated in favor of the Community. Some of the papers advocated moral suasion and praying bands to convert them, which they found amusing. JHN said that, without thinking about it, they were having a splendid Twentieth of February. It was growing plain that there would be a ridiculous failure every time Mears moved, and it seemed likely that there must be enough common sense in his former advocates to oust him and get a new commander. Professor Mears had something worse than a patch over his eye.

Mr. Hamilton wrote a letter which was read in the meeting calling attention to the great amount of truth favorable to the Community contained in the newspapers. This, he pointed out, came not only from impartial sources outside but even from their enemies, like the unwilling testimony of a witness under cross-examination. And these words fell into prepared soil, since for years Professor Mears and the clergy had been plowing up and fitting the public mind to receive just such a document. It showed the hand of a managing Providence, able to make the wrath of man praise Him.

The next evening there was more reading from the papers, and the article in the *Nation* was thought quite liberal while, as usual, the *Independent* was bitter and vituperative, so much so that it was thought that the family would not care to hear it read. Good news came from Mr. Searing, a New York lawyer, who wrote to say that the Community need have no fears in regard to the result of the late attack. An article in the *Syracuse Courier,* purporting to be written by a member of the convention, was considered a weak and lame defense and alluded to the reaction in favor of the Community, hoping that the mistakes of the convention would not help the Community.

The general Community routine went along much as usual. The report on appropriations for personal expenditure indicated that the average applied for by the men was $32.17 and for the women $15.63. This was $850 more than had been asked for the past year, and while Mr. Noyes did not think this unreasonable, he still urged that there should be economy in the use of it. It was suggested that since they now had so many sewing machines it would be advisable, instead of giving away their old clothes, that pantaloons and dresses might be made over for the children and a great deal of money saved that way.

A strong article of commendation of the Community, written by someone in Oneida, appeared in the *Syracuse Courier,* but a sour note was sounded in the report by one of the O.C. salesmen of a chance meeting with a Professor Stowe from Canandaigua, who made "a regular onslaught upon the Community," saying that "it is going to be wiped out now, this foul blot on the state of New York. It is already before the legislature." Later George H., the salesman, encountered Mr. Stowe on the cars. The latter began once more to preach to him, telling him he had better get down on his knees and go to praying; that he did not look like a good man, and called on him to repent. George H., by this time somewhat aroused, turned on his attackers and said: "If you go on in this way much longer you will find sometime that you are fighting against God!" This appeared to baffle Mr. Stowe, and in the end, George reported him "so mollified that he asked to have a copy of the *Socialist* sent him."

JHN wrote a letter to the family on the "Only Way to Get Out of Trouble," which was to *go to God in faith:* "The troubles of the Community as a whole are really due to lack of religious experience. If we avail ourselves of the troubles we are now in to get an increase of religion, we shall come out of them without harm."

The months of March and April 1879 continued to pepper the Community with opinions, both favorable and adverse, from the press. A "prominent New York Editor" (unidentified) wrote that he regarded the Oneida experiment as of the utmost importance. A Boston editor—again unidentified—said that he rejoiced in the ministerial attack; it was so entirely unwarranted and unjust that public sympathy was against them and the agitation would aid the cause of free speech and free acts not injurious to the world.

Two local papers, the *Elmira Gazette* and the *Hamilton Republican,* said respectively on March 6, 1879, that in view of the ulcers that afflicted society at large, Oneida was a comparatively healthy spot, and that the Syracuse convention was without proof that the practices which they deemed so reprehensible were now or ever had been practiced.

The *Catholic Mirror,* March 6, 1879, found the situation ironic: "Are not these the same men who were loud-mouthed about persecution, civil and religious liberty, the right of private judgment?

We do not defend the doings of the Community, but we would, if we were Protestants, in order to be consistent." The *Springfield Republican* on the same date wrote in a very moderate article that nothing could be more unfair than to couple the Oneida Community with the Mormons: "Mormonism is a gross tyranny of superstition and outrage, but the Oneida Community is a mutual compact of free men and women. We venture to say that the revelations of a recent dreadful scandal have done more to lower the moral tone and blemish wedded faith than a hundred Oneida Communities could do in a generation."

For the most part the Community, via the *American Socialist*, March 6, 1879, returned a mild answer to their critics. They had long known that the laws of New York State did not incriminate their form of society. They did not trust to the law for protection, but to public opinion which in this country was always above the law: "We will not be drawn into any fight on legal grounds. We throw ourselves upon the good sense and kindly feelings of the State of New York. If that refuses us the liberty to go on with our experiment, we shall close our laboratory, with consciousness of innocence thus far and with sincere gratitude for the liberality which has been extended to us for one generation at least."

The matter of name-calling also they could take in their stride:

Epithets of reproach, though often grievous to bear, do not, after all, have much weight in the courts of either law or morals. In the list of hard words cast at the Community by the clergy these two—*"a blot"* and *"a disgrace"*—are the most prominent and the most persistently used. "The Oneida Community is *a blot* upon society, *a disgrace* to civilization, etc." Having assumed these premises, it then becomes easy to proceed, as did one of their leading organs, in this manner: "No matter how pious, how thrifty or how honest, or how much esteemed by its neighbors, let it be extinguished." It is the old stain of intolerance that has always been a reproach to religion. It needs no prophet to foretell that the future will not remember the tolerance and liberality extended to the Oneida Community as a disgrace but as an honor that has marked Central New York as one of the bright spots in this free land.

Their old enemy, the *Observer*, March 20, 1879, did not agree: "All honor to Bishop Huntington, Professor Mears and Dr. Beard;

it is time the Oneida Community was uprooted.' " The article went on to an account of a visit to Wallingford which was, to say the least, apocryphal:

> *Visitor:* Do the children know their own fathers?
> *Communist:* No; nor their mothers.
> *Visitor:* Do the mothers know their own children?
> *Communist:* No; the child is taken away and she never can tell which it is. The children are all cared for alike and kept together and all are loved alike, for no man or woman knows which is his own.

This was one of the oldest and most persistent lies that followed the Community almost from the beginning, but it still annoyed them, and again they took pains to refute it in the *American Socialist,* March 20, 1879: "This is pure fiction; no such conversation ever took place. It is not even *founded* on fact; for the facts are the reverse of it. These lies have been contradicted so often that any decent paper ought to be ashamed to repeat them. The writer calls ferociously for more persecution and winds up with the following invocation: 'God speed the Bishop, the Professor and the Doctor and grant them an ally strong and true in the dear old *Observer!'* We are sorry for the Bishop, the Professor and the Doctor and the dear old *Observer.* A blessing from the lips of such a mendacious scamp cannot be much better than a profanity and a curse."

A paper in Wisconsin, on the other hand, carried an article noting the Community's statement that "We are never accused of theft, arson, fraud, murder; our members are never dragged before the courts to answer for deeds of crime." This paper wrote: "This seems to present a fairly clean bill of moral health. One at least that the followers of Dr. Mears and the other ministers cannot always boast of. Hadn't these men who are getting up this raid better subside until they can show as good results to the community at large and as high an average of practical goodness as the Community people possess?"

On March 27 a letter appeared in the *Utica Morning Herald* which the *American Socialist* called an olive branch. They wrote in a bantering tone that doves were not the only ones who could pluck olive leaves or tell when floods were abating, but it is not often that the chief instigator of trouble comes "bringing no overtures of war, no taxation of homage, but holding the olive in his hand"; yet what else can be made of the following communication?

"Hamilton College
March 20, 1879

"By your permission I would correct a single but important error in regard to the action of the Syracuse Conference upon the Oneida Community. It is claimed that the purpose of the conference and the aim of the movement is to crush the Oneida Community. No such purpose was expressed at Syracuse, nor did anyone attempt to commit the Conference to any such measure. No one offered a resolution—as sundry reports represent—'to suppress' the Community itself. The resolution referred to, when first offered and when adopted, read: 'to suppress the immoral features of the Oneida Community.' Someone who was not paying due attention when the resolution was first read misunderstood or failed to hear the exact form of the clause as above given, and proceeded to make remarks based upon the misapprehension, but he was quickly corrected and satisfied as to its meaning. As a great deal of sympathy and feeling has already been wasted, both in and out of the Community, upon this misapprehension, will you not confer a favor upon all parties interested in reprinting the resolution, and by allowing me to say that neither myself nor any others engaged in the movement have the slightest hostility to the cooperative and business features of the establishment in question, but view them rather with interest and favor? The resolution: 'Resolved, that it is the urgent duty of the citizens of this state to take and to press measures for the suppression of the immoral features of the Oneida Community.'

Signed,
John W. Mears"

This communication, coming from the Grand Commander of the crusade, was truly pacific in its tone. The *American Socialist* wished to meet it in the same spirit. There appeared to be a slight discrepancy in the reports of the conference, however, as given by the Syracuse and Utica papers. The Syracuse papers only mentioned the resolution as finally adopted, while the *Utica Morning Herald*, March 27, had the following:

Bishop Peck finally offered the following resolution: "Resolved, that it is the urgent duty of the people of the state to take and to press measures for the suppression of the immoral features of the Oneida Community."

When first offered, the resolution read: "for the suppression of the Oneida Community," but upon Chancellor Haven's suggestion that the Community could not be suppressed, the words "immoral features" were inserted. The Oswego *Daily Times* of the same date had the same report. In some of the papers the words "immoral features" became in print, "immoral practices." The *Syracuse Standard* says that before adoption a few important words were stricken out of the first resolution as first presented.

But for all these discrepancies neither the Oneida Community nor the *American Socialist* were at all responsible. They wrote, on March 27:

We agree in desiring that every "immoral feature" of the Community may be suppressed. We do not claim perfection. We freely confess that there are many things in our system and life that might be improved. But of course we will have to be liberal and considerate all round when we come to inquire what is, and what is not, immoral. Some Christians think it immoral to do aught but worship on the Sabbath day; other Christians think it perfectly moral to spend a part of the day in innocent recreations. Some think Sunday is the true Sabbath; others think it immoral to do any work on Saturday. Some think it immoral to touch, taste, or handle any intoxicating liquor; others think a little wine may help our infirmities and may be taken without sin or immorality; and so of other things; there is a great difference of opinion among conscientious Christians. The Great Apostle to us Gentiles says, "Let every man be fully persuaded in his own mind; and let not him that eateth despise him that eateth not; and let not him which eateth not judge him that eateth." Paul was a very wise man; and he would have all fully persuaded of what is right, and adhere to it, not condemning others who conscientiously have adopted different rules of conduct.

The *Rome Sentinel,* April 17, after quoting Professor Mears's revised version of the resolution, was very jocose about it:

Now, that begins to sound like something real. As the Conference and the committees and the ministers and the churches have been so profoundly quiet since the meeting, we had feared that nothing truly beneficial to the public was to result; therefore, this paragraph comes to us with double encouragement. It is like a cool, refreshing drink after a long and wearisome journey in a desert, or a gentle shower to parched and withering flowers, to learn, as a result of the great hulla-

baloo, the speeches, the shutting out of the reporters, the often expressed convictions of direct immorality, the majestic character of the
conclave—that "it is the urgent duty of the citizens of the State," etc.;
the inference being that previous to that great boost towards notoriety
secured by the Conference, good citizens didn't know what duty was.
The mountain is thoroughly recovered; the mouse will be found in the
resolution quoted.

"An unknown friend and lover of fair play" wrote a reply on
April 3 to an article by Professor Mears which had appeared in the
New York *Tribune* in which he demanded to know what Bishop
Huntington had meant by suggesting a popular uprising. "Does it
not always mean rapine, force and even bloodshed? The action
taken by the reverend gentlemen upon the instigation of the Professor is an uncalled-for and meddlesome interference which does
begin to look like a wanton crusade."

Another gentleman sent in an article to the *American Socialist*,
May 29, 1879, in which he quoted Professor Mears in his most
virulent mood: "The practices of the Oneida Community are shel-
tered from the public view by their own vileness, which honest
types refuse to tell. Scanty information upon this part of the subject does not result from any real difficulty in getting at the facts.
Loathesome as they are, they have been published with rhetorical
flourishes, with pretenses of science, and with complacent references
to the most objectionable parts of Plato, at the printing-house of the
Community itself, and have been for sale over their counters. In
those pamphlets may be found their methods of regulating the relation of the sexes and of securing what they claim is the best breed of
men, in all their nauseating detail."

In reply to this blast from the Professor, John Humphrey Noyes
addressed the editor of the Utica *Herald,* April 3, 1879:

You may be willing to allow me space to say that the Community will
be found as law-abiding and law-obeying in respect to its publications
as in respect to its general conduct. Long ago we withdrew from sale
all works which we had reason to suppose, after taking legal counsel,
might be considered by others as coming under the prohibition of
those laws. This we did, not because we were ashamed of anything
we had published, nor because we stood in fear of punishment, but
because it is our conscientious purpose, so far as lies in our power, to
render loyal submission to the laws and the government. And we

hereby give notice that if anything can be found in the works which we still offer for sale that any considerable number of fair men—like the editors of the Utica journals, for example—shall declare to be inimical to the interests of morality, we will at once and without putting anyone to the trouble and expense of a legal investigation, expunge them from our advertised list of publications and stop the sale of them.

Added to this, the *American Socialist* inquired on April 3: "In view of Mr. Noyes's statement above, what can be made of the assertion of Professor Mears in his recent *Tribune* article, that these works 'have long been for sale over the Community's counters?' Shall we call it slander, or ascribe it to the 'lamentable ignorance' of the Community which Dr. Bennett bewailed at the Syracuse convention? It at least evinces an inexcusable negligence in verifying his statements that would discredit them before any fair-minded jury."

6

Under the Surface

In his journal for February 5, 1879, Frank Wayland-Smith wrote:

The Oneida Community is a wonderfully interesting study at the present time. Mr. Noyes is jovial, hearty, interesting himself in everything that is going, deciding all important and most unimportant matters, planning varieties for the Evening Meetings and taking a practical oversight of the performances, reading everything, talking with everybody. Dr. Theodore Noyes is steadily regaining his health to all appearances, and busies himself in trying to make malleable iron at the old Wilson Foundry. I hear of no collisions between him and his father, but everything appears to be going harmoniously. There are no upheavals in the Community at large, at least none which come to the surface so as to be publicly known. Criticisms of individuals in public are almost or quite unknown, and we no longer have a standing Committee for Criticisms. In fact, there is very little of the old-fashioned "mutual Criticism" done in these days. Occasionally a few persons are called together to exhort or reprove some one or more of the younger members, but that is about all there is of that character.

Yet under the surface there is what seems to me a very important and dangerous state of things. The young people as a class, and some of the older ones, are free to speak of their preference for a more limited sexual fellowship than Mr. Noyes has always advocated. The more bold and ultra of them coolly declare in favor of a monogamic relation. They say one man is enough for one woman, one woman for one man. Others put it as a temptation to a belief rather than as a fixed belief by which they square their conduct. Dr. Noyes's exclusive relation to M———, i.e., exclusive in his possession of her, has done a great deal to cover and allow of this change in public sentiment. Perhaps, after all, I ought not to call it a *public* sentiment for it is by no means expressed publicly. I mean that it is a spreading feeling, already embracing quite a class. Mr. Noyes feels himself so strong that he does not meddle with it, even if he is fully aware of it. When I speak of this above as a "dangerous state of things" I mean that it is one which cannot but be destructive to the present organization of the Community, if it continues unopposed.

There is, however, a point in our situation which stands as a partial excuse and extenuation for this change of sentiment. It is the lurking doubt which has come up as to the perpetuity of the Community. Everybody sees that, with our system of complex marriage and our practical stirpiculture in which it often happens that one man has children by several different women and one woman by different men, if we should lose our power of unity and go to pieces, our failure would be the most dismal and heart-rending one in the annals of communism. It would be impossible for the men and women to pair off so as to take all their children with them; and as there is a strong feeling of love and affection among us as between parents and children, great suffering would inevitably result if we should make shipwreck. Just as soon, therefore, as a person begins to feel any doubt about the perpetuity of our organization, he or she naturally and instinctively begins to look out and avoid further entanglements. In the case of a young woman, I judge from what I hear and observe, the temptation to exclusiveness is particularly strong under such circumstances, for several reasons: 1. Every woman wants to lean on some man to protect her and provide for her. At present the Community as an organization does this, but if the Community is not positively certain to last, she wants to know what man is to take its place as a guardian and provider and husband to her. 2. Women are more helpless than men and greater odium attaches to any sexual irregularities they may have engaged in. After having borne children to several men, their chances in the outside world would therefore be very bad unless some man stood ready to claim them and take care of them. 3. They naturally like an ardent, romantic, exclusive attachment and the present situation gives them a plausible excuse for giving way to the desire whenever a chance offers. The uncertainty about the future leadership has not a little to do with it all. Theodore's installation, brief term, resignation, secession, return, vacillation, opposition to his father, his disease and precarious look after a partial recovery, all these incidents have inevitably unsettled confidence, especially as we have every indication that Mr. Noyes still holds as firmly as ever to his plan of making Dr. Theodore his successor. But, as I said, all this is working under the crust. Only those who happen to feel each other out sympathetically hold converse about it, for or against.

Among the many activities which the journalist spoke of were the new arrangement of the Evening Meetings—a low platform was built for the speakers—and JHN's exhorting of the whole Community family to consider the chain business the *family business* for the winter in which everyone should take part, "an industrial reunion for men, women, and children." He also asked to have a catalog made of the younger or middle-aged members to discover whether there were any Positivists among them. He believed that "all our young men, including twelve college graduates and several literateurs of some distinction, were believers in Christ and more or less definitely in the Bible." Joseph was the only college man who had left on account of skepticism, and he believed that evidence had recently come to light proving that Charles Cragin had turned back from infidelity before he died. The list, duly made, named forty-eight men who were firm believers in Christ and the Bible and had no faith in communism except as founded on Christianity. Belief in the facts of modern spiritualism was quite general, there being but two who admitted a decided unbelief.

The reported conversation with Charles Cragin before his death was rather oracular; it could be interpreted in several ways, although JHN took it as meaning a true reconversion. Charles had said that the branch that was thrown off from Mr. Noyes would be thrown out of the Community; that the new split was weak and there would be a movement toward Mr. Noyes and toward religion; and that he, himself, from having been the freest of free-thinkers, had begun to return to the religion of the Community. Shortly after this he wrote a note to Theodore inviting him to help in a study of the problem of how to capture the Positivists instead of being captured by them; to find the true key to reconciliation between religion and science. Theodore's answer has not been preserved nor any account of how this problem was to be solved.

An invitation to the family to send in anonymous letters of suggestions or criticisms apparently resulted in more criticism than suggestions and might "lead to discords and offenses, unless we all make it a rule not to say anything in such letters that we would not say by word of mouth in public meeting or write over our own signatures." A number of small matters occupied the meetings; the question of gum-chewing in the Community; permission for the ill or aged to lie down on the back seats in the gallery if they would not disturb the meeting by *snoring;* a brief lecture on the Universal Tendency to Spherical Forms, with illustrations.

One report touched a very delicate matter—a visit of Mr. Easton to Ann and Joseph in New Haven which suggested that this couple might ultimately wish to return to the Community. John Humphrey Noyes took this occasion to remark that he had never considered or treated Ann as a reprobate, had never sent her away from the Community, and, after she had left, had sent her word that he considered it her mission to convert Joseph and bring him back. He made this statement because some of Ann's friends seemed to think that he was her enemy. He must ask them to trust him to deal with her. Her restoration to fellowship was not likely to be forwarded by the continuance in the Community of a party feeling in her favor which quarreled with the judgment which had been passed and sought to put the Community in the wrong. The next evening a paper from JHN in regard to Joseph and Ann was read, together with letters from Joseph and extracts from journals written previous to the birth of their child. It transpired that Mr. Noyes had, himself, been responsible for this mating, in the hope that it would keep the recalcitrant Joseph in the fold. Unfortunately, after the child was born and a good deal of vacillation on his part, Joseph still felt constrained to leave the Community and did so in 1873.

On February 14 a new enthusiasm of Mr. Noyes's was the subject of a dissertation on a scheme of *unitary education.* "*Theoretically,*" he said, "education was going on principally in schools, academies, or universities, but *practically* the largest kind of education was going on in reading the newspapers." "The ideal I have before me is to make our family meetings equivalent to a great daily newspaper as a *means* of educating all classes by motives of attraction, natural and spiritual; and my plan is to make all our other schools subordinate and auxiliary to the high school, preparing all to enjoy, and as many as possible to contribute to the instructions and entertainments of the family meeting. Let it be borne in mind," he said, "that we are studying out contrivances and preparing models for the countless communities of the future." After this he went on to lay out elaborate instructions and suggestions for the new system of reporting and the conduct of the meetings along this new line.

On the surface, life in the Community was its usual tranquil self. But there were subterranean rumblings which might portend something more serious. Frank Wayland-Smith's private journal, on February 26, 1879, noted a situation which, he said, "opened to my knowledge an alarmingly serious matter."

Charles Burt hailed me as I was going into the printing office and explained to me a difficulty between him and Mr. Noyes. According to Charles, he and Edwin Burnham, who now acts as head book-keeper and financier, had a little conversation in the course of which Charles said he thought "Mr. Noyes had prostituted the finances of the Community to the pleasure of his son, Theodore," and Edwin retorted in some sharp words. Charles then said that he had been told by a better man than himself that 75 percent of the Community did not sympathize with the new project of making malleable iron, started by Dr. Noyes. Edwin replied (according to Charles), "That's a damned lie! That's a God damned lie!!" Afterwards Edwin reported Charles' remark to Mr. Noyes and Charles was yesterday called before them in Mr. Noyes's room and talked to for an hour and a half. Charles says he kept his temper but stuck to his statements and further told Mr. Noyes that he (Mr. Noyes) had no real knowledge of the state of feeling in the Community.

Mr. Noyes was much disturbed by these things and went to work to test the public opinion, apparently finding things worse than he had before supposed, if I may judge by his subsequent course.

This forenoon, at 11:20, Mr. Noyes stopped me, saying he wanted to speak to William and me together. He said: "I don't feel as if I should be able to conduct Evening Meetings much longer, as I have been doing, and perhaps I shall not be able to attend them. I don't know but I shall have to ask to be dismissed from the Community and I don't know but I shall die. You two have worked with me for a long time and on the whole we have got along together quite harmoniously. Now I want to make this request of you. My idea of the meetings is that they should be occasions of entertainment and home enjoyment, and that they are not a suitable place for the discussion of politics, finance, or any weighty questions, because the women and children are present and would not take part in any such debates. The meetings ought to be pleasant family gatherings and I want you two to keep this idea in mind. I beg of you, as in my last hour, as you may say, not to let the meetings become a debating society where persons wrangle over heavy questions. Keep the meetings cheerful and entertaining and try to carry out the plan I have entered upon. That is all."

Mr. Noyes then went to his room and I to mine. He paused a minute in front of my door and said, "We have kept the *American Socialist* free from these debates and let a good-natured spirit rule in it. That is exactly the policy I want applied to the meetings."

Presently Mrs. Skinner went past my door into Mr. Noyes's room crying bitterly and saying, "Why *don't* you go to Wallingford? Why *don't* you go to Wallingford?" Mr. Noyes soothed her gently, telling her not to be troubled.

Same day. 4:30 p.m. I have just been to show Mr. Noyes an article in the *Syracuse Courier* written by a man signing himself "Lenox," very friendly to the Community. After reading it Mr. Noyes said, "Do you know what I was thinking about when you came in? I was seriously thinking of proposing to the Community to disband, and I can see several things that must be looked out for. In the first place we must pay our debts. It would not do for persons to begin to snatch and run away or strike out for themselves. If we should be forced to such a thing, every one ought to hold still patiently until our debts were paid and the helpless ones provided for."

I was astounded and told him he must be suffering from hypo. He said, "No, but I cannot stand it any longer with things going as they are. Do you know," he continued, "that there is a large party in the Community who favor monogamic marriage?"

I told him I was well aware of it and that party was rapidly growing. I added that the difficulty worked in a double way; for when one person became a monogamist, he or she forced another to become so.

"I shall have to ask the Community to dismiss me," said he. "They evidently want and need a new leader. I shall have to go somewhere else and take with me all who want to live as I do. Perhaps we could take Wallingford and let those who desire to live differently from our system have Oneida. We could arrange it in some way so as to suit all. We have worked our system clear through to stirpiculture and the public has endorsed us grandly. Now then, if we can not agree among ourselves, let us at least disband in an orderly manner."

I said I thought he would find a strong love of communism in our members, when he came to propose disbanding. "Well," he said, "then you must take hold and make a different public feeling. I can't stand it as it is."

I have long foreseen that a crash must come, sooner or later, but I did not expect it just now, and am inclined to think Mr. Noyes himself will take a more hopeful view in a day or two. Still, it is a serious question in my mind whether it will not be a wiser course to modify our system now. I am losing faith in the permanence of our institutions after Mr. Noyes's death. The members may continue to live together for a long time, but I fear some of the old forms will be changed. Perhaps it is designed that they should. The law of progress which pervades every people may decree it.

In the Evening Meeting Mr. Noyes was present and seemed much as usual.

Two days later, on February 27, Frank was drawn into JHN's problems once more:

This afternoon Mr. Noyes came to my room and said that what he needed in the management of the Community was a "right and left bower" (terms in the game of euchre)—men like William Hinds and myself who would take hold and assist him in the business and politics of the family as we had helped him on the paper. I told him I would be glad to help him if we had a fair chance, but he shook his head and said we did not sustain him as we might. Then he went away and I set to work to think what could be done to help him. An idea struck me and I sat down to write it out. Just then Mr. Noyes came in again and I told him I was going to write out my views. He said, "In that case you had better submit it first to William Hinds. I have opened my mind to him a great deal more fully than I did to you the other day. I can, however, tell you briefly the three propositions I made to him. One was that he and you and others should take hold to correct public sentiment and sustain me in my present position. Secondly, if you cannot do that, you must dismiss me with enough to live on or set apart Wallingford for me and those who choose to live with me, and govern the Community by a committee such as William has long advocated. Or thirdly, when I was dismissed, I should prefer to have William assume the leadership. William was offended at this naming of him, but I told him I thought he was a better man that Mr. Towner, and I should prefer to have him the leader to having Mr. Towner. We talked all three of the propositions over in detail, but I will not go over them again. You can show your paper to William and then hand it to me."

Frank's letter to Mr. Noyes, in part, follows:

In the first place, one cannot undertake to advise, exhort, or instruct members of the Community, whether in regard to spiritual, social, business, or domestic affairs unless he has a recognized position authorizing him to do so. It would be looked upon as an unwarrantable intrusion and subjected to all sorts of misconstructions. I have endeavored to persuade some of my young lady acquaintances against the present monogamic tendency, but my efforts seemed only to aggravate the difficulty, and I left off.

If one undertakes such labor on his own hook, with howsoever honest a purpose to do good, he is sure to be suspected and eventually accused of ambitious designs. I hear every now and then that this charge is already circulating more or less in regard to me, based principally, as I suppose, on my long-continued chairmanship of the meetings, from which I have on this account often been anxious to escape. I am by no means ambitious to lead the Community, or to fill any official position whatever, preferring a life of peace; but it is useless to assert any such innocence after the contrary opinion is once started, for nobody will believe you. In this particular, William and

I are fellow sufferers, for I have heard the same charge against him as often as against myself.

To enable anyone to act with you in the way you seem to wish, it would be necessary that he should have your confidence and support. If you should speak approvingly one week and disapprovingly the next, it would inevitably breed a ruinous distrust in the minds of the people. You should be free to criticize and instruct your assistants, but this ought, I think, to be done privately, as a rule, unless the difficulty is aggravated. In a word, the Community can only be well managed by those who have your, and its, hearty confidence and love.

How would it do for you to nominate a man and a woman, or two men and two women, to act, jointly and severally, as circumstances may require, in consultation with you and under your advice, as general directors and correctors of family affairs; said persons to be confirmed in their positions by the vote of the family *and to serve one year,* at the expiration of which term their functions would cease by limitation unless they were reinstated for another year on account of the general satisfaction they had given to you and family?

I showed the above to William, as Mr. Noyes had requested, but he was very non-committal about it, and I saw at once that he was bent on "paddling his own canoe," i.e., that he had some plan of his own which he intended to push in his own way. So I handed the paper to Mr. Noyes who held it for a second careful reading.

Frank's entry in his journal for March 14, 1879, reads: "Mr. Noyes read my paper a second time and told me he thought very well of it. He passed it around among his immediate confidants and I understood it was generally approved. Dr. Theodore thought it would be a good plan. One not well acquainted with Mr. Noyes might judge from all this that he intended to adopt my suggestion. I do not think he will do so unless a growing discontent forces him to it. He is making a vigorous attempt to put under the late hostility."

The matter of selling the Wallingford property was still being deliberated. All the family had been asked to put in their ideas of a fair asking price for it, which resulted in wildly differing ideas of its worth, varying from $75,000 to $280,000. Finally a compromise was reached at $135,000 as the lowest possible price, but a week later they heard that the man who had been thinking of buying the place had instead bought at Ansonia, so there was no alternative but to continue there as before.

Mr. Hinds reported his call on Mr. Berry of Oneida, their local assemblyman, who said that no action had been taken by the legislature in regard to the Oneida Community. He seemed very friendly and disposed to do all he could to help, if there should be any occasion.

On the other hand, the clergymen of Oneida came out with a card in the papers expressing their disapprobation of the social practices of the Community. The tone of this notice seemed very mild, and someone reported that the ministers had been driven to it by Professor Mears who had written to them "cracking the whip over their heads." The Catholic priest alone refused to sign it and told them there was more iniquity in their own parishes than in the Oneida Community. Mr. Noyes remarked that the Catholics were likely to be the ones not to persecute them instead of the Baptists, since the Baptist minister had signed the card.

There were still small perplexities. Mr. Van Velzer sent a note to Mr. Noyes "which he hoped would not be called grumbling," but he was obliged to report that after he and Portia had spent all day Sunday planting flower seeds in the forcing pit, costing some three or four dollars, he found next morning that Milford's dog had been let in and had completely destroyed them. "To say nothing about the perplexity," the note wound up, "who shall stand the damages? The Dog Department or the Floral Department?" The next day Milford replied (1) that he would see that the floral department suffered no loss; (2) that it was not his dog that did the barking; (3) that he had made a high pen for the dog; and (4) that he was willing to sell the dog as soon as he could get a reasonable price for him.

7

Collision

As a part of Mr. Noyes's announced campaign to make the Evening Meetings—and all Community ordinances, for that matter—as entertaining as possible, he suggested reading the *Journals* of the early days of the Community, hoping thereby to arouse the old unity and enthusiasm. An item in their current *Journal* recorded this: "Evening Meeting, April 17, 1879. The reading of the Old News, describing the early morning bees in 1855 and depicting the industry of the Community at that period." Terse and to the point; no wild enthusiasm twenty-four years later.

Mr. Noyes said, "That was just the time when we were beginning our great system of industry, by which we made our fortune; the time when the spirit of industry filled every body and every vein. After a long time of departure from that spirit, we are just now beginning it in something like the spirit we had then. A cycle has returned in which we are entering upon a new industrial epoch. These cycles do not always end where they began. They ascend like a spiral, so that we begin on a higher plane than we were on before. This new industry we are working at now, the chain business for instance, which gives us an opportunity for our own labor, is a return of that old spirit."

It was not easy even for devoted followers to recapture an old emotion, and at a time when divisive influences were working more strongly every day, it was impossible. There had been for some time criticism of Theodore's financial situation. The partnership in Mr. Easton's Turkish Bath, formed in 1878, had not worked out well. Theodore had returned to the Community, but his patrimony of $3,500 was left behind and, as it now turned out, had been spent—and more money besides had been borrowed—in the name of A. Easton & Company, for which notes Dr. Noyes was a co-signer.

A long and acrimonious correspondence between the two former partners began and was continued for nearly a year; finally, in May

100

1879, Edwin Burnham was sent to New York to settle the matter. He reported that Mr. Easton was unable to pay the notes and called upon the Community to help him out. This they were unwilling to do, and since Mr. Noyes was anxious that Theodore's connection with the Bath be terminated, Burnham, armed with a power of attorney, succeeded in dissolving the partnership. It was impossible to recover the $3,500 until the Bath earned more money, so Theodore emerged from the affair with only Mr. Easton's endorsed notes which, in Mr. Burnham's opinion, were not worth much. This, some felt, rather tarnished Theodore's earlier reputation as a financier.

Also in this same month, a serial article which Frank Wayland-Smith was writing for the *Socialist* had touched a sensitive nerve in Mr. Noyes. This series, entitled "What Is and What Might Be," described various forms of government, taking for examples Russia, France, and Great Britain. As Frank wrote in his journal: "Mr. Noyes assumed that it applied equally to the government of the Community in a pejorative sense." What may have disturbed him are such remarks by the author as, "Whatever forms are opposed to the real progress of mankind must eventually be abandoned, no matter what good service they may have done in the past. Whatever such changes are brought about, there are always collisions between two classes of people; those who agitate for change and those who oppose it." The general tenor of the series looked toward the consent of the governed to the lightest possible form of government and perhaps in the end a form of cooperation. This sensitiveness of Mr. Noyes's was probably the result of the active and growing feeling of dissent from his policy about Theodore and his habit of deciding matters himself.

Frank Wayland-Smith wrote in his journal, May 9, 1879:

It is thought that he grows more and more autocratic and secretive in his moves and some of the leading men in business affairs are now quite estranged from him. William Hinds, J. W. Towner, Martin Kinsley, H. W. Burnham, G. D. Allen, and others are among the dissenters. Mr. Noyes undertakes to "localize the evil" in Mr. Towner, whom he charges with ambitious designs on the position of leader. Towner denies this *in toto* and asks to have his denial read in public. Mr. N. refuses to do this unless he shall also present the reasons for his charge. This does not suit Towner. The persons I have mentioned and many others support Mr. Towner who does not show any signs of yielding. Wm. Hinds and others are strongly advocating a representative government. Mr. Noyes feels these attacks keenly. He has been accustomed to implicit and unquestioning obedience in spiritual and temporal affairs.

This state of things has so influenced and exaggerated the question of leadership and government that what I write in my serial seems to Mr. Noyes to have a personal application. But he does most of the arguing. He has grown so positive in all his beliefs that he does not care to hear the ideas of others. When he sits down for a talk he delivers his opinion and almost always rises immediately upon concluding what he has to say, not waiting for any reply. If, however, one happens to agree with him exactly and accept everything he says with manifest approval, he will often considerably prolong the conversation. Today I happened to express to him some admiration of President Hayes as a Chief Executive of the nation. He at once approved what I said. This was in his room. Afterwards he came to my room and said that his position exactly corresponds to that of President Hayes; that Mr. Hayes was determined not to relinquish any of the authority due him under the Constitution, but was insisting on having his proper influence. In the same way, he, JHN, was bound to exercise the authority and influence with which he had been invested. "I have told you more than once," said he, "that I have not been put in my present position by the members of this Community. The real stockholders in our institution are the men and women of the invisible world. They have built up the Community and it is to them that I am accountable. I am resolved not to relinquish one iota of the authority they have given me."

This defines our present situation quite clearly. Mr. Noyes claims to be fully inspired and not at all accountable to those under him. He claims that the invisibles have put him into office and that he is executing their plans. The difficulty is that he claims a monopoly of the communication with these invisibles. I do not know of a single person in the Community whom he would consider fit to get at the mind of the spirits—except himself; and he has no hesitation in saying that he gets at it exactly, every time. It will be seen that this claim covers everything. It gives him complete command of the situation, so long as it is allowed. But a party of malcontents are beginning to dispute it, and hence the difficulty. Some of his moves turn out badly, and now and then his treatment of individuals is considered unjust; therefore some persons cannot conscientiously admit his whole claim. I cannot see exactly how the breach is to be healed. One feature of the present situation is that family government and discipline are nearly suspended. There is but little criticism by committees as of yore; the young people do pretty much as they choose, and everything is relaxed. This is, in some respects, demoralizing. It is not a freedom conferred freely and cheerfully on the members by the administration; it is a partial suspension of the functions of our government in consequence of an opposing public opinion which cannot yet be subdued. Every youngster recognizes this, and I fear the effect will be like that of a first runaway on a mettlesome colt. It will make them impatient of restraint and guidance hereafter. They will be tempted to take the bit in their teeth and run.

Noyes wrote a paper to William Hinds regarding an article Hinds had published in the *Socialist* of May 8. This article was entitled "Democratic Theocracy," and its thesis was that a nation might annex itself to the Kingdom of Heaven: "A nation, after transferring its general sovereignty to God would still be left to manage its municipal affairs by some form of political mechanism." Mr. Hinds's plan was, instead of legislating by a personal assembly of representatives, to let a periodical paper be established as the sole medium of proposing, discussing, and recording laws. The publisher of this paper must of course be chosen by the people, while the whole people resolved themselves into a permanent legislative convention.

Whether this theory was original with Mr. Hinds is doubtful, since in a Preface to the article Mr. Noyes noted that it was first published in 1844, "but its suggestions are more forcible and better adapted to the exigencies of the present time than they were to the time when it first appeared. With such men as the converts of Pentecost for the controlling power of the state, we believe that the plan proposed would be entirely feasible and fruitful. Without such an outset, with only the disputers of this world as the managers— the plan would probably be the worst the world has ever tried."

To Mr. Hinds he wrote: "I have not altered my mind about this scheme of government and I have never objected to any feature of it if developed in proper circumstances, such as were set forth in my introduction to the article in the paper. On the contrary I am waiting anxiously for the *revival* in the Community and in the country which will make it possible. I do not think the majority of the generation who are discontented with my administration have any idea of annexation to the Kingdom of God or any belief in the existence of that kingdom as present in the world. With those who have I am now dealing on the principle of this scheme and always have been, and they are contented with the liberty they have."

Theological matters were a lifelong preoccupation, but John Noyes was also an extraordinarily practical man. Mundane matters also claimed his attention. On April 10 a notice was read of an annual meeting of ministers representing about fifty churches, to be held in Oneida village, at which Dr. Mears would deliver an address on the subject: "Shall institutions subversive of the family be tolerated among us?" Two weeks later, portions of this address, together with an editorial alluding to it, were read to the Evening Meeting. Mr. Noyes commented that it showed that their enemies had been considerably tamed by the late discussions. No reference had been made to the legislature and the most Professor Mears seemed to be attempting now was to get the people of Oneida village to influence the O.C. to change their way of living. The editorial, which was very guarded in its language, might be taken as a general expression of the mind of the people.

On June 5, Mr. Berry, the friendly assemblyman from Oneida, reported that an effort had been made in the last legislature at Albany by "two men from near Utica" to take measures against the Community. He had not learned their names. Further, two members from Brooklyn and two from Albany were buttonholed by these same persons and urged to take special action, but all in some way excused themselves. When the lobbyists came to Mr. Berry, he said he guessed if there was anything that needed attending to here, the member from this district would look after it. The attempt was a failure. Mr. Noyes said that it was worth something to know that the effort had been made and that it had failed.

A more personal matter was apparently troubling him at this time. A letter from him, which must have been intended solely for Theodore, urged his son to prepare a clear statement for the benefit of the family on the subject of his experiments in producing malleable iron: "I am anxious that you should manage wisely, not only in the practical development of the business, but also in the manipulation of the Community about it. You must not rely on me to force the business on the Community. You must convince the Community that it is going to be profitable and that it is going to be profitable soon, with an outlay we can afford. You will be tempted to ask for more capital and to put off the time of returns; but this will give your enemies the advantage and will be a sad burden on me."

Old age, depression, hostility—if he felt these emotions—could not for long quench Noyes's ever-fertile imagination. Two days later on June 7, at the Evening Meeting, he broached a new idea:

It has been a subject of considerable thought with me the last few days whether we are not really indebted to our workmen—our hired people—what we may call a great constituency of laborers around us. I see as plain as can be that the Community is indebted to this constituency for its safety and existence. We should not have been able to withstand the late attack of the clergy—we should have been swept from the face of the earth if we had not been supported by these work people who are interested in our welfare.

It is worth our serious consideration in our estimates of how much we are really indebted to them not only for our prosperity but for our protection and insurance. It is through our connection with this large body of persons that the world around us realizes the benefit of our existence. These hired people, as I said, are a kind of insurance. They save us not only from the attack of the clergy but they are really an insurance from incendiaries and attacks of mobs and all such things.

I do not want to introduce anything into the meeting that would lead to discussions or that would raise parties among us, but I do think that all our thoughtful persons ought to be studying the question "How can we establish the right kind of cooperation between us and our workmen, so as to identify their interests with ours beyond all possible danger of their falling into the ways of strikers—into the enmity that exists in the world between capital and labor?" So far as our workmen become interested in our business, our production will be increased.

The next day Mr. Hinds, one of the two leaders of the opposition, made answer:

The Community, I trust, is destined sooner or later to present the best example the world affords of the true relation of capital and labor. In order to surround ourselves with a class which shall be permanent friends and continuously interested in our prosperity, we must be able to select from those who offer for service, and as fast as we find such trustworthy men as we want, fasten them to us by giving them *permanent* employment that is *remunerative*. Now we hire very many more hands in the summer than in the winter, and the consequence is that if we get good hands for the summer they, for the most part (certainly so far as our businesses are concerned), have to find employment elsewhere in the winter or get along without work and wages.

Now if we had some branch of manufacturing that afforded even small profits in which common hands could labor and which could be carried on whenever other departments failed, this would enable us to give permanent employment to those whom we wish to retain in our service. I have thought the chain business might, provided the market warranted it, be made to give employment during winter months to some employees who now suck their claws all winter; and what's to hinder having a room fitted up where they could work by the piece with very little superintendence. The advantages of securing permanent rather than transient help are very great, especially if we contemplate their improvement by giving them educational and other facilities.

JHN replied immediately:

It seems to me that your letter broaches a *side-question* which may be left until we get some primary scheme of *cooperation* or sharing of profits which will apply to *all* employees, whether permanent or transient. The main question before my mind was whether we ought not to give our employees—all of them, of course—a certain share of our annual profits, besides their wages, and if we decide in the affirmative, then two great practical questions follow to be studied and decided, viz.: first, what percentage of our annual net profits should be set aside for these dividends; and second, by what rule should they be distributed? For example, we might make up our minds to appropriate *one-tenth* of our clear net gains every year and distribute it in the ratio of the wages paid during the year to each employee. Would this be fair? If so, the distribution would be simple. If we found at the close of the year that we had gained $10,000 clear above all expenses, then we divide $1,000 with our employees, giving to each person such proportion of it as his or her wages bear to the whole amount of wages paid during the year.

It seems to me that we had better direct our attention to some such central and universal scheme rather than to such secondary questions as yours or as some of those started last night—that about cooperative stores, for instance. We shall find undoubtedly a great many ways to benefit our employees, but the first and main question is, shall we share with them our profits? I doubt whether anything less than this will identify our interests with theirs.

Undoubtedly we can *approximate* the state of permanent employment and should do so as fast as we can. And the way to do so evidently is to diversify our industries, so that our employees can be turned to work in one department when another is out of season. With this in view, our true policy is to build up a great variety of manufactures. Still, it is a question whether persons who work in manufacturing shops can be induced to go on the farm or into the fruit-preserving in summer. But these are questions for study and trial in future. Let us begin at the beginning and make thorough work.

It is not recorded whether the discussion that followed this proposal was receptive or hostile. Ten years before, such a suggestion, chiming as it did with the whole life style of the Community, might have met with an enthusiastic response. Now, it would seem doubtful whether the canny Yankees of the anti-Noyesite party would have applauded. The timid suggestion of George Cragin that "it might help if the band went over to the Willow Place factory occasionally and gave them a little music!" must have fallen on deaf ears, and the temper of the meeting must have been so warm that, as Frank Wayland-Smith recorded on June 9, "The next morning, fearing that the profit-sharing plan might lead to discussion and party differences, Mr. Noyes had to throw cold water on the discussions of it."

The journal continues: "I wish I could make a complete pen-picture of the state of the O.C. at the present time. It is in the strangest condition imaginable. The disaffection continues and spreads. Such men as Wm. Hinds, Mr. Towner, H. W. Burnham, and Martin Kinsley are practically alienated from Mr. Noyes and the acting administration. Mr. Noyes has not, as formerly, the power and influence to subdue them. This division is generally known in the O.C. and its effects on the young people is deplorable. The young are fast breaking away from all sense of moral accountability. They are independent, scorning advice, and some are really impertinent in their self-assertion. There is a great deal of uneasiness and anxiety among the thinking classes. All are waiting for something decisive to happen."

One appeal for unity made on June 10 by Mr. Noyes seems, in view of his past, truly pathetic:

I don't know but it will answer to touch gently upon a subject which might be termed our daily manners. I notice in these times of party feeling in the Community that it affects unpleasantly, and I think needlessly, our manners and probably all parties are affected pretty much alike. I am accustomed to meeting persons now-a-days, frequently coming in close contact with them, and find that they avert their faces, evidently not liking to look at me, and take some pains not to pass a word with me. I presume that is the experience of a great many others, and I don't attach any blame to individuals about it, nor to either party: but it strikes me that we might make a little approach toward harmony and conciliation by avoiding such manifestations. The thought came to me in this shape: Even if we hate one another, would it not be better to pass one another pleasantly, and with a smile if we can? I don't think it would be hypocritical, or detrimental to harmony, but an invitation to it. It certainly could do no harm and it might do good; at least to pass one another without manifesting a grudge or evil thought. I confess that it is quite unpleasant to me to meet persons whom I have been accustomed to be on very pleasant and familiar terms with, and see it manifest that they had rather not look at me and not sit by me at table. I don't know but I may be tempted to feel so myself, but I have made up my mind that I will not *act* so. I do not think that such personal grudges help the cause—help the side that acts them. We shall certainly make proselytes by treating one another politely, even if we don't feel so in our hearts. (These remarks were very generally cheered.)

It may be that this unusual outpouring of good will was a real encouragement, for two days later Mr. Noyes said in Evening Meeting: "It is evident that the Community is coming into a condition of greater financial prosperity—just beginning in that respect, as the whole country is doing, and I think, too, that the Community is prospering spiritually in something the same way. We frequently say we are living in the day of judgment. I take it that we shall find that God will carry on his work in that way, by putting his people together in such a way that they will criticize one another until everything comes to light."

Speaking of the children, he said that when persecution came to them and threatenings of the destruction of the Community he always thought of the children. He saw what a dreadful thing it would be for them for this to happen. It was then that he realized that God had taken care of them all these years that were past, and that to cut the Community off would be like stopping a story right in the middle. He believed that God would perfect the education of their children. They were common property, and God would see to it that they were rightly nurtured into womanhood and manhood. His faith in God was strengthened by thinking that He would not allow their children to be scattered. God and the angels had an interest in their children and in having them perfected.

The Community *Journal* for June 23, 1879, had a few words to say about the performance of the Gilbert and Sullivan operetta *H.M.S. Pinafore* as presented by the Community troupe: "Quite a number expressed their appreciation of *Pinafore*. Some who had seen it away from home said the performance here was much more enjoyable. It was thought by some that it will not only be the cheapest but the best way to bring such entertainments here, instead of sending out small parties to see them."

8

JHN's Departure

On Monday, June 23, 1879, Frank Wayland-Smith wrote in his journal: "To the surprise of everyone, Mr. Noyes left here last night, during the night, with Myron Kinsley. It is supposed that he has gone to Wallingford. Myron is expected back tonight. Mr. Noyes left without delegating his authority to anyone, so far as I can learn."

Later that day he recorded the probable cause of this astonishing departure.

> On Saturday, June 21, 1879, the *Syracuse Standard* contained an article headed, "The Oneida Community. Another meeting of the Central New York Committee. The leading communist, Noyes, to be arrested. Legal proceedings to be commenced. Testimony being taken which stamps the Oneida Community as far worse in their practices than the polygamists of Utah. On this latter testimony the arrest of Noyes, the leader of these Socialists, is to be made and his trial to be pushed by gentlemen who will be prepared to go to the very foundation of this thing."
>
> These headlines give a sufficient idea of the article. Yesterday, June 22, Mr. Noyes came to my room to ask my opinion as a lawyer in regard to his will, which he had just drawn up to dispose of the presidency of the Community in case he should be taken away by any cause. This will is the same one referred to previously but with the added provisions that William A. Hinds and James W. Towner should also be excluded from the presidency for the reason that, like Theodore, they have become ineligible by departing from the fundamental principles of the Community. They are also excluded from the list of Mr. Noyes's political executors named in the will, and Dr. Noyes is added to that list. Also, Mr. Noyes nominates George N. Miller to the presidency in case he should be taken away before Dr. Noyes or someone else is installed.

Whether John Humphrey Noyes habitually retreated in face of difficult situations, by which is meant the retreat from Putney in 1847 and the final retreat from Oneida in 1879, or whether he, as

110

the responsible head of both communities and therefore the chief target of the attacks by the clergy and the public in both cases, beat a retreat to draw off the fire of his enemies for the protection of his flock, is a matter of opinion.

It is certain that in 1847 in Putney "Public indignation meetings were held almost nightly; committees of visitation were appointed; resolutions were passed, affirming that the Community must be dissolved. Arrests were made, suits commenced, writs of attachment were issued, mob violence threatened. A Vigilance Committee was appointed" (Parker, *A Yankee Saint,* p. 139). On October 26, 1847, Noyes was arrested and charged with adultery. He waived examination and was indicted under bond of $2,000 for trial the next April. On November 16 warrants for the arrest of John and Mary Cragin, members of the little community, were in the hands of the sheriff. Other members, especially John R. Miller, were flooded with threatening letters and it was rumored that Miller was to be tarred and feathered. In December, writs for $3,000 were issued, and the Community real estate was attached. But with Noyes absent, nothing was done. His flock was not attacked.

John Noyes vigorously denied that he had abandoned his followers and run away to save his own skin. He had actually stayed in Putney for a month after his indictment and had gone to Brattleboro with the intention of surrendering himself to the authorities without bail, on condition that his followers be left in peace. This plan his lawyer brother-in-law, Larkin G. Mead, had advised against, urging him and the Cragins to leave the state. "The main point is," Noyes wrote later, "that we left, not to escape the law but to prevent an outbreak of lynch law among the barbarians of Putney." This statement was confirmed by the reported remark of Dr. John Campbell, their most bitter enemy, who declared that if there was no law that would break up the Community the people of Putney would make law for the occasion. Before this, he had actually made a physical attack upon one of the members of the community. "Who then," Noyes asked, "were the law-abiders and who the law-breakers? I was content to abide the issue and settle with the law as best I could. But Dr. John Campbell could not wait on the law and he may thank his own turbulence that I escaped its clutches and saved him and his confederates from committing acts of disgraceful violence and perhaps murder" (G. W. Noyes, *The Putney Community*, p. 302).

By January, even their most bitter opponents at Putney had calmed down and were beginning to patronize their store again, at first preferring to come after dark, so that the communists were obliged to keep the store open in the evenings, but, they reported, they had the store full. From New York, their leader wrote them, on January 1, 1848: "The head and front and whole of our offense is communism of love. No other charge is brought against us by our enemies. If this is the unpardonable sin in the world, we are sure it is the beauty and glory of heaven."

"Barbarians" of the Putney stripe pursued them even at Oneida. In 1850 certain persons complained to the district attorneys of both Madison and Oneida Counties. R. A. Parker wrote that in Madison County, the actual site of the Community dwellings, the plea was made that "there was in their midst a collection of individuals of both sexes, living together in a mixed manner; that they did not hold with marriage; that their numbers were steadily increasing and their example was corrupting and demoralizing the surrounding citizens." The Grand Jury, asked to find a bill of indictment against them, heard their witnesses but heard other witnesses who testified that these communists were industrious, peaceable, and law-abiding, and that they minded their own business. It finally decided not to notice the complaint.

The complainers in Oneida County fared better. Its district attorney, although he had no legal jurisdiction over the communists since they did not dwell in his county, nevertheless summoned Noyes and a group of his followers to court in Utica and, as R. A. Parker has written, "put them through a merciless examination by an exasperated District Attorney. It was not fair nor lawful that they should be called to incriminate themselves, but they were; and they told the truth and the whole truth. Sensitive and high-minded women were asked obscene questions. They ran a gauntlet of the curious gaze of idlers, the malicious probing of lecherous lawyers and dignitaries. But their dignity, their perfect manners, and their honesty carried them through." When told that they ought to break up and clear out, they replied that they were willing, if that was really the will of their neighbors. To ascertain this will, they circulated a paper which the majority of their neighbors, some of them influential citizens, signed, declaring that they had no sympathy with the recent attempts to disturb their peace.

The next attack was largely by the printed word. It occurred during the existence of their small branch community in Brooklyn, New York, and was instigated by a bigoted and intolerant religious paper called the *Observer*. At first the communists were amused by the violence and inaccuracy of the attack. In their paper, the *Circular,* February 22, 1852, they wrote: "The newspapers, following one after another in the wake of the N.Y. *Observer,* have been for the past week giving us plenty of notoriety. It is very amusing to notice the kaleidoscopic changes which the reports about us assume, as they pass from paper to paper." Even the local paper at Oneida Depot carried an article which admitted that "what the actual practices of the Association are, we do not know. We have always heard the Community folks spoken of as industrious, well-behaved people though all sorts of rumors are afloat."

By the next week, March 7, 1852, "the combined attack from at home and abroad had evidently reached such a pitch that the communists published a manifesto covering their past, their present, and what they believed to be their future. In the past, they said, their course had been neither seditious nor unchaste; their household habits would show not a licentious spirit but the opposite of licentiousness. Still, at present their liberty was looked upon with jealousy and offense by surrounding society. Therefore they had decided to withdraw from the position they had held and formally to resume the marriage morality of the world" (C. N. Robertson, *Oneida Community: An Autobiography, 1851–1876,* p. 266).

This retreat before the attack of popular opinion seems surprising in such a devoted flock with such a radical shepherd. It should be remembered, however, that in each of these confrontations, they followed one of JHN's most profitable dicta: the cultivation of a flexible will. "Pliancy of will" the *Circular* reported, on January 20, 1859, "seems to be especially pleasing to Christ; it gives the social atmosphere a more than downy softness. What better index to the inborn nobleness of a person's character or the reverse, than to know in what sphere he uses his will. If he is obstinate, you are tempted to mark him as a man who takes a pin-hole view of the universe."

In Putney they had acceded to popular will. In Utica and Oneida they had offered to leave if their neighbors desired it. In Brooklyn they agreed to "recede from the practical assertion of their views"—but they did not say, in this *Circular* article of March 7, 1852, for how long. On May 23 they wrote that they had "fallen back within the lines of worldly toleration." On June 27 they spoke of "temporary disgrace; We are not ashamed of [our] social principles—we believe they contemplate a glorious emancipation for man and woman and the highest improvement of the race." And on August 29, they announced what they called their "Theocratic Platform," in which was included "Abandonment of the Entire Fashion of the World—especially marriage and involuntary propagation." The next plank in the platform was "Cultivation of Free Love, Dwelling together in Association or Complex Families."

If the *Observer* or other local or metropolitan newspapers commented on this reversion to original dogma, it is not recorded. In any case, the Oneida Community resumed, from this time until nearly the end of the Association in August 1879, what they called their social theory—Complex Marriage. And it was, once again, this vexed social theory, under attack by the clergy, which drove John Noyes, for the sake of his followers, first to remove himself from the public eye and, two months later, to advise them to abandon their disputed system.

This time, not only his own arrest was threatened, but a legal movement was in preparation against the communists. A June 21, 1879, article in the Syracuse *Standard* also spoke of "other testimony of a more positive character" and said: "We do not want to have our witnesses spirited away when the time of trial comes." The withdrawal of Noyes, the chief protagonist of the drama the Syracuse committee was rehearsing, practically disposed of that, and the announcement on August 28 of the end of Complex Marriage in the Community spelled its end.

In 1847 when he was for the first time indicted, John Noyes was comparatively young—only thirty-six—vigorous, tremendously vital, filled wtih confidence. His light-hearted reaction to the threatened arrest shocked his elderly lawyer brother-in-law by what seemed frivolity. Confidence, high spirits, and enthusiasm remained with him for the next thirty years. True, he grew older and ill health took its toll, but not until a schism in his own group turned half of his old adherents against him did he lose his resilience. This desertion was a profound blow. For two years he tried in vain to recapture the minds and hearts of the young dissidents, but during that last spring, when the clergy was assembling for their grand attack, he saw his flock in danger and believed that his presence could no longer protect them but instead spelled their peril.

So, for the second time, he left them, a tired old man, perhaps heartbroken. As he wrote some years later, in his *Niagara Journal,* 1881, "I was dreadfully hungry for rest and my heart took a great swallow of it." But this could not last for long. "It was only my body, after all, that was hurled into Canada. My soul was marching on at Oneida. It could not be otherwise. In spite of the fancies and even the wishes of my desperate moments, I was bound in many ways to the Community beyond all possibility of resigning or expulsion. I had a host of spiritual relatives there who held on to my heart. But in my own heart I laid down my sceptre and lost all desire to rule in the old way."

The sensation caused in the Community by this precipitate departure of their leader can only be imagined. Less than half of the members actually had been calling for his departure or, at least, for his deposition. Now their wish had been granted, and they were left virtually leaderless in the face of the threat that had driven him away. There is no specific record of the reaction of these dissidents to this event. On that same Monday when the news broke, Mr. Hamilton called a meeting of a dozen or so of the so-called loyalists to talk about the situation and especially about the conduct of the Evening Meetings. He said he thought they had better *occupy the land.* They, after all, *were* the Community who continued to be faithful to Mr. Noyes and the old principles, and they need not be too modest in assuming it.

Mr. Noyes's sister, Harriet Skinner, wrote to him:

I could see that Mr. H. had power and was a medium of your spirit and I have felt safe ever since as if you had been at the helm—safer, too, in some respects, because Mr. H. is not such a target as you were.

You left no orders, but Mr. H. felt a call. The meetings have gone off well. Tuesday night he asked Mr. Burnham to read the 3rd chapter of James. It seemed as if every ear was captivated and that the experience of the Community gave a new meaning to every word.

"Behold, how great a matter a little fire kindleth! And the tongue is a fire, a world of iniquity: so is the tongue among our members, that it defileth the whole body, and setteth on fire the course of nature: and it is set on fire of hell."

Mr. H. put Frank up to a strong attitude in regard to the paper. Told him he could swing William just as well as not, if he knew his strength in union with you, and Frank got William to agree, or they both agreed together, that they would carry on the paper to please you, more carefully than if you were here. Frank has talked very boldly to William, charging him with being a leader in this anarchy which is going. Wm. denied it, but Frank thought it made him feel serious about it.

The wicked spirit here has not ceased to pervert the right ways of the Lord yet, and I am not anxious to have you come back. This stir-up outside seems to me only a providence to get you away from inward persecution. Sarah and I guessed you were going away in the night and expected to find your room empty, as we did. I have got a trunk with a key and put all your papers in it.

On June 26 Frank wrote a long report to Mr. Noyes detailing the events up to that time:

The reporter of the *New York World,* Mr. F. W. Eddy, was here yesterday, the editor having sent him up in consequence of the article in the *Syracuse Standard* about the intended arrest of yourself and others. I drew out of him that he had interviewed the clergymen and lawyers before coming here. He said he called on the District Attorney of Oneida County and asked him if he had been spoken to about the intended arrests and prosecution, and he said he had not. No one had mentioned the matter to him. Then the reporter asked him if he thought anything could be done, and he replied that he thought not, unless there was special legislation. He said if we had withdrawn our pamphlets, it would be impossible to get a conviction on that. We could not be prosecuted as a public nuisance, for we were not a nuisance. We could not be convicted of keeping a disorderly house for we were confessedly orderly and law-abiding. No prosecution for polygamy would lie, for we are not polygamists. The reporter suggested that the clergymen intended to prove that we abuse our women, but the District Attorney said he did not think an outside body like the committee of clergymen would be competent to take up such a prosecution and furnish evidence in a matter that did not materially concern them. The reporter then called upon the District Attorney of Madison County who also said he had not been spoken to on the subject, and gave substantially the same replies as the other had done.

The reporter says the plan is to get testimony from seceders, of whom he had procured a considerable list. He would not tell me of whom he had procured his information. He said his opinion was, from all he could leran, that nothing could be done. From here he went to Clinton this morning to question Dr. Mears.

The story of June 20, 1879, in the Syracuse *Standard* stirred up a flurry of reprints and comments in a number of other papers both local and metropolitan. On June 27 the *Syracuse Evening Herald* took note of this: "Mr. Eddy of the New York *World* was in town yesterday. He had been interviewing the members of the Oneida Community and Professor Mears of Hamilton College on the raid to be made on this social institution. Whether the society or individuals are to be proceeded against is not yet known. In fact, the whole movement appears to be in embryo as it has been for years. Moral suasion is to be the chief weapon for a while. Whatever legal proceedings are to be taken must be against individual members." Three days later the same paper wrote: "At the meeting of the clergy last week one member assured a Syracuse reporter that a decisive course had been marked out and facts had been obtained which would warrant the arrest of Mr. Noyes."

The *Syracuse Courier* of July 1 said much the same thing: "The Committee had collected evidence which stamped the Oneida Community as worse than the Mormons: that samples of obscene literature had been collected and the newspaper readers who had laughed at the movement as bigoted, impractical, and radical would soon have occasion to admire the most masterly crusade ever waged against Socialism."

Beyond this the Eddy article of June 29 in the *World* only added an interview with Professor Mears:

"Yes sir," Professor Mears said with a great deal of emphasis for so quiet-spoken a man, "we have decided upon something definite; our plans are all laid."

"And will be executed when?" I asked.

"Well, that I can't say; I don't know what individual members may do, and as to the Conference, I can't say. As soon as we do anything the public will hear of it; until then we prefer to say nothing."

"Have you consulted lawyers?"

"Yes."

"And have they advised you?"

"Well, what they may have said to individual members I don't know. I doubt if we do much at the law. I rather think it would be difficult to do much at present by the law."

"But your plans are fully laid?"

"We have definite plans, yes. We shall begin with moral measures. We mean to make a great moral effort and finally, if all other means fail, we shall resort to the law."

"Did your committee attempt to have a special bill pass the legislature at the last session, the effect of which would be to correct the evil you complain of?"

Mr. Eddy had heard reliably that such an effort had been made by clergymen or their agents and that the assemblyman to whom the bill was taken had asked the applicants why they did not present it through members from Oneida or Madison Counties, to which reply was made that it was useless to broach such a distasteful subject to them.

To this question Dr. Mears answered tartly that if they did, they should be commended for it. Mr. Eddy persisted:

"In case you should resort to the law, do you suppose you could procure an indictment under existing statutes? Do you think they violate the law?"

"Think? I *know* they do. It would not be necessary to bring a criminal suit. Any person could bring civil suit against them—any person who was aggrieved. There are plenty of such, you know. Then witnesses could be found to sustain the charge. It would be very easy to have a suit with them in that way."

"Have you any such persons in mind?"

"Well, it would be an easy matter to find them, you know; then, besides, they are liable for circulating obscene literature."

"Have you been collecting testimony?"

"Well, I should say I have! I have a stack of it so high" (spreading his hands about about five inches). "It is disgraceful—horrible. That is all I have—their own publications—but they are bad enough to condemn them."

"Do you mean to say they still circulate them?"

"I had no difficulty in getting mine. They say they have ceased to circulate them but that is the only assurance I have that they don't. They have such singular notions about other things that I don't know why I may not safely doubt their veracity."

"Have you submitted the case yet before anyone in authority?"

"That is a question I am not at liberty to answer."

"You can tell if an arrest is likely to occur?"

"I don't know that I can tell; wait a few days."

"I will write precisely what I have to say and that is all I want said from me." Upon which Professor Mears wrote: "Precise nature and condition of the movement against the Oneida Community is not made public as yet. The committee is not disposed to thrust it prematurely upon the public. They are moving cautiously and propose for the present to rely upon moral measures which they hope will prove effective. It is believed that these will, in a few weeks if not days, be laid before the public."

Mr. Eddy had been informed that the moral effort contemplated by the clergy was a request to the various Young Men's Christian Associations throughout the state to pass resolutions condemnatory of the social system of the Community. Such an effort, Mr. Eddy remarked, evidenced rather more zeal than wisdom or discretion. His only other investigation was whether the United States District Attorney, Mr. Townsend of Troy, had received any complaint of the Community on the grounds of circulating objectionable literature. Mr. Townsend's brother, who was his assistant, assured Eddy that there had been no such complaint. This exhausted the list of authorities who would be empowered by law to conduct a criminal prosecution against the Community. When he returned to Oneida that evening he said he thought Professor Mears was crazy, he appeared so violent—wanted to crush the thing right out.

In his letter of June 26 to JHN Frank Wayland-Smith reported that he had talked with William Hinds about conducting the *American Socialist* as before, to which William agreed:

He and I have had to define our positions pretty squarely but we think we can work on the paper in entire peace as formerly. I do not feel irritated at all, and I begin to talk with considerable plainness to him and others. The other night Theodore wanted to talk with me. He feels a little uneasy and is tempted to wish we might modify into some form of cooperation; at least he says he would prefer that to having William and Mr. Towner capture the Community and try to run it, and I quite agree with him. But I am in hopes true communism may yet remain to us, after the smoke of this row blows away.

The day after you left the story got started that you had appointed Theodore and myself to direct affairs until your return. William came to me and asked if it was true. Of course I told him no. On investigation I found the story was started by someone who listened at your conversation with me in my room on Sunday when you asked my opinion about the wills, etc. This listener reported that he or she (I don't know who it was and William will not tell me) overheard you say that. Things of this nature happen every day, nearly, but I trust they may not long continue.

In his journal on June 23 he had been more explicit: "I had a long talk with William Hinds yesterday afternoon about the political situation in the course of which I drew out of him the points of dissatisfaction he and others have. I find that William has a very complete system of procuring information in all parts of the Community, and that the party of malcontents is organized around him and Judge Towner. I am considering whether I shall be justified in holding still much longer. I am tempted to take hold of the situation with determination to restore order. We shall see what transpires. Possibly we shall get some word from Mr. Noyes directing what course to take."

Two days later he wrote:

I devoted yesterday almost entirely to politics. I talked with members of both parties. One important thing was that I defined my own position to William Hinds. I showed him that while I agreed with him that the government of the Community might be made more representative to advantage, and that other modifications of our present forms might and ought to be made, yet I disagreed with him *in toto* as to the methods by which we should seek to procure these changes. I thought that the true way was to lay our views before Mr. Noyes and the old administration and to study the matter with them, until we were all agreed that the changes would be valuable and Mr. Noyes would join with us in making them. I told William that he had gone farther than that and had inaugurated a revolutionary movement. He sets aside Mr. Noyes's authority, openly avows a want of confidence in him, and yet says he will not leave but means to stay here and make such changes as he thinks desirable. I told him I thought if a member lost confidence and could not agree with the leader, the true and honorable way was for him to leave, not stay here and imperil our home by starting a revolution. He replied that to leave was cowardly and that to wait for Mr. Noyes to consent to change and modification was useless. He declared that I would be as grey as a rat before anything could be accomplished that way.

I learned by a talk with Edwin S. Burnham that H. W. Burnham had been talking about a division of the property, how it could be equitably done, etc. This is going very far. HWB is hand in hand with Wm. Hinds, and stands as the chief religionist of the new movement. His party claims that Mr. Noyes has abandoned the old faith— that he began his work in the spirit but has ended in the flesh. As Mr. Burnham is a notoriously self-indulgent, ease-loving man, seldom denying himself anything, the new position of his sounds rather forced. He now acts as religious adviser to some of the younger girls. He is pious but by no means a practical Christian. He and Messers Hinds and Towner make strong efforts to cover their position by very exalted sentiments.

In my talk with Mr. Hinds he remarked that someone had classified the members of the O.C. into three companies, viz.: (1) Those who fear man more than they fear God (Mrs. Skinner, Mr. Herrick and all those who believe implicitly in Mr. Noyes). (2) Those who fear God more than they fear man (Hinds, Towner, Burnham & Co., presumably). (3) Those who fear neither God nor man (the rabble whom Hinds, Towner, *et al.* have led away from Mr. Noyes but cannot control or restrain).

Mr. Hinds thought this classification very good. It certainly gives him and his brother revolutionists a fine moral vantage among those who accept it. It is by such flattering sophistries that Mr. Hinds is able to draw to himself nearly everyone who is tempted or uneasy for a change. Even a staid businessman like Martin Kinsley goes about retailing things against Mr. Noyes and making proselytes thereby.

Under date of July 2, 1879, he wrote:

Myron has been here, having left Mr. Noyes fishing on the St. Lawrence in Canada. He (Myron) brought some papers from Mr. Noyes relating to some methods or plans for settling the trouble in the Community. He proposes, for one thing, to resurrect the old Business Meetings, in which all important matters used to be decided, and which everyone was free to attend and take part in. This is a move in the direction of a representation of the people in the affairs of government. He also proposes to have a committee appointed to conduct the affairs of the Community other than the businesses. This committee was one of Wm. Hinds's proposals and was identical with one I proposed last February. When I made the proposition William would not endorse it. Now he makes it himself and pushes it through.

On July 8, Frank's journal noted: "Myron has been to see Mr. Noyes again and returned with a paper from him advising peace and harmony all round, and the abolition of parties in the O.C. Mr. E. H. Hamilton acts as father of the family at present. Mr. Noyes has sent for a list of all the members of the Community from which he will select the names of a Committee of Internal Management."

On July 22, 1879, the journal noted:

Yesterday Myron Kinsley arrived again from Wallingford bringing a list of the members nominated by Mr. Noyes [in Canada] for the new Administrative Council. It is understood that its duties will be to conduct the social and domestic affairs of the Community, being more particularly a spiritual and disciplinary body. Following is the list as presented and accepted.

MEN	WOMEN
E. H. Hamilton	H. H. Skinner
W. H. Woolworth	Sarah K. Dunn
Wm. A. Hinds	Helen Miller
Martin Kinsley	Augusta E. Towner
Wm. G. Kelly	Belle Woolworth
Theo. R. Noyes	Emily E. Otis
H. W. Burnham	Harriet E. Allen
G. D. Allen	Chloe Seymour
C. Otis Kellogg	Mary Bolles
E. S. Nash	

Total, 19 members. This committee is to serve till January 1, 1880. E. H. Hamilton is chairman for the first month, or till after Sept. 1st. W. A. Hinds, ass't. chairman to succeed EHH as chairman for September. Augusta is secretary.

9

The New Government

Communication from J. H. Noyes, written June 26, 1879, Read in the O.C. Hall June 29, 1879:

The good opportunity which I have enjoyed the past few days for clear thinking has been employed in reviewing, with Myron's help, the situation of the Community, and in trying to get some practical scheme for settling our difficulties. The following is the general view I have come to.

As communism of property was the prominent characteristic of the state produced by the Pentecostal afflatus, so it was the prominent characteristic of our community afflatus in all the early and prosperous stages of our growth. "No man said that aught he possessed was his own, but they had all things in common." Without intending to accuse any person or party, I think I may say without danger of dissent in the Community, that we have departed from this blessed state. Is not this fact sufficient to account for all our troubles and for the danger of dissolution which is upon us? Would not a return to real communism invite the Pentecostal breeze again and give us the old prosperity? Can we not find our way back to communism where we can again touch the Primitive Church, and in their baptism be as they were, of one heart and one mind? One way to seek this result is to look back and try to find where and how we departed from communism. I will sketch briefly what seems to me to have been the process.

I think we have been falling away from communism ever since we adopted the plan of making different departments distinct institutions with separate appropriations and keeping strict accounts with each other. I have no doubt that this arrangement, considered as an external matter, could have been carried out by men of thorough spiritual wisdom, without sacrificing communism. But it was a temptation to the selfish and the careless to fall into the feelings and ways of the world in business. The departments came to have separate interests and the heads of them in many cases probably became more ambitious for their own business showing than for the Community interests. This was the first step. I cannot enlarge upon it. I beg that it may be studied soberly. It seems to me that there we began to say

123

that the things we possessed were our own, and the spirit of communism departed.

This evolution into distinct departments naturally allied itself to the spirit which was already at work in small ways, building up what may be called "side operations"—little individual speculations. I think it will be found that these have had a new and vigorous growth since the change referred to. Persons who do not find place at the head of some regular department naturally are ambitious to create a department for themselves in which they may individualize.

The natural result of these developments of individualism has been to take the departments more and more away from community control: and I think here will be found the secret of the decay of the great business committees, and of the management which used to reside in the Sunday meetings, where all who chose attended and discussed matters. Those meetings died out, not from any arbitrary orders from me or anybody else, but because the departments got to be independent of them, and so their business left them.

Now if we suppose (what must be true) that this process of individualization in business propagated itself gradually into other things—social matters, for instance—we shall see how the structure of the Community has been revolutionized. The institution of criticism is one form of community control over individual persons and parties. I think it will be found that criticism has decayed and died out simultaneously with the committees and Sunday business meetings, and from the same cause. The growth of individualism has taken away the business of criticism. The interference of the Community with individual affairs of all kinds has come to be resented as intrusive.

I have talked this matter over very fully with Myron and our views have agreed very perfectly. He thinks he can present a remedy. He is full of enthusiasm for sounding the bugle call to all the scattered departments to turn back and place themselves under Community control as they were in the beginning. As to the form which Community control shall take, we have not settled upon any plan: but I have assured him that I will support any move he will make in the interest and spirit of the state of things which existed before the individualizing process which I have described commenced. He goes to O.C. with my entire sympathy for this purpose.

Frank Wayland-Smith's journal noted that "this paper from Mr. Noyes led to the reestablishment of the Business Meetings on Sunday. The first one was held at 11 o'clock on Sunday, July 14, 1879. Soon after the above paper was received from Mr. Noyes, William Hinds drafted the following and sent it to him by Myron."

This paper, entitled "Suggestions" and referred to rather bitterly later by its opponents as the "Bill of Rights," differed in a number of ways from the old Community doctrine. Although it had much to say about the religion of Christ and the New Testament, it did not mention the Second Coming or Salvation from Sin, the two cardinal points of JHN's theology. The successor to the presidency was to be chosen freely whenever it should become necessary. Their recommendation for the formation of a Business Board and an Administrative Council, both of which had been previously suggested by Wayland-Smith, differed principally in "suggesting" that the president, an ex-officio member, should "rule in harmony with it." The suggestion that the tenure of the Four, as holders of the Community property, should be recorded as trustees with no right to appropriate the property for any individual purpose showed, perhaps, the fine legal hand of James Towner. Suggestion Number 8, possibly the most revolutionary of the suggestions, practically did away with any community control of the practice of Complex Marriage, either in the matter of "Special Love" between adults or in the control and education of the young in sexual matters. It is surprising that such an ultimatum should have been received by John Noyes as submissively as his reply would seem to indicate.

An excerpt from the *O.C. Talks,* June 30, 1879, noted: "a wish having been expressed that some of the so-called disaffected members of the Community should be called together for the purpose of ascertaining what changes in the administration and practical life of the Community are, in their judgment, essential to future peace and harmony, some thirty persons met Myron Kinsley in the Printing Office at 5 P.M. on Monday, June 30, 1879. It is thought the following suggestions embody the substance of the remarks made; but they are not offered in any unyielding spirit. The greater number of those who desire that important changes shall take place confess themselves thoroughly devoted to communism and are willing to make great sacrifices to insure the peace and harmony of the Community."

"SUGGESTIONS"

1. Of course offenses, real and imaginary, must be buried and forgotten by all parties.
2. The religion of Christ and the New Testament being the very blood of communism, every facility should be given for its revival and continued presence and work in the Community, and especially

pains should be taken to bring religious influences to bear upon the young people: but in all relations and positions the Christ-life of love and unselfish service is to be the criterion of religious character.

3. The question of Mr. Noyes's successor in the presidency (it was assumed by all present that he would continue to fill that office) having been a serious cause of trouble for many years, and still being a cause of anxiety to a large number, it is not seen how entire concord is possible unless the matter is dropped by all parties, and full assurance given that the Community itself (meaning thereby all the covenanting members of the O.C., W.C., and all affiliated Societies) shall be permitted to freely choose such successor whenever in their judgment it shall become necessary.

4. The suggestion of the revival of the Business Board, as it existed prior to 1876, with power to appoint committees to have charge of the finances and other interests of the Community, including its various business departments, is approved.

5. The suggestion is also approved of the creation of an Administrative Council which shall have supervision of internal affairs, such as household management, education, amusements, stirpiculture, etc., etc.; but it is thought the nomination of the members of such council should be subject to the approval of the Community; that no member of it should serve in opposition to the general wishes of the Community: and that the time of such service should expire by limitation, as was formerly the case with the heads of departments, with the last day of the year. Of course, the President of the Community should be *ex-officio* a member of this council, and we think should rule in harmony with it.

6. Respecting the property of the Community, as the members voluntarily put their interests into the hands of "The Four" for purposes of security and convenience, it would allay anxiety and give encouragement in some cases if it were distinctly acknowledged and put on record that "The Four" are virtually Trustees of the property, and therefore have no right to use or appropriate it for individual purposes and can make no transfer of it, or any part of it, except by and with the express approval of the Community.

7. Mutual criticism, being an indispensable means of government, it is thought it should be revived and administered in the spirit of Matt. 18:15–18.

8. In respect to social matters, it was thought that old principles of the Community should be emphasized, that every member is to be absolutely free from the undesired sexual familiarity, approach, and control of every other person.

9. In the Administrative Council, in the Business Board and in all departments of government, we hope to see revived and put in practice the principle requiring substantial unanimity on all important

matters before action—not meaning by this to favor anything which would enable a few persons to unnecessarily obstruct the functions of government.

Myron returned to Oneida on July 5, and the next evening a paper of comments by JHN on the famous "Suggestions" was read to the family:

> I heartily agree with most of the suggestions brought to me by Myron. Some of them I think imperfect and some of them I should have to interpret, perhaps, differently from what the authors of them intended. The impression upon me is very strong that the spirit of these suggestions is what is wanted in the Community—that it is only as the good spirit of justice and devotion to the public interest gets new entrance into all hearts that we can hope to get rid of party spirit and really carry out the suggestions which we put into words and resolutions.
>
> It seems desirable that Myron should return to O.C. as soon as possible and I have therefore not time to digest all that ought to be said about the suggestions. I intend to write more at large hereafter than I can do at present. I will confine myself to some remarks on the most important subjects—the *leadership* and social matters.
>
> The Community certainly ought to believe me when I say that I realize as much as anybody can that it is impossible for any man to be a leader in any effectual sense if he is not acceptable to the Community as a whole. This is true of myself as well as anybody else; and accordingly I did several years ago consider myself displaced when I found that the Community did not sustain me in an important matter, and I have never fully recovered the leadership since. What has been going on among us for several years has been a series of experiments to get along with a Community divided into two parties. This is not intended as an accusation but as a statement of fact. Mr. Hinds knows that within a few months I offered in good faith to step down and out and leave the Community to its own free government, whether by leaders of its own choosing or by committees without leaders. He refused to listen to such a proposal and I did not see that I could insist upon it; but I did most heartily wish I might be discharged. Perhaps what I had wished is now coming about by the agencies above my wish or his refusal.
>
> But what I am at in this recital is to show how heartily I recognize the principle that the universal or at least general acceptability of a man is the necessary condition of an effectual leadership. And now I say that I have had regard to this principle in my dealings with the Community in relation to Theodore. I have never hoped or expected to make him the leader of the Community except as he should earn

by his faith and good works the confidence and the votes of the entire Community. Doubtless I have had more confidence that he would ultimately do this than some have had and doubtless I have been more zealous and determined to give him a chance than some have; but that I have ever even thought of helping him to the leadership in his state of unbelief or of forcing him upon the Community anyhow, is not true. So, in the case of George Miller, I named him in a certain instrument as my candidate for the leadership under certain conditions (not likely to be realized immediately) because I supposed on consultation with several persons, that he might be more generally acceptable than anybody else I could name; and if that supposition is incorrect (as it seems to be) the nomination will fall to the ground and ought to. In a word, as I have no faith in leadership except as it is accepted and supported by the led, I hope and trust in God that the Community will never have a leader who is not the hearty choice of all parties. I think that this avowal is compatible with my belief that the qualification and primary nomination (so to speak) of spiritual leaders must come from above, and not from below; and I think it is also in harmony with the spirit of the suggestion in the paper sent me that the Community shall be permitted freely to choose my successor. Here I, for one, am willing to drop the subject and hope all parties will do the same.

Whatever rules are adopted as necessary in the present state of the Community should certainly be held subject to the laws of progressive enlightenment. In general, we should not expect righteousness from law but from grace; and we should be careful not to shut out grace by our laws. Wise attraction and not repression will finally govern the training of the young, as well as the conduct of the old in the kingdom of God.   JHN

Frank Wayland-Smith wrote to JHN on July 19, 1879:

Dear Mr. Noyes: I am constrained by internal pressures and the shaping of external events to write you a political letter of some length.

Now that the Community has thrown off its old administration and is about to organize on a new one cast on somewhat different ideas and principles, it is important that we take time to look on all sides of the subject before entering on the new scheme. Of course we are all anxious for peace and harmony, and that anarchy may end; but it is extremely important that we do not allow this anxiety to urge us on to a false settlement of our differences or into a position in which we rest on delusive hopes. Sufficient time has now elapsed since the *coup d'etat,* if I may call it so, for us who have remained on the ground to have taken observations of the drift of things and to have formed some conclusions. I will present to you my view of the situation as it has developed up to the present time. I will try to make it brief and it will necessarily be somewhat hastily sketched.

In the first place, I have asked myself, *What is the real change which is being made in the Community?*

As nearly as I can make out from a patient study of the situation up to this time, the party represented by Messers. Hinds, Towner, and Burnham is seeking to establish a new code of morality—I might almost say, a religion—different from that you have taught. I am aware that they claim the opposite of this, viz., that they represent the old principles of the Community from which you have departed in these later years. I have not heard that any were rebuked in any way. Of course since Myron's visits and the talks about having peace and unity, they do not openly say things of this kind; but it is the spirit on which their action is based in demanding the changes they have indicated, and they have made no retractions, nor have shown any signs of a change of opinion as to your character, so far as I am aware. A real change about to be made, if we leave things to take their course under the management of William and his friends, is one from your religion and morality to theirs.

Assuming this to be a fact, as I think I am abundantly justified in doing, it becomes at once very important to understand wherein their religion and morality differ from yours and what chance of perpetuity, unity and happiness we are likely to have under them. And first as to their religion.

Mr. Burnham is put forward as the religious man, *par excellence,* of that party. William has said to me that if there ever was a religious man, Mr. Burnham is the one. Theodora tells me that she has taken him for her religious adviser, and that she cannot feel full confidence in you. She says that she takes her mother's advice in this, ignoring that of her father who suffers much at her course. Now I am firm in the belief that Mr. Burnham's religion is one of piety rather than holiness, having little of self-denial or self-judgment. Self-indulgence and a love of ease have characterized him all the days of his life. Therefore, his religion cannot be said to be altogether a saving one. I have no particle of personal ill-feeling towards Mr. Burnham or others of that party. What I am going to suggest to you is that this new religion and new morality (or are they merely the old, worldly ones of the churches?) do not possess the elements of strength needed to hold this Community together. I am afraid their characteristic is legality; and as you have often said and I believe, the Community cannot be governed by law. I need not enlarge to you on the difference of religion between you and these other men. Now as to morality.

The new rule is that there shall be no compulsion; and any considerable amount of moral suasion is construed as compulsion. I doubt if it would be proper under this new rule to do more than suggest to the young certain desirable lines of conduct. It is a negative, repressive rule; they may be forbidden to do certain things but not obliged to do certain other things. But there is among the young women a powerful sentiment in favor of marriage, pure and simple. And as other interesting symptoms, I may mention that since you left there has been a noticeable leaning toward long dresses and long hair among the young ladies. I asked one of them what this meant? She replied that the desire for long dresses and long hair had always existed, and the late outcropping was merely on account of the supposed greater liberty secured. I do not wish to convey an exaggerated idea of this tendency; only a few of the young women have appeared outdoors on the grounds in long dresses, and they, not regularly. The hot weather has also been a partial excuse. But it had seemed to me that there was a serious leaning that way, aside from mere accident or whim.

Now I see clearly that unless the young of both sexes are trained and controlled substantially as you have trained and controlled them in the past, our social system must eventually go down. And what troubles me is that I do not see how any other man or committee can hope to succeed with them on our system. If they are not allowed to have their own way, they will now give voice to complaints. How then are they ever to be properly educated? I think we are getting ourselves into a serious dilemma. If the young, before conversion, are allowed to have their own way, they will assuredly plunge into marriage and familism; if it is said that their parents must now be responsible for them, I reply, as you have, that not all parents can control their children in these matters, so that this plan could only save part of them at the best; if, lastly, a leader be put forward to attempt to do what you have done, the chances are now, after the present demoralization and breaking down of authority, that such a leader, whether an individual or a committee, would fare even worse than you have fared.

I declare to you soberly and emphatically my belief that if your authority in these matters is overthrown, the social system of the Community is already at an end!

But aside from any logical reasoning, I am supported by evidence in asserting as a fact that our system is pretty well broken up already. A number of the young women of Lily Hobart's class do not hesitate to say that they will have no children except by a husband to whom they have been legally married. The next class younger is still more set in this feeling. I have questioned Emily Easton on the point. She tells me that quite a number have decided not to have anything more to do with our sexual system. This feeling has taken such a hold that some of us find ourselves practically monogamists, or nearly, perforce; and some of the young men who have been thus affected have said to me that we ought to be protected in this situation. That is, suppose that Theodore or Edwin or I find it both difficult and dangerous to try to associate with more than one woman; shall the party now coming into power be free to discipline us on account of exclusiveness in love? This will seem hardly fair, as the poverty of acquaintance will be due simply to the political whop-over.

I do not believe that any other man but you has the power to control the affairs of the Community except by the exhibition of a legal authority which would just as surely disrupt things on its side. If we cannot be ruled by grace, we must either fall under the power of the law or run into the looseness such as is generally understood as attaching to the term "Free Love," in either of which latter cases our system of communism will be a failure.

What then are we to do? Here we are threatened with being subjected to a new system of religion and morality which will bring with them peculiar methods of discipline. It is a plan different from that under which we enlisted and have thus far lived. Can persons be forced into such a new system without there being a compulsory communism, which thing we hate? If there is to be a new departure in principle and practice, must there not be a fair and honorable chance for all who do not wish to take part in it to withdraw in peace and with a decent provision? These are questions I would really like to have you answer. Personally, I do not feel the strength of nerve nor the courage necessary to undergo ten or twenty years of exhortation and discipline under the set of men who seem to have captured our organization. I would rather be excused, if I can have your blessing and approval of my choice.

When I come to this point in my reflections, I remember that when you had that sharp collision with Charles Burt last February and became aware of the real state of things in the Community, I happened to go into your room to show you a Syracuse paper and you said to me, "Do you know what I was thinking as you came in? I was soberly and earnestly thinking of proposing that we settle up our affairs and disband." Then you went on to explain how it would be necessary first to pay our debts and provide suitably for the aged and infirm and children; how there must be no scrambling or snatching, etc. Well, I am almost inclined to believe that was a genuine inspiration. At least I am more than half convinced that it will be better for the record of our experiment if you close it up in a round and handsome way during your lifetime, leaving us all in good and safe position and then withdrawing your sanction from all sexual irregularities. You would then have conducted the experiment of a lifetime and brought it to a safe conclusion, instead of leaving it to decay or fall into worse disaster, as so many other leaders have done. It would astonish the world to see such an example of continence.

Such a proposition would also astonish the Community, or many of the members, but I think it would have a salubrious effect on them.

It would wake them up to the fact that if communism is going to be preserved, something must be done to preserve it. Why not face the situation squarely?

Now a word as to the possibility of closing our experiment. Some will cry out that it is impossible because of the complications which have resulted from stirpiculture; but if we go on, these complications will only have increased, as the platform of Mr. Hinds includes a supervision of stirpiculture and if we go on longer and then fall with a crash, the disaster will be much greater. The only feasible plan seems to be to modify into a Cooperative Society with familism and private purses. We could all continue to live here together and pay our common expenses as at present, setting aside at the end of the year something to apply to our debt and for a sinking fund and, as the debt gradually disappeared, increase the personal allowances. This is a wild and radical proposition and I admit offhand that it would be the beginning of the end—*if repentance did not set in before the process was completed*. It would take a considerable time to wind up and pay our debts and I think you ought to preside over the operation. Possibly by the time we got our debts paid and everything fairly adjusted, we would all be filled with such keen regrets at the prospect of separation that, even if we were still comfortable in externals, we would all, with one accord repent and resolve to go on in the good old way, under your lead. That strikes me as a possibility. At any rate I am serious in saying that I prefer the idea of cooperation and familism to communism in legality and subsequent shipwreck. I would not even like to live under Mr. Hamilton as an independent leader. And I do not think that under cover of a clamor for unity, the former malcontents should be allowed to do all the reorganizing and then take charge.

Do you not think that if you should withdraw your sanction from our sexual practices until such a time as your influence and authority shall be restored, it would have a wholesome effect? I do.

One great advantage of the cooperative plan, or modifying into Shakerism, would be that *you* could be relieved from all sense of outlawry before the world. We could announce the change in our paper and send it marked to all prominent papers. That would put an immediate and final end to all thoughts of persecution and you would be perfectly free to come and go as you please. Otherwise, I do not see but this threat of arrest, prosecution, etc., will hang over you indefinitely. It does not seem right to me that you should be forced away from your home, after all you have done and borne. In fact, this whole matter, if allowed to pass, will be confusing to my sense of right and wrong.

There are several other points I ought to touch upon to be at all thorough, but I am afraid I shall weary you as it is. Let me say in conclusion that I do not claim to represent any party or class. I know that a number feel as I do, but I have no right to speak for them. I have avoided as much as possible broaching ideas that would cause trouble. I will show this letter to Theodore and Edwin, as late events have thrown us more together, and possibly to Tirzah and Helen. I hope you are well and that we may have a more direct communication with you as soon as it is prudent.

With feelings of gratitude, love and respect, I am,

Yours,

F. Wayland-Smith

Myron Kinsley's account of his part in the choice and presentation of the list of members nominated for the Administrative Council was revealing of the state of mind of the Oneida Community at this crucial moment.

On July 22, 1879, he wrote Mr. Noyes from Wallingford:

Dear Mr. Noyes: I received your letter Saturday and owing to something that had come from O.C. that made me feel some anxious about affairs there, I concluded to go on there at once and see if I could not get this committee appointed and accepted without any delay, and with the sympathy of the family at W.C. I started at once for O.C. and in thinking over the matter on my way to N.Y. I concluded to choose the Committee without consulting anyone and for this reason. I, of course, wanted Mr. Hamilton on, and if it should come out that he had helped select it, certain ones might find fault with him about it and say that he selected those that would please him and carry out his plans—some had already begun to find fault with him—and I could say to all that he did not know or have anything to do with the choosing of it; and I find this to be true. Quite a number have already asked if Mr. Hamilton did not have his wishes in the choice granted, and I told them, No, not in the least: that he knew nothing about it.

These are the names that I have presented to the Community as your committee:

E. H. Hamilton	W. H. Woolworth	H. H. Skinner	S. K. Dunn
W. G. Kelly	T. R. Noyes	H. C. Miller	Augusta
W. A. Hinds	H. W. Burnham	H. E. Allen	Chloe Seymour
Martin Kinsley	F. W. Smith	Belle Woolworth	Emily Otis
Otis Kellogg	E. S. Nash	G. D. Allen	Mary Bolles

They were presented last night, but the vote was put off until tonight, as some wished to think the matter over. There is a strong opposition to TRN being on the Committee by some, but I have advocated for him and I have no doubt that the Committee will be accepted by all heartily. I said in meeting last night that I would rather put off the vote until tonight if there was one single one that felt like waiting, as I did not wish any coercion about it, and I think that tonight it will be unanimous.

N.Y., Wednesday morning. Last night, after some talk by Mr. Hamilton and many others, a vote was taken and it was unanimous in favor of the Committee and they have their first meeting at 11 A.M. today.

As the meeting progressed, Mr. Hinds and a number of others made remarks in favor of acceptance for the purpose of promoting unity. Alfred Barron was in favor of accepting the Committee and added that here was a chance for each one to give up his individual preference and have peace. It had been proposed that Mr. Noyes should be an umpire in cases where the Business Board could not come to an agreement and in those cases they would expect to abide by his decisions.

Mr. Towner could not let this pass. He said that he approved of the Committee but at the same time he took occasion to make a very pointed reply to Alfred, utterly disclaiming any authority or umpirage on Mr. Noyes's part whatever: "I accept the Committee but wish to say distinctly that I do not accept it as the decision of an umpire. It is simply a nomination by Mr. Noyes, subject to the approval or rejection of the Community."

Theodore, it was noticed by his aunt, Harriet Skinner, was taking a strong part in the new Council. She reported to his father that he "lost no opportunity to speak, and influenced the proceedings a great deal." He and Frank were very wide awake and met the other side on their own grounds, although this forced the pacific Mr. Hamilton to "entreat them to work for peace in the committee meetings and to avoid discussion that did not lead to harmony."

Actually the meetings of the Council, for the most part, ran along on a fairly routine course. A case of spontaneous combustion at the mill was providentially discovered in time to prevent damage; a special committee reported that the tree trimming for the year was finished. A council of ministers from Saratoga discussed the O.C. and the Reverend Mr. Duffield from Altoona, Pennsylvania, was delegated to investigate and report what was being done to eradicate the obnoxious social features of the Community. The Council de-

cided to hold to its rule against explaining or discussing these matters with any outsider. This they adhered to, refusing to give any
information unless Mr. Duffield promised not to use such information against them. This promise he refused to give, whereupon he
was introduced to Dr. Noyes with whom he wished to discuss the
health of the Community but when he persisted in his inquiries
about the sexual system he was finally told that all that was secondary to the Community's religious foundation. He was also told
that Mr. Noyes, their leader, was considered a man inspired of God
and safe to follow, whereupon Mr. Duffield, a minister of the Gospel, remarked that he never expected to have a man tell him that
and look him in the face; that he thought of every man as having
his own inspiration. After he left, Mr. Hamilton said he thought the
man had considerable push, but the Lord had helped them to do
the right thing. Mr. Duffield had bought $2.00 worth of O.C.
publications and professed himself well satisfied.

In a letter to JHN his sister Harriet wrote, on July 28, 1879:
"This free fight has made such a field for Theodore. I think he and
Frank were thoroughly frightened at first—as Theodore expressed
it to me, he looked forward to the time when we should have to
pick up the pieces; and I think he made up his mind to throw himself into the breach, so that he has been a great damper on what
evil there was in the movement. Today in Council he was prepared
with recommendations for the treatment of the young folks, which
commended themselves to all, and William himself proposed that
the committee appoint Dr. Noyes to meet with them and deliver
the discourse he gave us. I think Wm. will get acquainted with him
and take an entirely new view of him and that Theodore won't
despise Wm. as he has."

Surprisingly, even Mr. Hinds began to take a more optimistic
view. In a letter to Myron Kinsley on July 30, 1879, he wrote: "I
think there is great reason at the present time for encouragement.
The irritation and jealousy of parties are growing less and less conspicuous and offensive, and of course in a corresponding degree the
brotherly spirit prevails. The sessions of the Administrative Council
have thus far been unexpectedly harmonious, and appearances indicate that all are disposed to inquire when any new question arises,
What is the best thing? All are free and it seems to be expected that

each will modify the others, and so the wisest conclusion be reached. There are a few extremists on both sides who say and do things which cause irritation, but only a few, who will 'cease from troubling' when they see that the great mass of the Community are bent on conciliation and unity."

On July 31 he even wrote to Mary Prindle, with whom he had been closely associated but who, as a staunch Noyesite had been estranged from him for some time: "I really believe a new and better day has begun for us all. No, I don't ask you to change a single thought or feeling toward Mr. Noyes and I am willing to wait a long, long time for you to appreciate my motives. I would like to feel that you do not judge me; the Lord will certainly do that, for none of us can escape his judgment. Let us make the most of our points of sympathy and agreement, which are many."

An Evening Meeting on July 29 ended in a feast of reason and a flow of soul when Frank said he could not help thinking how much they were indebted to Mr. Noyes and confessed his love for him, whereupon there was a strong hearty expression of love. As Harriet Skinner wrote:

It burst right out in the Hall and I thought we had got along a good ways from where we were a while ago when we could not mention your name. Portia said she thought of you when we were enjoying good things and how you were not here to enjoy them. Alfred said he hoped the time was near when we could invite you back as a medium of Christ, as you had always been. Emily said she wanted you to come back, etc., etc. Mr. Clark's voice was heard, Mr. Burt's, Mr. Ackley's, etc., etc. It was all in a minute like a clap of thunder. I thought Frank was inspired. He seems inspired to me nowadays— so does Alfred, each in his own way. Mr. Hamilton says that Alfred bangs around amongst them like a bull in a china shop. He don't pretend to any sham peace. JWT was silent all through the meeting and I thought he felt awfully straitened.

I had such a view last night of the reign of grace under your administration and of the reign of law that is being inaugurated now. It came out in our session yesterday that the young folks, especially the boys, are in the most awful state of disrespect and rowdyism. Their manners would not be tolerated in decent society. Well, how has this come about: I saw as plain as day that it was by separating the girls from you and the ascending fellowship, and letting the young of both sexes run together without so much as a word of reproof. And now we are getting up a machine to bring them to order—committees etc., and Wm. is quite sanguine about its working. All the council are in favor of a thorough system of compulsion, punishments, etc. We shall see how it will work. It may be a schoolmaster for the present distress, but I guess there will be a cry for the old regime before we are done. I see no prospect but this council will have to meet every day, indefinitely, and the machinery that is necessary to carry out its decisions will make this Community by and by like that which worked all day and legislated all night. It rather wears on my nerves.

On July 30 Harriet wrote later a report of Theodore's new ideas:

He said he philosophized in this way—that society outside, with an experience and action of forces going on for thousands of years, had got the very best system for that kind of society possible: but that communism was a new form of society and your system was the best for that: and now that your system was departed from, we are on a sliding scale that will certainly land us in the order outside. There is no stopping place—no modified form that will work; and all he expected to do himself is to help make the descent safe; not to have it violent and destructive—perhaps some measures of cooperation could be saved from the wreck. I think he gives up the ship entirely in its old shape; will try to preserve cooperation if possible, with several different religions. He says he can see there are four different religions now in the Community.

Along with a budget of papers which Myron sent to JHN on August 3 he wrote: "The papers all speak well of us now. The committee at Syracuse may think best to print the evidence they have collected. What this is or who it comes from I do not know—seems to me that someone inside has been talking. I do not see how they could get anything from outside, and yet I do not like to think so but am obliged to, and I still think it best that you are away for the present until things become settled. The inspiration of your new move grows more and more every day to all, or nearly all." (The "new move" was not specified and may refer to Mr. Noyes's plea that all in the Community let bygones be bygones. There is no other communication from him on this date.)

Myron wrote later, on August 4: "I think I can help some there to carry out your spirit about letting bygones be bygones in regard to TRN and others. By things that are written here I see that some still have personal feelings yet, and refer to the past in a way to produce hard feelings. I have not heard one word about you of this kind; it seems to all be dropped. Everything about it makes me feel thankful and hopeful and I expect that the true spirit of charity will govern all in time."

In reply Mr. Noyes explained that although he enjoyed letters from home he thought it best only to answer Myron as his single contact. "I thought it best in the present state of feelings in the Community not to give occasion for any evil thinking by giving expression to my natural thoughts and feelings in correspondence with friends." He asked to be sent three volumes of the *Perfectionist*, a Greek concordance, a copy of Shakespeare, some underwear, and his cowhide shoes.

The dilemma which some members of the Community were bound to find themselves in was in certain cases very painful. A person—especially a woman—who had affectional ties with the leaders of both sides of the quarrel could not but be torn. One woman who had borne a son by Mr. Noyes, and had for some years been a close friend of Mr. Towner, suffered greatly. As she wrote to Myron Kinsley on August 5:

> I am one of those who believe fully in Mr. Noyes as a competent head of the church—God-appointed, if you choose to call it so. Not that I think or ever thought that every word he says is direct inspiration from God or that he never made a mistake in his moves, but to me he has most always proved *a true medium of the spirit of Christ,* and I believe that through all these years he has been that to the Community. I know of no person living who seems to me to be so perpetually in the spirit of prayer and therefore in such close rapport with God as Mr. Noyes—that is why I have confidence in him as a leader of the church.
>
> Feeling as I do, you will see why I have not sympathized with those who felt free to criticize Mr. Noyes and denounce his inspiration. When I did not sympathize with all his plans and ideas, as in the case of his criticism of Mr. Towner, I did not allow it for a moment to weaken my confidence in Mr. N. In regard to Mr. Towner I said, "I *know* Mr. Noyes is a Godly man, though I don't see Mr. Towner's character in the light he does—I *think* Mr. Towner is, and as they both are praying men, I think sometime they will know each other better." In that way I found it easy to keep my loyalty to Mr. Noyes as the head of the church and not throw Mr. Towner over as a bad man. I could not see or feel that he was a bad man, though I willingly

admitted that he was not free from faults nor beyond criticism. From the first I have testified freely to him of my faith in Mr. Noyes and I have not sympathized with all his ideas about leadership. But his love of the truth has made me have confidence in him as a Christian, and I fully believe it will bring him through all right, and in unison with Mr. Noyes ultimately.

She was also disturbed by the rumors of the starting of a third party which she considered unconscientious, since all the Community had agreed to let the past be forgotten:

Their talk has the sound of loyalty and yet it seems to me that it is not loyal or right under the circumstances. After we all voted *in good faith,* I deem it unconscientious for anyone to start a third party in this way. I know the direct effect of it will be to open the old breach wider than ever. Mr. Towner tells me that he feels disposed to ignore all the talk about it. But there is something of a ferment begun in other quarters. For myself I shall stick to the old ship of communism so long as our good commander directs us to do so; but I never will be a member of a *Joint-Stock concern* with TRN for President. I never will live in a cooperative institution with no religion to guide it. I never will belong to a Positivist institution. If I cannot have the old Bible Communism, I want no communism. If Mr. Noyes is driven out, I want to go out too. Rather than live in a place full of dissension and evil-thinking and backbiting, for the sake of my children, if for nothing more, I will go with them into isolation.

Augusta Hamilton—who, although her father Erastus Hamilton, was Mr. Noyes's viceregent, was generally thought of as belonging more than half to the opposition party and had married Judge Towner's son—also wrote to Myron on August 5 about the state of things in the Community. As the letter shows, she was a person of strong opinions, aggressive, violently partisan, and somewhat autocratic. Her attitude at this time was a sore trial to her father who was a mild and pacific man striving to calm the turbulent waters of the Community:

I had strong hopes that the Council would go on successfully and, in an honest endeavor to do the best thing, give satisfaction to all. And I still believe it would, were it not for the party represented by Theodore, Frank Wayland-Smith, Edwin Burnham, Orrin, and others. They are constantly throwing cold water on the whole movement, and by the bucketful. Orrin told a friend of mine that he and his sort of folks didn't think the new form of administration a good one; it wasn't accepted by them, and anyway was only put through by a minority; that they had a perfect right to go ahead and get up another party and break up this one. This after their, or the Community's, public endorsement of the "Suggestions" and Mr. N.'s endorsement of them. This party called the "Suggestions" a "Bill of Rights," in a very offensive way. Those on this side (mind you, I exclude all such folks as father, Mrs. Skinner, Mrs. Dunn, etc.; it is really a third party) are so cold and stiff and offish in behavior toward those they know support the present administration that it is quite embarrassing and one has to put on a bold face to go alone in a kindly brotherly and sister manner.

It does seem evident that all the trouble, past and present, is through Theodore and his scheming. I hate to think so but I can't get around the facts. He began the first anti-communistic talk years ago, advocating cooperation, and saying what he should do in that line when his father died—calling his father old, and spreading the idea that he was superannuated. No one has ever talked so hard against his father as he has about some things and I am almost persuaded that his present advocacy of his father is because only through him does he expect his ambition to be gratified. The only way I see out, as it comes to me this morning by an agony of prayer, is a *grand revival*—a drawing of all hearts together in love of Christ and seeking after the highest and best religious experience. I feel sure Theodore and his party would not allow any such thing could they prevent it; for they are now saying such things as these to some of the younger part of the family; "If you get under the rule of Bushnell & Co., you'll have less freedom than you ever had." We can have a revival without Mrs. Bushnell leading it, even if she wanted to, which she does not. But such talk stirs up suspicions against any form of vital, inspirational religion.

In a rather surprising postscript she added: "Orrin, in his talk this morning, admitted that Theodore is a very selfish man. Frank thinks so, too: and Theodore and Frank each, this last spring, expressed to me lack of any genuine confidence in each other, both thinking the other sought selfish ends. Yet all these now go together, still thinking so."

The most vivid accounts of the situation at Oneida were penned on August 5 by Harriet Skinner to her brother:

The "tug of war" has begun in the Council. Yesterday an anonymous vote proposing a suspension of stirpicultural proceedings was read, and William made a motion to that effect. Theodore raised the question whether *stirpiculture* was any more possible in the Community. It was barely possible under your administration and he thought it was not possible under the present; that is, propagation regulated for the public interest, not according to personal choice. He was not in favor of suspending *propagation* for any length of time; we should keep our numbers good, at least. He wanted the time limited, and that the discussion of the subject should be a standing order. He and Frank were evidently anxious to bring on this tug. Frank took the position that our social system is *dead:* that we had no sanction for it now. Mr. Burnham was very anxious to have propagation suspended on account of the burdens it brought on the women (I could see his wife behind that) and on account of the uncertain state of the Community. He said something about the necessary allowance for mistakes keeping the number good. Augusta said her heart had ached all day on account of the baby born in the morning (Marion's), with no father to own it. Her idea was that we ought all to get married. Frank thought there would be very few such cases hereafter, the complexity of our relations is so much diminished. Martin thought it was no time to get children, with so much uncertainty before us; that it was unjust to the child. I thought his idea was that we shouldn't have any more children except in marriage till the status of the Community was settled. As near as I can understand Theodore, he is operating for marriage and the common order. There seem to be three parties, quite distinct, one going for marriage, one for communism without you, one for communism with you. I must confess that of the first two I like Theodore's best. I had rather have legitimate marriage than Berlin free love; and I think Theodore and Frank have done a great deal to destroy that principality—to break the power of that evil spirit that drove you away.

Berlin Heights in Ohio was perhaps the best-known of the free love communities, and James Towner and his family had, for a time, been members. With this recent background, he was somewhat suspect in the minds of certain members of the Oneida Community who were particularly jealous lest Oneida be tainted with the free love odium. They may have felt that the Oneida Community's social theory of Complex Marriage was what had originally attracted Towner, which explained his vigorous objection to its abandonment in favor of worldly marriage. In a paper presented to the Community on August 27, he wrote: "I believe in communism of love just as much as in communism of property. I do not believe that marriage and communism can exist together."

Harriet was feeling optimistic:

I recognize their inspiration in baffling the enemy. I don't think it has half the assurance and courage it had, and I think William's hope of doing anything without you is being weakened—that he finds this democratic system is his master now, instead of being his servant. He is very much opposed to giving up our social order. Mr. Hamilton is full of ideas ready to bring out; he does not feel as Frank does, that the system is dead. As you sanctioned it, he thinks it is respectful to wait for you to withdraw your sanction—that it will be damnation to those who eat and drink unworthily, but it is lawful for those who are in union with you.

It is difficult to convey much of the talk. Mr. Burnham and Martin seemed to have a great sense of the uncertainties of the future. I shouldn't suppose they thought there was any building on the Community's stability. Theodore and Frank seemed determined to keep this topic agitated till something is settled as to what we are going to have as substitute for the old system. At the same time, I think they are both discouraged about any reestablishment. Mr. Hamilton said today he was more and more convinced that nothing came of contention. *Power* is the thing, and he proposed that we have little gatherings; not to discuss evil but to pray for *power*.

Two days later she wrote:

The Council yesterday seemed a good ways from agreement. Mr. Hamilton entered a paper recommending we should not stop stirpiculture, but go forward moderately. He thought the effect of stopping would be a drift toward marriage. Wm. and Mr. Burnham were set upon having it suspended for the present. Frank thought we not only ought to stop propagation but the whole system of complex marriage, which was also the line of Theodore's talks. He (Theodore) said that system was founded on faith in your inspiration, and if that was displaced, he certainly had no confidence in the inspiration of persons of less intellect and common sense than you. Frank told me that Theodore's scheme is *limited communism,* attempting all that is possible and abandoning the impossible. Complex Marriage he thinks impossible, but communism of property possible. Wm. thought the Council was no place to consider the subject of a fundamental change in the system of the Community. Frank thought Wm.'s "Bill of Rights" was a fundamental change already, and Theodore thought there was no other place to discuss the subject. Frank says his object is to crowd home on William the logical consequences of his course in banishing you. Augusta seems to affiliate with Theodore in his views and go for the abolition of complex marriage, so it is a very queer situation, you will see. Folks on both sides are alarmed at Theodore's position. I have been reconciled to it because I thought William's was much worse, and it nonplussed William's. Theodore thought it would be much better to wind up at once than to have a long, distressing slide. He did not want this generation of children to be brought up in a mixture. There was such a push of principalities in the Council yesterday I thought something would break before long—it could not go on. But Mr. Hamilton said yesterday somebody is running this Community right through all this chaos, and we can trust that hand.

The tug of war—a draw, up to this point—was about to conclude. One side or the other had to win.

10

The Tug of War

The first strong pull in the tug of war came probably on or about August 4, when Mr. Hinds presented to the Administrative Council the following motion: *"Resolved,* that propagation be suspended in the Community family for the present."

Frank Wayland-Smith, a member of the Council, described the next moves:

> This led to much discussion. The matter hung along for days and days, much to the annoyance of Messers. Hinds and Burnham, who made efforts to push through the motion. Dr. Noyes and I determined to force on their attention certain constitutional changes which they were making in the O.C. I moved an amendment to Mr. Hinds's resolution, as follows:
>
> AMENDMENT TO MR. HINDS'S RESOLUTION
> CONCERNING PROPAGATION
> *Whereas,* the Oneida Community was founded and built up under the direct personal authority and influence of John H. Noyes, he being, as he claimed and we believed, an inspired medium of higher powers in the invisible world, and
> *Whereas,* our only justification for departing from the sexual morality of the world by instituting complex marriage or communism of persons, has been the claim that we had risen to a higher plane of morality than that of the world and were living under a higher government, and
> *Whereas,* the amount of communism possible to be realized in any orderly responsible and permanent form is directly dependent on the amount of control and government to which people will submit themselves, the evident truth being the less control we will submit to, the less communism we can have, and *vice versa,* and
> *Whereas,* the leadership of Mr. Noyes has been greatly modified by late movements in the Community, and his authority and influence limited, no authority and influence equally extensive and effectual having been substituted for that of which he has been deprived, or which he has laid down, but on the contrary the functions of our gov-

144

ernment having been expressly limited in the "Suggestions" adopted, so far as control of sexual affairs is concerned, and

Whereas, there are abundant signs that we have not at present such complete control over our youth and younger class of adults as Mr. Noyes has exercised in past time or such as is necessary for security against reckless, lawless, and loose conduct,

Now, therefore, as an incentive to ourselves to sober and honest investigation of the foundation and sanction on which our higher phases of communism have been built up and must forever rest, and in order that we may certainly hold ourselves in the path of integrity and prudence

Resolved, that sexual intercourse be also entirely suspended in the Community until such time as we can give honest, full, and satisfactory reasons for believing that we have not forfeited our right and title to this privilege by repudiating, in a fatal degree, the authority by which alone it was conferred and has been thus far safely regulated.

The Wayland-Smith journal continued:

This amendment was a radical one and made no little stir. Mr. Hinds and Mr. Burnham were naturally indignant at it, for it was a direct indictment of them. They stormed some, but I persisted in urging my amendment. Dr. Noyes seconded the amendment, so there was no escape for them. They could not throw it out and I declined to withdraw it. It put them in a very awkward dilemma. If they voted it down, they would have to utterly repudiate Mr. Noyes's authority and claim complex marriage as a natural right, which would be essentially adopting the Berlin Heights Free Love platform which has always been held in detestation among us. If they voted for the amendment they would put themselves in a very bad light before their following in the O.C. as confessing that they had made a bad move and deprived the whole family of a high privilege. So we argued the matter hotly.

Harriet Skinner, for all her peacemaking proclivities, was rather exhilarated by the smoke of battle which she scented from afar. "For all this state of things," she wrote to John on August 5, "the atmosphere is quite buoyant compared to what it has been many times. SKD says she feels like laughing in spite of herself. She don't know what is coming but can't feel bad; and Mother Noyes and I feel a good deal so; and clear at the core, the Community seems to be harmonious. Everything goes along in the business and we are the same miracle to the world as ever."

Mr. Hamilton's amendment, a sort of diversionary move, was offered to the Council on August 9:

Believing that stirpiculture is an interest of the greatest importance in its bearing upon the welfare of the Community, not to say the world, and that our minds have been enlightened by much truth as to the principles and spirit that should govern its practice and recognizing that Providence has established us in conditions favorable to carrying on stirpiculture, conditions that exist nowhere else; we feel that considerations of the highest kind call upon us to go forward in this matter. We have gone too far to think of turning back, with our little ones, our old people, and our Community interests, to the selfish ways we have left behind. There is no other course but to trust in the power that has led and protected us thus far, and go forward. And the way to go forward is to turn our backs upon the world, its spirit and its fashions and set our faces toward the Kingdom of Heaven and its policy.

In this view of the matter we think that stirpiculture, conducted on Community principles and in the Community spirit—the *we* spirit and not in the *I* spirit—would inevitably be an ordinance and measure of life and strength. As with a great ship in the neighborhood of rocks and shoals, so it is better for such a body as the Community to keep under some headway in the right direction, rather than to stop and drift at the mercy of wind and tide. We think that a steady but perhaps at present moderate experience in stirpiculture would conduce to promote elevated aims, personal improvement, Community courage, enterprise, and unity; that it would tend to lead persons away from the spirit and fashions of the world and recall them to first principles and our early faith. It keeps an open door of hope to some of the strongest desires that God has put into the human heart.

This proposal provided for three stirpicultural births a year: "Thus shall the lamp on this altar be kept ever burning."

There is no record of how this well-meaning effort of Mr. Hamilton's was received or what discussion followed its reception. HHS wrote to JHN, August 12, 1879:

Dear John: We have had two or three stormy Councils since I last wrote. The fact is that the *heads* of the Community are bewitched, but all the while I think the *hearts* are drawing together. We have had two beautiful Evening Meetings this week, when a good spirit brooded over us. When Myron came here he was quite put out with Alfred and Frank and others that he thought had violated the compact of peace; indeed he was ready to think that Mr. Hamilton and I had overstepped, by what he heard; but I felt that he would feel different after he had been here a little while; that is, he would see there had been an inspiration on Alfred and Frank and others, and what they had done was necessary. He talked with Frank several hours yesterday and each reported to Mr. Hamilton, who was distressed at first with what seemed to be irreconcilable difficulties between them: but before night they had come together and touched hearts as they never had before, and respected each other's inspiration, and said that there was a spiritiual atmosphere here in which misapprehensions and false interpretations and representations are miraculously occurring. I think one result of this whole affair will be to develop individual inspiration and make us respect each other's inspiration. I see that Alfred has an afflatus. It is quite different from Myron's, but I can't help respecting it, and I think Myron does now. Alfred's hobby is *obedience*—the subjective value of obedience—obedience to persons. He read to me today an Apostolic letter he had written to Mr. Burnham on that subject. Frank's inspiration is to convict this other party of the disaster of exiling you, etc. Mr. Hamilton's inspiration is to keep clear of wrath, to keep in a condition that invites the influx of the Holy Spirit and to depend on that for everything—not stickle about measures. Frank and Theodore have worked together. Frank spoke the other day of your wish that they might be reconciled, and he said it had come about: that the first thing Theodore did when he saw the situation and made up his mind to have a hand in guiding affairs, he came to him in a tender, brotherly spirit and all their jealousies and grudges were forgotten. I think Frank has joined himself now to Mr. Hamilton in a way that gives him hope and faith which Theodore does not have, and that will affect Theodore. I felt last night that Theodore's conversion was the thing to pray for, and the change that is going on in Frank is very encouraging. Mr. Hamilton thinks that Frank is really getting a spiritual education.

The Council continued its discussion of the question about stirpiculture till when the other party renewed the motion for stopping, Frank moved an amendment that Complex Marriage be also stopped, which Theodore seconded. That raised a tumult, you may suppose, Mr. Hamilton did not like it and rebuked Frank. I cannot describe the affair. Theodore said that those who got up the "Suggestions" sent to you imagined they had made only a slight modification of the Community social system, but they had made a *fundamental* one, great enough to destroy it. He was finally invited to give his views in full which he did yesterday. It was a very philosophical discourse, I thought, and unanswerable.

Two days later, enclosed with a copy of Frank's speech which was practically a résumé of his amendment, she wrote: "I can imagine you laughing over these guns of Theodore's and Frank's. Frank told me they had fired off their guns and felt better. Wm. said he was glad of Frank's explanation and the effect seemed every way good. Mr. Kelly said Frank spoke as if inspired and that with a good spirit. Mr. Hamilton manifested it. It was a very edifying Council—moderate and graceful."

On August 13 Myron wrote from Wallingford to Mr. Noyes:

I feel that my mission is about ended as mediator, but I hope that someone that has the confidence of such persons as HHS will take my place, as I know that there must be work done of this kind if different parties come together. You will see by letters [of Harriet Worden and Augusta] which I send, how some feel, and I have quite a number of such ones, and I have to preach the spirit of the first suggestion in the article sent you for approval, that past offenses, either real or imaginary, must be dropped. Now when I find that Mrs. Skinner says that W. A. Hinds is bedeviled, and it goes around to him, and that Alfred Barron called him a scamp—and that to his face—it seemed to me that WAH, Alfred, and Mrs. S. never could come together with this feeling, and it seemed to me that such expressions *ought not* to be expressed. If they think they are true, for the other side to take it up and make the most of it; no matter how good the intentions may be, it produced discord and hard feelings—does not provoke to love. And on the other hand, expressions by Martin and Augusta are to be regretted *just as much* as on the other side. Each come to me with their stories and I have to advise even such persons as Mrs. Skinner, which seems out of place for me. I write this freely because I feel that I can do no good if persons think I am out of place, and it is not agreeable work that I have. Yet it *must* be *done by some one,* for the sake of our children, if for nothing more.

At the Evening Meeting Mr. Underwood, at Mr. Hamilton's request, read an article from *The Berean* by Mr. Noyes, entitled "The Faith Once Delivered to the Saints," which he must have hoped would pour oil on the troubled waters. He announced that it was thought best that fragmentary reports of the proceedings of the Council should not be given by the members, as there was a liability of misunderstanding in that way.

Alfred Barron, apparently still pursuing his "hobby for obedience," said in meeting:

I find my mind working on that old subject of renunciation which exercised us so powerfully at the beginning of the Community when we were moved to give up everything. Men and women came into the Community and gave up all private rights. Men gave up their wives; and women their husbands and parents their children in the same spirit of renunciation that they had on the Day of Pentecost. I have had things in my own experience that made me feel that I was called on to give up. I have sometimes thought that we might have a revival this winter of that old Pentecostal spirit of giving up. That was a very serious thing in those early days, the giving up of all private rights. It made a kind of spiritual hush and solemnity that was very apparent, though there was a great deal of cheerfulness.

On August 16 Mr. Hinds's revised resolution was presented, followed by Frank Wayland-Smith's amendment, as before, after which Mr. Hinds spoke at some length:

I received the Social Theory of our founder because I was convinced that it is a natural and legitimate outgrowth of Christianity. The logic of Mr. Noyes's Bible argument always seemed to me unanswerable, namely "that the same spirit which abolished exclusiveness in regard to money (as on the Day of Pentecost) would abolish, if circumstances allowed full scope to it, exclusiveness in regard to women and children": and that "abolishment of sexual exclusiveness is involved in the love relation required between all believers by the express injunction of Christ and the Apostles and by the whole tenor of the New Testament." This language makes communism of the affections as much a principle of Christianity as communism of property. If it can be shown to be a truth which can be properly put in practice only under a particular person's supervision, then we might as well abandon its practice at once and in fact ought never to have entered upon its practice, unless it can be affirmed that that person will live forever, and be able personally to supervise the social relations of all who shall hereafter attempt to embody his principles in practical life. If the Oneida Community is still a Christian organization and is able to faithfully protect all the interests involved in its social freedom, with a good promise of perpetuity, then I can see no reason for a withdrawal from the present advanced social position, even if Mr. Noyes is temporarily absent from the Community. Mr. Noyes is still nominally the President of this Council and of the Community, and may return at any moment he chooses. I, for one, should be glad to have him return, and utterly disclaim any voluntary agency in his temporary withdrawal. But the all-important question bearing on this amendment seems to me to be whether this is still a Christian Community, that is, an organization having for its avowed object the practical embodiment

of the unselfish spirit of Christ in all relations of life. If so, we are
bound by the logic of the Bible argument to maintain our communism
of the affections as much as our communism of property. If expediency absolutely requires the abandonment of either, that is another
question.

The revised form of Mr. Hinds's resolution was as follows:

Whereas, propagation among us has always been subject to Community control, and whereas it is the conviction of many members that
we cannot offer the best hygienic conditions and training to a greater
number of children than we now have, while others are of the opinion
that economic and higher considerations, including the present social
and spiritual status of the Community, require that propagation should
cease for the present,

Therefore, be it resolved that further efforts at propagation by any
and all persons shall be considered unauthorized, except as they are
hereafter sanctioned by the general consent of the Administrative
Council.

Harriet, as usual, gave a lively account of the meeting:

I want you should know that with all the turmoil, we have good Evening Meetings. *There's* a piece of blue sky, if it is ever so cloudy
elsewhere. You know what a point you made of keeping that ground,
and it seems to be permanent and to be the most hopeful thing going.
Last night Harriet Worden made a vibration. She quoted that text:
"To be spiritually-minded is life and peace." Said it ran in her mind
and there was a good deal of response. Frank speaks, heartily endorsing Mr. Hamilton's remarks. Mr. Hamilton has a great deal of
freedom to preach humility and love.

At the Council yesterday, Wm. put his motion for suspension of
stirpiculture in another shape, that is, with reasons attached, etc., and
also read another paper relating to Frank's motion. I send you both
papers. There was a very warm talk after the reading of the second
and many delicate points just touched and questions raised, which
would take months to discuss: as to whether you was turned out—
whether the ascending fellowship was destroyed by the 8th section of
the "Suggestions," or had been at least, by influences coming in some
time before; and so on. Mr. Hamilton proposed at last to refer the
motions and the subject in general to you, as he did not think we were
likely to agree. Wm. was very anxious we should vote, or recommend
a suspension of stirpicultural proceedings meanwhile, but did not get a
vote exactly, and Mr. Hamilton's motion to send to you was carried

without condition. Mr. Hamilton asks if Wm. supposed he was going to open such a Pandora's box as this Council seems to be.

Mr. Hamilton wrote to JHN the same day:

I have understood that you were kept informed of the doing of our Council, so that you will know about the discussion on stirpiculture that has been going in the meetings of the Council for some time. You have probably noticed the different views and ideas that have been presented, by Theodore, William, Frank, and others, so that I need not repeat them. As there did not seem to be much prospect of our coming to an agreement I moved yesterday that we refer the matter to you, and ask you to give us your advice. This suggestion was approved. My thought was that the moral effect of referring the subject to you in this way would be good for us, and that possibly you might have something to say that would turn our thoughts into a channel that would lead to harmony, or at least tend in that direction. Since then I have had some misgivings about the matter, fearing that it might be a trouble to you and break in upon your studies and the quietness of your present life. I can imagine what a relief it has been to you to get away from this atmosphere of contention. But you must be free to say nothing, as I know you will be, unless you get something from above.

In yesterday's meeting, William made a reply to Frank's amendment, reading from notes. His argument, as I remember, was that our sexual freedom was a Christian privilege, a common right in a Christian Community, its legitimacy not dependent upon any individual. The weakness of his position seemed to me to be in not recognizing the importance of "the administration of the spirit." I presume you have noticed that the discussion was brought about by an anonymous communication, calling attention to stirpiculture. With this introduction I leave the matter to you.

Harriet Skinner wrote to JHN, August 19:

I don't know what effect all that budget by Myron had on your feelings, whether you laughed or cried, but I think I could make you laugh if I could convey the bright side, as it shows itself to me this morning. The Council yesterday was quite gentle. Edwin Burnham sent in a request that when the Council reported its decisions it would report also the argument, and the yeas and noes. This led to a reconsideration of that resolution of privacy which has not been favorably taken by a good many in the Community. Theodore has been in favor even of holding the Council in public—very much in favor of openness and having everyone responsible for their opinion. It was Wm.'s motion to forbid talking outside of the Council about matters discussed there and one reason he gave was that Theodore's own talk was horribly twisted and misrepresented after passing through several mouths. Theodore thought he should have fared much better if he had spoken to all the family, as he would have been willing to do. He would take any risk, at any rate, of having freedom to tell outside what was said inside. I think all the Council except Wm. were in favor of having that motion of privacy rescinded, and he gave in very cheerfully to so large a majority. I liked his spirit about it. The effect will be to make all careful what they say there and to make the Community, many of whom are as much interested in the discussions as the members themselves, feel satisfied. I do not believe in individual *sovereignty* but I am delighted with individual *inspiration*.

I think there is a secret change like this going on. The bad spirit, which used to expect to have to go away, has more lately, you know, said to itself: "I have as good a right here as anybody. I am going to stay, and the Community has got to change to suit me." I think that spirit is getting discouraged and giving up hope of being suited here, and feels more like going away. It is not apparent yet, but I see signs of it.

11

The End of Complex Marriage

On August 20, 1879, the Administrative Council received from John Humphrey Noyes a document which was to have a profound effect on the life of the Community and to cause a tremendous sensation in the national press:

Preface

It is to be observed that the paper which I have given to Myron to be read at O.C. is not intended as dictation or even as advice; but it is a rough sketch of an inspiration which has come to me today (if I know what inspiration is) and sets forth what I should direct and advise, if that was my business.

Least of all is it in my heart, by this paper or in any other way, to stir up strife. I offer my suggestions in full consciousness that no party spirit mingles with them. I should offer them all the same if there were no party divisions at O.C. I think they point the way of wisdom for the times we are in; but every man must be fully persuaded in his own mind.

My supreme anxiety for the Community is that it should have grace to hold together, even if it is not agreed in respect to the best form of social life. My hope is that if it does hold together, the best scheme will finally emerge out of all these debates and turmoils, and carry with it a moral and spiritual power that will really be, and be known to be, the judgment of God.

On the other hand, what I see in the world impresses me more and more with an awful sense of the woes that would come upon the great majority of the Community, if it should break up. I am afraid that many of those who have always lived in the Community have but little idea of what it would be for them to be thrown out into the world and compelled to get their living by hard work. Let me tell them, as one who now sees face to face, and in many respects *feels,* the miseries and anxieties of common life, that the O.C. with all her faults, is a mother whose care and brooding they will bewail with many and bitter tears, if they ever lose it.

My view is that both of the great motives of life—the religious motive which looks to heaven, and the worldly motive which looks to "bread and butter"—persuade with voices of thunder and entreaty to every man, woman and child to seek harmony and hold together, and keep that great machine—the business organization which shelters and feeds them—going with unfailing momentum. On this point it seems to me that both parties and all parties would agree at once and put away all thought and all talk about breaking up. For my part, so long as the Community does hold together, I shall live for it, even though I have to leave it like a thief to save it from the danger of my presence.

Myron will perhaps be able to tell the Community more fully the spirit in which I offer my suggestions. They have been so hastily and imperfectly expressed that they may need comments and explanations. I have thought that Frank Wayland would be a good man to digest and present them. But I leave this to Myron and the Council.

PROPOSAL FOR A MODIFICATION OF OUR SOCIAL PLATFORM

Preliminaries

1. A change of policy analogous to that which I am about to propose may be seen in the course we have taken in regard to our publications within a few years. As the Comstock movement began to loom up, we began to withdraw our objectionable writings from sale, so that now, when the hostile agents begin to approach us, they find nothing to complain of.

2. We have always claimed flexibility enough to adopt any form of social life that may be found necessary or expedient.

3. It will be remembered that I have often said, within a year or two, that our present social forms are not essential—that we can go back to Shakerism or any other inferior regime—and that we may be called to do so.

The New Plan

1. I propose that we give up the practice of Complex Marriage.

2. That we put ourselves, not on the plan of the Shakers, on the one hand, or of the world, on the other, but on Paul's plan, which *allows* marriage but prefers singleness; and to carry this out, we should first of all go into a new and earnest study of the 7th. of 1st Corinthians, and all take the spirit of it into our hearts.

3. Having thus provided for two classes in the Community—those who choose to marry and those who choose to keep their freedom from marriage—we then must take the same ground in regard to what is called fornication and adultery that the state takes; that is, we are not called upon to make any law or to pursue it to its hiding place: in fact, we must take no cognizance of it, unless it trespasses in some gross way which makes scandal or excites private complaint; we must recognize in our constitution only marriage and celibacy, and hold ourselves not responsible *as a Community* for what individuals

choose to do outside those forms; such irregularities are left to individual sovereignty.

4. Standing thus on the same practical platform as that of ordinary respectable society, we must still hold and preach our entire social theory, not conceding any consciousness of wrong in any of our practice, but conforming to worldly custom for the sake of avoiding offence, and we must still hold Complex Marriage as the true, rational, and final status which we look forward to as loyally as ever.

5. Then we define what remains of our communism thus: First, we hold our property and businesses in common, as now. Secondly, we live together and eat together in a common home, as now. Thirdly, we have a common children's department, as now. Fourthly, we keep control of the propagative department in the hands of the Community, as now, and of course enjoin on all concerned the practice of Male Continence, except as leave for propagation is obtained from the Community authorities. This injunction, of course, like all others issued by the Community, is to be enforced by criticism and such other measures as may be found necessary.

Results

This modification of our constitution will take away its "immoral features" and compel the clergy not only to let us alone but to encourage us, as they have lately promised to do.

It will also give new liberty and harmony within the Community. The adherents of the different social arrangements can respect and tolerate each other on Paul's principles, as set forth in Rom. 14:1–6, and all work together to make a happy home, to get out of debt and to make money, not to multiply our indulgences, but to support missionaries and multiply communities.

And observe that with such a platform as I have sketched, Communities could be started anywhere, in all the States and in Canada, and in all the civilized world, without fear of persecution—which is the job set before us by all our inspirations and prophecies, and ought to begin in 1880.

Such a platform could be fearlessly put before the world in our paper, and would certainly be very acceptable to a multitude, especially if accompanied with the assurance that JHN, the original and principal offender against sexual decorum, has left the Community and retired to private life.   JHN.

The reactions of the Council members, on hearing this document read, varied largely in accordance with their various party affiliations. The loyalists came in strongly for the new departure. That the suggestion came from Mr. Noyes had, of course, great weight with Mr. Hamilton, and he could see that since the Community was so much in advance of the world in its social practices, they might serve the cause of communism better and do more good by withdrawing from their advanced position and be able to meet the world on its own level. He also believed that a hearty response by the Community to Mr. Noyes's advice would bring them all into greater unity. If they could get a good spirit that would make them all love one another *fervently,* he was confident that everything would come out right. Otis Kellogg and Mr. Kelly agreed that the Community might get great enlargement from such a move.

Among the Noyesite women on the Council, Emily Otis, Chloe Seymour, Harriet Allen, and Sarah Dunn were strong believers in communism, but owing to persecutions from without and dissension within they thought this change was expedient; that Mr. Noyes, removed from the turmoil, could see more clearly than they the course to take, and they believed his inspiration was their best guide. Surprisingly enough, Augusta Towner, until now the most vociferous voice against the Noyes party, agreed with the other women. She said she was touched by the whole spirit of the document and thought it showed a wonderful degree of wisdom and patience. It is to be remembered that Augusta had run away from the Community some months before and got married.

Theodore Noyes spoke at some length, reminding the Council that the pressure of public reprobation was likely to increase with the national victory over Mormonism, after which the whole current of disapproval would very probably be turned upon the Oneida Community. This, he said, would give smarter men than Professor Mears a chance to acquire a reputation at their expense.

Frank Wayland-Smith agreed and mentioned the recent case of a Mormon who had been tried before the highest court, found guilty and imprisoned. Other Mormon leaders were to be tried in October, at which time there would almost certainly be another push against the O.C. Frank said:

> Mr. Noyes first proposed that we stop the practice of Complex Marriage and become celibates. In this case there would be no rupturing of old relations further than that, and all could go on in the same fraternal relation as in the happy days of yore. That single step would involve no giving up of friends, so far as fellowship is concerned; and

it is entirely within our power to adopt this plan if we can all agree to do so unitedly. But Mr. Noyes makes a merciful provision for those who cannot endure to be celibates, which is to marry. It will cost us something. The most we can do to mitigate the situation is to go slowly, try to get the full consent of all concerned before acting and be, in a word, Christians.

One great point in favor of the plan is that it will, once and for all time, relieve Mr. Noyes from all danger of indictment, arrest, or persecution. He will be as free to come and go as any other person. To free Mr. Noyes from the legal theatening would be worth a great deal.

Of the opposition party, only Mr. Hinds and Mr. Henry Burnham were reluctant. Mr. Hinds spoke first, seeing so many difficulties in carrying out the proposed measures that he asked for an interpretation of them. He said: "I will say this much, however, that as communism and marriage are based upon fundamentally different principles, it seems to me that the introduction of marriage into the Community is a perilous undertaking that may endanger, sooner or later, the most important features of our Community life."

Mr. Burnham said that he had felt for some time that some change in their social status was inevitable. Exactly what it would be, he could not see. "Even now," he said, "I am not sure that absolutely the best thing is being done. But things are mixed in this world, and if the very best things cannot be reached, the next best may be, and I am content."

After this discussion by the Council, at its behest Mr. Hamilton sent the following request to Mr. Noyes:

> *Whereas:* Mr. Noyes has expressed a willingness to write out a statement of the modification of our social system, as proposed, for publication in the *American Socialist,* therefore
> *Resolved,* that the Council hereby cordially requests him to so write at his earliest convenience,
> Carried unanimously.
> E. H. Hamilton, Chairman

One extraordinary fact came to light. Myron, having brought Mr. Noyes's document from Niagara to Oneida, told the Community in Evening Meeting assembled that when he had met Mr. Noyes, according to an arrangement of some weeks' standing, he found that Mr. Noyes had not previously heard any of the deliberations of the

Council on the social subject but had written his paper, as he said, because he thought it was the best thing for the Community, under the present circumstances. He advised and entreated that there be no interfering with present communism—no going into cooperation, no talk about paying wages or paying for board or in any way having separate interests. They should all work for harmony and look with jealousy on anything that would prevent making a happy home. He said that the whole Community should take hold and support the Council just as they had supported him in the past. He, himself, felt that he had not at present sufficient physical strength to govern the Community and look after all its affairs. He believed that they would get along better without him but assured them that they could advise freely with him. Myron added that he did not expect Mr. Noyes to return to Oneida under six months or a year.

At this point Mr. Noyes's paper was read and, as Myron wrote him, "the family cheered and cheered." Later, Mr. Hamilton explained that the paper had been read and voted on by the Council and carried unanimously, with one exception. However, since there were some points on which they wanted Mr. Noyes's advice, they had sent Myron back for further consultation. It was important, he added, to keep this matter as closely as possible from the public until they were ready to publish it to the world.

Myron now had a few oral messages from Mr. Noyes. He did not want to be held responsible any longer for the practice of their social theory; he now withdrew his sanction for any further proceedings in that direction but hoped, however, that there would not be any immediate rush into marriage, a step which should be taken only after a good deal of consideration. In reference to the children, he said, in cases where one woman had two or three children, each by a different man, there should be no changing of names; the child was to retain the name of the father. The principle which they had always observed should be held good, that the children belonged first to the Community, not only those now born but those born hereafter under the system of marriage.

After some further comment and commendation from the family, a vote was taken. Myron described it in a letter to Mr. Noyes: "When the time for the vote came, persons were requested to rise and everyone, except WAH, rose, and when the opposite vote was

called, not one arose. I thanked the Lord and bid them all good
night. Complex Marriage ceases at ten o'clock, Thursday, A.M.,
date of our paper. It is accepted here."

A paper from Mr. Towner was handed in the next day:

I think the question presented in this proposition is a great question.
I confess I am not without serious misgivings to it, as to how the
adoption of the modification of our social life shall affect the future
of the Community. I do not believe in marriage as a remedy for our
troubles. I do not believe that marriage and communism can exist
together. The only question with me is whether or not this proposed
change will prove to be an inlet of the spirit of marriage which will
overcome that of communism and at no late day disintegrate the
Community. Whether this shall prove to be so or not will depend upon
ourselves and upon the spirit we shall allow to come in and upon us.
I must claim the right of prophecy and if I have the spirit of prophecy,
I think the Community is to some extent in a state of reaction and if,
in the violence of that reaction, the marriage spirit shall take possession of it, it is doomed to dissolution. For myself I would add one
word more. I would have preferred to have had the change made to
one of entire abstinence all round, with "consent for a time." I want
none of the privileges of marriage. I think I shall share the state of
the "unmarried and widows." I am sure it will afford the married an
unusual opportunity for self-sacrifice and continence. Let us, if we
can, take the "preferred course."

Mr. Underwood was briefer: "I voted for the resolution but with
very much regret that the family were again driven into a corner
and forced to a decision without the calm deliberation that a matter
of such momentous importance demands. But I voted for celibacy.
I felt that *celibacy* was what Mr. Noyes earnestly desired, and that
the enthusiasm of the family went with him, and I voted for it as a
temporary expedient."

Mr. Hinds, the only member who did not rise when the vote was
called for, was brief and to the point: "To prevent any misunderstanding of my position, and to save personal explanations, I will
say that I did not vote in favor of the proposition before the Community last night because, with my personal convictions, I could
not do anything which might be interpreted as approving the introduction of marriage into the Community: and I did not vote against
the proposition because I was not prepared to say its plan is not,
under all the circumstances, expedient. Time will tell."

The Wallingford family received the news with its usual equanimity. Their journal noted:

For historical purposes it may be well to review the past and mention briefly that Mr. M. H. Kinsley's arrival from O.C. on the morning of August 27, bringing with him Mr. Noyes's "message to the Community" and numerous manuscripts from O.C. relating to it. With the exception of three persons away on business and those temporarily absent at Cozicot, the family, numbering just twelve, assembled in the parlor at 10:30 A.M. to listen to Myron's report and the reading of the documents—the matter of which, though startling, was quietly and favorably received. Indeed, we know full well that we have a good and trustworthy leader, and we are not afraid to follow him, let him advise what he will. A hearty vote of acceptance was rendered the message and the same was forwarded immediately to O.C. by telegram. Since then we have had enough to think of: and indeed, if we have lacked, the newspapers certainly have supplied every deficiency. Two reporters only have interviewed us, one of the *N.Y. Herald* staff, a civil and pleasant young man, took dinner with us.

The telegram: "Wallingford, Ct., 8/27, 1879, 3-06 P.M. E. H. Hamilton. Accepted. (signed) M. H. Kinsley."

The *O.C. Journal,* August 28, 1879, ten o'clock, reported:

With the stroke of the clock we record the beginning of a new experiment in communism: That we give up the practice of Complex Marriage, which has existed for thirty-three years in the Community, not as renouncing belief in the principles and prospective finality of that institution, but in deference to the public sentiment which is evidently rising against it: That we place ourselves, not on the platform of the Shakers, on the one hand, nor of the world, on the other, but on Paul's platform, which allows marriage but prefers celibacy.

It is a clear beautiful morning in the "out-world," and as we write, the sound of many voices mingled with the hum of industry falls upon the ear: while over all and above all there is an atmosphere surrounding us with a spirit of faith and hope from the "in-world," inspiring us with heroism for a new career.

On August 30, 1879, Harriet Skinner wrote to Mr. Noyes: "This is a great time. I wish you could see the interesting matter that has come in the papers today. The *Boston Post, Syracuse Standard,* etc. The *Utica Herald* man is here, Cunningham. Prof. Mears comes out with a handsome response. I think we shall be a universal pet now."

The *American Socialist* printed an extra edition of the September 4 issue which they offered for $.05 a copy and remarked dryly that it was surprising how well the metropolitan journals were represented in such a village as Oneida: "In point of fact, as we have abundant opportunity to know, letters which appear in some of their columns dated 'Oneida' are sometimes written by persons who have not seen Oneida for a twelve-month."

They made another interesting comment: "The past history of the Oneida Community is at least secure. Its present social position and its future course, whatever they may be, have no power to change the facts of the past; and the more these are studied, the more remarkable they will appear. These things prove, as does also their present course in giving up that phase of their communal life which has caused offense, that the Communists have not been the reckless bacchanalians a few have represented them. The truth is, as all the world will one day see and acknowledge, that they have not been pleasure-seekers and sensualists but social architects, with high religious and moral aims, whose experiments and discoveries they have sincerely believed would prove of value to mankind."

What the press now said of them did sound rather as though they had, as Harriet said, become a universal pet. The *New York Times,* datelined Oneida, N.Y., August 28, 1879, reported: "The Oneida Communists have taken an important step toward reorganization by formally abandoning the system of Complex Marriage that Father John Humphrey Noyes has consistently advocated for so many years. The Community has always been a popular institution here, owing mainly, perhaps, to the fact that its members are honest in their business transactions, industrious, enterprising, peaceable, and good citizens from every aspect. They have been menaced with criminal prosecution by the leaders of various religious denominations repeatedly, but it has never been possible to secure legal evidence of their practices, and they have managed at every crisis to outgeneral their opponents."

The *Boston Post* as the *American Socialist* noted on September 4, was quite sympathetic: "The founder and, we believe, present leader of the Oneida Community, is a man of education and strong conviction, who labored with great consistency and unity of purpose to establish a system that seemed to him best for society. The order and prosperity which have attended this experiment have given its enemies, who are naturally many, very little to work with in making a crusade against it effective. A very important change in the social platform is now announced. From this date, the Community will consist of celibates and the married, who will follow the law of strict monogamy, and they declare that they will now look for the sympathy and encouragement which has been so liberally promised in case this change should be made. They certainly should receive it. The experiment now becomes one toward which all the world may feel kindly."

The *Syracuse Standard* first commented on August 30, then sent a reporter to investigate:

> The announcement yesterday morning by J. H. Noyes, the head and front of the Oneida Community's 30 years of offending, was a complete surprise to the entire Christian community of central New York. More than that: it was a most astonishing announcement! A most unexpected and entirely unlooked-for concession! A most graceful and entirely Christian method of putting to utter rout one's enemies by the inexpensive method of simply writing, as they used to in the late war: We have met the enemy and we are theirs! And yet the more one thinks over the graceful and Christian concession the Community has made, the more it is apparent that the victory is not all on the side of the enemy after all. The Community has now placed itself fairly and squarely on the ground of suffering themselves in a so-called just cause, rather than permit the enemies of that cause to be afflicted.
>
> Hitherto, only peculiar temperaments sought entrance to their fold. The order was therefore less generally infectious in its influence than it will now become, that its offensive marital regulations are changed. As an industrial phenomenon or experiment, it has been proven a triumphant success. If the meagre acreage of land of which they are possessed and their limited manufacturing yields them a living of such excellence to which nine-tenths of our population are strangers, the question will become more popular why a general system of this character shall not prove a remedy for the wars of society.
>
> Yesterday morning a reporter of the *Morning Standard* left Syracuse to interview the Oneida Community leaders in regard to the circular we reprinted yesterday morning. Arrived at Oneida village, not a person could be found who knew anything about the new movement. Said a leading citizen, "If Noyes prints that over his own signature, I'll believe it. We've always had faith in those Community people and it has never been misplaced. Their word is a good deal better than that of many who assume to criticise them. I tell you, sir, the word

of Mr. Noyes or Mr. Hinds or Mr. Hamilton or any one of those Community fellows is just as good as their bond!" And the distinguished citizen emphasized this statement with a thumping whack on the table with his fist.

It was eleven o'clock when the Community was reached, and the inquiry for Mr. Noyes or Mr. Hinds, the editor of the *American Socialist,* was made of one of the divinities in short-dresses. "Mr. Hinds is in, sir," said the lady, and a moment later Mr. Hinds made his appearance and gracefully submitted to his 999th interview.

Reporter: "It may seem strange to you that I should put these questions to you, and yet there is a good deal of skepticism as to whether or not your movement is a sincere one!"

Mr. Hinds: "You may say, sir, and I speak for Mr. Noyes as well as the rest of the Community, that this movement is a *bona-fide* one, and we enter upon it in the utmost sincerity. The Community has always held itself ready to recede from the practical expression of its peculiar social principles as a matter of expediency and in deference to public opinion."

Reporter: "Was that sentiment fully understood at the Syracuse Conference?"

Mr. Hinds: "It was distinctly stated at the time of the convention at Syracuse."

Reporter: "Have you had any conversations with the committee which Bishop Huntington or Dr. Beard of Syracuse and Professor Mears of Hamilton College represent?"

Mr. Hinds: "None at all, sir; our movement is simply a measure of prudence on our part, adopted in the spirit of that message of St. Paul which says: 'If meat make my brother to offend, I will eat no flesh while the world standeth.' "

Reporter: "Have any members of that committee been here since it was organized?"

Mr. Hinds: "Not that I know of. If they have, they did not make themselves known as such."

Reporter: "At whose suggestion was the reform made?"

Mr. Hinds: "At the suggestion of Mr. Noyes."

Reporter: "How was his suggestion first received by the Community? Were there any objections to it?"

Mr. Hinds: "Well, perhaps it is sufficient to say that it was generally seen to be wise and expedient, and was accepted by the Community as the way out of a dilemma."

Reporter: "To use a common expression, has there been any bulldozing of the Community on the part of any?"

Mr. Hinds: "No present pressure is being brought to bear by the people in this neighborhood or anywhere else to compel this action. We have, of course, been cognizant of a general movement on the part of the public that was likely, sooner or later, to demand some such action on our part, and Mr. Noyes and others deemed it best to anticipate it."

Reporter: "Well, when is your grand old wedding to come off, when the Community people will be united in matrimony like unto the outsiders?"

Mr. Hinds: "You will notice that this article says that the Community will hereafter consist of two classes, the *married* and *celibates* and that celibacy is considered the superior condition. Still there will be freedom for those to marry who prefer marriage."

Reporter: "What are the elements which will keep your Community from going to pieces?"

Mr. Hinds: "I think Mr. Noyes has answered that question in his circular."

Reporter: "As to other people, will you mix with them now? Will they be permitted to mingle with you?"

Mr. Hinds: "Well, now that we have made a radical change in our social platform, we hope for immunity . . ."

Reporter: "Don't say it yet! Just one moment! What are your present numbers?"

Mr. Hinds: "Here and at Wallingford we number some 300, with the sexes about evenly divided."

Reporter: "Finally and lastly, when did this reform go into effect?"

Mr. Hinds: (Decidedly and pleasantly) "On Thursday, the 28th day of August, in the year of our Lord, 1879. The abridgment of our social system has already gone into effect!"

Reporter: "Now, fire away!"

Mr. Hinds: "I was about to remark in all kindness, however, when you interrupted me, that we hope *that the eternal and everlasting system of interviewing us which has been insisted upon for the last 30 years has now come to an end!*"

Reporter: "Requiescat in pace!"

Mr. Hinds: (cordially) "It gives me pleasure to extend the hospitality of the Community to yourself and lady. You will remain to dinner with us?"

And it was a bountiful and elegant spread, served by one of the ladies over whom all this trouble and fuss and discussion and argument had waged, and for whose dear sake this most delightful and Christian conclusion has been reached.

The Reverend Doctor Mears's "View of the New Departure" appeared in the *Utica Herald* on August 30, 1879:

Professor Mears of Hamilton College expressed surprise and pleasure at the voluntary action. When asked what effect it would have on future movements of the ministers' association, he said: "I can only give my own views. The matter on our part has been confided to a committee, of which Bishop Huntington is the head. For myself, as a member of the committee, I can say unreservedly that if the Community faithfully conforms to the principles it is here declared to have adopted, it seems to me 'our occupation is gone.' A mistaken idea is abroad that our purpose is to crush the Oneida Community. That is wrong. Our efforts and intent have been against the immoral features —the same that the Community now abandons. There is, as I now see, nothing for us to do. I do not intend to express or harbor distrust. But while I say that, so far as this declaration of the Oneida Community is satisfactory to me, still more satisfactory would be the announcement in the columns of the *American Socialist* or the *Utica Herald* or other public journals, in the usual form, of the names of those parties who now propose, or may hereafter propose, to live together in the sacred relation of husband and wife. It may be their purpose to make such announcements. Everything pertaining to a change of practice so radical as the Oneida Community is now entering on cannot, of course, be done at once."

The *American Socialist* stated the Community's public position:

Congratulations pour in upon the Oneida Community thick and fast on account of its "New Departure." It need not be said that they are very welcome. It is more than pleasant to realize that the days of persecution are ended and that the Community may now continue its course with the approbation of even its former enemies. The Oneida Community have made a pretty fair social reconnaissance; they have perhaps a clearer conception than their outside friends of the difficulties of maintaining a social system so much in advance of existing civilization, and certainly have a better knowledge of the means at their command; and if they have concluded that the cause of human advancement will not suffer by their present action, this judgment should be received with at least respect, especially as their career for more than thirty years has been one of unexampled daring. The Community has no regrets for the past; it, on the contrary, considers itself fortunate in having been called to such pioneer work; it rejoices in the general results of its reconnaissance; it abandons no previous convictions, it is simply persuaded that it is best for all interests, including those of social progress itself, that it should give up the practice of Complex Marriage and place itself on Paul's platform, which allows marriage but prefers celibacy. And it does this in the utmost sincerity and good faith. If the underlying principles of Complex Marriage are true, as the Community holds, the day will yet come when that system will be honored as it deserves: its endorsers and advocates can safely commit its claims to the civilization of the future.

12

Marriage After the Fashion of the World

One of the most important subjects to come before the Administrative Council at this time was the Community's relation to the world. It was hoped that no one would be tempted into thinking that the lines of demarcation between the world and the Community, either as a body or as individuals, would be any less rigid now than in times past: "Though in our new constitutional change we may appear in some measure to conform to a custom of the world, we are, nonetheless, a peculiar institution and a peculiar people, and it is as vital a matter now as ever that the line dividing the Community from the world be distinctly marked." No motion was accepted to embrace these ideas, and the matter was left until the next meeting in order to give all a chance to organize and condense their ideas on the subject.

On August 29, the Council thought also that the matter of their social etiquette should be freely discussed: "Under our new constitutional change it will inevitably be quite different from what it was before. Indeed, considering this change we should be exceedingly circumspect, for the eyes of the world are upon us, and if we indulge in the free and easy ways which have before obtained among us, we may cause scandal, and certainly will arouse suspicion as to our honesty. The Council hopes that the whole family would make this a matter of serious thought, and that it would be considered soon in public."

Harriet Skinner had her usual budget of news for Mr. Noyes: "Perhaps Myron told you that Mr. Burnham and GDA and Martin and Augusta and Belle were all very zealous for your new platform, and that it made a kind of split between them and Wm. The situation was very curious. They all had their private reasons, I suppose, and Theodore and Frank had theirs: but whatever our private reasons

166

all round, we all run together except Wm. The family's accepting it was a most miraculous affair. It was voluntary, and still it was forced. If there had not been that necessity to make it public in the paper *right off*, it would have taken months to get through it probably: there would have been so much discussion, if Wm. had had time to have it stirred up. We see in it Paul's managing, and your power to sway the Community as one man, even though you are hundreds of miles off."

Her letter the next day, August 30, treated a subject she had mentioned several times before:

I have not wanted to communicate any trouble from here, but I don't know but I ought to say a word about the state of the young folks. It is a frequent topic in the Council, and as yet there seems to be no control over them. The Youths Committee are, too many of them, I think, in a state of irreverence themselves—Martin and GDA for instance—to have much influence the other way, and the policy seems to be, a good deal, to gratify the wishes of the young folks, at the same time that they are amenable to no authority and under no moral instruction. They are abandoned to each other's society entirely, and such persons as Frank think the danger of social corruption and accidents is very great between themselves, not to speak of the danger between them and outsiders. So far the Community keeps yielding to them and pacifying them, rather than they rendering obedience to the Community. Mr. Hamilton says he sees no way but to let it go on and grow worse and worse till Martin and such folks see we need more power. He thinks they, the young, will not get beyond the ropes, though they will push to. He says his policy is to cultivate the spirit of obedience in himself, and be what he wants others to be: that he will ask no favors but have faith that he will command respect sooner or later—that the profane will fall down and confess that God is in him, seeing the good spirit in him. I am driven more and more to prayer as the only outlook: the human outlook for reducing our young folks to obedience is gone. I mean to pray without ceasing.

A matter of great interest now came before the Council—the first applications to marry by Community members. The following application was presented to the Secretary:

To the Administrative Council: Martha J. Hawley and I wish to get married, and desire to learn what steps are necessary to enable us to.
F. A. Marks
Martha

The Minutes of the Council recorded on September 1: "Resolved that in the matter of the application of F. Marks and Martha J. Hawley to be allowed to marry, the Council recommend that in order to give chance for the discussion of objections, they wait one month from the date of the application, and in the meantime study Mr. Noyes's analysis of the 7th Chapter of 1st Corinthians. If, at the end of that time they still desire marriage and no valid objections are presented to the Council, they shall have the approbation of the Council in entering upon it according to the procedure laid down by the Council. Carried. Members of the Council expressed their approbation of the respectful and organic way in which F. Marks and Martha Hawley have made their application for permission to marry."

The next entry recorded a different kind of application:

O.C. Sept. 2nd. '79. To the Council: Wishing to be married elsewhere and as quietly as possible, we take this occasion to inform you that it is our intention to do so without further delay.
Respectfully,
A. E. Hawley
E. H. Mallory

A discussion of the matter was carried on in the Evening Meeting. Mr. Hinds made the report:

I would ask, on behalf of the Council, that some special attention be turned to the case of Alfred Hawley and Elisabeth Mallory. I understand that they have been married this afternoon. The report of the Council's proceedings says that strong disapprobation of their course was expressed. It was considered wholly unjustifiable. The Council has neither taken nor is likely to take a position unfriendly to marriage: indeed, it is pledged to furnish all necessary facilities for marriage: and there was nothing to indicate that any obstructions would be put in the way of these two persons marrying. But without consulting the Council or the Community they have entered into marriage in their own way and time, and in direct violation of Mr. Noyes's suggestions and the general understanding in the Community that such matters should be subject to the approval of the Council, and should take place under regulations which it shall prescribe, and should not take place in a hurry nor in the fashion of the world, nor outside of the Community. It seems to the Council that the same spirit which would lead two persons to act thus independently in the first step of marriage would lead them to take the matter of propagation and other things into their own hands in the same independent way: and that if it were allowed to become a precedent for others to follow, it would lead to the greatest disorder. We must have order and good government, if we would preserve any part of our communism.

Mr. Hamilton remarked that however confused the ideas of right and wrong had been in the minds of some for a time past, there could be no question as to whether this act was right or wrong. Some were of the opinion that if they had got to a spot where they could disregard the wishes and feelings of the Community in going out in this way, they had better stay out.

The *O.C. Journal* noted: "It was thought that Alfred had been somewhat a victim of the government of Libbie and her mother over him, and a great deal of surprise and disapprobation was expressed in regard to the course pursued by Mr. Hawley and Mrs. Mallory in going with them to get married. A strong point was brought out in a clear way that marriage cannot be tolerated in the Community under the control of a worldly spirit; that it must be subject to the powers that be."

Quite naturally, the subject of marriage was prominent in the minds of the Community folks. On September 3, 1879, George Miller wrote from Wallingford perhaps the most extraordinary suggestion regarding it: "If there should be marriages at O.C. why would it not be the appropriate and handsome thing to invite Dr. Mears to come over from Clinton and perform the ceremony: we to pay him suitably for his trouble. He could thus satisfy himself past all doubt of the sincerity of our proposal and could testify of it to the Churches and the world in a way that would silence all suspicion. In this way 'the lion and the lamb could lie down together' and perhaps Dr. Mears would become one of our best friends." He also mentioned more seriously that such a performance might be "a splendidly sensational *advertising* device that would help our businesses wonderfully." There is no record of how this suggestion was received. However it was, Dr. Mears was never asked to perform a marriage ceremony at O.C.

Harriet Skinner was inclined to feel depressed about the general state of the Community. She wrote her brother on September 3:

I feel like telling you about the billows which rock the Community nowadays, and how the water spashes into the boat. Sometimes it *looks* as if we were going head-first to destruction—that worldliness would carry everything away, but what we keep deep in our hearts. This week there has been a great rush to a camp meeting at Oneida, led off by Helen Noyes. For several evenings our own meeting has been thinned by this rush; no consultation that I have heard of. Then the prospect is that there will be a rush into marriage soon. Belle and Milford opening the ball. Then there is a rush of seceders toward us. Then Belle A. is in communication with Arthur B. and Homer is, too. He told Frank that he wrote to him the other day that he had better come here now—that things were changed and he could have a good time; and when Frank rebuked such a proceeding, Homer only laughed as though it was a good joke. Augusta, who was very forward in getting a resolution passed, making the opening of letters a crime, said, as though she gloated over it, that she had reason to know that the freedom of seceders to write here now is on account of the passage of this resolution. She pushes for opening our doors to them without fear. The prospect is for a rush from outside friends. Mr. B. has come and quartered himself on us and the Baileys are working on Lily's sympathy again—say they are $2,800 in debt. She talks of going outside to earn something for them.

There has been a strong effort to get long hair and long dresses going, headed by Helen Noyes again. She and Belle and Augusta seem to have a mission to open every door to worldliness they can. I guess as many as twenty long dresses have been made, and some of the girls have said they had made their last short dresses. The horses' tails about are shocking to good taste. I want they should have either long hair or short. I am mortified that strangers should see the frowsy heads of the Easton girls and others. But I have a kind of feeling in regard to short dresses—that they will hold the day. Also, if the young folks feel free to get married without consultation, I don't see what is going to stop them having babies without.

Well, I have told my story. You can imagine what cares Mr. Hamilton has to mow away. He stands in a good deal such a place as you did before you escaped. He feels every little while that he must seek rest somewhere, and then he bows himself to the situation—dives under and comes up renewed for the battle. I expect he will have a chance to get away at the right time. I am not discouraged about the final result. I pray God that I may not be, but God is doing a strange work.

"Mother Noyes"—Harriet Holton Noyes, the wife of John Humphrey—also wrote him about the situation on September 3:

A view of the state of the young people, their worldliness, etc., which has sometimes distressed me, came to me this morning, which comforted me. I saw if they must have a baptism and run of worldliness— having their own way as to amusements, dress, marriage etc.—they had better have it inside of the Community than to go out: they would suffer less than to have to work to get their living, as they would if they left the Community. I suppose some of them will not learn by what is told them of others' experience, but have to go through the experience themselves in order to appreciate the freedom there is in Christ. If any one could feel what I went through in the marriage spirit, I think they would run from it as they would from a fire. But I hope and believe that all who are true-hearted and have been hooked by Christ will yet be drawn in: they may run the length of the line, and I will feel hopeful about them. Mr. Hamilton says thus far every wave that has rolled in upon us has left us on top of the wave.

Two days after their rash elopement, Libbie and Alfred repented and wrote an apology to the Community:

We wish to acknowledge to you that we were at fault in getting married before waiting for some expression from the Council, after sending in our note to them. Though our reasons, of course, seemed legitimate, we now see that the example was not good. We are sorry. We pray that God may give us grace and wisdom.
Sincerely,
Libbie and A. E. Hawley

Mr. Hamilton wrote rather mournfully to Mr. Noyes in reporting various probable marriages which had been proposed: "I am afraid all this is not very pleasant for you to contemplate, but I suppose it is just what we might expect unsanctified human nature would do."

Myron Kinsley, who had been JHN's strong right arm from the time of his leaving, was a pragmatist, a doer instead of a theorist, who sometimes found the hesitations and vacillations of the Community at this time trying, to say the least. On September 5 he wrote to his leader:

What I wish and pray for is that the Council will come together and put on a certain dignity that commands respect, and put off all the theorizing in their councils, or as much as possible, and take hold of practical issues in the Community, like making the most of our business this season: try to draw everyone into it, as you did years ago at the old Trap Shop. If they could, it would hide and cover many discords. It is something we could all unite on. Let us make the most of all these notices in the papers. It certainly is the greatest advertisement we ever had, and there is many a businessman that would pay $1,000 for it. I am sure that there will great good come to the Community as a whole from this move of yours. It was certainly inspired. As you say, everything goes to prove it. And if some do rush into marriage, cannot we overlook it and treat them as brothers and sisters still? It seems better to me for them to marry than to go outside and do so. I feel good about it, looking at it in this light. God will surely have his way about all this in the end, and I will trust him. As ever your faithful son, Myron.

That same day Harriet Skinner wrote to her nephew, George Miller, at Wallingford in answer to his suggestion about Professor Mears:

I don't know as your suggestion was anything but fun, but I did not dare to have it read in meeting; the Community are so ticklish just now. There seems to be a great prejudice with some in favor of a minister. I think Augusta, who is a kind of self-appointed mother of this marriage movement, has the English prejudice, thinking it disreputable to be married by a Justice. The meeting last night showed that the old power of criticism could be evoked when necessary. It seemed as if the poison in the system had come to a head in the Hawley family, and been lanced. William and Mr. Towner and all the that party were as indignant as anybody. It destroyed all party lines completely.

The Council are at work on the procedure, guarantees, and so on proper in cases of marriage. Mr. Hamilton told Frank and Theodore they were a good deal responsible for this movement, and they must take hold and reduce the thing to order: and they have enlisted.

Harriet also enclosed the following document in her letter to George Miller:

"SUGGESTIONS"

for the guidance of those persons in the Community who contemplate marriage under the new Constitutional provision authorizing it

Preamble

Whereas it is exceedingly desirable for the interests of individuals as well as the Community, that any marriages among us shall be arranged and executed in an orderly manner, with due deference to the feelings and views of all concerned,

Therefore the Council deems it advisable to suggest to the Community the course of action which, in its judgment, should be followed by those who desire to marry. Following are the

Suggestions

1. When a man and a woman desire to marry they should, before any practical steps farther than to ascertain each other's willingness, apply to the Council for a marriage license.

2. After receiving such application, the Council may approve at once, or may order a delay if there is reason to suppose any allied complications remain unsettled, and to give time for proper consultation all round; after which it shall authorize the marriage in a license signed by the chairman.

3. Marriage being, according to the statutes of New York State, a civil contract, a choice is open to us of the form by which we will be married. Mr. Herrick is, it is understood, still a clergyman of the Episcopal Church, his Bishop (Potter) having refused to accept his resignation when it was tendered several years ago (1865). He is, therefore, empowered by statute to marry people according to the Episcopal form. This will furnish the means of ecclesiastical solemnization here at home for those who prefer that form. On the other hand, as no particular form of church solemnization is necessary to a valid marriage, we may, if we choose, adopt some form of marriage by written contract which will be just as legal and binding as a marriage in church. Mr. Noyes has requested that there be no going abroad to get married. The Council coincides with this request and would advise that all marriages be executed strictly within the Community. After the license from the Council has been received, the contract may be signed or the ceremony performed, in the presence of only one or two witnesses, if desired, or of the whole Community.

4. A form of contract of marriage will be drawn up under the advice of the Council and will be ready whenever occasion requires, for the use of those who prefer marriage by contract.

5. A record-book will be procured in which all marriages shall be recorded in their order.

6. It shall be expressly understood that all persons who conscientiously conform to these suggestions and who marry in accordance with them, do so with the entire sympathy and fellowship of the Community.

7. Every marriage shall be announced in the Evening Meeting on the day of consummation, or as soon thereafter as possible.

8. The following are cases in which the Council may interpose a prohibition of marriage:

(a) When minors propose to marry without the consent of their parents or guardians.

(b) When a member proposes to marry with a person not a member of the Community.

(c) When a person proposes to marry who is in open rebellion against the authority of the Council.

It is understood that the act of marriage with a person not a member of the Community is an act of secession from the Community, and the membership of the person so doing ceases at the time of the marriage.

Form of Application for Marriage License

To the Administrative Council of the Oneida Community: We, the undersigned, A.B. and C.D., members of the Oneida Community, with full purpose to continue our membership and do all we can to insure the prosperity and permanence of the Community, and recognizing its right to limit the number of children born in the Community and control their condition, solicit your approval of our proposed marriage, which we desire shall be consummated on or before ―― day of ―― A.D.

Signed, A.B.

C.D.

Form of Marriage License

License is hereby granted to (A.B.) and (C.D.) to join themselves in marriage on the ground stated in their application dated ――.

For the Administrative Council,

(E.F.) Chairman

Form of Marriage Contract

We, the undersigned members of the Oneida Community, take each other for husband and wife, and do solemnly promise, in the presence of these witnesses, to love, comfort, and cherish each other.

Frank Wayland-Smith's journal recorded that the form of application for license to marry was afterwards altered somewhat to make it seem a little less stringent to those who disliked to subscribe to conditions on marriage.

As though he sensed from a distance what was going on at Oneida, Mr. Noyes wrote on September 10 to Myron:

I wish to say a few words to the Community on the Proposals which I offered them, and on what their duty is in undertaking to carry them out. My object is partly to help them find the true path in an important crisis, and partly to limit my own responsibility and satisfy my conscience.

It will be remembered that in my first paper (prepared more expressly for the Community) I disclaimed offering you dictation or even advice, and professed simply to report what I considered to be an inspiration that came to me from the higher powers. In accepting my proposals I believe that you are dealing not with me but with those higher powers.

My main proposal was the positive one in the second item, viz., that we place ourselves on *Paul's platform*. I do not think the powers above would have advised us to give up Complex Marriage if there had been no other refuge than Shakerism on the one hand, or mere worldlyism on the other. Paul's platform, allowing marriage as a preventive of fornication in incontinent cases: but positively confining it to the circle "in the Lord," and very emphatically preferring celibacy, is really a transition platform, preparing for, and leading to, the Complex Marriage which succeeds it in the heavenly kingdom. The emphatic preference of celibacy for the sake of increased fellowship with Christ, and in view of the passing away of the fashion of this world, stamps that platform as a truly spiritual device, worthy of the wisdom of Paul, and a fit antecedent of the heavenly marriage toward which the Church was pressing. In moving out of Complex Marriage into the status recommended by Paul, we do not leave the University in which we are being educated (as we should do, if we went into Shakerism or worldlyism) but only fall back into a previous class (as a sophomore might become a freshman), for expediency's sake, and in our case, doubtless, because the mass of the Community are really freshmen.

In these suggestions I remind you of what you really accepted in adopting the proposals I sent you, which, perhaps, you are in danger of forgetting, if you are in a hurry to avail yourselves of the liberty of marriage. Please remember that in the change which I offered you and which you are inaugurating, I turned over to Paul's inspiration (for I believe that the afflatus came from him), and to Paul's written advice, and I emphasize this transfer by insisting both in my first paper and in my second, that the first thing to be done is for the whole Community to enter upon a new and earnest study of the 7th. of 1st Corinthians. In your accepting my proposals, I understood, and I think fairly, that you pledged yourselves to me and to the public, to give Paul a respectful and serious hearing before taking steps, individually or collectively, in the direction of marriage.

I was much pleased with TRN's statement of the probable course of the Community, when the reporter of the *Utica Herald* asked whether there would be any "hurrying into bonds" on the part of any considerable number. He said: "No. Father's counsel is in favor of celibacy. Many of the members have expressed similar views. In consideration of the founder's advice and the teachings of St. Paul, the disposition of the Community will be to follow those teachings, and the public need not be surprised if it does not for a considerable time hear of any marriages in the Community."

At all events I wish it to be distinctly understood that I am not responsible as sanctioning by what I have done any course of things in the Community which is not taken after a deliberate, respectful, and united study of Paul's platform and in harmony with the plain purpose and spirit of his instructions.

J. H. Noyes.

Harriet's letter, two days later, may have been disappointing to Paul's advocate:

I don't know but you foresaw it all, but *marriage* fills the eye now of most of the young folks; that is, from folks as old as Alfred down: and I should think there was very little reference to any counsel but personal wishes. It is a kind of baptism. Mr. Kelly was telling me today that it came on him with a kind of irresistible power: he was glad to know what the influence is, but he said when it was on him he knew in his heart that that desperate feeling would not control the matter: he should wait till he knew the mind of God: and now it has all passed off. I should think Alfred had had a similar experience: that is, has got by the fever, and feels like waiting.

Just now there seems to be very little motive working but what impels to marriage in the world, and it looks as if marriage would eat up Communism: but I believe Christ is deep in the hearts of many of them, and will make their experience turn them back to communism by and by.

In Mrs. Skinner's letter of September 15, discussing the business meeting of the day before, she referred to "Theodore's proposition," of which no record has been found. However, from the context of her letter it seems evident that he had proposed to settle the matter of appointments to the financial and other committees by the democratic method of putting it to a general vote. Earlier the Hinds-Towner party had been strenuously in favor of the democratic method as opposed to what they called the dictatorship of Mr. Noyes's rule. Now, in the clutch, they were afraid of a popular landslide to Theodore's side and objected that a general vote would lead to wire-pulling and so on. Although she gave no definite account of the outcome of this conflict, the fact that Mr. Hamilton felt "as

though the Lord avenged him in this meeting" suggests that the
loyalist party won the argument.

Mrs. Skinner wrote:

I suppose I have conveyed to you the impression of some of our blue
days. I wish I could, of this bright day. The Business Meeting yesterday was a great affair. The question of how the financial committee
and other committees shall be appointed was up. You will have seen
Theodore's proposition. It was democratic in the extreme but very
distasteful to William and his side. Mr. Hamilton said they saw that
Theodore would probably get 20 votes, putting him on every important committee, and they would have to face him everywhere. They
were disgusted with their own favorite form of government. They
ignore entirely inspiration and spiritual character as having any
weight: it is the voice of the people that should rule: but come to the
practical issue, they bolted. Wm.'s objection was that it would encourage wire-pulling and caucusing, but Theodore said that was going
on now, it would only legitimate it. If they would go back to the old
way of making our wisest man leader, if they would let you appoint
the committees, he would like it better, but this was the only pure
democracy. In a disagreeable talk with Martin the other day, Mr.
Hamilton said that Martin was full of the spirit that ignored spiritual
character and put everything on the basis of vote, and he felt as
though the Lord avenged him in this business meeting. Mr. H. said
Theodore's conduct was very graceful. Mr. H. scarcely spoke, himself.
He has got a new enthusiasm in the business and worked out some
ideas that will be useful in the chain business. The businesses are
prospering, and all the machinery of the Community goes on with
"untiring efforts" in spite of the strange state of things. Some of the
folks have visions. Mary Pomeroy and Mrs. Newhouse have seen
what they believed were spirits of the Primitive Church, and others
have a great sense of their nearness. The marriage fever has cooled
down, if I should judge by the feeling.

The *Nation* of September 4 contained a long article on the
Oneida Community, prophesying doom. Its last paragraph stated:

Mr. Noyes's compulsory retreat from a fundamental position strikingly
exhibits the weakness of communism. The uniform lesson of socialist
wrecks with which the pages of History are strewn is that the strength
of the Community is in its founder; that if he has executive ability,
the organization may endure as long as his powers are unimpaired,
but that it seldom survives him. Mr. Noyes has, we conceive, outlived
his headship. His successors, who should be the Community as a

whole, competent to maintain its principles and its business, is the self-appointed head of the party which has become dissatisfied with Complex Marriage. In other words, there is no real succession. A revolution has taken place: the Community as it was has suffered a mutilation which practically destroys its identity, and will, by the coming historian, be added to the list of extinct Utopias. Meantime, all must wish well to the industrial experiment from which "everything audacious" has been eliminated.

The next week, the September 11 issue carried, under the title "The Oneida Community's Change of Base," a reply by Theodore Noyes:

Sir: Your editorial in last week's *Nation* on Oneida Communism shows the penetration and sagacity which a reader of your paper from the beginning naturally expects: but you have been slightly misled by the Froudes and Macaulays of the daily press. It is unfortunate, if they must chronicle an internal cause for the late action of the Community, that they are obliged to fabricate one by piecing together old notes and conjectures, for they must try again. I explicitly deny that, "self-appointed" or otherwise, I have led any movement in the Community which has extorted this concession from my father, with whom I have been in substantial agreement for some time. We have had trouble from time to time for several years on account of my tendency toward what he calls "Positivism," but I have never allowed these differences to force me into any party antagonism. Your conjectures of collusion between the opponents of Complex Marriage in the Community and the clergy are unfounded.

Yours respectfully, Theo. R. Noyes

Neither the *Nation*'s editorial nor Theodore's reply to it made any mention of the change from Complex Marriage to monogamic marriage which, as HHS reported almost daily, filled the minds of the Oneida Communists. On September 7, 1879, she stated:

I suppose you will get from the journals some idea of the drift of things toward marriage. I do not feel any opposition but I see the course of true love is not going to run smooth, that the heart-strainings will be many, and that probably is just what is wanted. The only opposition Mr. Hamilton has made to it is to the haste there seems to be and the disposition to go outside for the ceremony. They seem to want to have it made *tight* and be *recorded*, so that generations hence the certificate can be produced. Yesterday Frank discovered that Mr. Herrick had never lost his license—that when he offered to give it up, the bishop refused to take it; so he can marry as tight as anybody wants and give certificates, and have his marriages recorded. That was a cause of jubilation to Frank and the reasonable class. I think there is a good deal of consultation with Mr. Towner about the legal points and there is ever so much worldly feeling. William has committed himself strongly against marriage, but he is working in the Council very heartily to make the best of it, if we are going to allow it.

The upshot of the strong disapprobation of the Hawley-Mallory marriage ended in sweet charity and forgiveness in the following resolution:

Whereas, Alfred Hawley has acknowledged that his course in his recent marriage was inconsiderate and censurable, and whereas he has expressed his purpose to conform to such regulations as may be passed by the Council respecting the control of propagation and of children, and has further offered to submit his course as a business superintendent to criticism: Therefore, be it resolved that the Council reconsider its vote asking Alfred's resignation, and allow him to continue in the discharge of his present business responsibilities.

13

Paul's Platform

A letter on September 19 from Theodore Pitt, Mr. Noyes's "right bower" at Niagara Falls, proved to be a long and heated criticism of the whole Community in its response to Mr. Noyes's permission to give up Complex Marriage in favor of monogamy or celibacy:

> The rush of attention toward marriage indicated a great misapprehension of the recent change of social platform, or rather an almost entire failure to apprehend it at all. Less than a month has passed since the change. We hear very little as yet about the turning of the hearts, old and young, to the study of the *real* social platform onto which the Community has moved, but instead there is an immense amount of talk and excitement and wringing of hearts about the marriage of this one and that one, just as though the Community had given up communism and had started on the broad road to private familyism and a general breakup.
>
> It seems to me that most, if not all, of this is very unseemly in a people educated as we have been, having hopes such as we have cherished, having a mission and calling such as we have received. The change of platform was not designed for the destruction of communism but to save it in time of peril. The Community has not adopted the social platform of marriage nor the platform of Shakerism —legal celibacy; but it has adopted the social platform of Paul and the New Testament Church. They have publicly, in the presence of both the visible and the invisible worlds, and unanimously, pledged themselves to his platform. This being the fact, it seems to me that the modest, reverential and civilized thing to do would be to go into a six-months' study of the new platform, under the guidance and leadership of Paul and the Holy Spirit, before even the question of an individual marriage was mentioned. If we study this new platform sincerely we can see that it is not in favor of marriage. While it allows marriage, it allows it only for one reason, incontinence.

There followed a long and intricate analysis of the Pauline theory of marriage, including the translation of the Greek roots in-

180

volved, and a harangue on the meaning of *Porneias,* "the sin of whoredom, pure and simple."

Harriet Skinner took notes of a speech in reply by her nephew, Theodore:

Theodore said he had studied Paul earnestly and he had his own interpretation of his theory. It did not agree with Mr. Pitt's. He did not see how any marriage could take place in the Community according to Mr. Pitt's position. He said that he wanted to get married, himself, and he would give his reasons why to anybody that wanted to know. He had made the whole subject a matter of earnest study. Mr. Pitt's theology gave him no honorable excuse for getting married. He said he thought there would have to be more or less marriage to make the Community hold together. If they were all enthusiasts like Mr. Pitt, they could get along, but a great many of them were not. He said he did not want to do anything contrary to his father's will. He spoke as if he shouldn't, anyway. He thought there would be a great many secessions, if Mr. Pitt's theory was crowded. He should not leave the Community, but he thought many would. Theodore thought there had been a good deal of deliberation and patience, on the whole. Permission to be married was given and there had been only one marriage.

Whether this report—or, indeed, whether Mr. Pitt's impassioned harangue—was ever seen by JHN is not recorded. His sister continued to write him lively and generally cheerful accounts of the doings at Oneida:

There are a good many encouraging signs now-a-days. This delay of waiting for word from you has been very salutary. Edwin Burnham told me last night that he thought it had been good, and he was one of the eager ones. Alfred's excitement has subsided. He said last night in meeting that he saw we were under the same control as before; there was a different administration but the same spirit. With all this confusion in the family, the children seem to be good. The children's house, as an institution of rules and regulations, is a good deal demoralized. The parents have the children a good deal more than ever before.

You hear, I suppose, of the great prosperity of our business. It is very stimulating to the men, I think. The criticisms that have come providentially on Alfred Hawley and James Vail and Arthur Towner have affected their business habits very much, and of course those with whom they associate. Martin is quite a drill master as to industry.

Mother Noyes was saying yesterday that she thought it must have an elevating effect on Martin to leave his business every day and sit down with the Council to confer on other matters. His judgment is useful many times.

Toward the end of her letter she wrote: "Today Myron comes. He will report the imbroglio today. It is thought Mary Van's letter to Mr. Pitt may have given you a false idea of the state of things here; that there has been a great deal more continence than his letter would imply."

The Minutes of Council for September 27 recorded that it was voted that the letters from Mr. Pitt and Mary Van Velzer be read. To this Mary objected and "an exciting discussion ensued. Unreportable." This, presumably, was the "imbroglio" and was, actually, unreported.

On September 29, Mr. Noyes sent two papers to the Oneida family. The first dealt with a special subject, the children:

I wish you would tell Theodore and others to see to it that their children that were begotten out of marriage never have any occasion to feel any difference in their feelings toward them on that account. I shall see that all of my children are looked out for just as much as Theodore. I hope that you will do all that you can to impress the importance of this on the Community. I trust Theodore and others will do nothing to alienate them from their present children and the responsibility that they hold as fathers to them. The Community must protect its offspring. *This is their first duty and an important one.*

I pray daily that the Community may hold together, prosper, and grow *if for no other reason* than to save the children that have been begotten in Complex Marriage. Now that we have given it up, *we have not given up our responsibility to our children and cannot.* We have them to look back upon as the fruits of Complex Marriage, and we ought to see that they are brought up in the very best way; do all that we can for them, so that they will be an example of our experiment, and something to be *proud* of: and in a way that they, themselves, will have occasion to be thankful for when they grow up.

Again, you may tell them that if they will keep communism, live for it, and work for it, I don't care how much they marry. If marriage will help them to do this, the more they marry, the better. This is a good political reason, and on the same ground that I have recommended in the past. I only want that they should become *fully* persuaded in their own minds so that there shall be no after regrets.

Again, sincerely I do not think that any of those that propose marriage do it for the reasons cited by Mr. Pitt. They have good reasons, no doubt, and I for one do not wish to inquire into their motive.

On the same day he wrote a more formal paper to the family:

I might leave Mr. Pitt to defend his own position, as my previous message simply asked the Community to move slow and give Paul a faithful hearing before rushing into marriage. But in justice to Mr. Pitt I will say that I thought, on first reading his letter to Myron, and still think, that he did substantially reproduce Paul's ideas in 1st. Cor. 7, and I approve of his practical purpose and wished that Myron and others might have the benefit of his example and influence in a time when the current of public opinion was setting strongly the other way.

But now I am free to say that in stemming the current manfully as he did, he presented, in my opinion, not quite so liberal a front to marriage as Paul did, when we take into view all that he said about marriage in other epistles. In other words, Mr. Pitt did not bring forward all that could be gathered from Paul's writings on the other side of the question, nor did he seek out and expound fully the reconciliation between Paul's opposition to marriage and his actual treatment of it as "honorable" and "no sin." I am very unwilling that the Community should hurry into a fever for marriage right after adopting Paul's platform in regard to marriage. Censuring them for marrying, *after* giving Paul a fair hearing, never entered my thoughts.

I should say in general and once and for all, the more really useful marriages, the better: the fewer fancy-marriages the better: and the more heaven-seeking celibacy the better: but God forbid that I or any other man should sit in judgment on anybody's motives for marrying so long as they are good communists. Let everyone be fully persuaded in his own mind.

After Mr. Pitt's letter, Frank Wayland-Smith sent a memorandum by Myron, asking Mr. Noyes a series of questions raised by that letter:

1. Now that the Community has abandoned the practice of Complex Marriage, how is it going to keep its numbers good in the future? Shall it be by propagation or by the admission of new members?

2. If it is to be replenished by propagation, shall this important service be committed entirely to the half-dozen fertile couples already married, or shall others be permitted to marry for this and other forcible reasons, with the sympathy and good will of the Community?

3. Or, is it expected that we shall, in six months or a year, find

some way to evade our present position and resume the practice of Complex Marriage and stirpiculture?

4. Or, are we to take the ground that the time between now and the great final day is so short that all the advice to the primitive believers who were awaiting Christ's Second Coming within their lifetime applies equally to us at the present day? That is, are we to endeavor to found a permanent Community home, or are we to look for great changes and a removal within a lifetime or so?

I ask the above questions because Mr. Pitt's language suggests them, and because each of these points is maintained by different persons and parties in the Community, and it seems to me they ought to be answered explicitly and clearly for the peace and good order of the Community.

Mr. Noyes answered this in a postscript to his letter:

Frank, in a memorandum sent to me, asks in substance whether we have any such prospect before us as the Primitive Church had in their expectation of the Second Coming. This is a very interesting inquiry and is very pertinent to our present discussions. I wish that the study of Paul's platform may be pursued till we get light on this and many other questions. My impression is that the time is not distant when Complex Marriage will be legitimated by sweeping revivals and revolutions of public sentiment. That is the logical and dramatic outcome of all we have done. I think it is rational to advise our faith heroes to wait for that revolution and keep themselves in the best training for it, and under the best inducements to work and fight for it, as it was for Paul to hold up the Second Coming as the goal of liberty before the Primitive Church. But this is too great a subject for a postscript. I leave it with a hint.

The note in the *Oneida Talk Book* for September 30 reported that "Mr. Noyes's letter was responded to by very general and hearty cheers." Alfred Barron not only sympathized with Mr. Noyes's letter but asked those who were proposing to marry to "sacredly promise that they will not do anything to wreck communism. *Endorsed emphatically*." Mr. Hinds called attention to another reason for maintaining their organization, "viz., that our aged and weakly members and those who would be unable, if left alone, to secure a good living, may be properly provided for. Someone, for example, has counted among us thirty widows. Now for the sake of all these classes, it seems to me important that we hold together and work together and strive together for the prosperity and permanence of the Community. *Endorsed.*" Even Mr. Towner expressed sympathy with what Mr. Noyes had said about the children and marriage and was "especially glad to have their attention directed to the fact that the fashion of the world passeth away." Frank Wayland-Smith remarked drily that he found himself living in the Community from attraction, not from a sense of duty, and thought this was a good reason for holding together. This was responded to with *"enthusiastic cheers."*

On October 1 "the Reverend Doctor Mears called at the O.C. in company with Mr. McKinney of Utica. He was treated civilly and given dinner. He stayed about two hours.

He asked what assurance he could give the public which he represents that our new departure will be sincerely carried out, while we at the same time maintain the truth of the theory of Complex Marriage. He was told that we had given our word to the public on the subject; our word was considered good on other subjects, and if it was not taken by the public which he represents, we have nothing further to offer. As to being interviewed on this subject, either by reporters or ministers, we did not consider it consistent with our self-respect to submit to it.

"Mr. Noyes," said Mr. Mears, "has taught that *marriage is a sin.* How then can he recommend the Community to adopt a condition of sin?" In reply we said, "Will you state where Mr. Noyes has said that marriage is a sin?"

Mears: "In the *History of American Socialisms.*"

Communist: "I have read that history a number of times and have never seen any such statement in it. I furthermore believe there is no such statement, or any statement that by any fair interpretation can be so construed, in that book or in any other of Mr. Noyes's writings."

The other point on his mind was that Mr. Noyes had said that communism was impossible with marriage. I told him that Mr. Noyes had never made so narrow a statement as that. He had shown by historical deduction that communities that had succeeded had, as a matter of fact, in some way or other modified the usual marriage relation: but Mr. Noyes would be very glad to see communism succeed with marriage, as that would bring its benefits and economies within the reach of a much larger class than at present enjoy its blessings.

Mr. Mears went away with good feeling, apparently, and invited us to call at the college and see him.

On September 21 Frank Wayland-Smith wrote to Mr. Noyes

posing the question of whether or not to continue the publication of the *American Socialist* whose circulation had declined in the past two years: "Two years ago we were printing some 1,300 copies per week; a year ago about 1,150 copies; now only 730 copies." He asked whether they should discontinue the paper or substitute some other form of periodical. He suggested the possibility of making an arrangement with one of the great New York dailies or weeklies to give them space for whatever they wanted to publish to the world, so that their subscribers would know where to look for any word from them.

To this JHN replied that the discontinuance of the paper had been settled by the announcement they had made in January of that year: "If those concerned rally to its support, as we hope they will, it will go on stronger than ever: *otherwise it will cease its issue with the present volume.* They have not rallied, but have fallen off: we are pledged therefore to cease. Moreover, within the Community we are pledged to the business men—at least I am—to not continue the paper beyond this year, unless it supports itself. And now that we have given up the 'immoral features,' there is less occasion for the paper as a means of defense than ever before. I should say, therefore, that it is best by all means to discontinue." He did not like the suggestion of employing a New York paper as their organ, but put forward the idea that they might issue a small paper as an advertising sheet for their businesses. To such an inveterate publisher as Noyes, the man who had said in 1851, when the communes were barely keeping their heads above water financially, "Let the private fortune of the Oneida Community be what it may, its first business is to see that God has a Press," it was impossible to resist adding, "On this plan we could keep our postal advantages and a good many other things that would help us to begin again some new departure hereafter. It would be like a *cadenza ad libitum* thrown in to lead to a new key and a new strain."

Some investigation into the practicability of such a scheme was made, but when the matter was finally laid before the Business Board on October 21, the general consensus was that advertising could be done more economically in other ways, and further consideration of the matter was indefinitely postponed. Frank asked

Mr. Noyes to write an editorial, announcing the end of the *American Socialist.*

Nearly two months later, December 4, 1879, they published in an editorial, entitled "Farewell for the Present," possibly written but not signed by JHN: "It is now time to report that the responses do *not* encourage the hope of a fair support for the paper. The *American Socialist* will therefore cease its issues at the end of the present year. As to the immediate motives of this cessation, it is obvious, and not to be wondered at, that lack of cash returns decides the matter. The Oneida Community and its founders have been sinking money in non-paying publications some forty years—about $100,000 in all—and naturally would like a change. Doubtless we could go on without seriously embarrassing our affairs; but, on the whole, think it best to let somebody else turn the grindstone, while we take a breathing spell."

So ended a series of publications which stretched with only a few interruptions from 1834 to the beginning of 1880: *The Perfectionist, The Witness, The Spiritual Magazine, The Spiritual Moralist* (two issues only), *The Free Church Circular, The Circular* (two volumes), *The Daily Journal,* and *The American Socialist.* Besides these, the Community published upwards of a dozen other works by John Humphrey Noyes, including a number of pamphlets on specific subjects and ending with the splendid *History of American Socialisms,* still the most compendious and authoritative work on nineteenth-century communism.

As a sort of preamble to his long paper on what he called Circumscribed Marriage, John Humphrey Noyes referred to a matter which had been under consideration for some time. A Mr. D. G. Croly who had been editor of the New York *Graphic,* and with his wife had visited Oneida and taken a great interest in the Community's project of Stirpiculture, had strongly urged both JHN and Theodore to publicize the subject. Unfortunately, his early correspondence with Mr. Noyes and what Frank Wayland-Smith called his "late prophecies" have not been preserved, but the Community *Journal* for April 1, 1879, notes that Croly's "late prophecies" had been read in meeting, and "it looked as though the whole thing was published to further his interests in mining, as it is well known that he left the *Graphic* to engage in that pursuit."

Mr. Noyes said at this time, "Croly has not always prophesied correctly, for when we were about starting the *American Socialist* he saw nothing of the tidal wave that was coming." (It will be remembered that his views in several particulars were directly in opposition to those of Mr. Noyes.) "Croly advised us to write very plainly and radically on sexual matters and to boldly assail and expose the evils of the marriage system. It looks now that if we had followed Croly's advice we should have been found in the attitude of offenders in the late assault upon us by the clergy; and in the trial we should likely have been swept away. While Mr. Croly has tried to push us forward in an offensive way, he has himself kept out of sight."

Croly next came to light after the Community abandoned Complex Marriage. On September 15, 1879, he wrote to Dr. Noyes:

So you have taken a new departure. I am sorry for it, as it shows weakness. As an American I feel humiliated that the tyrant majority has so much power. I write to know if you will care to send me such of your publications as relate to your social practices. I propose to write a short pamphlet on what you have done in that direction. I think you have made a contribution to sociology of the highest importance to the human race. I think those facts which bear on the matter should now be collected and given to the public. Somebody will tell your story. Why not let a friendly historian make it public? I do not propose to discuss your religion except incidentally, or your communism. I propose simply to give the facts touching your social practices, your efforts to improve the race, and the result so far. Please speak to your father about this and let me know.

Theodore's reply on September 17, 1879, first reproached Croly for implying that his own personal troubles about beliefs had drawn him into antagonisms which had imperiled the social structure of the Community. This he denied. Regarding the Community's change of platform, so-called, he wrote: "The late move of the Community has a deeper origin than in the attacks of the clergy. Father's social experiment came practically to an end before the abandonment of Complex Marriage was decided upon. It was only after I and several others concluded that Father's system had gone beyond recovery that we felt ourselves at liberty to advocate monogamy as the best way to avoid worse evils. The action of the clergy hastened matters as there was every prospect that they would bring us to a legal issue which, in the condition of the Community within, we were not prepared to meet."

The letter contained more to the same effect and it may be that Theodore at this point felt that perhaps he had been too confiding, or too indiscreet, both failings of his. At any rate the letter closed with the request that Croly "regard it as confidential."

A week later, on September 24, Croly answered with a denial that he had ever criticized Dr. Noyes for his views on the marriage question. He said frankly that although he was "intensely interested in the experiment of race culture, the special religious views of the Community had never interested me. I regarded them as antiquated and certain to give place to wiser views." In a postscript he added: "I remembered in all our conversations you wished the social experiment to go on under a somewhat more liberal state of feeling on religion."

Whether or not this correspondence was forwarded to Mr. Noyes is not known; neither is there any copy of a report by Frank Wayland-Smith "about Croly's proposition." In a letter dated November 12, Frank spoke of a letter he had written Mr. Noyes on October 21 which he feared had never reached him. In this second letter he mentioned having read Mr. Noyes's article on Stirpiculture to the family at the Evening Meeting but says nothing about Croly's proposition to which Mr. N. refers in a sort of prologue to his Article. The essay was entitled "The Future of Stirpiculture," and dated November 4:

> So far as Mr. Croly's application for information is concerned, T. R. Noyes is the proper person to report to him, and that is one reason why I have neglected to answer the letter which was forwarded to me some time ago. TRN knows more about the statistical history of our experiment and its results than I do.
>
> There is another reason why I have hesitated and delayed to say anything about Mr. C.'s application; which is that I have doubted whether it was expedient to encourage him to report and speak for us in this matter. His eye is very exclusively on the stirpicultural part of our experiment and doubtless he exaggerates the importance of that part, at the expense of our religious efforts and probably of all other interests concerned. And he evidently thinks the stirpicultural part of our experiment is completed; at least that we have stopped the whole

work we attempted in that line, and that the Community, so far as that is concerned, has failed and come to an end. It doesn't seem to me likely that a man in that position of mind would report us satisfactorily. Undoubtedly he would help us to publish what we might say in the scientific world. His scientific proclivities and his nearness to scientific and literary men might enable him to speak with effect in that direction as much so as any one. But the question with me is whether his known character as connected with the Positivists and Free Lovers would not weigh more against us than for us, especially among religious people; and I am as anxious to find favor among the clergy and religious people as among the scientists.

I suppose he may have it in him to make a hit, perhaps in Dixon's fashion, by which he may make money and perhaps get popularity that would not be worth much to us.

Then I don't know but he intends to publish anonymously. I have been a good deal dissatisfied with his persistent refusal to be known as favoring us. I do not feel so much indebted to him as I otherwise should.

On all these accounts I have had no definite inducement in my mind to make any reply to Mr. Croly's application. Yet I should like to leave it to TRN and FW-S to do what is best about it. I mention these things in explanation of my delay. If they see reason to expect that a report from him will really be a benefit to the cause of stirpiculture, I will sympathize with what they think best to do, and will cooperate as far as I can; that is, I will write what may be required of me.

So much is preliminary to the main ideas I have in mind to present in this paper.

I particularly dislike the attitude of Mr. Croly in considering our experiment in stirpiculture *at an end;* and I am going to express my dislike pretty strenuously and give my reasons for it in a shape that might be presented to him, if TRN and FW-S think it expedient; or at any rate might be fit to go before the Community whenever T. and F. believe it will do good.

CIRCUMSCRIBED MARRIAGE

I am very confident that a great illusion in the public mind and in the Community in respect to myself (of course I must be allowed in this case to express myself about myself, and let the expression go for what it is worth), I do not consider myself superannuated. I do not consider my work done. I never found my mind clearer or stronger, or felt better prepared for an active career. I am not at all likely to give up the business of my life at present, *if ever.* I say this just by way of introduction to the further and more general remark that there is, in my opinion, a great illusion of the same kind about the Community. I do not consider the Community superannuated or past its vital climax and going down to oblivion. And the object of this writing is to point out what is really before the Community as its future career, or rather as a continuation of its past career—particularly in relation to stirpiculture.

The giving up of Complex Marriage is not necessarily nor (as far as I am concerned) *really* the giving up the attempt to start a superior breed of men and women. Indeed I am by no means certain that the change we have lately made, when we come to understand it, will not be found to be a help—and a very important help—to the carrying forward of that enterprise. We give up Complex Marriage but we have the *products* of Complex Marriage in a splendid collection of children; and we have the Community organization and the business organization that was connected with Complex Marriage. In these products which remain, namely our children and the inexpugnable social and business relations which have been formed in connection with Complex Marriage, we have the manifest requisites and the greatest possible inducements to go on, as a Community, with our stirpicultural experiment.

Now then, let us look into the situation faithfully and see what we *can* do.

In the first place, we must regard what I call the products of Complex Marriage which remain: namely, the children and the social relations connected with the children—*as the capital* which we have accumulated in our experiment of Complex Marriage. That capital is valuable property, notwithstanding the fact that the process by which it was accumulated has been abandoned. We have plenty of reasons to be certain that the O.C. collection of children is, in many respects, a superior collection, and if we can keep it from being swept into the mongrelism of the world, it may become permanently a superior race. Whatever there is of good in the blood or breeding of these children remains as capital for us to go to work upon now as stirpiculturists to keep it pure and to multiply it. And this can be done under the *regime* of monogamic marriage—that we can go on to evolve the germ we have produced with perhaps less diversion of our forces than heretofore, if we are disposed to make the best of our position. The giving up of Complex Marriage sets us free from two great hindrances—the clashing and worry of love-intrigues within the Community and the annoying excitements and persecution from without that have followed us on account of our supposed illegalities. We can now turn to the work of planting and replanting the capital we have won, with unfettered hands and hearts without fear.

But the great practical question is, what can we do with this capital *without Complex Marriage?* How can we invest and turn it so as to go on with scientific breeding and yet keep within the limits of the monogamic law? I don't know that I should ever have studied this problem thoroughly without being under the present pressure. But now that I have been compelled to face it, it seems to me the answer is very simple and one that will so simplify the practical possibility of Stirpiculture that everybody—that is, all sober, self-denying people—not only within the Community but outside, can go to work at it; not perhaps in the *very best way,* but in the *next* best, and certainly in a very effectual way, without giving any offense to legal morality or public opinion. Of course with our capital we are in the best situation to take hold of this work and therefore ought to lead off with an example; but there is no reason why any company of persons that can agree should not do a good business in the stirpiculture line, on the plan I am about to propose, even without communism of any kind, as I shall proceed to show.

My idea is just this: To introduce what I would call (for want of a better term which I hope somebody will invent) a system of *Circumscribed Marriages* in the place of complex marriage. By this I mean (in our own case, which I will attend to for the present) that we should keep the Community enclosure sound, and place ourselves under—not a law, but a *rule* of persuasive grace and home loyalty that *as our children grow up their marriages shall be kept, so far as lies in our power, within the enclosure.* By this simple rule, well carried out, we shall have henceforth just such breeding in and in as that which produced the Jewish race after it was fairly started, and we shall have it as they did, without the necessity of incest or any violation of law. Our great family gives us a liberty in this respect which the common little family does not have. It is an enclosure sufficient for all stirpicultural purposes *now,* and will grow larger and more liberal for selection from generation to generation.

I said in my article on *Scientific Propagation* that the two essential precepts of stirpiculture are: *breed from the best* and *breed in and in.* It seems to me that Providential signs and even scientific inspection allow us to assume that our thirty years' experiment in Complex Marriage has been in some good measure an obedience to the first precept, giving us what we may hope will prove to be a germ of an improved race; and that in the great revolution which has now come we are entering upon a dispensation of obedience to the second precept in which, by a persistent system of lawful but Circumscribed Marriages, we shall conserve and perfect the germ we have produced for the benefit of the world in ages to come.

Far be it from us to claim any monopoly of this idea, or of the privileges which it opens to us. Undoubtedly the whole world is, even now, either consciously or unconsciously working out its civilization and salvation by Circumscribed Marriages. The great cosmopolitan and age-long example of the Jews is only a conspicuous form of what is going on more obscurely everywhere. Every distinct nation is substantially an inclosure for breeding in and in, and so producing a special race. Every district in every nation, every distinct class in every district, every aristocracy and every humble caste the world over is propagating under the law of Circumscribed Marriage, more or less stringently enforced. My idea is simply to take this universal law and go into obedience to it voluntarily and systematically. And this might be done even in society at large on the basis of a simple agreement between any number of married couples without communism or association of any kind for any other purpose than stirpicultural improvement. Suppose forty families, for instance, instead of undertaking complete communism as the O.C. did, should choose each other simply as persons of good blood and good culture and agree as a business corporation or village colony to consider themselves an association for circumscribed marriage, pledging themselves to bring about by all honorable means the fittest possible mating of their rising generations within their own circle. Such an association would rely on the promises of science and the love of offspring as its inducements to undertake an achievement like that which the Jews have carried through under the inducements of religion.

This would be my scheme in its simplest form. The varying grades from this form up to Circumscribed Marriages in complete communism might be numberless, and the inducements would vary throughout the scale.

I cannot doubt that the time is coming when there will be as much enthusiasm for perfecting the blood of human beings as there is for starting choice breeds of horses, dogs, and strawberries; and when that time comes I believe that if law and public opinion stand in the way of Complex Marriage, that enthusiasm will find its path to liberty of experiment through the system of Circumscribed Marriage. It is quite certain that the opportunity of selecting good specimens for the founding of such voluntary association as I have described will be so liberal in the ordinary advance of civilization that there will be no necessity for such audacious experiments as ours has been; and on the other hand, it is not unlikely that the enthusiasm for human stirpiculture, which will be developed in this intermediate system of thoroughbreeding by voluntary limitation of marriages, will finally force public opinion to legalize Complex Marriage.

But I must check the flow of speculation and return to what I consider to be the practical outlook and duty of the O.C. at the present time. It seems to me that we are really launched already into the scheme I have sketched, by the force of events and, as it were, in spite of ourselves. Our circumstances are all in favor of that scheme, and it only remains for us to wake up to a clear understanding of the situation and accept it heartily. Then we shall set to work to devise the best means of carrying out the essential rule of the scheme—the keeping of marriages within the home circle.

The prompt and unanimous acquiescence in my proposal of the 20th of August, followed by execution as swift as to seem miraculous, makes me hope that similar preparation of heart will meet the present proposal. If the spiritual vigor of that first movement, or anything like it, should now accept the positive mission which I have pointed out as opening before us, it will surely turn out that the O.C., instead of being superannuated and in a decline, is rising into manhood and just beginning its great work.

I believe the Community will accept its mission. If I did not I should certainly set about starting a new Community and do my best to draw into it all the material of the old which would fairly fall to my share; for I consider myself and all that belongs to me—especially my children, natural and spiritual and indeed *all the children of our Complex Marriage*—as sacredly pledged to the cause of stirpiculture.

If the old spirit of faithfulness should now rise in the Community and take hold of the good work which I fully believe Providence is setting before us, I should be in favor of adopting marriage—legal, faithful, monogamic marriage—as the very best means now available for pushing forward the work of stirpiculture; and I would go for encouraging marriage as the best duty of all healthy, fertile persons, young or old, instead of frowning on it as a tolerated diversion. Nay, verily, I would go further still: assuming first the reserved right of the Community as a whole to advise and direct (parentally) in the business of mating and having children, *I would go for making the married free to have all the children they can get from Providence.* The principle on which I would do this is that it is to be assumed henceforth that we have started a good breed, that we have the organization and the material means necessary to the development of that breed, and therefore that our highest duty to God and man is to propagate as fast as we can. And I believe that Paul, our superintendent in the heavens, applying to our situation in the nineteenth century the same wisdom which dictated his message to the Corinthians 1,800 years ago, would sanction this principle and speed us on in our predestined work with his blessing.

J. H. Noyes

In a postscript which recommended a part of the correspondence of Mr. Pitt with the leaders of several incipient communities he added the following extract: "What are they starting a community for? The whole creation waits for the manifestation of the sons of God—for the days of scientific, heaven-inspired propagation, which shall people the world with men and women who will *never sin.*

If this is the supreme work and function of communism, then it is easy to see how important in the organization of Communities is the selection of right material. They are to be the breeding-place of the new race."

In a somewhat more secular tone was a postscript from JHN to his sister Harriet Skinner:

> As I reflect on my scheme to Circumscribed Marriage, I am more and more inclined to ask: *What else can we do?* If we go on with communism, which we are bound to by all our property interests, to say nothing of our religious and social proclivities, the bulk of our wealth will remain indivisible. Therefore, when our children come up to the age for marriage, if they go outside for mates they will have to go without portions. The Community cannot divide up its estate into dowries for its daughters and sons, as fathers do in the world. Here will be an immense inducement for our children to marry within the home circle. And added to this great inducement there will be a natural and probably unanimous wish of the parents to keep their children in the home circle. I am not sure but that these inducements would keep families in the world from breaking up, and in our great family there is no need of running against this law, if our children do find mates at home. Are we not then in a sure enclosure, one that will take care of itself? What else can we do than to accept Circumscribed Marriage as our destiny, at least until Complex Marriage comes again, and set about making the best of it?

On November 9 Frank Wayland-Smith read JHN's paper to the family at the Evening Meeting. As he wrote to its author three days later:

> I had the pleasure of reading your article on "Circumscribed Marriage" in our Evening Meeting. I thought it opened a splendid outlook for us as a Community. But I am sorry to be compelled to report that it was not well received by the opposition. Yesterday morning Wm. Hinds called me into the sanctum at the Arcade and said he hoped there would be no public discussion of the paper, as it would be certain to be a painful thing. I replied that I saw no occasion for painful discussion, if it was heartily accepted by the whole family. He said it would never be accepted. I asked what he objected to, and he said, "to the whole of it." Afterwards he made these four specific objections:
>   1. That the married couples should never be allowed to have all the children they could get.
>   2. That we had announced to the world that celibacy was pre-

ferred, whereas this document would certainly make marriage preferred. He thought we ought to stick to it that celibacy was preferred.

3. He objected decidedly to have Croly's matter referred to Theodore and me, or to any two persons. It was a matter for the whole.

4. He did not like it that the paper was read in Meeting before
being read and discussed in the Council.

It was evident that he and those who go with him had talked it
over and come to an understanding. They say that they do not want
anything published about our stirpiculture any more. William said to
me that he did not like that brag about our children: that he thought
them only an ordinary lot, etc. etc.

I ought to say further about the article on Circumscribed Marriage
that Theodore and Mr. Hamilton and I are all agreed that the best
way will be to let it rest without further discussion. It has been read
without any comment whatever, and will have some influence inevitably.

The next week Frank Wayland-Smith took the Noyes document
to New York with him and, in his conference with Mr. Croly, read
him the article during their two-hour session at the Lotos Club.
After some discussion Croly gave up his intention to write the pamphlet on Stirpiculture which he had proposed and agreed to under-
write financially, to the tune of $500, any book or pamphlet that
Mr. Noyes might write on the subject. Frank wrote to JHN on
November 22: "He would not want our religious views in it but
would want a full treatment of stirpiculture, etc. He thought such a
work would round off your record handsomely. I think so, too. You
could write it at your leisure and make it just what you would wish
it."

The end of the Croly affair. The end of Circumscribed Marriage. The opposing factions in the Community next turned to the
difficult matter of electing an Administrative Council for the coming
year 1880.

14

The New Council

As might have been foreseen, the appointment of the Administrative Council for the year 1880 provided the next bone of contention to be worried by one party or the other for the next month.

It was voted by the Council on November 13 that Mr. Noyes be requested to nominate a new Council to come into office January 1, 1880, and that Myron Kinsley act as intermediary as he had done before. As a directive to the new Council it was cautioned that "past experience has shown it to be a tendency of worldly influences working in connection with individual ambition to take departments out of the community spirit and control. We recognize it to be of first importance that Departmental service and appointments should receive wise and careful consideration which properly devolves upon the Administrative Council where a more deliberate examination of matters of a personal nature can be had."

What actually went on in the Council meeting was revealed in a letter from Harriet Skinner to Mr. Noyes:

> The Council has been laboring on a motion made by William that all offices in the Community shall expire by limitation on the first of January and that the nominations for the next year's officers shall be made by an *advisory committee* appointed by the Council. There was some discussion on the question whether this committee should report to the Business Board for approval or to the Council, and which should overrule the other's decision; which was superior.
>
> Theodore, not hardly hoping to beat William on his original motion, told me he wanted to load it down with all the red tape he could and hamper its action: he could see in it a chance for demagoguism. Mr. Hamilton kept rather quiet, praying for guidance, and finally put in a paper which was only opposed by Wm. and Augusta and Edwin Nash, the last two receding somewhat at last.

Mr. Hamilton's paper admonished them that "as departmental

changes and appointments will naturally involve the consideration of individual character and fitness and of other than business interests, the work properly devolves upon the Administrative Council."

Mrs. Skinner noted that "Wm. had got his motion pretty much through, as he thought, but Mr. Hamilton's motion upset him. Theodore had a good deal to say about the danger of having several executive bodies or coordinate authority, cited the Tweed fraud, etc. Frank, seeing that in important practical issues William seldom has his own way, seems to be quite reckless of the future; all his anxiety about being rode over by that party is gone; he says he shouldn't worry now if the whole Council was made up of that side."

The next day she wrote: "Mr. Hamilton's paper was revised by Frank; also the method of appointing the new Council was settled on. Wm. was very urgent that the Community should have a chance to represent their choice to you by letter or an intermediary. You are to appoint the next Council in consultation with Myron, as before; Myron to be stuffed more or less before he goes about the last of December." It had been suggested that O.C. members express their preferences as to the appointments of the next Administrative Council.

Mr. Henry Seymour, a devoted follower of JHN and an original member, led off the chorus of pros and cons on November 18, 1879:

In respect to politics I am becoming very much of a partisan and cannot help it. I have seen and heard enough to make me wish to pull up stakes here and go off in the wilderness, if you please, and help those of like mind with myself to start another Community. I cannot avoid the impression that worldliness is rushing in upon us like a flood through many leaks in the vessel. One thing that happened at the last business meeting. A measure prescribing the resigning and appointing of committees was under discussion. Mr. Towner had an amendment that amounted to about this: "Resolved that the Administrative Council be regarded simply as a committee for nominating officers and committees, to be accepted or rejected as the Business Board may see fit." This was warmly seconded by WAH and Martin, others demurred. According to Towner, Hinds & Co. the organs that represent the moral and spiritual character of the Community are of very small account. It is plain to me that the animus of the whole performance was to stamp out what remains of the influence of the founder of the Community. I hate this scuffling more than I can express and sometimes wish myself into the middle of the next century. "Great is Diana of the Ephesians" cried a mob on very slight provocation on one occasion. "Great is the Business Board with the Bread and Butter Interests" on the smallest provocation breaks forth a certain party among us. I think the real occasions for the two cries are somewhat similar.

Comments, criticisms, and recommendations followed. From a woman member: "Most of us feel as though things were all afloat and we should not feel easy without such men as Mr. Burnham, Martin Kinsley, and William Hinds on the Council, helping the ship to anchor safely." From various men: "If the Dr. and FW-S are in the new Council, I think our side should have Mr. Towner as a representative," "Wayland-Smith makes more trouble and discord in the Council than any six others." "Dear Mr. Noyes, in the opinion of many, your place is now on board this ship. Many of us think you have done very wrong in the past, but it is quite human to err. David and Solomon both did. If you will but be true to your best instincts you can be the means of lifting this Community out of its present trough and cause it to become an ornament and a blessing to the world." "I am aware of the difficulties which beset any and all who attempt to appoint a Council. Those calling themselves 'loyalists' of course claim the right to name whom they choose. The other side whom some call 'disloyalists,' also claim the same right. I belong to the latter party, I claim we are not 'disloyalists.' We number fully as many as the other party, perhaps more, which at least should demand respect. One word about co-operation or joint stock. There is much talk here now about such a scheme. I will only say that the majority are *decidedly* opposed to any such plan and *will never submit to anything of the kind.* Those wanting to start anything of the sort had better leave the O.C. in peace and start on their own hook."

Augusta, née Hamilton, now Towner, took up the cudgels for her new family: "Regarding this evil-speaking and evil eye that Mr. Noyes's 'friends' (?) as they call themselves, have toward Mr. Towner, I am in a perpetual wonder that they dare set such an example, and at the same time presume to criticise folks for uncharitableness toward Mr. Noyes. 'With what measure ye mete, it shall be measured to you again.' I sometimes think that I would like to tell the so-called 'orthodox party' here that I can no longer consider them to be either *Christians* or *Communists* but 'Noyesites,' and a disgrace to the name, at that, as were the Christians left after the destruction of Jerusalem."

The issue of communism versus cooperation or joint stock having been raised, a number of the letters sent to Mr. Noyes via Myron evinced strong opinions. "The joint stock movement does not have my hearty sympathy. My wish is for communism under your lead. I long to be in a family that will be a true home for you. I think if Frank and the others would wait upon you and really represent your spirit they would get out of their difficulties sooner and easier than in their own strength. I have confidence in the afflatus you are under." "Communism is my choice. If this family could, by a stroke of divine power, be melted into perfect unity, I should rejoice above all things. Frank makes the issue squarely between you and JWT. This is giving the latter more preeminence than he deserves, but as for me, I shall not follow any such uncertain leadership as the latter could offer." "The devil has got himself so thoroughly rooted in the body politic that it seems as though nothing but dissolution can dislodge him. I am sure that my confidence in you and love for you has grown steadily and rapidly during all this upheaval and I believe that is true of every loyal heart in the Community. No outward form can destroy the communism in our hearts. W. A. Hinds threatens to go to the Shakers if we dissolve communism."

A woman wrote: "I do not care personally to have any change in the Council. If any change is made, should like the following persons: E. H. Hamilton, T. R. Noyes, H. H. Skinner, E. E. Otis. I shall be perfectly satisfied with anything Mr. Noyes decided upon."

Another woman: "I despise the effort on the part of some vaunting themselves as 'loyalists' to suppress, bully, worry and eliminate individuals of the other party from the Council. In the coming spelling-match, let each party choose its own side, or let every member be elected by a Community majority. For one, I shall not consent to the withdrawal from the Council of such persons as W. A. Hinds, Martin Kinsley, and Augusta Towner, who are certainly better representatives of communism than any I can select from the other side, without suitable substitutes or a corresponding withdrawal from the opposite party of Frank Smith, T. R. Noyes, and Mrs. Skinner."

Three long letters to Mr. Noyes from the three members of the Third party–FW-S, TRN, ESB—summed up the situation from their point of view.

From FW-S:

In regard to the new Council for 1880, the most pertinent question which rises in my mind is, *what is the use of having another Council?*

Mr. Hinds's scheme of governing the Community by a Council was an experiment which we were asked to try. We have tried it now somewhat more than four months. It is admitted by everyone whom I have heard speak on the subject that the present Council is as strong, well constituted, and justly balanced as it could well be made, so that the trial we have already given the plan may be considered as favorable a one as we are likely to have in an equal time.

I will suppose you to ask me this question: *What has been the general result of the attempt to govern the Community by an administrative Council?*

I will answer it by stating a few facts.

1. When the Council was first organized the Community was divided into two great parties: those who remained true to you and the doctrines you had taught, and those who followed Messrs. Hinds, Towner, and Burnham. These two parties were very evenly represented in the Council. During the past four months the party lines have not grown fainter but have been more and more sharply drawn. The same old issues as to your character and Mr. Towner's remain unsettled, and although they are not openly discussed, there is frequent private skirmishing. The result is that the whole Community is in a sort of armed truce, and we are apparently farther than ever from an understanding. New issues constantly arise.

2. The result of the division of the Council into two parties has been that it could not act effectually in the upholding of a high spiritual and moral standard: nor could it keep up the necessary criticism and discipline of personal character. The very attitude of one half the Council in defying the authority of the old administration put an end to all spiritual obedience and subordination. The result is that our system of criticism has been entirely abandoned.

3. A young woman said to me yesterday that she had never known our young people to be so utterly irreverent and free to talk bad stuff as at present. They have thrown off all regard for Community tastes and fashions, and each one does as he or she likes.

4. It becomes more and more difficult to conduct the Evening Meetings because there is such liability of offending someone. Almost everything that may be said or read is suspected of a political significance. To remedy this for themselves and their followers, Messrs. Hinds, Towner, and Burnham have for some time held private religious meetings of their own at which numbers assemble. Their meeting is a strictly party one. We have, therefore, a church within a church. A good many no longer attend the regular Evening Meetings.

Within a month or so a jealousy of the Council has been springing up. Both Mr. Hinds and Mr. Towner have taken pains to publicly define the relative spheres and powers of the two bodies and they both insist that the Business Board is supreme in all matters relating to business and externals. Mr. Towner said in Business Meeting a week or two ago that he wished the Council would busy itself more with teaching the religion of Christ to the young and that business matters should come before the Business Board. This would be well enough if the Council could agree as to what is the religion of Christ and who was fit to teach it to the young; they cannot, as yet.

The plain truth is, as I view it, that government by a council, in the present state of the O.C., is a dead failure. Martin Kinsley is the chairman of the Youth's Committee. Their government consists mainly, if not wholly, in requiring certain hours of labor *per diem*. There is no high purpose upheld. Your idea of continuing stirpiculture by means of "Circumscribed Marriage" is not accepted by the Community. Money-making is becoming the main thing.

With the above facts staring us in the face, it does not seem to me advisable to continue the experiment of governing by Council longer. I think it will be the wisest way to face the situation squarely and settle our differences in some permanent way. There are some signs that we shall encounter serious difficulties if we try to continue in the present way much longer. Some persons are growing uneasy about the way our property is held. Martin Kinsley said to me a few days ago that it was well enough to have had four persons hold all the property as long as we were a united Community, but that he wanted something different now. Others have said the same thing.

I assume from all this that there will of necessity be a change before long, such as will settle the great differences which now exist in the center of the Community. If the spirit of communism has left us, the forms of it, under a false administration will only gall us. I will speculate a little as to the possible changes and you can read it or not as you choose.

1. I think that if William Hinds, Mr. Towner, Mr. Burnham, Martin Kinsley, and Augusta Towner, with their immediate dependents, were away from the Community, we might again have substantial unity. Some persons have suggested whether we could not buy them off? I do not think they would accept any offer.

2. Another possibility I have heard spoken of is to divide up into two Communities. It would be very difficult to make a satisfactory division without first resolving ourselves into a joint-stock company, in which the whole property should be represented by shares, on which the net income should be paid.

3. Some of us think that unless some better prospect can be shown —some better grounds for expecting unity and harmony—the best thing we can do is to resolve into several joint-stock companies, say one for each large business we have, and issue to each person shares in each company, so that each person would have an income from each business. Then by merely holding their shares they would all draw a sufficient annual income, even the most helpless, young or old. It would be an equitable way.

I would not lend my name to such a plan or such a thought if I did not believe there is an irreconcilable incompatibility between the two parties in the Community. Myron will tell you of certain expressions made to him which show that you can hardly expect to live here again without some such change. Martin said to me that it was certain the O.C. would never go back to its old state or anything like it. Some persons here desire very much to live with you, but they see that they cannot do so without some great change which will leave every one free to act as they think best. It would not be right to settle with such persons as we do with ordinary seceders, giving them merely $100 and an outfit. They ought to have their full share. The question of your own future support is involved. Alfred Barron thinks that if we adopt joint-stockism or cooperation, the original founders should first draw out in shares the amounts they put in, then the remainder or increase be divided equally between them and the others. The logic of the Property Register is that those who still respect you have put in much more than the opposition. Mr. Herrick has made out the following:

Total capital deposited in the O.C. by living persons and their heirs now in the O.C.	$170,000.00
Deposited by the disaffected and those of uncertain politics	$ 30,000.00
Balance deposited by loyal persons	$140,000.00

This may not have any great bearing on the case in hand, but it is an interesting fact.

Our financial condition on the first of January next will have an important bearing on our decision. Our condition on November 1:

Liabilities	$ 87,430.00
Assets	100,987.36
Subtract liabilities	87,430.00
	$ 13,556.70

The financiers calculate that by January 1 the balance of assets will be from $35,000 to $40,000 as the sales are holding out very well.

Shall we ever be in a better condition for a final adjustment of our troubles than January 1?

There has been no public discussion of our troubles and I think a great many, especially of the women, are misled. They might be reclaimed by a plain showing of the situation. We need some way to do away with the opportunities for demagoguism which now exist. Your friends here feel somewhat bound by your past expressions in regard to not agitating political issues, while the opposition have at no time felt that embarrassment.

Martin said to me the other day that there was a great deal of distrust of Theodore and me, lest we should take charge of some business. He said there was a class in the O.C. who would not consent to have Theodore take charge of our businesses. If we continue as at present, such issues will become serious. In joint-stockism the matter of managers and directors would be settled by votes representing shares. All our businesses would be continued as at present, and be run as vigorously as possible. Of course great study and care would have to be bestowed on the details of any such change.

Yours faithfully, FW-S

Theodore Noyes's comment on Frank's letter was further enlightening:

During all the late events I have held aloof from taking either of the two sides, although my sympathies have been mainly on what is called the "loyal" side, and was such as to deserve the appellation of "Third party," though I have not tried to form a party and have only known FW-S and ESB as thorough sympathizers. Our effort has been to take a dispassionate view of the possibilities and impossibilities of our situation. I have followed the rule that if the opposition threw down any of our old institutions so that it was impracticable to restore them, to use my energies to see that they do not set up an imitation in its place, but to work for the adoption of common, well-tried usages instead of theories under, to me, unsuitable leaders. Foreseeing this, I felt at liberty to advocate a modified communism in the form of cooperation, until the adoption of the Council and Father's injunction not to agitate that subject. In a certain light it may be regarded as a success. That is, we carry on our business without external discord, but underneath there is a constant state of flux. Such conditions cannot exist permanently. When Father's document on Circumscribed Marriage came and was not accepted, several little indications thrust themselves upon my notice, showing the policy of the opposition, so-called (which, by the way, though disclaiming coherence as a party, is, nevertheless, well-drilled and has leaders with a well-defined policy). I will indicate several lines of policy on the part of the opposition which have become evident to me.

First. To belittle the Council and take *the practical direction of affairs out of its hands.* They have turned their attention to the Business Board, and have openly told the Council to refrain from "secular matters." They also refused to give it power to appropriate small sums of money in the course of its business. It cannot spend a dollar without revision by the Business Board or Financial Committee. It cannot decide upon matters of public policy which involve the spending of money. Then, for some reason or other, the Council is powerless in the matter of personal discipline. I don't see any prospect that the Council will concern itself with much higher matters than giving persons permission to visit Wallingford and giving gentle guidance to education and public amusement.

Second. The next line of policy has been, under the plea that Mr. Towner was unjustly ignored, to force him into (to me) undue prominence in his legal capacity. I have no objection to him, in fact I rather like him personally, but I have seen a tendency to make him a martyr and work him into a position to be regarded as, in a sense, sacred. This is not much, but from the strong feeling Wm. Hinds displayed about it, I felt uneasy lest something deeper be hidden in it.

Third. Another point is a strong hostility to marriage, and beyond that a hostility to the bearing of children by the married. It is in a line of policy with the opposition to make marriage unpopular by refusing consent to the bearing of children. This has remote bearings on a possible inauguration of free love after the married have been worried sufficiently.

We limited our communism of persons by introducing marriage. Now I would like to limit the communism which holds us in a form without the substance. We can retain our combination for making money and distribute the proceeds to the members so that they can use them to suit themselves. For myself, I have no desire to live anywhere else but I would like to be able to visit my father or anyone else without asking consent of W. A. Hinds or any of that set. In fact, the close relations of communism are becoming almost intolerable. I regarded Father's action about marriage as peculiarly shrewd. Now it seems to me that he would do a similar shrewd thing to give his consent to a gradual and fair resolution of the Community into a cooperative business relation.

The Community will then gradually resolve itself into four classes:

1. Those who "stay by the stuff" and see that the financial machine runs regularly and honestly and that a fair division of profits is made. (I choose my position here.) These would take advantage of

all our facilities for combined living to a much greater extent than many imagine in their longings for a change.

2. Those who have a passion for small surroundings which overbalance their love of combined society and who retire to ordinary life. There are a few who would do that.

3. Those who wish to establish themselves elsewhere in harmony with Father on the old basis, perhaps even going back to Complex Marriage.

4. The class represented by Wm. Hinds and Towner, who would perhaps form a free love community somewhere.

Now all four of these classes could retain their interest in the business organization here and draw dividends semi-annually which would materially help them in their new organization.

There are several things to be attended to if such a plan is entered upon. It ought to be done without shock to the Community credit. I don't think we could form one joint-stock company under the laws of the state to do the variety of business we do. We should form several (silk, hardware, tableware, fruit preserving, farming, hotel) as found best. These could have identical boards of directors but each member of the Community would own an equal share in all.

It has been suggested that the old members of the Community should withdraw the capital they put in before the remainder be divided, but I should not favor this. It would create bad blood and imperil a dispassionate discussion of the subject. I would not put it under the light of a breakup at all, but merely make it a change in our mode of distributing profits and appointing officers and try to really feel brotherly all round in doing it. I am tired of the enmities of this state we are in and should be glad to be good business friends with Hinds, Towner, and all. But first we must get further apart.

Of course there are many details like the children, the aged and infirm, etc., which would require careful adjustment. If Father does not want to make a formal proposition, I think the thing can be accomplished by just setting his sympathizers free to advocate such a change and I would guarantee an almost unanimous movement in favor of it, in spite of Wm. Hinds's and Towner's opposition; for the strangest thing about their politics is that they have built themselves up on the dissatisfactions of people who are bent on quite different objects. These people joined in with them in casting down the old *regime* but would like their new state no better than the old. This is the explanation of the success of the marriage manoeuvre. The great mass of the opposition went for it like a flock of sheep, in spite of Wm.'s and Towner's protest. It would be the same with a movement in favor of more liberty of individuals in a pecuniary way. Open discussion is what is wanted.

Francis Wayland-Smith, a young intellectual and independent thinker, kept careful record as a member of the Third party of the events leading up to and including the breakup.

Right: Joseph Skinner, son of JHN's sister Harriet Noyes Skinner, was educated at Yale and became a free-thinker, seceding from the O.C. in 1873. *Below left:* Edwin S. Burnham, son of Henry W. Burnham, was a member of the Third party but loyal to JHN. *Below right:* Henry W. Burnham, a former Congregational minister and member from the early Vermont days, supported James W. Towner's efforts. to control the O.C.

The "Singing Girls," Flora, Lily, Edith, Mabel, Jessie, and Marion, later appeared in the popular O.C. production of *H.M.S. Pinafore* in 1880.

Right: Joseph C. Ackley, one of the earliest and most devoted of O.C. members, was always loyal to JHN. *Below left:* Julia C. Ackley, wife of Joseph Ackley, joined the tiny commune in 1847 at Jonathan Burt's mill on Oneida Reserve before the Putney group arrived. Like her husband, she was a devoted Noyesite. *Below right:* Alice Ackley Kinsley, daughter of Joseph and Julia Ackley, was brought to the O.C. as a baby. A beautiful woman and gifted musician, she became violently opposed to the Community's social theories and in the last years was a vehement anti-Noyesite.

A group of "World's People" lunching in the Quadrangle, probably in the late 1870s. JHN stands on the boardwalk, *left center,* in light coat over dark suit.

View from north side of Quadrangle before building of the "New House" wing in

North side of Mansion House, after 1878.

George Noyes Miller, son of JHN's sister
Charlotte, was a devoted Noyesite.

Alfred Barron, a strong Noyesite, was the son of a Vermont family which joined the O.C. in the early 1850s.

Homer Barron, younger brother of Alfred
Barron, was also a Noyesite.

Helen Miller Barron, daughter of JHN's sister Charlotte Noyes Miller, and wife of Homer Barron, was, like her mother, a gentle, intelligent, and devoted Noyesite.

Tirzah Miller Herrick, daughter of JHN's sister Charlotte, was especially devoted to her uncle and acted as his confidante and assistant.

William G. Kelly, an outspoken defender of JHN, joined the O.C. in 1854 and was "Father" of the Children's Department.

Children's playhouse, *left foreground,* with south front of Mansion House in background; photo around 1878.

Abram Burt, son of Jonathan Burt, joined the O.C. as a boy in 1848 and was always a devoted Noyesite. He later became a director of the joint-stock company.

Harriet M. Worden came to the O.C. as a little girl of nine and later edited the *Circular* for three years. She was devoted to JHN and also a friend of a major dissident, James W. Towner.

James W. Towner joined the O.C. in 1873. A forceful man, possibly ambitious to succeed JHN, he made himself the leader of a group of dissidents in the schism which led to the breakup.

Above left: Augusta Hamilton Towner, daughter of Erastus Hamilton, married Arthur Towner, son of James W. Towner. She was intelligent and aggressive and became one of the most vocal of the dissidents. *Above right:* Charles S. Joslyn, a young Noyesite lawyer trained at Columbia University, was involved in the Wallingford altercation over selling the Community's silverware business in 1880. *Left:* William A. Hinds, a member from the earliest days, supported James W. Towner's efforts to control the O.C.

Stone cottage at Niagara Falls, Canada, where JHN and a few followers lived after leaving the O.C. in 1879.

I think of Father often and wish to help him. I think I could do more for him at the machine here than in a personal relation and have the liberty to visit him when I could afford it. I wish we could settle upon this basis and have him come home to civilized regions where his friends could get to him often.

T. R. Noyes

Edwin Burnham, the last of the trio of Third party members, also wrote to Mr. Noyes:

For my part I am sure that Councils are and will be a failure, conducted on the present plan. The decisions of the Council are even now condemned by those in the family who do not like them, and so far the Council is unable to enforce its decisions. The Community is just exactly what you said it would be if it followed the lead of Hinds, Towner and Burnham: a great town-meeting where the most blatant demagogue secures the most votes.

There are many here who are unwilling to continue much longer this life of turmoil, and if I did not believe God was really managing the affair, I should despair. The more I think of it, the more impossible it seems to heal the breach without our getting farther apart as individuals. I cannot be led or driven by William Hinds, and he cannot be led or driven by me. Why not arrange matters so that we shall touch each other only in business ways, unless inclined to. Perhaps if we could live for a while in a state where his main business is to mind his own affairs and mine the same, we shall see in each other things congenial. At least let us try the experiment.

Yours lovingly, E. S. Burnham

P.S. I might say here that I am in accord with Theodore and Frank in the position they take in their letters to you.

Here, in their own words were the opinions—and emotions—of some of the most articulate of the Community members at the end of four stormy months of self-management and at the beginning of their last year as a Community. Looking back, as many of them must have done, upon nearly thirty years of happy and harmonious Community living, it must have been a heartbreaking moment. To at least some of the dissidents, it was the threshold of a new liberty.

On December 5 a paper from JHN in answer to the mass of letters he had received from the Community was read in the Evening Meeting:

To the family: The large budget of documents which Myron brings me relate mainly to two subjects, viz. the appointment of the *Administrative Council,* and the proposal to resolve the Community into a joint-stock or cooperative company.

First, as to the Council, I may as well, to begin with, make known, if it is not already known, that I did not name or suggest any one of the persons who were placed on the present Council. I left the formation of the Council entirely in Myron's hands. My reason for this was, as I said to him, that I wished to suit all parties, and I was sure that he knew the wishes of all parties much better than I did. The whole thing was done by letter (which Myron will show if it is called for) in which I said that he might make a Council to suit himself, and either present it without further authority from me or, if he thought necessary, he might send it to me and I would send it as my nomination. He did not send it to me. He says that on receiving my letter he started immediately for O.C. and made out the list of the Council on his way. I had suggested in my letter that he might consult Mr. Hamilton or not, as he pleased, or anybody else. So much for my responsibility in the matter. I put the business in Myron's hands because I thought him a very liberal large-hearted man, thoroughly anxious for the life and welfare of the Community in its perils, and as impartial between the various parties as any man could be, and more so than any man I knew. I was glad to hear that his list was accepted unanimously by the family. From all that I heard at the time and since, I have been led to suppose that it was generally regarded as fair and liberal to all. The present expressions of dissatisfaction are entirely a surprise to me. Certainly I cannot hope to make a better selection; and I judge that my best way is to do as I did before: put the whole matter into Myron's hands, leaving him at liberty, so far as I am concerned, to make any alterations in the Council that he thinks best. I am not anxious that the Council should be composed of my particular friends. On the contrary, I hope HHS will be excused from it, let who will take her place. But I confess I am anxious that the Council should work heartily and effectually for good order in the family.

If there are any serious objections to Myron's mediatorship, I am certainly willing to leave the whole matter in the hands of the family. The present Council has had but a short term, and I should be in favor of continuing it, with a few alterations. But if the family want a new Council, I am willing they should appoint one in any way they choose.

Secondly, as to the joint-stock proposal, I must beg time to think. Myron wants to go back soon, and I do not feel ready to write out a mature judgment on the mass of ideas, pro and con, which are before me.

I have in mind, however, what seems to me to be a necessary

preliminary of all discussion on the subject, which is this: *that any decision to take such a step, in order to be valid, must be unanimous.* When the question was asked last summer whether "The Four" did not hold the property as Trustees, I answered, "Yes, but as trustees *for the Community,* not for individuals." This answer, if correct, amounts to the conclusion that in any breaking up, the body that remains really communistic owns the property, even if it is a minority. Nevertheless, I doubt not that *by a unanimous vote* the Community could dissolve and become a joint-stock company. Those in favor of taking this step should count the probabilities of convincing *all* of its expediency.

Another thing that seems to me plain is that communism of those who are really one in heart might go right on in the midst of joint-stockism. But I have not matured a plan for this, and with this hint I must leave the matter for the present.

My best thought and hope for you all is that you will have grace to go through all possible free discussion of these great subjects, and that in it all you will keep your peace and moderation, so as to do as little mischief to each other as possible, and finally do the best thing.

Yours in haste, JHN

The *Community Journal,* December 5, 1879, reported the reading of this paper to the family, and Myron reported that Mr. Noyes thought it much better to discuss these matters publicly than privately. He also said that in all cases where the authority of the Council was disregarded, criticism should be brought to bear. It was thought best that all who had ideas on the subjects of Mr. Noyes's letter should present them in writing, to be read "to as many of the family as wanted to hear them, and that the public discussion of these questions would prevent *a great deal of misunderstanding,* suspicion, and misrepresentation."

Harriet Skinner's report of December 6 to her brother was cheerful: "From all accounts I should think Myron's coming and your communication brought a good wave, very encouraging. Charles Joslyn took up the testimony like a young convert, praising your spirit and acts, producing a general vibration and response. John Cragin went off in a rhapsody about you. If we only have patience, I am sure you, *alone,* without anybody's help, will overcome all this evil with good, and we shall have the joy of seeing your righteousness brought forth as the light and your judgment as the noon day. That will be happiness enough for me."

Two days later the Council discussed the methods of forming the next Council, and a motion was made to leave the nomination to Myron and consider it an appointment, but a substitute was offered, that the Council be nominated by some form of balloting. It was agreed that all persons over eighteen years of age should be allowed to vote. At the Evening Meeting, Mr. Hinds explained the two methods, with the advantages and disadvantages of each. The first method was to leave it to Myron and have it considered final, with no grumbling afterward. The second was to nominate it by ballot. It was finally decided to pass slips of paper to all, for each to write the word "Myron" or "Ballot." The slips were gathered in and it was soon announced that there were 105 votes for it to be left to Myron, and 49 for ballot. Myron had declined to nominate members for the Council and have his action considered final unless it should be the expressed wish of the family that he should do so. After this vote by the family he agreed to act and left for Wallingford the next noon.

On December 8 Mr. Burnham opened a sealed package at the Evening Meeting and read the names of the new Administrative Council:

Names selected for Council of 1880 by M. H. Kinsley, as requested by the family:

E. H. Hamilton	H. C. Miller
H. W. Burnham	Belle Newhouse
T. R. Noyes	S. K. Dunn
W. A. Hinds	Mary Bolles
Otis Kellogg	E. E. Otis
Martin Kinsley	Martha V. Marks
John Freeman	H. E. Allen
G. D. Allen	Chloe Seymour
George Campbell	A. S. Burnham
C. C. Hatch	Elizabeth Hutchins

Myron added a footnote: "The reasons for making these changes are these: Some *requested* by letter to Mr. Noyes *to be left off,* and also *by request to me,* and by letters to me from different ones in the family as to their wishes in regard to the next Council. In making the changes that I have, I have tried to get at the wishes of all as nearly as possible, and still have all classes represented. Respectfully submitted, M. H. Kinsley."

On December 8, Myron wrote to Mr. Noyes describing the meeting:

> Your paper to the family *was well received,* and all said that the meeting was more like one of our old revival meetings than anything they had seen for months, and it would take but a few more like it to *turn the whole Community* back to you as a unit. I was surprised to see how many spoke in favor of brotherly love and unity and respect and love for you. Many came to me, and quite a number that have been on the wrong side shook me by the hand, saying that they had more hopes of the Community *as a Community* than they had for years. Father, Mr. Hamilton, Mrs. Skinner, *Mr. Burnham,* and others said that they felt that a good spirit came with your paper, and that power came with it: and that they had no fear of anything, if we could only have a few meetings like this one: it would save the Community from joint stock: and I should not be surprised if the Community would invite you back as its head at no distant day without one voice the other way. *I think a disturbing element is away now that has been here before: it certainly is so, and many feel it, and some that have not before. His influence was very great here.*

The same suggestion—no name mentioned—was made by Harriet Skinner in a letter on December 10: "We all think the good spirit gains here. It is pretty evident that the absence of one person is favorable to the spirit of unity. Even Frank *hopes* we shall not be forced to joint stock. Not a word has been lisped against the new Council that I have heard, and 'whisperings,' gathering in cliques, etc., are much gone out of fashion. The Burnhams were quite gushing after that good meeting in which your paper was read. He catched Mrs. Kelly and hugged and kissed her like old times."

The obvious reference here went back to the events of a month before. At the special Business Meeting of November 13 which had been called "to consider what could be done to protect the steel spoon interest at W.C. against the patent monopoly of Wallace Bros.," it had been decided to send Mr. Towner to their assistance "with the recommendation that in any important matter O.C. shall be consulted." At another Business Meeting on November 16, Mr. Towner had "moved an amendment that the Council become a committee of the Business Board for the purposes named in a resolution that all terms of office expire on the last day of each year." Both the motion and the amendment raised so much argument that they were put over to a later meeting, and Mr. Towner thereupon left for Wallingford to deal with the Wallace matter. He apparently remained there at least until after December 14 when Myron mentions his making out a deed at Wallingford relating to the holding of the Community's property. The *Community Journal* for December 20 recorded that "Myron and Mr. Towner arrived this afternoon and Mr. Towner gave some account of his investigations in regard to the 'Wallace Patent.' " Whether or not he was the "disturbing element that is away now and that had been here before," on December 8 and 10, cannot be certainly ascertained, but the fact that two correspondents make almost the same reference at about the same time gives some color to the inference.

The announcement of an application to marry by Mr. E. H. Hamilton and Miss Elizabeth Hutchins was responded to with cheers and a flurry of testimony. Mr. Hamilton himself led off by saying that he was willing to testify by example that he thought marriage honorable and expedient: "Marriage with us, in an important sense, has been swallowed up in victory, 'Oh marriage, where is thy power?' Legality is the sting of marriage as it is of death." These remarks were endorsed by quite a number. Old Mr. Wright was convinced that the marriage movement was one of God's flank movements on the world—opposing powers were to be met and outgeneraled. Alfred Barron said that Complex Marriage had not been worked out and arrived at by the Community in any intellectual or philosophical way. They had not had much to do with it. Now, for some reason, it had been withdrawn for the present and that change had not been brought about by any intellectual process or by their having much to do about making it. A hope was expressed that all who entered into marriage would do all in their power to make the children legitimate that had not been born in marriage. Mr. Hinds thought it should be settled once for all that the marriage of the parents would not do this, either in the eyes of the law or the world. He also believed that the children of Complex Marriage were of more honorable birth than any that had been born of monogamic marriage, and hoped that all in the Community would regard them in this light.

From this time until the end of the year, the troubled waters of the Community seemed to subside into a welcome calm. On December 21, Harriet Skinner wrote to JHN: "I will rest and float with the current." There was a certain amount of disagreement between the law-trained members in the matter of the form of a deed for the Wallingford property. Mr. Towner had inserted a phrase expressing a trust which altered the tenure of the property. A complicated legal point was involved, and in the end, Charles Joslyn had a talk with Mr. Towner, they disagreed, and Charles finally assumed the business and dismissed Towner from it. Mr. Hinds, a short time before, had urged that a phrase from JHN's letter, to the effect that the whole Community property was given for communism and would belong to those who remained with communism, even if they were a small minority, should be registered with the deed.

Despite all Mr. Hinds's efforts, the subject of Circumscribed Marriage came up before the Council. As Harriet reported it on December 27:

> Wm. has tried to hush up all discussion about that—but Frank has pushed it through and finally prevailed and in the Council today carried everyone with him except William. Mr. Hamilton had the wisdom to propose that the discussion be conducted not in the way of common debate but let everyone speak in his turn around—he thought that would prevent its being an argument between Frank and William and one or two others which might be exciting—and it proved to be very favorable to candor and harmony. The point, you know, is the liberty you propose giving to the married pairs. William thinks that is going back to unlimited propagation and that we shall be flooded with children—there will be no chance for stirpicultural discrimination, etc., etc. On the other side it was shown that there would be a great many natural limitations. Frank thought the young women had schemes for education, traveling, etc., that would make them loath to be tied down with babies. The married couples already take a great deal more care of their children than they did. Then not a few of the new married pairs are beyond the chance of having children and some don't want any more. The danger of being flooded, as William fears, does not seem very great.
>
> William has been dead set against the subject being brought before

the family; thought it would be the occasion of a great deal of bad blood, but Mr. Hamilton is encouraged by experience in the Council to think it will be got through without excitement. William thinks that instead of our original platform, marriage allowed but celibacy preferred and propagation controlled, we are going for *marriage preferred, propagation unlimited, and celibacy allowed.*

Mr. Burnham gave his opinion in a long paper presented to the Council on December 28. He said that he was not one of those who believed that stirpiculture was the brightest object of pursuit before the Community, although apparently the Community had drifted into that idea during the past few years. In his opinion it was an afterthought and a serious departure from their first principles, which had been Salvation from Sin, Christian Perfection, and Holiness of Heart. In these later days, flesh had crowded out the spirit. That was the lamentable fact at the foundation of all their troubles.

In regard to propagation, he thought they had children enough. He would be glad if they could stop for at least five years. Or, as a compromise, he suggested that all the married women over the age of forty be allowed to "try" for children. By his count there were nine married women and twelve unmarried, between forty and fifty who were "more or less liable to have children." As to unlimited propagation, as contemplated in Mr. Noyes's paper, it would, he believed, in due time "swamp us entirely."

Harriet, in reporting these meetings to John, gave her usual lively description:

I don't know but it is in this debate on Circumscribed Marriage that William is going to get his checkmate. They say he loses his temper in this discussion as he has never done before. He is quite determined the question shall not go before the family, and it is evidently because his own position is so unpopular with many of his own party. Mr. Burnham gave his opinion in writing yesterday. He thought we had all the children we want for the next five years—that we can engage in much better business, *attention to religion*—in the way we used to do before stirpiculture was entered upon. Theodore goes for keeping our numbers good and thinks we should not be likely to do much more than that if we gave full liberty to all women over thirty years of age. Martin is in favor of *increasing* our population—not limiting it as Theodore would. William, you know, pretends to think that our children are not exceptional at all, and yet he talks about our ignoring stirpiculture in this new move, and is quite offensively aristocratic in his discrimination. He is guilty of the same inconsistency in respect to free discussion—the champion for it, he has been the first one to really forbid it, and so in regard to democratic election. He is very much opposed to the ballot and Theodore in favor of it. They have the fourth Council meeting on the subject this afternoon. SKD says she hasn't the least doubt that all checks but Providence will be taken off before they get through with it, which will be a great discomfiture to William and Mr. Burnham. They had better take up with Theodore's proposal to make all women over thirty free. Mr. B. went into a calculation showing that it was possible if we did, we should have twenty babies right along. He counted women even over fifty and said one woman of fifty-two years of age told him there was nothing to prevent her having one if she had a husband. There are really only fourteen or fifteen over thirty who have a ghost of a chance.

The next day, December 30, she could make a final report for the year:

Well, the child is born. At the fourth Council meeting yesterday P.M. the proposition which Theodore made at first and which William and Mr. Burnham have opposed so bitterly, was unanimously voted and recommended to the family. "Resolved, that the Council recommend to the Community to adopt a birth rate of five annually as certainly within its present resources and likely to be so in the future, and also resolved to supply this rate, all married women over thirty be set free to propagate within the following limitations: When the conceptions have reached three for the year, the freedom shall be confined for the remainder of the year to those over thirty-five, and those over thirty who have no children. It is understood that this arrangement is temporary and not to debar those under thirty from having children for any great length of time—as many think a larger number than five is desirable for the first year. It is understood that the Council has power to enlarge the limit to eight for the year 1880 after the limit of five is reached."

William and Mr. B. came to the Council in quite a different temper, and William himself proposed the resolution and that your paper be read to the family in the evening, which was done. It was decided by the Council to have the paper read but to postpone discussion for a week or more to give time for consideration. I think, on the whole, that William is used as a necessary force in this revolution—that is, he seems to retard movements till they can go through without violence or precipitation—till things are safely adjusted. Thinking so makes me feel forgiving toward him. At least I expect we shall forgive some of these folks as Joseph did his brethren. He said to them, "It was not you that sent me hither, but God, Ye thought evil against me but God meant it for good."

Tomorrow the new Council will meet. I think it is stronger for you, if anything, than the first Council. It is on the whole rising in power—and in the confidence of the family. Instead of becoming a Committee of the Business Board it has grown in dignity ever since Mr. T. made that motion. Mr. Hamilton's spiritual power and Theodore's intellect have things their own way.

The *Community Journal* for December 30, 1879, merely remarked that "Mr. Burnham reported the resolution passed by the Council in regard to Circumscribed Marriage, adding that it was not presented to the family for immediate action, but for thought and consideration, to be acted upon at some future time."

15

Proposal of Joint Stock

The year 1880 began with an affair which was thrilling to at least the younger and more romantic members of the Community: a double wedding in the Hall. Mr. Hamilton (who was marrying Miss Elizabeth Hutchins) and his bride felt some compunction about so frivolous a celebration, since both preferred the businesslike form of a private marriage by contract, but still they wished that in some way they might include the whole Community and finally agreed to join with another couple, John Cragin and Lily Hobart, who wished the Episcopal form with all the trimmings.

Corinna Noyes, then a romantic seven-year-old, described the ceremony that took her fancy in her book *The Days of My Youth:* "Pretty Miss Lily was dressed in a long dress of beautiful jade green cotton with a slight train [which] set off her lovely figure and beautiful complexion in an entrancing manner. Her hair, though short, was naturally curly and was a mass of ringlets. The Episcopal service was not a word too long, and the giving of the ring and the bridal kiss were the supreme touch of romance. Home-made currant wine and fruit cake were then served to the grown-ups. What a thrilling scene! It was like a play on the stage." The *O.C. Journal* merely recorded that "the general verdict was that we had a good time. The Community spirit was with us."

Not everyone felt so amicable. Mr. Noyes complained of the injustice of having a partisan lawyer—in the face of his protest—employed to make deeds for him to sign. Obviously, Mr. Towner was the man referred to. The resolution in regard to propagation, presented to the family despite Mr. Hinds's strenuous opposition, was now thrown open to discussion by the family who were exhorted by Mr. Hamilton to discuss the matter goodnaturedly. Most of the opinions were to be presented in written form. During the next two weeks the replies showered in, leading off with a half-dozen closely written pages by Mr. Burnham who foresaw the Community being inundated by a flood of babies, and an even longer screed from Charles Joslyn who echoed this thought with an added and ominous warning that the last set of graduates from the Children's Department "were not a success, considered either as communists or as God-fearing young folks." Of the men who cast their votes in the family meeting, only Mr. Herrick and Mr. Hamilton voted aye. Of the older women, whose complaint was largely that the present accommodations for lying-in and baby-tending were insufficient, only Mother Noyes and Harriet Skinner voted for further propagation. If the young men and women had an opinion on the subject, as they might well have done, since theirs was the natural age for propagating, no record exists.

On January 15 the Council was offered, as a substitute for the Resolution on Propagation passed by them on December 30, the following Resolution:

> *Resolved* that a birth rate of five annually be adopted as within the present resources of the Community, and likely to be so in the future; and that to supply this number for 1880, in addition to the liberty of propagation already given by the Council to a few special cases, all married women over thirty who have no child or children, and all over thirty-five, excepting those who have two or more children, one of them by her husband, shall be allowed to propagate within the following limitation: When there is reason to believe that five conceptions have taken place, freedom of propagation shall be restricted for the remainder of the year to those whom the Council shall by special action designate. But, on the other hand, it shall be the duty of the Council to reconsider the subject on the first of September, and if it is then found that the probability is that the classes engaged in propagation are not likely to produce five children through the year, to extend the same freedom to such orders as may be thought necessary in order to insure that number.

The Council desired to treat the subject of propagation in a liberal spirit, and again endorsed the sentiment previously recorded, "that it is not expected that any regulations now made will debar for any considerable time those under thirty from having children, but as there must be some restriction for the present on propagation, it was thought those who have the fewest chances for success should be given preference."

It was unfortunate that just at this time, January 12, 1880, a committee appointed by the Council to investigate the financial condition of the Foundry Department, Theodore Noyes's pet project, should report a rather questionable situation. The family's first awareness of this new venture had come with an announcement by Mr. Noyes, more than a year ago, on December 17, 1878: "Theodore's proposal is to take the old Foundry and go into the malleable iron business *on a very small scale at first, feeling his way along, avoiding expense, making his experiments pay for themselves and thoroughly acquainting himself with the mysteries of the business.*" At that time Theodore volunteered his own statement: "I guarantee the Community against any considerable expense."

Whether or not this new business was ever limited—either orally or in writing by Mr. Noyes or a member of the Financial Committee—to the sum of $500, could not be determined. There was no record of such a transaction. In any case, the investment had increased to $3,834 by the end of 1879 without, the committee report said, "any action by the Financial Committee authorizing such increased investment and, indeed, so far as we can learn, without their definite knowledge of the amount of the investment."

Dr. Noyes disclaimed all responsibility. His father, he told the Committee, claimed the right of decision in all matters and had told him to go on and make a success of it, as economically as he could. He considered himself fully authorized to do what he had done, although of course he might have conducted his experiments at less cost. The bookkeepers claimed they had no responsibility since their books showed no special appropriation of $500 or any other sum for the Foundry Department, so that the account was left to take care of itself. The Financial Committee was partially responsible since, if they had followed the instructions of the Business Board, they would have discovered the situation at least two months earlier, when the investment was several hundred dollars less than it was at the end of the year. It was suggested that in starting a new business it might have been wiser to have hired a man who thoroughly understood the processes involved—but on the other hand he would probably have demanded a high salary. Moreover—and here is the old O.C. note—Theodore thought the superintendence of the business had been a means of health to him, which might be placed on the credit side of the ledger, as "he began the business when in a low state of health and with the exercise it afforded him he had been able to do much more general labor for the Community."

It was doubly unfortunate because the family still remembered a report made the summer before by Edwin Burnham of the disappointing settlement of Theodore's partnership with Abel Easton in the Turkish Bath in New York in 1877, in which his $3,500 inheritance had apparently sunk without a trace. Now, half a year later, it was recalled by those who opposed his appointment on the Financial Board, and Theodore's qualifications as a financial genius were questioned. Some busybody had been at work gathering up a lot of notes from various members all requesting that Mr. Towner be appointed to the Business Board. Mr. Hamilton was obliged to read these notes aloud to the meeting, but he considered it a saucy move and insisted that if Towner were appointed, Theodore should go on also, which was done. All this combined to make what Harriet Skinner called "a tumultuous day. There was a regular Towner cyclone here. The witches' caldron bubbled furiously." The political maneuvering led her to suspect that the opposition's secret plan was to put Towner into Edwin Burnham's place as head financier. She called them "fogues from hell" and almost rejoiced in them, seen in that light.

A subject of far greater importance, and one which had been seething in the "witches' cauldron" for many months, came to a rolling boil at this time. A letter from Frank Wayland-Smith to Mr. Noyes on January 20, 1880, alerted him to the situation, and his reply, in a letter read to the whole family in Evening Meeting, made the matter public for the first time.

Frank's letter was very disturbing:

> I did not originate the idea of cooperation and joint stock and I have not really desired to go into it except in an extreme case, to save us from an intolerable situation and to facilitate a separation between discordant and irreconcilable elements in the Community. It had been reported to me that Mr. Towner had said that if we were going into cooperation he should immediately take his family and go back to Cleveland. This seemed to me a consummation so devoutly to be wished that it acted as an inducement to urge the idea. And the threat of joint-stockism did really calm down Wm.'s and Towner's party a great deal, especially after you gave the liberty of free discussion on the subject. But after you gave it I had no desire to use it.

The more I reflected on joint-stockism, the more difficulties I saw in it for many in the Community who would be comparatively helpless in it. None of us have tried to push that idea.

After the new Council was appointed there was a lull until they began to reorganize businesses for 1880. Then it became apparent that the Hinds-Towner party had a settled policy to get the active management of our large businesses. I remembered that, after you left, their first move had been to try to capture the social affairs of the Community and how it resulted in our limiting our communism by throwing out communism of person and confining it to communism of property. So, when they turned their attention to capturing the control of our property and I saw how unscrupulous Towner was in the matter of the deed, I thought it would be a good thing to show them that there was a legal way of escape in the matter. I saw that the matter of personal appropriations was entirely optional with the Community. We could, if we chose, divide up as much of our net annual profits, after paying all our common expenses, as we cared to appropriate, and that without impairing our communism or violating the covenant. This would demonstrate to the other party that we could stop the Community accumulation where it was, and not go on to create a great cash surplus to fight over. On this ground, Theodore, I, and some others advocate increasing the personal appropriation for adults for 1880 to $100, men and women to share alike. This idea met with some favor and some opposition.

The question came up in the Council yesterday and was put over till today. After yesterday's Council, William Hinds went to Theodore and proposed another plan, viz.: that we should not greatly increase the appropriations but should fix on a certain number of hours labor per day of necessary Community work, and if persons were willing to work more than that number of hours, the Community to pay them for the overtime at a fixed rate per hour: every person to elect at the beginning of the year whether he would go in under this system or remain under the old-fashioned Community system: those who adopted the overtime system to stick by it and be docked if they made undertime, except in case of sickness.

This seems to me a more radical and anti-communistic change than simply to increase the appropriations as fast as we can afford, but others do not see it in that light. William's object in it is plain enough. He proposes to allow people to make accumulations by drawing wages for overtime, which accumulations may, from time to time, be deposited in the treasury and the amounts be credited to the individuals on the Property Register, to be drawn by them in case of leaving the O.C., the same as property brought in, but to be beyond their control whilst they remained members! It is evident that the larger the accumulation became, the greater would be the temptation to leave for the sake of getting it. But he would not force people to so deposit it if they chose to spend it as they went along. I have seen for a long time that they are trying to make it easy for us to leave, but I can assure you that I have not the slightest intention of doing so, except in a much greater extremity than has yet threatened.

The *O.C. Journal* recorded on January 24 that "Myron returned from Father Noyes today, reports him as very well and stopping for the present at Niagara Falls. The interesting paper that Myron brought with him from Mr. Noyes to the Council and family was read in the meeting this evening."

JHN to The Council and Family: In my opinion individual liberty and enterprise are in the long run valuable only as subordinates and complements of God's communism. As such I have already favored them and always shall. In any other relation, I have never favored them and never shall. With this understanding of my private position, I will freely say what I think, and how I feel in regard to the evident tendency in the Community toward large appropriations, liberty of private speculation, paying wages to members, and in general toward cooperative relations in business and individual sovereignty.

I am sick of resisting the inevitable. I am convinced that it is useless to oppose permanent human longings. They must have their way, even if it is to destruction. Therefore, I promise the Community that I will not stand in the way of anything that shall be fairly agreed upon in the present drift of feeling and opinion. But I ask leave to say a few things that may mollify and perhaps direct the current.

My policy, it will be remembered, from the beginning of the present revolution, has been to keep all eyes of all parties on the importance of maintaining our business organization in all its vigor. That has seemed to me to be the engine which has kept the ship in motion and enabled it to obey the helm. And I think, as a matter of fact, we have held together and kept from foundering—to speak plainly— by our money. Nay more—I think that God our Savior, has got the love of money—that root of all evil—into such gearing in our case that it pulls the right way—toward unity—communism. We hold together and love one another, or try to, because we hate to give up the money we have made and the power of making more. It is evident to every soul of us of all parties and descriptions that Communism is a blessed thing for getting a living easy, and that poverty and care that stare us in the face outside of communism are a dismal thing. This tremendous motive, low as some may think it, has carried us through the storm of the past six months, and in my opinion is destined to

carry us through all future storms. I notice that right through the toss-
ings and strainings of our social experience, Providence is taking care
to pour in the money, and I defy anybody who has a sober thought
in his brain to cut adrift from communism that has a yearly profit of
$44,000 in its balance sheet. I look upon this motive-apparatus as
God's contrivance, and I shall shape my policy by His leading.

Changing my metaphor, perhaps from the sublime to the ridiculous,
I look on communism as the goose that lays the golden eggs, and my
advice to "Young America," or, more properly, "Young Oneida,"
may be summed up in this: *"In appropriating the eggs and speculating
on them, for Heaven's sake, and for your children's sake, don't kill
the goose."*

And now I must confess that I don't see exactly how the new
schemes of privateering are to be kept in subordination to the main
motive. Won't private speculation withdraw people from interest in
the general business? And will it be safe for the Community to pay
wages to its members while it has no control of their labor or power
of dismissing them as ordinary employers have? But I suppose you
have all studied and discussed these questions and know what you are
about. I only ask you to convince *me* that you are not trying to kill
the goose, and then I will get myself contented with any of your
experiments.

I can see, as I intimated when the joint-stock scheme first came up,
that the difficulty of reconciling it in some way with communism may
not be insurmountable. We have got well through such huge incom-
patibilities in the last six months that I say to myself—Nobody knows
but that a great system of private property and individual sovereignty
can be worked out by the rising generation of Yankees, right here in
the bosom of communism. Sometimes I almost think, for instance, that
if it should be decided to give up our whole income to private appropriations and leave everyone at liberty to speculate what he pleases
with his own share, the real Communists might turn such an arrangement to the benefit of communism by returning as much as possible
into the Community Treasury, or by maintaining missions abroad; and
if the real Communists are in the majority, as I hope they are, and
if they would go about their work of keeping the goose alive with
courage and wisdom and peace, I really believe they would in a short
time either convert the individual sovereigns or bury them out of
sight in the wealth and blessings of communism. The fact is, the
liberty of private speculation can be used *for* communism as well as
against it.

And this leads me to an idea that is pleasant to me. Suppose that
both parties in the Community, just as they are—the Communists
and the individualists—should heartily agree on the main point, to
keep the great engine going: and then enter into a friendly and fair

competition to test the question whether communism or individualism is the best system for education and happiness. Is this chimerical? At all events, I do not think the Communists ought to be afraid of such a trial. I am not.

Myron reports to me that Wm. Hinds, in a private conversation, expressed a wish that I might return to the neighborhood of Community and offered to guarantee that I should be furnished with a comfortable private residence and living, at Cozicot or near either W.C. or O.C. I think this is a liberal offer and am thankful for it. I will, however, give some reasons for preferring a different location. I would like, in case any such movement is made, to take a house and start a little family here at Niagara Falls. Such an arrangement, instead of robbing the Community of one of its present pleasure places, would give it another; and this station would be nearer and more convenient and much less expensive for intercourse with O.C. than Cozicot or W.C. I have several other reasons for this choice which Myron can report if they are called for.

With much love to the O.C. unit. JHN

In relation to the last paragraph of Mr. Noyes's paper, after it was read, W. A. Hinds explained that in his conversation with Myron alluded to, about his guaranteeing Mr. Noyes a home, he only intended to express his own wish—that he was not authorized and had no right to guarantee or to speak for others, etc.; and then he proceeded to read to the family the following, as embodying the ideas he had in his mind at the time:

MR. HINDS'S PAPER

The dangers of outside persecution being past, the undersigned would like to have Mr. Noyes return to his Oneida home; but understanding that he does not wish to be burdened with cares and responsibilities, and that there may be other reasons why he may not choose to live either at Oneida or Wallingford, we yet hope he will consider favorably the proposition to make Cozicot or some place near one of the Communities his home.

The above, I wrote December 29, and I would be glad to sign a paper like this, but I cannot speak for others. It was slightly modified by Charles Joslyn, with a view to its circulation, but never circulated, that I have learned. I cannot say that anyone would have signed it but myself. To be frank, I should have to add that I had not thought of his coming back to govern the Community as formerly which I certainly do not desire; and some who speak for him say he does not desire it. But I certainly do desire that he should have a pleasant home where he can have the society of some of his nearest friends.

The *O.C. Journal* noted that "there has been yet no 'official' action on the proposition to furnish Mr. Noyes with a home near Niagara as he suggests, but quite a number in the meeting expressed their desire that he should be generously provided for."

Two days later the Council, "after considerable conversation," voted to recommend to the family "to allow Mr. Noyes to rent such a house as would be suitable for the small family he wishes to gather around him. That we furnish the house, provide a horse and carriage for them and allow the family expenses $150 per month."

On February 1 Mr. Hamilton returned from Niagara Falls and was able to report that a good Providence had favored them in securing for Mr. Noyes a very satisfactory house on reasonable terms —$200 per year. "Large stone house, well built, with parlor, dining room, kitchen, seven or eight bedrooms; large barn, six acres of land containing choice fruit trees, etc., and the location a very desirable one." Two women and a man were voted as a committee on furnishing the house at Niagara, "their special duty being to collect such articles as can be spared here and get them ready to send to the Falls." Mr. Hamilton also wrote to tell Mr. Noyes that his wife, "Mother Noyes," was pleased to go there to live. "She seems to enjoy the prospect of it."

16

"Pinafore"

The one bright spot in an otherwise rather gloomy picture of the Oneida Communists during the winter and spring of 1879–80 was their production of Gilbert and Sullivan's comic opera *H.M.S. Pinafore*. The project was evidently suggested by a professional performance of this operetta by a troupe which had come to Oneida the previous autumn. The Community family fell in love with it. Its comedy was infectious, its music enchanting. Young and old, the Community folks for years had acted, sung, and danced for their own entertainment. Now, why should they not act, sing, and dance for the public in *Pinafore?* The idea captivated the young musicians, and, after beginning tentatively with one or two of the simpler scenes, they finally dared to undertake the entire opera; by the end of January 1880, they were ready for a dress rehearsal which the whole family attended.

The *O.C. Journal* recorded it on January 26, 1880:

> The elaborate comic opera of *Her Majesty's Ship Pinafore* was rehearsed before the family last evening—the actors in full costume—and the entertainment lasting for two hours. We have heard but one opinion of the performance—that of enthusiastic commendation. The whole cast of characters seemed fitly chosen, so well did the long and persevering drill enable every one to do his or her part. It was a rich treat, and we only wish you all could have personally witnessed it. Here are some of the actors: *Sir Joseph Porter, K.C.B.,* T. R. Noyes. *Capt. Corcoran,* C. A. Burt, *Ralph Rackstraw,* A. L. Burt. *Dick Deadeye,* Harold Kinsley. *Boatswain,* John Cragin. *Josephine,* Lily D. Cragin. *Little Buttercup,* Marion Noyes. *Cousin Hebe,* C. M. Leonard. *Sisters and Cousins and Aunts,* H. M. Worden, Flora, Mabel, Cosette, Ann Eliza. *Sailors,* Milford, G. W. Hamilton, C. R. Marks, F. A. Marks, John Freeman, Ransom. *Middie,* Josephine Kinsley. Frank, E. S. B.., Horatio, and Tirzah furnished the instrumental accompaniment.

Several days later, since two members of the company were to

226

be absent for some time, it was asked whether *Pinafore* should be repeated once or more before the members left. It was decided to give another performance, inviting all the hired help, and then, two days later, again for "all outsiders willing to pay for it." Rehearsals continued every other evening that week, to which the family was invited. The *Journal* reported that "everybody enjoyed it as well or better than the first performance," and an invalid willingly sat through the two rehearsals without ill effect.

On January 30, the *Journal* was jubilant:

> This is *Pinafore* week. We have had it now three nights in succession and tonight again it is for the general public who pay. The *Oneida Union,* referring to the performance of Wednesday night for the benefit of O.C. operatives, recommended it as "first class." Dr. Carpenter, who was present and had seen this opera several times at Oneida, was greatly pleased and only regretted that his wife and daughter were not with him. Rev. Mr. Hibbard was also present and, withal he is something of a *connoisseur* in such matters, says he never tired of *Pinafore*. He had already listened to it seven times—once by the highly praised Boston troupe—but said that though he noticed some things that might be criticized—the performance of our company on the whole pleased him better than anything he had heard before. Our Dick Deadeye, he said, couldn't be beat. Such commendations are encouraging and stimulate our actors to further improvement. Indeed, all say that the rendering is better every time it is done—a more distinct articulation on the part of all. Mrs. Lily Cragin does her part as the "gallant capitain's daughter" like a born actress all through, and her appeal to the "God of love and God of reason" is usually broken in upon by cheers from the audience. Cheers would be elicited at many points if they could be expressed without interrupting the play.

Mrs. Skinner was delighted, as she noted on February 8: "There seemed to be a good voice and character for every part. I don't know which is most to be praised, but there is the glory of communism shining in it all—and affectionate freedom that only a Community troupe could feel or act. There is not a villain in it. Nothing evil; but a great deal of fun and sweetness. Alfred said in the meeting last night in his dry way, that it was most as good as a religious meeting. It has been a most profitable and wholesome diversion to the Community during the political strain of the winter."

By late February the *Pinafore* had sailed as far as Canastota and

Vernon, two nearby towns, and the *Canastota Herald,* February 23, "spoke in the highest terms of the late performance, making flattering mention of every actor whose name was on the printed programme. The Vernon folks want Pinafore repeated to them on some more auspicious evening"—the first performance took place in a blizzard —and "the Oneida people too would like to have our troupe rehearse to them again and keep the profits themselves." There had also been talk of a performance in Rome, but unfortunately the measles took the floor. "Nothing can be done without the 'Bosun'— and the 'Bosun' has the measles and others of the troupe are liable to come down with them at any time."

There is no record of any disagreement among the actors, but a set of rules drawn up and signed by the whole company on March 1 does suggest that some discipline was necessary:

We, the undersigned members of the Oneida Community Musical and Dramatic Company, agree to the following bylaws to regulate our conduct while belonging to it:

1st. We agree to play or sing in parts which we undertake, at any time or place when we are not excused by medical authority designated by the Company.

2nd. We agree to give a reasonable time from our leisure to practice so as to be always prepared for performance.

3rd. We agree to give three months notice of our retirement from the company and to continue to act in every respect in harmony with the rules until the expiration of the notice.

4th. We agree to abstain from unpleasant censure of the other members except at meetings of the Company held for that purpose, or to its officers.

5th. We agree to give notice to the proper officers of the Company when we intend to be absent from home, in time, if possible, to have our places filled.

6th. We agree to use reasonable diligence to attend rehearsals promptly and give notice to the proper officers if we are prevented from attending.

7th. We agree to dress at any time and submit to painting by any one designated by the manager.   PINAFORE COMPANY

By the end of March there was apparently enough criticism of the *Pinafore* project so that it was called on the carpet by the Council: "After considerable discussion," Theodore's plan was accepted, which called for the use of the Hall once a week and an arrangement whereby the proceeds, after paying the necessary expenses of the Company, should be used for "such means of culture as they may deem best." The Council also made the proviso that "the entire experiment is to be under the Community control so that it can at any time be stopped or the funds thus gained be diverted to other objects than culture and amusement. The going abroad this spring of the *Pinafore* Company was limited by vote to Morrisville, Madison, Earlville, Norwich, and Oneida, and they are not to remain away more than one night on any trip."

Mrs. Skinner, who recorded her thoughts on March 31, had learned the real story behind this edict:

> Theodore was quite set about it and pled for the liberty to go out and try their fortunes in two or three concerts. The family did not sympathize. On William's and Mr. Burnham's side there was strong opposition—they spoke very contemptuously of any missionary object in it. On our side too it was not generally sympathized with—that a promiscuous company of twenty-five or more should go out and be gone several nights at a time. Theodore's object, so confessed, was to get away from the turmoils here, and that was Frank's object, I suppose, and pleasure-seeking was the general object. Well, in the last Council, Theodore seems to have given up his will and came out with a plan that was very acceptable to most everybody. His plan is to give an entertainment here every week for the public—to take pay —have it on a fixed night that will be well understood—and work up an audience. The proceeds are to pay for the teacher from Syracuse, for costumes, etc., and the excess to go into the Treasury. The troupe are to have liberty to fill partial engagements at three or four places about here.

A few weeks later the *Journal* reported two performances of *Pinafore* and commented that "it wears well and always draws a full house of admiring listeners. All drop their 'whys and wherefores' and come and hear it. It promotes love and fellowship in our family circle and so proves a good medium of communism."

Under the surface—or perhaps one should say backstage— all was not so happy. Harriet Skinner wrote to JHN that "Theodore has ever so much trouble with his musical organization this spring —everything is at sixes and sevens all the time. The changes which the Syracuse Professor has introduced and some changes in the cast of performers have made it almost equal to beginning again. Lily was saying what tribulations she had been through and others were telling their troubles when Theodore said, 'We must confess the *true Pinafore spirit.*' There was a beautiful flow of inspiration and harmony in it last winter and I suppose he wants to get that again. He knows the way to get a good spirit if he would own it."

Nine performances—in Canastota, Vernon (twice), Oneida (twice), Morrisville, Earlville, Madison, and Cazenovia—brought in receipts of $368.45, with expenses for travel, advertising, etc., of $194.27, or a profit of $154.18.

Council meetings on January 27 and 28 were occupied in discussing the subject of personal appropriations for the coming year. Various persons gave figures on the average costs of clothing, traveling, and amusements, and Frank Wayland-Smith advocated $100 to each member over twenty-one years of age. The Council recommended that the cost of all traveling for pleasure and amusement should be borne by the individuals themselves; that all amusements indulged in for the mere pleasure of the parties concerned should also be charged to them. Travel to Joppa and all expenses incurred for such things as hiring sailboats or rides on steamboats or extra provisions such as beer or oysters should also be included in the personal appropriation. There was some talk about pleasure riding with teams at home, and it was thought that there must be a decided reform in the matter since, at it was, a part of the family managed to have a good many rides while others hardly got one during the entire season.

Strong feelings on these subjects were expressed by the family. Mr. Abbott thought it unwise for children between fourteen and twenty-one to share equally with the aged veterans whose strength and life had been spent in securing the treasure they now enjoyed. Such liberality would tend to make them independent, insolent, and vicious. Women, he also said, should not share equally with the men unless they could earn as much. The Council met four times and ended with a recommendation very much like their first effort except that they proposed that the Community pay for various small items in the sewing room and for long dresses for women's wear outside the Community. The matter was left for the family to decide.

The Financial Committee met with the Council and they agreed that the limit for both sexes should be $65 and that at least one-fourth of this appropriation should not be expended until after November first. No decision was reached.

Mr. Hinds presented a long paper on appropriations in which he advocated that they should not exceed $50. His text was a statement by President Hayes: "In good times, prepare for hard times; in good times pay debts." He also quoted a remark Mr. Noyes had made two years before: "It is not honest for us to live as the world does in uncertainty about our financial condition; it is not honest to live with a doubt in our mind whether we may not be cheating somebody by going beyond our income, or preparing to rob the poor, by and by, by failing." Although the past year had shown a net profit of some $40,000 it must be remembered that the four years previous had shown a total loss of $14,000. It was true that this included 1877, which was a depression year, and because of that the Community's businesses had lost a large amount. However, it would be better to take advantage of the present prosperity to prepare for the hard times to come. It should also be remembered, he reminded the family, that when the Community made most of its money, it was a Community of producers, and that for several years past the non-producing part of the Community—the children under ten or twelve years and the aged who could not work as many hours as formerly —had considerably increased.

Mr. Towner sounded the same note of alarm. The question was not what they wanted but what they could afford. Last year's earnings were large, but the coming year's earnings might be $10,000 or $5,000—or nothing. The family expenses for the past year had been $60,000 and were not likely to be less for the coming year, especially since they had been obliged to add to the capital of their businesses in order to enable them to do as much business as last year. He was in favor of a fair, if not liberal, appropriation of $50 for men and women alike, which would include the clothing fund and some other items while not adding to the family expenses more than about $3,500.

Mr. Hamilton did not ask for any figure for personal appropriations but wanted six or eight thousand dollars set aside for finishing up the new house wing. Mr. Jonathan Burt, that stalwart of the first Community days, wanted the personal appropriation to be such that every individual should have not only what was necessary but what was needed to give them a respectable appearance in the presence of surrounding society both at home and abroad. Thirty-five dollars, he thought was sufficient, with the exception of the traveling agents. If more was demanded, he would recommend paying a wage for overtime work. All surplus funds were to be returned to the Community treasury, which would give the young people a chance to grow up in the Community spirit.

A large group of more than twenty men and women signed a letter to Mr. Noyes expressing their views on these subjects: "We want you to understand that we are Bible Communists and expect always to remain so, and therefore have no sympathy whatever for any scheme of cooperation or joint-stockism or paying wages for overtime, the form that the selfish spirit in the Community is putting on at the present time. The solution of the problem of the relation of capital and labor can be found, we most earnestly believe, *only* in the *Pentecostal Spirit*. We have labored with you, long and hard, to make a Community home, and we want to continue such labor, and so persevere and enjoy our home." After the long list of signatures they added: "The sending you this expression has had the effect to make all the signers of it more united and brotherly. The few to whom it was shown who did not sign for want of room, were very hearty in their sympathy."

On February 5 the Council voted that all then over fourteen and under sixteen should receive $40; all over sixteen and under eighteen, $50; all over eighteen, $65. That parents and guardians should be free to expend for children under fourteen such sums not exceeding $40 as they may deem expedient.

17

The Wallingford Altercation

While the matter of personal appropriations was still agitating the Community, another of more serious import arose. Mr. Hamilton wrote to JHN about it on February 4:

> I wrote you hastily yesterday about the offer from the Meriden Britannia Company to rent for five or ten years our Wallingford Factory and power with privilege of buying. I will mention one or two items more in the conditions.
>
> At the end of the lease, if they did not buy, they to return the same value in machinery and tools as at the beginning. We to reserve the machinery for making chain links with necessary room and power.
>
> Myron and I, who are on the Tableware Board, met this forenoon with the Financial Board and talked over the matter. CSJ was absent on business. We were pretty well agreed that it was a favorable offer, but we thought we would take more time to consider, and wait till we have heard from you. I did not know how you would feel about having George and Myron tied up in the manner proposed. Myron thought it could be arranged so that they could withdraw by giving sufficient notice. For some reasons I like the feature of having Myron and George work on salary. It would relieve them from a certain kind of legal supervision that Mr. Towner keeps over them and Wallingford affairs. In this respect I regard this offer from Mr. Wilcox of the Meriden Britannia Company as a special providence. (This is confidential. There are signs that he, Mr. T, is working through John Norton again.) I think Myron and George can be trusted to "return with the spoils to the home of our dear ones." Myron says Wilcox would like a reply right away, so we shall be glad to hear from you soon. Myron thinks Wilcox is quite in earnest.

It is evident that the "hasty" letter sent the day before had included a proviso in the offer from the Meriden Company that Myron Kinsley, the superintendent of the Community's Wallingford spoon factory, and George Miller, his assistant, be part of the deal; that is, to work for them on salary and presumably to continue to manage the factory. Unfortunately this letter is missing, but Mr. Noyes's reply, dated February 7, showed his immediate reaction to the offer:

I feel like the mother hen with a hawk sailing over her chickens, and I hope in the present writing to sound the alarm-cluck which will send the chickens to cover.

In the first place, I object to the *hurry* we are being pushed into in a measure so *very* important as the virtual sale of our entire Wallingford property *and two of our best men, to boot.*

In the next place, I do most seriously object, as you supposed I might, to the "tieing up" of Myron and George, proposed by Wilcox's offer. I do not doubt that they are true to the Community and would faithfully turn their earnings into our treasury; but nevertheless they would be practically the servants of Wilcox; their time would belong to him and they would be generally responsible to him in such a way that the Community would have but little personal use of them. Now Myron has been, for the past seven months at least, one of our most efficient and useful general managers. I have often said that he saved the Community from anarchy and destruction by his whole-souled action in favor of peace and communism last summer. I cannot afford to let him drop out and become a clerk or agent of a scheming millionaire; and I do not think the Community can. If Wilcox offers him four thousand to go out, we had better offer him five thousand to stay in. He is worth more to us than he is to Wilcox or anybody else. And all I have said of Myron is substantially true of George. I object to disabling those men for Community service. Instead of their going out to help build up the hireling system, I want them in the Community to help *keep out* the hireling system and build up a solid and happy communism. Money is no object in such a matter.

My example is not one of running away to escape war-pressure in the Community, but of leaving the United States to escape threatened prosecution which would have injured the Community more than my absence, and my purpose is to go back into the Community just as soon as that danger ceases. Meanwhile I am still in full service of the Community and probably laboring harder for it and doing more good than I ever did when present to it in body.

I should wish to consider very carefully a good while the mere offer of the *lease,* some of the conditions of which, such as that relating to new buildings, I do not understand. But the main objection is to the disposal of our *men.* I hope that will not be tolerated for a moment, and so I will postpone discussion of other points until I hear from you again.

This letter of February 7 may not have reached Oneida by February 9 when the *O.C. Journal* recorded that in Business Meeting yesterday [February 8] Mr. Hamilton, not waiting for Mr. Noyes's reply to his two letters, recommended that we offer to lease the factory and power for five or ten years at $10,000 a year (including the services of M. H. Kinsley and G. N. Miller) with the privilege of buying at the expiration of lease—the whole property for $175,000, or that portion of it lying east of the lower road for $150,000. Adopted: with proviso that in conducting the business, the relation between Meriden Britannia Co. and the O.C. shall be substantially as follows: the name of the Community shall not be used in doing business for said company, but it simply authorizes M. H. Kinsley and G. N. Miller to contract with M.B.Co. for their services at the proposed rates—the agreement to be with them as individuals and not with the Community as such; M. H. Kinsley to hire such other Community men as can be spared, as he may deem best.

Voted, also, that M. H. Kinsley appoint a Committee (including himself) to conclude negotiations with the Meriden Britannia Company.

On that same day, John N. Norton, assistant manager of the spoon factory under Myron Kinsley, evidently worried about the offer, wrote to Theodore:

I have but a moment to write before the mail leaves, and perhaps what I have to say would have no weight anyway, and then the matter may be decided by this time. I refer to the Wilcox scheme. The more I have thought of it, the more uneasy I have become, until I can hardly sleep or eat in view of the possibility of the O.C. accepting it. To me it seems like weakness to accept it. The fact is, very few of our people have any idea of the value of this property and business, if put into the shape it ought and very easily might be put into, and at very little expense, too. I am convinced (if even moderately prosperous times continue) that we can easily take $300,000 out of this business in ten years, and more in *clean profits,* and that, too, without increasing the investment to any alarming extent. To accept the Wilcox proposition seems to me, and I think any candid and moderate figures will sustain my view, like making the Meriden Britannia Co. a present of the whole thing, that is, the water-power, buildings, etc., at the end of ten years and just throwing away by far the best business we ever had. Don't, for heaven's sake, let O.C. throw away this thing just because Wilcox wants it and is willing to pile on soft soap to get it. There is a great deal said by Wilcox and repeated by others, of the enormous cost it would be to go into German (silver) for instance, or fine goods and large profits generally. To a great extent (as we are situated) that is not true at all. Figures will show, and safe ones, too, that a very moderate amount would start us on German and give us a percentage of profits that we have not even tasted as yet.

Not until February 11 did Mr. Hamilton receive Mr. Noyes's letter of February 7, and he acted immediately, sending Myron two telegrams; first: "Delay negotiations till you get letter from Mr. Noyes"; and second, an hour later: "You had better see Mr. Noyes before closing bargain." He also wired Mr. Noyes and wrote him, reporting what he had done: "I regret now that I did not insist upon having Myron go and see you before returning to Wallingford, as I had a strong wish that he should, but I allowed myself to be influenced by the remarks that some make about the expense connected to it. I have forwarded a copy of your letter to Myron and written him also to be free to go and see you. Whatever comes of this proposal, I believe it will be a good thing all around for him to do so. It would be good for him, I think. I have just learned that some had rather have *me* go and see you. Possibly I shall."

The Wallingford *Journal* was in a position to observe the comedy of errors that attended the Wilcox affair:

> This has been a day of telegrams between Wallingford Community and Oneida Community, the first from Mr. Hamilton, saying, "Wait for Mr. Noyes's letter," arrived in time but was delayed in the delivery. It was at the office when Myron and George took the cars for Meriden. They were late for the train, however, and had no time to call at the office. E. S. Burnham, with horse and carriage, took the telegram to Meriden, but reached there too late. The second telegram sounded a little scoldy, because, as they said, "The Committee was not consulted" and said, "Go ahead." But if Wilcox & Co. accept Myron's offer, the mischief (if mischief it is) is already done. A day or two (if Wilcox keeps his agreement) will decide.

Actually, a third telegram from Mr. Hamilton, not noted by the W.C. *Journal,* arrived an hour after the first: "You had better see Mr. Noyes before closing bargain."

By February 13 Mr. Hamilton had received no word except a telegram from Myron: "Offer made before telegram came. Will send report soon as given." Mr. Hamilton evidently felt under some condemnation for his part in this mix-up. He wrote to JHN: "I shall probably be found fault with for suggesting it in my telegram without calling the Committee together. But I don't care. I think it was the right thing to do. You are the President of our organization and our spiritual head, and there ought to be no barrier in the way of a person's communicating with you."

The next day he was still obliged to justify his actions:

> When the Business Board decided to make an offer to M.B.Co. they appointed a committee to take charge of the negotiations. This committee consisted of the Financial Board with the addition of M. H. Kinsley, G. N. Miller, D. M. Kelly, and myself. Theodore, for some reason, declined to act. This left CSJ, Mr. Campbell, J. W. Towner, and Martin with those named above, eight in all. You can see that six of the committee would wish to be guided by your judgment and would not have made just such terms as we did, had we received your letter in time. The providence in the matter seemed to me peculiar. Yesterday I got the committee together and moved that Myron be free to go and see you. This was carried after some resistance. Mr. Towner was most prominent in opposing it but was overruled.

After the mail came that day with a letter from George Miller there was still no word from M.B. Co. "The suspense is rather unpleasant." George also sent them a copy of the famous telegram from the committee. "You better go on and negotiate and report details here as directed by Committee. Committee has not been consulted in what has been sent you." It was signed J. W. Towner and M. E. Kinsley. The offer having already been made, this order could not affect the deal. It did indicate that these two members were annoyed because Mr. Hamilton had acted unofficially. There was one funny thing about the affair. The committee could not have known the contents of the two Hamilton telegrams unless someone—D. Edison Smith was the telegrapher at O.C. and a firm Townerite—had divulged it. Charles Joslyn, one of the Community's Columbia-trained lawyers, looked the point up and found that such an act was a misdemeanor and punishable by three months in jail or five hundred dollars fine. As Mr. Hamilton wrote: "It looks as though Providence had let them fall into their own trap. We have kept pretty quiet about it. The apparent thing in all that is going on is the dislike of these folks of your influence in the Community."

Mr. Joslyn himself wrote to Mr. Noyes about the proposed sale: "If our last year's business is any indication of what the future will be, the spoon business is the best business the Community has; and it is capable of almost unlimited expansion as fast as we want to put capital into it, which is true of none of our other businesses. If we make the arrangement with the Meriden Britannia Company we abandon the spoon business; that is what it will amount to and that is, no doubt, what Wilcox wants; and I do not yet see what we have to take its place. If the inducement is sufficient, of course we can afford to abandon the business; but the question is, 'Is it sufficient?' As I have said, I do not feel at all clear that it is."

Mr. Hamilton's next letter sounded discouraged:

There seems to be considerable commotion here just now in the Community atmosphere in connection with this matter, but I don't think it relates altogether to this bargain, either. I will mention one or two things that possibly may help you to understand the situation. When your letter came I read part of it in the Council. I did not read what you said about Mr. Towner but *did* read what you wrote about returning to the Community just as soon as danger ceases. Perhaps this has excited some opposition, though I read it because I thought it would be a comfort to many to know that you entertained such a purpose. Another thing. I think there is a combination against Myron. I find that John Norton has been writing here against selling or leasing; is very decidedly opposed to it. I knew before that he was advocating a policy for the factory different from Myron's and was in correspondence with Mr. Towner about it. Mr. Burnham took John's side, too. CSJ stands in a criticising attitude toward Myron as a business man.

George Miller, Mr. Noyes's nephew of whom he was very fond, had been involved in this fracas, acting as Myron's second in command, and at this time he wrote his uncle, calling his attention to another phase of the problem facing them:

At the beginning of the year we find ourselves confronted by an ugly-looking lawsuit (backed by an array of five lawyers) which threatens the most important and profitable branch of our tableware business, viz., that of making steel spoons. If we lose this suit we shall have to abandon the steel spoon business because we shall be forced to pay a royalty to Mr. Wallace that will enable him to so undersell us so that we shall be virtually shut out of the market. If we gain the suit, we must do so at an expense which is estimated by the lawyers at not less than $5,000. Mr. Wilcox simply proposes that Myron shall manage the business as he now does, and Myron himself has no idea of consenting to anything like personal servitude for either of us. We both feel alike in regard to the matter, viz., that if we go into it, it will be to serve you and the Community more effectively than we now do, and neither of us have any desire to get away from the Community, with all its politics.

In a second letter Miller mentioned "one strong reason" that influenced his wish to sell: "That is, that Mr. Towner has assumed the charge of the steel spoon suit and we have no confidence that he will bring it to a successful issue. I cannot help remembering his conduct of the suit about the dam, in which he took a passive, negative view of our rights in the matter and we were defeated to the surprise of and indignation of everybody. So far as Wallingford is concerned, Mr. Towner has only the prestige (if I may call it so) of defeat and evil and I should employ almost any one but him in our legal affairs."

This opinion apparently affected Mr. Noyes's attitude toward the sale. On February 15 he wrote to Mr. Hamilton:

I have just received your letter and one from GNM relating to the Wilcox overtures, and I hasten to assure you that there is no occasion for distress about my difference of opinion in the matter. If the general judgment of the business men of the Community is in favor of the offer which has been made and if that offer should be accepted, I shall acquiesce in it cheerfully, though I felt it my duty, on being consulted, to give my honest thoughts about it. Having done that, I consider the matter out of my hands, and shall accept the result whatever it may be with hearty goodwill and without blaming you or Myron or anybody, not doubting that God's hand is in it and that it will be turned to good account for the Community welfare. My chief anxiety—I may even say my *only* wish—in the matter was and is to keep the whole strength of Myron and George in the Community; but I know that God can do this under the conditions proposed as well as under present conditions—perhaps better. I am entirely willing to see the experiment tried and will do my best to help it to a good result. If the deed is done, pray count me in favor of it and go ahead with the vigor of unanimity. Or, if you want any further advice from me about it, rely upon me to give you my best thoughts without intending dictation or imputing blame to you or anyone for differing from me.

He added in a postscript:

Your intimation that my proposal to come home when the liability of prosecution is ended caused disturbance reminded me of William Hinds's circular, which was never circulated, but was read by him to the meeting and copied in the *Journal* of January 24. In that circular he says: "The danger of prosecution being past, *the undersigned would like to have Mr. Noyes come home.*" What I said about coming home was only a fair response to this and ought to be credited to me as simple politeness to William. As to my *ruling* the Community, I never supposed that I used to rule it in any other way than he does, viz., by persuasion and natural weight of character; but if I did, I don't want to and never shall, if I can help it. The rule that comes by telling the truth and doing my best for all who respect me and letting my natural weight of character rest upon the Community cannot be avoided and I am not to blame for it or for the perversions of it by others. I shall rule the Community in this way forever, whether present or absent.

On February 20 Mr. Hamilton wrote to JHN: "Mr. Towner went to W.C. the last of the week to look after the spoon suit—and as usual, has made a muss, as you will see by copy of Myron's letter which I inclose. It looks as though his case was getting ripe for judgment."

Myron was filled with grievances:

Mr. Towner wrote to me several days ago asking me to go and see Mr. Hubbard, Wallace's lawyer, and tell him that we had got an offer for our place here and that it might end in our wishing to drop the suit on the steel spoon question and asking him to postpone for two weeks. I called the Spoon Board together and we all thought it was not best to say anything to Mr. Hubbard about our offer from Mr. Wilcox. We had given him our promise not to let it go out of our family, and from what he told me I knew he did not wish Mr. Wallace to get hold of what he was doing and we all felt that our honor was given, therefore did not wish to say anything to Mr. Hubbard, as it would go at once to Mr. Wallace and all over town. This I wrote to Mr. Towner, asking him to choose some other way of attaining his point without saying anything to Mr. Hubbard about our offer and told him it was the wish of the Spoon Board (all were there but John Norton; he was away). We had not heard anything from him in reply but the first thing we know is that Mr. Towner appears and, without coming to the factory or house, went straight to Mr. Hubbard and told him just what we, as a Board, had requested him not to do. This has tried us very much. I asked him if he had consulted the other part of the Committee at O.C. that was chosen by me when the thing

first came up, by request of the Special Business Board called together for that purpose. This committee was accepted.

Mr. Towner said he did not consider this committee was a power
now or had charge of the matter. Now what I wish is this: if this
committee is not satisfactory to the Community, another one be appointed and that there should be some consultation before things are
carried on as they have been for a few weeks past. Another instance:
Mr. Towner asked me to see the other manufacturers of steel spoons
and call a meeting and see what they proposed to do and compare
notes on this occasion. I called the Spoon Board together and we all
thought it would be better to get the opinion of a first-class lawyer
like Dickson and then we could talk understandingly with these manufacturers. I reported this to Mr. Towner, and he said he had taken
measures to do this and we supposed he was doing so, but now, without consulting us at all, he has written to these different spoonmakers,
calling a meeting for tomorrow. His plans may be the very best, but
we must not be left out entirely or must have a chance to say what
we think best or at least be treated with common courtesy.

The letter was endorsed and signed by all but one of the W.C.
Spoon Board.

The next day the quarrel came out in the open. Myron wrote:

I have had a plain talk with Mr. Towner this morning. He justifies his
course in going to see Hubbard as he did in this way; says that if
Hubbard did tell, no one would know that it was we who were leasing
our power to him. I told him there was not a person in town but what
would know at once and that our word had been given and Mr.
Wilcox had often said that he would trust our word quicker than
most people's notes, and if this offer should get out and he should
hear that we told of it, it would lessen his respect for us very much.
As long as Mr. Towner takes this independent way, he will not get
much help or sympathy from us here. As a Spoon Board we are a
unit, with one exception. After our talk this morning he came back
and said he would like it if he could have our sympathy and cooperation in what he was doing here this time. I replied I thought it was
impossible until we had a settling up in regard to the past. He said
he might as well go back to O.C. then. I replied perhaps it would be
best. He said he would see about it on his return from New Haven
where he has gone alone to attend the spoon meeting.

I pray that we may act wisely in regard to this matter, but at the
same time we are bound not to come under Mr. Towner's spirit. I
do not know but here is the place for the fight to commence. If so, I
am ready to show my colors.

This was certainly not the end of the dispute, but the end of the Wilcox affair, as they called it, came the next week. The W.C. *Journal,* February 26, 1880, recorded tersely: "A letter was received today from Mr. Wilcox saying the Meriden Britannia Company had abandoned the idea of leasing the factory property. The announcement produced a pleasant 'humming of the tissues' in some quarters. Mr. Towner leaves this morning for O.C."

18

The Hinds-Kinsley Correspondence

"The humming of the tissues" which arose from the Wilcox affair, if it began in Wallingford, did not end there but continued as a sort of tremor which shook both sides of the embattled Community. It was expressed first in a series of long and heated letters of mutual accusation and denial between partisans at Oneida and Wallingford. The first was a letter from William Hinds to Myron Kinsley, February 20, 1880. Mr. Hinds had a mind subtle in contriving and supple in debate:

> How strange it is, if Mr. Towner is, as many think, an evil-minded man, that no one is ready to put his finger on a thing and hold it there until it can be examined. That story about his trying to change the terms of the Community property in an underhanded manner, which you told me, was distressing to many people in the Community, and yet, on hearing his explanation in my room, you expressed yourself fully satisfied. The story about his collecting evidence against Mr. Noyes with intent to use it against him at some future time is, I am persuaded, another fabrication.
>
> You can do a great deal to put a stop to such slanders, if they are slanders; and if they are not slanders you can do much to bring the *truth* to light. Such stabbing of character in the dark—how can it be justified? If there is anything that can be proved against Mr. T.—any charge that will stand investigation—any accusation that will bear the light—let it come before the whole Community, or before an impartial committee, that the truth may be known. I will not stand by him a moment if it can be shown that he is unworthy of confidence or that even a small part of the stories told about him are true.

The letter was long and very persuasive, but in the postscript a little more iron showed through the velvet glove:

> It is not alone by slanderous reports and dark insinuations that Mr. T. suffers. The prejudice against him is constantly manifest in business matters. Others who do not possess a tenth part of the confidence he does may be put into any place of responsibility and it is submitted

243

to with little complaint, but let him be offered as a member of the Youth's Committee or Finance Committee or invited to attend the sessions of the Council as a substitute and there is immediately great displeasure manifested. How long are such things to continue? And what is sought to be gained by them? Does anyone fancy he can, by these means, be driven out of the Community? He and his friends, I am sure, would endure any fair investigation of the complaints against him, if anyone has manliness enough to make open charges and present proof; but they demand and will continue to demand that he shall be held innocent in the face of all accusations that are in independent ways, and by persons who wind up their stories by injunctions of silence.

Myron Kinsley was neither a wily debater nor a ready writer, but he was willing to speak his mind, doing so on February 23:

Yours about Mr. Towner comes just too late, or rather at the wrong time to have the effect you so much desire. I had just been having a plain talk with him in regard to his course in this late suit on steel spoons, when we as a spoon board thought he had not treated us with common courtesy, but had taken a very high-handed course. I will simply name two instances in regard to our business here which have tried us very much, and I told him frankly how we felt about it. He raised his head, buttoned his coat, folded his arms and stood a little straighter and looked quite as though he meant to squash me at once by saying that we had nothing to say or do with the legal part and that he had done what he thought was right and he still thought so and had nothing to regret.

Myron then, laboriously and at length, recounted the Wilcox-Hubbard-Towner imbroglio and the resentment of the Tableware Board at such cavalier treatment: "We here think he had no right to come here and meddle with our business in this way. It is not doing things in a Community spirit, and I do not think we ever had another man in the Community that would treat us in this way. He cares for no one's feelings (except they are his special friends) and assumes that he is always right."

The matter of the telegram mix-up was gone over in detail; who had done what and who was to blame:

I write all this to explain how I feel toward Mr. Towner. In all my experience in the Community I have not seen such a high-handed course as this, such disrespect to Mr. Noyes in business matters, and

Mr. Hamilton, too. And it would be just the same toward any of the elders in this church or any number of them. This is another example of his high-handed course. But instead of being turned toward some Committee, as the spoon board, it is turned toward Mr. Noyes—the Father and founder of the Community. Now can you, William, expect any order, any respect, any organization, or in fact any other good effects from a Community where this spirit has such sway?

The episode of Mr. Towner and the steel spoonmakers meeting was gone over with bitter resentment:

Mr. Towner called a meeting by letter from Oneida, of all the steel spoonmakers, to meet at New Haven, without consulting us in the least about it. He wrote me, some time ago, asking me to call this meeting. I called the Tableware Board together, and we all advised not to call such a meeting, and I told Mr. Towner so when at Oneida last. This makes no difference to him; not even inquiring our reasons, but without any consultation with us he appoints this meeting—comes here Friday, but says nothing to us about it, but just at night as I sat down by him at the supper table (he sees that I am lame, using two canes) he says, "You can't attend the Spoon Meeting tomorrow at New Haven, can you?" I said, "Hardly." He asked me no more questions about it; dropped it there. The next morning about fifteen minutes before time to start to take the cars, he said he would like someone to go down with him. He went down to the shop with John Norton but went to New Haven alone. This was Saturday morning and now it is Monday afternoon and he has said nothing to any of us except John Norton about the meeting or what they did there. He is off again today. If there is not a change in Mr. Towner's spirit and attitude toward us we would much prefer to go outside for what counsel we need here, than to have him go on as he is now doing. To have success there must be unity and there is absolutely no unity between us.

The last pages of Myron's letter—and Mr. Hinds mentioned that there were twenty-four pages, hand-written—tried to answer some of Mr. Hinds's questions, the reasons why he felt as he did toward Mr. T:

I was sorry that Mr. Towner's name was put on the Financial Committee, even if he were qualified or the best man for the place we had, and for this reason: I know that there are a good many in the Community and good persons, too, that have lived here a long time, much longer than he has, and do not have that confidence in him as a spiritual man or as a business man, no, nor as a loyal man to Mr. Noyes, and I was surprised that he should accept the place, knowing how so many felt about him. No matter how well he is fitted for any place, that place should come to him as a free gift—an unanimous one—especially with Mr. Noyes's approval; but this is not the case with him and he knows it. I have no idea that anyone thinks or wishes to drive him away from the Community, but would like to help him to become the man you think him, if he is not now. But, William, I think honestly that you, Martin, Mr. Burnham and others are Mr. Towner's worst enemies or advisers by this very way you have of pushing him forward beyond the confidence of the Community as a whole.

You ask me as the avowed friend and champion of peace and general unity to make myself conspicuous in discouraging and disapproving of the feeling toward Mr. Towner. William, I have tried to do this as you very well know, in many ways. By demanding that others should take your estimate of his spirit you have killed what I tried to do in all sincerity, which was to bring about good feeling toward Mr. Towner and that feeling was growing until you pushed him forward so fast. The only advice I can give you is the same that I gave you and Mr. Burnham last summer. You are the ones that can help him most and that by advising him to fill a small place in the Community.

What were probably the last pages of this letter are missing. Something of what they may have contained, however, may be inferred from Mr. Hinds's reply on February 25. He had written, he said, in no spirit of controversy but to befriend a brother. In the matter of Mr. Towner's course in consulting Mr. Hubbard, "if it be admitted that he should have more fully consulted the Spoon Board, it is to be considered that he and Charles were agreed about it and they considered, rightly or not, that as counsel they were authorized to ask for such extension, provided your position in the negotiation for sale was not in any way unfavorably affected, which is claimed to be the case. There seems to me at least room for a charitable view."

The tangled affair of the three telegrams was discussed at length, and, according to Mr. Hinds, Mr. Hamilton's actions were "wholly indefensible." The sorest point, apparently, was the unauthorized wire to Mr. Noyes:

It was right enough and cerainly proper out of respect to Mr. Noyes to consult him about such an important matter, but it is hardly proper for a single member of a committee to say how he shall be consulted or by whom. It remains to be shown that either Mr. Towner or Martin objected to his being consulted. But I cannot see but they have as much reason to be tried as you had to be tried with Mr. T.'s calling on Mr. Hubbard in the way he did. In a note to me he says he had not a thought that you would object if he acted judiciously in the matter. I know nothing about the Spoon Meeting or Mr. T.'s reasons for calling it. I only know that it has been repeatedly mentioned in the Business Board as very desirable that, if the suit were to go on, there should be an effort to secure the cooperation of other spoon manufacturers, but of course everything of that kind should be conducted with due consultation.

The remaining pages of Mr. Hinds's letter dealt at length with the matter of his own course in acting as advocate for Mr. Towner:

In respect to the course of Mr. T.'s friends in "pushing him forward beyond the confidence of the Community as a whole," we shall probably not entirely agree. It seems to me that his friends have been very patient in the matter, and he also. As it appears to his friends, he has been purposely and persistently ignored in matters of business as no other person in the Community having similar claims to confidence has been. Compare his present responsibilities, if you please, with those of TRN, for instance. The latter certainly has twice, I think thrice, as many. But is there any more confidence "in the Community as a whole" in the latter "as a spiritual man, as a business man, as a loyal man to Mr. Noyes"? The fact is that we have to make the best of things as they are, and learn to work with those whose opinions and course we do not fully approve. What you say about my doing harm to Mr. Towner and the peace of the Community by my zeal for Mr. T. I shall consider and be ready to mollify my course if I am able to accept your conclusions.

Again, alas, the opening pages of a confidential letter from Charles Joslyn to Mr. Noyes are missing. Charles Joslyn was one of the highly intelligent and aggressive young businessmen in the Community. His position politically as between the Noyesites and the Townerites—or even the Third party—was suspect at various times by each. This letter, which described the situation in the Community more clearly than any other of this date, placed him squarely on the Noyes side, rejected the Third party proposals, and made the Townerites' influence entirely understandable. There is no date on this letter other than February 1880 at the heading of the page:

And I may assure you here, that my feelings toward yourself have not changed and probably will not and that I consider you now, as I always have, as a constant medium of good spirit to us all.

Promising this much, I would allude to what you have said in regard to Mr. Towner, and from which I have no wish to dissent. And what I am about to say I wish to say in strict confidence, and that is that much of the influence that Mr. Towner has in the Community at this time is owing to the unsatisfactory conduct of persons who call themselves your friends. And this is what I mean:

You have heard of the scheme for cooperation etc. which has been urged upon the Community by FW-S, TRN, and a few others. The history of these is as follows: First, and beginning several months age, was the cooperation scheme. This may never have been laid before you in its full length, but it is nothing less than an abandonment of communism and a substitution of a form of selfishness in its place. It is not necessary to go into the details of the scheme, but this would have been the sure and certain result. This proved unpalatable to the great mass of the Community and was dropped, and a new scheme started, which was this: "There is no use in piling up money—for we know not what—let us quit all this and divide the entire earnings of the Community for each year among its members and let them spend it as they please." This did not prove acceptable, except among a very low class of persons in the Community, who want to get all the money they can—for personal use—no matter how. Then the scheme was revised in another form—that of a large personal appropriation—$100 for each person during the current year. This would have amounted to the same thing as the previous scheme, inasmuch as it is the opinion of our best financiers that our earnings this year will not be as large as last year, by a considerable sum, and that a $100 appropriation will absorb our entire earnings and possibly more. Now, FW-S canvassed the Community thoroughly in support of that scheme, appealing to the lower passions of the thoughtless and selfish for its support and obtaining a large part of his support in it from persons who are your worst enemies. Another plan, which has come along with this is the proposal to hire and pay wages to Community men and women, requiring them to spend about four hours *per diem* for Community labor, and paying them a certain price per hour for all work over this.

Now the continued agitation of such schemes as these is very distressing to the great majority of the substantial men and women of the Community, especially the older portion, who have borne the brunt of the labor of establishing the Community and who want to enjoy their religion and their communism in quiet.

They feel that such things are anti-Communistic and that unless they are checked they will destroy communism from among us. The result is that these persons who are agitated by these schemes have lost to a great extent the confidence of a large part of the substantial and conservative men and women in the Community who are in their hearts loyal to communism, to their religion, and to you. Some of the less discerning have lost, to some extent, their faith in you because they saw that schemes which they feel to be revolutionary and dangerous are put forth by persons claiming to be your friends, and who do not look deeply enough into the matter to make the necessary discriminations in the case.

Now right here is where Mr. Towner comes in and gets a strong influence. He says to such persons, "I am a Communist and a religious man. I am opposed, utterly, to everything that strikes at our religion or our communism," and in this attitude he strikes a sympathetic chord that vibrates in every loyal heart. He appears to the Community in the light of a conservator of what they consider most precious, and these persons who claim to be your friends are felt to be taking measures to destroy the Community. It is impossible for those who have the interests of the Community at heart to avoid taking the same ground that he does in such matters, and be consistent with their Community training; and thus the sober-minded men and women, many of whom do not sympathize with Mr. Towner's attitude toward you, are compelled to act with him when these issues come before the Community family, and to a certain extent look upon him as one of the bulwarks of our faith.

I, for one, should be very glad indeed if every man and woman proposing to be loyal to you could have shown as much of your spirit as Mr. Hamilton does, or if not, could at least have seen the necessity of it, and give way to those who do so, and I think a close homogeneous organization, clinging to you and acting in an organic way, could do a great deal toward pacifying the excitement and quieting the antagonisms that exist. My feeling is that if all your friends would accept the situation, abandon combativeness and revolutionary schemes, and set themselves at work exercising patience and long-suffering and Christian forbearance, making up their minds to endure some things that are disagreeable, and to work if necessary for a term of years to bring about harmony, I say, if they would take this attitude and stick to it, I think in time the Providence that watches over us would bring about a solution of all our difficulties. But it will never be brought about by restiveness, impatience and a disposition to turn everything upside down because they don't go just as they ought. You referred to Mr. Towner. I don't think he has as much influence in the Community in general as Wm. Hinds, owing to his shorter membership and more limited acquaintance with the inwardness of our Community organization. I am inclined to consider him, as you suggest, the medium of a principality which he himself does not understand.

In conclusion I would say that I claim to be loyal to you and regret very much that I cannot take you by the hand and give my heart to everyone in the Community making the same claim; but the plain truth is, I find myself quite incapable of endorsing the attitude of such persons as Mr. Herrick, FW-S, ESB, and others of like conduct, and I know, as I have said, that the great majority of sober-minded men and women feel as I do. Understand, that I don't allow any of this to affect my faith in you, for there are men and women here, like Mr. Hamilton, Mr. Kinsley, Mr. Campbell, etc., whom I very much sympathize with, and who, I know, are faithful to primary principles and to you.

I ask you to consider this letter absolutely confidential. I am in peaceable relations with most of the persons I have mentioned and do not want to give them any occasion of offense; as would certainly be the case if they should hear the contents of this letter. I should not have said anything about the matter if your allusion to Mr. Towner had not given me the impression that one of his strong points in the Community was not perfectly understood by you, and this I have tried to explain.

19

Real, False, and Non-Communists

Exactly how the Oneida Communists were choosing sides in the struggle that was being waged was a matter of grave importance to the little group of Central Members who were doing their best to maintain order during John Humphrey Noyes's absence. The inquiring mind of Harriet Skinner set about making a census, in which she divided the membership into seven classifications:

1. *Staunch friends of Mr. Noyes at O.C.,* fifty-seven of these attend our private meetings.
2. *Staunch friends at W.C., Niagara and California,* twenty-one.
3. *Friends of Mr. Noyes but more or less disheartened and inactive,* twenty. Of this class eleven are in the *Pinafore* troupe; the same number have been married under the new regime. All belong to the second generation—all have forsaken the Evening Meetings, I believe.
4. *Neutrals, represented by Chester Underwood and Harriet Worden,* twelve.
5. *Persons badly infected with Townerism but not rabid, represented by Margaret and Mrs. Allen,* fourteen.
6. *Not pronounced or transparent, likely to go with the successful party, represented by Daniel Abbott and Lily Hobart,* eighteen.
7. *Townerites, or persons who openly renounce the leadership of Mr. Noyes,* forty-seven. Young folks under twenty not counted. Whole number counted, 208. Community census at the close of the *Socialist,* 199; four left since then; one born, one died.

Recapitulating Mrs. Skinner's census, Mr. Hamilton made the whole number 208; "loyal, 116, leaving a minority of ninety-two, of which there were probably loyal, thirty-one, a probable minority of sixty-one, giving a probable two-thirds vote. In other words, more than half of the Community certainly, and more than two-thirds probably, are in favor of the old government with modifications adapted to present experience."

This analysis, forwarded to JHN, brought an answer in his old form on March 9, 1880:

Every word of what you have said from time to time about the little meetings and the reviving faith of the old believers has stirred my heart with love and hope. It is evident to me that all the experience of the last year has been necessary to the awakening which is coming and has begun. I am confident that a renewal of faith-experience has been going on in you and the circle around you. So I have nothing to quarrel with, nothing to regret in the disturbances that we have been going through. I see but one party at O.C.—them that love God, surrounded by the "all things that work for good." The fight that seems so real becomes an illusion when I see that God is on both sides of it. I bear no grudge against those who have done me good, even if they meant it for evil.

I see that the judgment is dissolving the Community into its separate elements. It has been filling up by the birth of a new generation and by taking in new members without much care, till a large proportion of its constituents are very different from the old set that commenced it and settled its principles. Of course all shades of character have been represented in it from the beginning; but the *proportion* of believers to unbelievers—of Communists to non-Communists—is very different now from what it was at the first. This change of proportion has brought on the present troubles and these troubles are bringing out into sharp distinction the different kinds of folks that now make up the Community.

According to my view, there are three kinds that are now prominent or coming into prominence, *viz.,* real Communists, false Communists, and non-Communists. Real communism is a thing of the heart; it is unity of life; it may exist without community of property and on the other hand, community of property may exist without Communism of the hearts. I say boldly that real communism can exist only by grace through faith in the blood of Christ identifying with God.

But every good thing has its counterfeit, so there is a false communism. People see a great advantage in communism of property and communism of sexual privileges while they have no idea of communism of the heart. The inducements for such people to join the Community have been much greater of late years than they were at the beginning; it is therefore probable in the nature of things that there is a greater proportion of real communism in the "old sett" than in the later accretions. But however this may be, it is certain that real communism, which in fact is real *spirituality,* cannot coexist with party divisions, for the idea that people of one heart can fall into quarrelling and hatred is absurd. It is therefore certain that one or the other of the professedly communistic parties that are quarreling in the Community—or both—are false Communists.

The party of non-Communists are those who have no distinct feeling of community of hearts—perhaps no faith in the possibility of it—and are therefore opposed to Communism of property, etc., on scientific grounds. These may be, and are likely to be, a great deal more honest than the false Communists; for they are honest enough to seek consistency—to prefer separation of property interests where hearts are separate. This is the reason for any seeming sympathy which I have shown to this party. I cannot help agreeing with them that *compulsory* communism is a bad thing, and that communism is and must be *compulsory* where there is no real unity of hearts. But on the other hand, I think this party is made up mostly of the younger generation who have grown up in the Community without being converted, and that, on account of the very honesty which now makes them non-Communists, they are convertable, and if God holds them in connection with the real Communists they will sooner or later realize community of hearts and so become real Communists.

So you see that I divide the Community into the three old familiar parties, the true believers, the hypocrites, and the "World's People," and my hope is that the true believers will wake up and have a revival that will convert the "World's People" and especially their own children and to restore the Community to more than its old strength and prosperity.

But how is the Community going to dispose of the hypocrites? I don't know and I don't care. I only know that we shall have them, like the poor "always with us," so long as we need them for discipline. I have no wish to exterminate them or expel them. Perhaps they, too, are convertable—some of them, at least. I leave the hypocrites to God. He will either convert them or take them away in his own good time. I only insist that we can live at peace with them and take the discipline which they bring upon us in a good spirit, improving by it, and patiently waiting for the day of deliverance.

The world's principle of dealing with evil is to *fight* it. Instead of this, the Christian principle is to *withdraw* from it. "Reckon yourselves dead with him in the city out of sight where evil cannot enter." There is escape for all from all; and really all these troubles are nothing but the friendly bow-wows that are sent by the shepherd to drive us into the fold. If they persecute you at Oneida, flee into that city. If the people around you walk disorderly, withdraw into that city. Don't hope or try to escape in any other direction. Especially don't seek relief by fighting.

And now, my true yoke-fellow, and all the deeply beloved, let me freely exhort you not to think that you have fully tested this mode of escape. I think you have but little idea of the help and comfort you can get by the inward secret power of locomotion. It is this flight to Christ that is the whole salvation wherever we are and it is as real as the power of traveling by railroad. By this secret power we can meet not only Christ but one another without change of bodily presence. There is danger of fanaticism and delusion in this kind of traveling; but there is also no salvation without it.

Yours more and more, JHN

Harriet was delighted with this letter:

I cannot tell you how much your epistle is appreciated by the "faithful" here. I gave it to Frank and Cornelia to read. Frank said he had got so he was able to appreciate it—sick of fighting. The reason they have not been able to come to the Meeting is because William's and Mr. Towner's pious talk exasperated them so. It is distressing. Last night, for instance, the subject of special providence was up, and William went into quite a discourse. He thought the difference between the spiritual and the carnal man was that one noticed God's special care and the other didn't. He tells Mary that he thinks you have been the greatest medium of inspiration the world has had since Christ, or except Christ I believe, but you have fallen in your old age as Solomon did—he thought nothing was more natural than that you should.

A prolonged struggle had been going on about the management of the Children's House. A number of the dissident party claimed that the present Father of the Children's House, Mr. Kelly, was too strict a disciplinarian and for that—or other—reasons had removed their children from his care. The ulterior motive behind this accusation may have been political; it was claimed that Mr. Kelly, backed by certain other Noyesites, had forbidden the Children's House children to play with the offspring of the other party. Mr. Towner finally appealed to the Council on March 18:

Among other children, Dorr [Mr. Kelly's stepson] has come down to my room now and then to visit Ruddy [Mr. Towner's step-grand-son]. Some over a week ago, on Ruddy's inviting him down, he said he could not come, as Mr. Kelly had told him not to. The other day I asked Emily [Dorr's mother] about the matter. She said Mr. Kelly had told Dorr not to come down and see Ruddy because Ruddy was out of the Children's House. I said, "Why no; he was not. I did not consider him so, and when things got settled after the measles campaign, intend he should go back to the meetings, and Ruddy understood this." Emily said she sympathized with what Mr. Kelly had done, and for other reasons than above. Said she told Dorr that I did not feel to Mr. Noyes as she did—she wanted Dorr to believe that Mr. Noyes was the best and wisest man. She gave me plainly to understand that if she made him a good boy, one of the conditions was to keep him away from those who did not think so of Mr. N. Remarked that I had said that I did not want my boy under Mr. Kelly's spiritual teachings—well, she did not want Dorr under mine—and so on.

Augusta, Ruddy's mother, said that it was perfectly evident to her that all this treatment of her and Ruddy was out of pure personal spite because of her honest expression of convictions in the late parents' meeting. She asked the Council if she deserved to be socially excommunicated—children taught that she was a bad woman and her children not fit to associate with? Were they going to teach the third generation a strict social division on party lines? What answer the Council gave is not recorded.

The disorganized condition of the Children's House continued to make trouble. Harriet Allen, who had been one of the Mothers, told a friend that when she got a chance she was going to oppose the taking of the children out of the control of the Children's House and letting them mix with the other children. Several of the small boys had been over to the shop, mixing with hired folks. They got to the barn, too, more or less. When the children were out to play and the bell rang, those belonging to the department would mind the bell and come in, but the others would stay out, and that made the others discontented.

Augusta's complaint in Council concerning Mr. Kelly had caused a real explosion of feelings, pro and con. Six weeks later, on March 18, another matter which aroused angry passion on both sides was brought before the Council as unfinished business requiring action. It was a motion made on February 1, "that a committee consisting of J. W. Towner, C. S. Joslyn and Albert Kinsley be appointed to consider the question touched upon by Mr. Towner and suggested by Mr. Noyes some years ago, which was the obtaining of special litigation in the matter of holding our property, and report to the Business Board." The *O.C. Journal* remarked tersely that "after a prolonged discussion the motion was carried."

Mrs. Skinner wrote to Mother Noyes: "This subject the other

side have tried to get before the Board for several weeks, but one thing or another (principally Alfred, I think,) have staved it off. Mr. Hamilton thinks that Charles will be opposed to any change. He said in the Business Board that The Four would probably have to give their consent and might not be willing to do it." This meeting with the "prolonged discussion" involved not only "William & Co." but Theodore, Augusta, the Kellys, Mr. Freeman, and Sarah Dunn. Mrs. Skinner reported that "our side preserved complete moderation, though there was more flourish of wrath on the other side than ever before."

The distressing tension of the atmosphere naturally affected some of the older members. Several weeks earlier Mrs. Skinner had reported that Mr. Hamilton was quite ill; had fainted away in a Council Meeting. He had apparently recovered shortly. Mrs. Skinner thought it was a hint not to let evil get his attention and was caused by carrying such a load of responsibility alone: "What with Augusta, and with Theodore and Frank lending him no support and Mr. Joslyn playing off Mr. Towner against Myron, he has a great deal on his shoulders and Theodore says it would not do for him to go on so—that he should take care of his body as well as his soul." Toward the end of March Mr. Hamilton was still unable to attend the Evening Meetings, and Mrs. Skinner reported on March 26 that several of the other elderly men were ill, and although the measles epidemic was tapering off, there were an unusual number of hired nurses employed in the Community: "The Community is the sickest that was ever known and we certainly have more doctors and medicines and beefsteak and oysters and all kinds of luxuries for poor health than ever before. The atmosphere of measles has generated disease, no doubt, but I can't help thinking that marriage and family exclusiveness, the resumption of the children by the parents and disorganization of the Children's House has a good deal to do with it. Mr. Barron thinks we are having a great family criticism. I believe more than I ever did before that if John's ideal of vital society could be *fully* realized, it would bring salvation of the body."

Two days later she wrote: "The atmosphere here has been very oppressive. I have been tempted to say, 'How long, O Lord, how long'—because it seemed as if the wolf was ravaging among the children—but we have got to learn to trust the Good Shepherd for them as well as for ourselves, and the signs of his watchfulness are manifest. We have good meetings in the South Sitting Room. Mr. Hamilton has been to meeting two evenings. I think William fired a dart at him last evening. It made me see what a mark he is. They don't want he should get his mouth open again. Speaking of his weakness, he said he could give the enemy odds and beat him."

In late April a matter came up in the Council which had been hanging fire for some time. A Community man, Charles Burt, who had been acting as salesman—"agent" in the Community terms—was found to have been acting also for another fruit preserving company at the same time. This was, of course, strictly against Community procedure, and the matter was argued vigorously in the Council. There was "nearly unanimous disapproval of Charles' course as disorganizing and at variance with the covenantal obligations of the Community." But there was also a general expression in favor of meeting the matter in a charitable spirit, and a committee was appointed to confer with the culprit.

Harriet Skinner scouted around for reports of this meeting on April 22, could not find her friend Elizabeth, but another friend gave her some detail. According to this reporter, Mr. Towner had occasion to make a long speech on the legal position, and the Board's conclusion was to legitimate Charles' act so far as to allow him to make a trial trip, after which the subject would be discussed again. Mr. Towner and William Hinds wanted a promise in writing, but Mr. Hamilton advised against it "in Charles' present state of excitement." Theodore also made a speech, not exactly justifying Charles' action, remarking that the man who led in a revolt generally had his head cut off, but in this case the result might be an enlargement of the rights of the young folks. He added that his generation of middle-aged men and women had grown up in the Community and were going to stay and enjoy themselves and not be governed by persons who came in later—obviously a dig at Mr. Towner.

Harriet observed that "the battle now seems between the wings, Theodore's party and William's party, and they both like the party of which Mr. Hamilton is head better than they like each other. Theodore also said there were three classes in the Community: the old religious enthusiasts who founded it, the class of younger persons like himself who were not in sympathy with the older class and a third party who had become dissatisfied with the old order and had instituted a new one; which meant that there had been a revolution which annulled the original covenant. Therefore there must be a new covenant which would recognize his class and *fit* it. His class had no *isms*. The present government was in the hands of men discontented with the old, who had run through everything else and failed, so had now fastened themselves upon the Community."

According to Harriet's informant, Theodore would not want his father to come back and thought he never would. He had said to Mr. Hamilton that he, himself, was nothing but brick and mortar in his father's scheme, but he owned his own soul and was going to be free. He had control now of his social relations, his health was good, and he was bound to enjoy himself all he could for the rest of his life. He added that he had got a taste for art—meaning the *Pinafore* organization—and he was not going to be governed by men who could not read a note of music. (The Towner party had been opposed to the excursions of the troupe.)

The committee met again and was glad to dispose of the Charles Burt case for good. The Towner-Hinds party had had all they wanted of Charles' saucy tongue and Theodore's haranguing. The decision was to allow Burt to sell O.C. goods on this experimental trip and consider later whether the arrangement should be continued. Theodore left his aunt with the impression that he and Frank thought they had done all the fighting thus far—that the peace party had left them to take the brunt. He thought there was no hope of unseating William and Mr. Towner and no hope, or at least no object, in resisting his father; that the succession was more hopeless than ever and that his principle now was to *enjoy himself*. Harriet wrote her brother that it reminded her of their sister Joanna: "I remember she took the same attitude once, very much in the same spirit. She thought the Noyeses were hypo-y and morbid and odd, and she broke all out of it and I heard her say she was going to enjoy herself —she was going to be happy."

One report from Wallingford cast a light which was reflected in the future. On April 26, George Miller recommended the adoption of measures for the establishment of a silverplating branch of the Tableware Department, and after some discussion it was voted that the Tableware Board be invited to make and send a careful estimate of the cost of starting the silverplating business on a scale sufficient to do what was necessary to supply their own wants, the estimate to include the cost of a new building, or the cost without a new building but the cost of fitting up one of their old buildings for the purpose. They were also asked to estimate the amount of plating they might do yearly with the profitable profit from same. The Finance Committee reported that on April 1 the books showed a considerable reduction in liabilities as compared with previous months.

On April 18 the committee appointed to consider obtaining special legislation in the matter of holding the Community property reported defects in the title of some of the Wallingford property and recommended that the committee be authorized to remedy such defects by procuring quit-claim deeds. On being advised of this, Mr. Noyes wrote Mr. Hamilton May 14, calling this move "the prelude of the revolution," and said that the statement that he had suggested the idea some years ago was untrue: "I *know* that my prevailing thought has always been that Ward Hunt's plan was good and sufficient and, being the plan of a thoroughly impartial man, was more satisfactory to the Community *as a whole* than anything that we could get up among ourselves; and I do not think I ever said anything to the contrary. I mention this that I may not be held responsible for a move which seems to me specially unwise at the present time."

As though there was not already enough cause of dissension, the matter of the Children's House was brought up again and set off a hot battle. A canvass of all the parents in the O.C. showed that at least twenty-five were "desirous of maintaining good control and discipline in the Children's Department." There were eleven parents and guardians "who hold that the Children's Department have no authority over the children, to discipline them, only as they get it from the parents or the guardians of the child."

As Harriet Skinner reported it on May 6:

It seems as if we must be in the beginning of the end—that this quarrel about the children would break up the Community. There was a strong representation of the Noyesites and but a few Townerites and there was a substantial unanimity, but after the meeting there was a great stir-up. William began by endorsing what was said against the children who were taken out of the Department being allowed to play with outside children and then with ours; said that perhaps the mothers did not know the state of things. Mr. Kelly answered to this that one mother told him she would *seek* playmates for her boy outside. This called up Towner who took up as the attorney for Augusta. Martin made quite a speech—said there never would be peace till both parties were represented in the head of that Department. The conclusion was to refer it all to the Council.

The other inveterate bone of contention—the matter of substitutes for absentee Council members—came up once more. As Mrs. Skinner reported it: "Mr. Hamilton is pushing to have the system of substitutes in the Council abolished. The other side have abused it to keep in Mr. Towner and Augusta the greater part of the time so far. Abby substituted Mrs. J. on account of her nerves and Mrs. J. has a stiff kind of bitterness worse than Abby's. George A. substituted Fred who is a stolid tool of Wm. and Towner, so that the Council is not the Council nominated by Myron and accepted by the family."

The next day, May 8, she wrote: "The Council yesterday arrived at this decision in regard to the question of substitutes, that members, in case of absence, employ some other member present to represent their opinion and vote for them—this arrangement to be good for one month only. Mr. Hamilton supposed that was final, but William, by one of his tricks, had it announced that the question lately before the Council would come before the family tomorrow." On May 10 came the final report:

Yesterday due notice was posted that the decision of the Council about substitutes would come up for the vote of the family. Accordingly, in the evening the reserves of both sides were set in array—more than usually full downstairs and the reserves on both sides up gallery. The decision was read and John Freeman stated the principal reasons for making it—that members appointing their own substitutes was irregular—and that the original Council was appointed with reference to harmony—excluding extremes and objectionable members. It was not until three persons—Augusta, Fred and Mr. Towner, who should, of all others, have been silent if they had the least bit of modesty—

had spoken several times, that anybody opened their mouth on the other side. Then Alfred spoke.

I do not think a member of the Council should get in the way of looking upon his office as one of his personal projects, as it were— one belonging to him and one that he has a personal right to transfer to whom he pleases. He might hold it for a while and sell it to some-one for a valuable consideration. The time has come when we can see that the plan of each member having a substitute does not work well in practice. We supposed that a member would only require a substitute once in a while in case of indisposition or brief absences. But the fact is that some members have dropped out almost entirely and their places have been taken by those who are likely to hold on to the end of the year. An example of the looseness that has come in, a substitute and his principal have been known to sit in Council at the same time.

Finally Mr. T. offered an amendment that no member should be chosen to represent more than one absent person at the same meeting, to which there was no objection. When the question was ready to be put, Fred Marks proposed that we wait till another evening, to give all time to think about it. Then Theodore made his presence known in the gallery. He said notice was given that a *vote* would be taken, which was his reason to be here. He called for a vote. There was ball in his shot—nobody said a word more. The vote was called for and was unanimous for Mr. Hamilton's resolution. The gallery has been a kind of terror to us heretofore—it has given us "the cup of trembling" several times, but it gave that cup to the other side last night.

20

The Towner-Kelly Imbroglio

The matter which Harriet Skinner had feared might be the beginning of the end—the quarrel about the management of the Children's House and the thirty-year-old understanding that the Community, not the parents, was the owner of the children—came up for final decision first in the Council and later in the family meeting.

Under the regime of Mr. Kelly, a number of children had been withdrawn from the Children's House by their parents but, because they liked to play with the other children, voluntarily spent much of their time there. This posed a problem of control, since if they behaved badly those in charge had no authority to deal with them other than to send them away. As Mr. Kelly reported to a parents' meeting, it was a painful fact that these children felt a certain independence and defiance of government and sometimes said things to the children in the department which encouraged insubordination. It was resolved that parents desiring to remove their children from the control of the Children's Department should give a formal written notice of the fact. In the discussion that followed it was pointed out that serious evils would result from the disorganizing government that some of the children were under, and the hope was expressed that those who had previously withdrawn their children from the department would reconsider their move.

On May 17 the Council debated this question and also the wish of some parents that the Children's Department be reorganized. It was voted that the matter be referred once more to the parents, who were asked to indicate their wishes about it.

This was the struggle that Mrs. Skinner had dreaded but, as she wrote on May 19: "We are safe out of another threatening storm. The Children's House matter is settled for a time, at least. In the Council Monday things looked rather blue. Martin spoke against the present organization and against the principle that the Community owned the children. He said that principle went out when marriage came in and ought so to have been understood. The conclusion was to have a parents' meeting next day, expecting that meeting would refer the matter to the Council for decision." Harriet wrote:

> Mr. Hamilton was much pleased with the way the other side's combativeness was wet down. D. Edson and Augusta and Martin and Alice came charged for a melee—and tried to get up one, but it was confined to a corner.
>
> After everything was settled and they were ready to adjourn, Alice vituperated about the principle that the Community owned the children—said it was wrong clear to the bottom and she never would put her children into the department till it was renounced. Finally she said if they were forced to it, she should take the *law* and show what that could do—at this there was a general burst of laughter. "Well," she said, "you may laugh, but I am in earnest." Augusta said unless the rules suited her in every respect she should not put her boy in.

Mr. Kelly's account of the affair was written to Mr. Noyes on May 19, 1880:

> I am out of the Children's House and am a free man. My three months probation were up the middle of this month. Our party were strong enough to keep me in there right along, if we had chosen to do so, but there was so much hard feeling toward the department under the present administration and so many children taken out that I concluded to resign again. I put in my resignation this time on condition that they would put someone in my place that all could agree upon and the parents who had taken their children out should put them back in the department. In the parents' meeting yesterday we left the other side free to nominate their man, our party being prepared to concentrate on ESB if he should be named. Several were named, ESB among the rest. Augusta said she would like him, and William Hinds nominated him. They wanted to put him in as principal father and Mrs. Harriet Ackley as principal mother in Libby Hamilton's place, but we would not consent to that, and William proposed to make all four, ESB, Clarence Bloom, Libby H., and Mrs. H. Ackley, as joint heads of the Children's Department. That seemed to satisfy all, and ESB was unanimously voted in not as head but as joint-head of the department. I feel very happy to get out and don't feel as though we had suffered a defeat.

It is curious that the *O.C. Journal* for May 20 recorded the successors to Mr. Kelly as the three mentioned above except that Mr. E. S. Nash (ESN) was substituted for Edwin S. Burnham (ESB) as one of the four joint heads of the department. It also noted that "as they were elected by the unanimous voice of the meeting, the inference is that those parents who had withdrawn their children from the control and discipline of that department, now intend to place them again under its authority." This may have been a slip of the pen, since Mr. Kelly had definitely mentioned ESB (Edwin Burnham) as having been elected. This would have been a singular choice for the Townerite party, since Edwin S. Burnham was well known as one of the small—and resented—Third party, along with Theodore Noyes and Frank Wayland-Smith, while Mr. Nash was a Townerite. Mr. Kelly had written that Nash was a moderate who "claims to have a high respect for Mr. Noyes and believed in the right of the Community to control the children." He was also acceptable to the Noyesite party.

In the Council meeting on May 25, Mr. Hinds said that he had reflected a good deal on the state of the Community—the disunity which he saw was increasing, and wished there was some way to stop it. He dwelt upon the intolerance of Mr. Noyes's friends, saying that because others thought differently, they became their enemies. It was possible to think differently and yet be good friends. After this, unfortunately, the discussion degenerated into a Donnybrook. Mr. Hinds accused the other side of making offensive remarks. John Freeman said that, aside from the extremists on both sides, the main body was charitable and careful of what they said. William tried to pin him down in regard to Mr. Towner, and John declined to answer. Martin and William said the other side were determined to *crush* them. Theodore denied this. The Townerites declared it was not right to judge such a man as Mr. Towner. Theodore said the right of judging individuals was the fundamental principle of all religious sects; that the Community was founded on that principle. One of the women called that fanaticism. Theodore replied that it was the fanaticism that built up the Community, and in the revolt against it, the Community had been broken up; that when the Towner party had rebelled against Mr. Noyes's right of judgment they broke up the Community; that they were now sliding down an inevitable descent to the level of individualism, and their troubles all came from trying to hold the pieces together. Mr. Campbell spoke of the great body of men and women in the Community who still held to the old faith. Theodore replied that these people tried to hold the other party to that faith but it was perfectly useless—the sooner they all consented to go to pieces, the better. For himself, he said he did not feel this spirit of intolerance, nor did he think as his father's friends did, but he did not feel crushed by them. After this Martin agreed that they had better accept the inevitable, have the fight out and be done with it.

In the end Mr. Hinds offered for consideration a preamble and resolution: "Whereas genuine Communism must be founded on substantial unity of heart and purpose, and whereas everything which endangers our unity endangers the life of our society, therefore be it resolved that it is the first duty of the Council to inquire how the causes of disunity may be removed and harmony promoted among all classes of the Community." There is no record of whether or not this motion was passed.

Harriet Skinner, in a letter to her sister-in-law Harriet Noyes on May 27, was the first to mention a difficulty arising in the Wallingford Community family: "As to W.C., I think myself they need something to wash them up, Myron and George, to their relations to those above them. They have hardly any communication with Mr. Hamilton. Mr. H. has not known what to make of their silence. Please be judicious with this information, but I cannot help thinking Providence will punch into their seclusion and make them see that they are branches and not a tree by themselves."

More officially, the Business Board, on May 28, was taken up with "a warm discussion of the 'whys and wherefores' of the recent neglect of the W.C. authorities to conform to the rule of the Board that no cash expenditures amounting to more than $100 shall be made by any department without first consulting the Finance Committee or getting the necessary appropriation allowed in meeting of the Business Board." It was moved that the Committee appointed the year before be instructed to make a report.

In a letter of the same date, Myron Kinsley wrote to Mr. Noyes: "I want to say that I am just the same as when I saw you last, or more so. My faith is as strong and I believe that good is coming out of all this great shindy. I have tried to keep quiet since I wrote that letter to WAH. I knew that ended my mission as mediator, but I feel just as strong as ever, and when the time comes that I can be of any help to you I shall be there, if it is in the thickest of the coming battle which I feel must come. If I do not write much, do not doubt me, but call for me when I am needed or can help you."

On May 31, George Miller, who had been visiting Mr. Noyes at Niagara, wrote him in a different vein:

> Wallingford is, on account of its unhealthiness, a very expensive station and for that reason is quite obnoxious to the Townerites, so they would not object to selling. According to our present experience, it will be more and more difficult to find people willing to live at Wallingford. If Myron and Mr. Kelly become liable to recurring fits of ague (both are now having it for the first time) I do not know how we can fill their places and I have lost much of my attraction for the locality. Mr. Wallace, our neighbor, sent a note to Myron not more than six weeks ago, asking him what we would take for our entire water power property. We replied then that it was not for sale, but I think they and others would like to buy. If the time is pregnant with business change and new departure, I wonder if it would not pay to summon Myron for a business consultation. He did not seem so fruitful when I came away as he did when he had free communication with you.

Mrs. Skinner presented the situation more dramatically in a letter to George Miller:

> I was not there [at the Business Meeting] but am told that Mr. Towner made a long speech and that Mr. Burnham and Martin boiled over with wrath and indignation at the independent course of Myron and W.C. You know Mr. Towner was overheard to say when the affair first came up, "that we should hoist Myron now." Theodore talked some as he did to you against W.C. keeping one complexion. He thought Myron ought to come here and "take this grind a while." He has thought you had an easy time and wanted to shut out all the strife we had here. As he does not hope to ever get out of this strife, I suppose he does not think it will work well to have W.C. exempted. Chas. Joslyn was quite conservative and Frank spoke for consideration—not coming down with slam-bang censure. No one, I believe, really defended W.C.'s course.

Myron's letter of May 31 to Mr. Noyes seemed unaware of any special problem at Wallingford but treated the whole political situation in the Community:

> I have this thought about the situation which I will express to you and then let it drop. It has been in my mind for weeks and it seems

to me that I must let it out, as I can see no other way to save all that is good in the Community and at the same time separate the bad element.

You know how you and I have talked about TRN, especially when you first left O.C. I still believe as I did then about him. Now quite a number of those that look up to him also think quite well of Mr. Towner, but will follow TRN whichever way he goes. Still, they want Theodore's and Frank's ideas of cooperation or division of the profits to come in with a settlement of this quarrel, and do not want a settlement and will try to prevent one, until this can be brought about. In fact, one of Theodore's staunchest friends told me his party (or Third party, as they call themselves) did not care for a settlement at present because it would certainly in the end bring about what they desired.

As things look to me, with the three parties, it would take a long time to settle this quarrel (if you please to call it such). I believe that God permits it and that good is coming out of it. The question, it seems to me, is how to help God have his way and work with him.

Is it not plain that Townerism is not compatible with a happy home? If this is so, cannot your party and the Third party, represented by TRN, FW-S, and ESB, etc., unite about this? Will God let us go till this is settled? Acting together on any question these two parties will have a large majority, and then when this sliver is extracted, cannot these two parties come together in a frank way and discuss this idea of cooperation peacefully, good-naturedly, and get at the best way for the Community to hold its property, save its home and its businesses and its credit and go on in prosperity? I say with you, as you wrote the family and sent by me once, that you were not afraid to discuss this subject in the Community. But with the Towner party as it is, there is no chance to discuss any subject in a true Community spirit because your ideas will not be allowed by Townerism or the other party. Yours will insist on supporting you for all time, and if you should be taken away, it would make no difference. This shindy must go on until it is decided in the Community which party is strongest—yours or Townerism. God speed the work. I did hope a year ago to save the fight, at least until you could choose the battleground. You have beaten the outside enemy against Towner's wishes, and you will come out victorious in this next battle, I am sure, against his wishes. Is there not a chance to use our allies in this battle, even if we have a treaty to discuss the future policy of the Community afterward? I am ready to support TRN if he can convince you and the Community that his ideas are best for communism and a happy home, but first let us unite in stopping (what is clear to all of us) the influence that is destroying our home.

How this letter was received by Mr. Noyes or what was the exact succession of events at this crucial time cannot be known since two vitally necessary pages of the manuscript are missing. The first page we have following Myron's letter gives what must be the last paragraphs of JHN's letter to the Community advocating the sale of the whole Wallingford property. This letter was evidently sent to Oneida by George Miller who had been visiting at Niagara. The paragraphs are as follows:

> . . . its advantages and invitations. Now, however, we have, for the first time, the opportunity for the sale and reinvestment of Wallingford unencumbered by any counter question of importance. The way is clear, and apparently the sunlight of God's Providence is shining upon it.
> By a happy coincidence, just as the lines of circumstance and inspiration seem leading us to the thought and proposal of this measure, two wise-hearted, conservative representatives of the interests of Oneida and Wallingford—Albert Kinsley and G. N. Miller—happened here and have entered into thorough sympathy with our thoughts in the matter. Trusting that it is an omen of the larger sympathy and magnanimity of the whole Community with the proposition, I submit it to your consideration.
>
> J. H. Noyes

George Miller wrote Mr. Noyes from Oneida on June 2: "I have presented your message to the family, and the ideas contained in it are working. I have not heard one word of dissent. Curiously enough, Towner and wife were at Joppa when I arrived, and William Hinds had arranged to join them that evening, so he did not hear the message, though he hunted assiduously for me up to the time his train left. Meantime, in utter ignorance of it, I was passing freely around the house with the communication in my pocket. William, however, probably sounded the note of alarm at Joppa, for Towner and wife appeared here suddenly this morning. I feel strong and ready to face forty like him."

On June 6 he wrote again to his uncle:

> The consideration of the question of selling Wallingford came up in Business Meeting today, and there was a solid vote in favor of selling it, not a dissenting voice being raised. W. A. Hinds inquired a little cautiously before the vote if the proceeds were to be understood as pledged to any other project, and I promptly replied that they were not. One step at a time; if the manager of the opposition had

any suspicion that the capital was to be transferred to Niagara they would have opposed it and discord would have run higher than ever. As it was, there is perfect harmony on the subject and the fury in regard to Myron is appeased. Theodore made a motion that until there was opportunity to decide about permanent investment, the proceeds of the sale should be invested in government bonds. I seconded the motion and everybody was satisfied. If we have good luck in selling, I have no fears but that your friends will be strong enough to give you what you want (and what is really yours without any question).

I leave for Wallingford tomorrow and hope that you will have occasion to keep up some communication with us there. Myron has been appointed Chief Salesman, and I want he should get an afflatus from you. He can move mountains with that.

In the Council the next day, June 8, this proposal was made a motion and carried. A motion by Mr. Miller proposed a committee of men and women from both Oneida and Wallingford to be in charge of reducing the working force at W.C. to not more than eight persons who should have the care of the business and property there and do all in their power to effect the advantageous sale of same.

During the ensuing week George Miller wrote first to Mr. Noyes and then a series of increasingly nervous letters to Mr. Hamilton, about the situation at Wallingford.

To Mr. Noyes he wrote on June 10: "I found some regrets on the part of only two or three here, and their reasons were purely personal. Myron says he is in favor of it but he has got so immersed in relations with the towns people through his control of the farm and shop that I do not think he is quite so earnest and wide awake about it as I hope he will be. I love him and have great confidence in him when under your control (to which he is very susceptible), but I doubt if it will be healthy for him to have a great development here independent of you, and on the defensive toward O.C."

Four days later he wrote to Mr. Hamilton:

I want to give you my impression of the situation here freely and so must ask you to consider this letter private.

Myron has not been the same man since he lost his active communication with Mr. Noyes that he was before, and it seems to me that instead of being a powerful medium of Mr. Noyes, he is now acting mainly under his own natural impulses. So long as he was in close rapport with Mr. Noyes and under his control I loved to work with him and did not care how much he dominated the family, but if he gets away from Mr. Noyes and undertakes to be a center himself (however great his natural abilities) he will be an offensive and tyrannical leader. One thing why he does not seem to be acting under inspiration is that he is so attached to his great sphere of personal activities here (the Farm and Shop) that he does not take hold heartily of Mr. Noyes's inspiration to sell and is not therefore in that attitude of spirit that will make selling possible. He has proposed several times to get three or four of the Community men to combine with him and agree to buy the place of O.C. Such a scheme would be perfectly impracticable because he could not get anyone to submit themselves to his independent leadership and no one would be willing to live here. Much as I love and admire him, I shall never follow him when he is not controlled by a higher spirit. His tendency toward an independent career shows that he is out of his true sphere which is simply to be an Agent and Medium of one greater than he.

The next day he wrote again to Mr. Hamilton: "It surprised me that Myron should manifest so little interest in Mr. Noyes and affairs at Niagara, when he was so full of it before and it seems as though the umbilical cord between him and Mr. Noyes was broken somewhat. I am glad that John Sears is going to O.C., as he can talk with you about the chain business. Myron will not consent to its being moved anywhere but Niagara and says he does not want it to go until he goes with it. I like this but feel as though the business would remain here indefinitely unless he changes somewhat. It seems to me that the farm is the thing that has seduced him and that now diverts him, but perhaps I am wrong."

A reply from Mr. Hamilton reached Miller at Cozicot from which he answered on June 18:

In regard to pricing the different lots, I have scarcely known what to do for the following reason. I approached Myron on the subject one day but found him full of schemes for buying it himself. I urged the matter somewhat earnestly on the ground that it was Mr. Noyes's proposal, when he became somewhat irritable; said he was not enthusiastic for selling and thought he should decline to act as agent for the sale. This, of course, threw cold water on to the matter and I have not been able to see how to do anything about it since. Please advise me. Myron has such complete control here that unless we can secure his cooperation it will be difficult to do anything. One thing that I hope we shall push for as fast as possible is a business at Niagara. I think if we could loosen up the chain business and get it started to Niagara this fall it would rouse Myron's interest in that direction and be good all around.

By this time, Mr. Hamilton, perplexed and perhaps somewhat alarmed by what he had been told, on June 19 wrote Mr. Pitt who acted as Mr. Noyes's secretary, enclosing George Miller's letters: "From which you can see that Myron is not under a very good control. He seems to have got away from Mr. Noyes somewhat. I have hesitated about calling Mr. Noyes's attention to Myron's state, hoping to see some change in him. On getting George's last letter I felt that I must not let it go any longer, but send the letters at once and you can lay the matter before Mr. Noyes. I have written George and thought some of writing Myron, but could not feel quite clear to do so. I think Mr. Noyes is the one to handle him."

JHN made a soothing reply on June 21:

My impression is that the devil is at work to make a quarrel between George M. and Myron, and that he can be defeated by a little patience and quietness. I do not think that Myron should be pushed and hurried about selling. I am not very anxious to sell and put the capital in U.S. bonds. My idea was to sell and transfer the capital here, and until one can see a fair opening for both parts of this scheme, I think we had better keep quiet and wait on Providence. Myron seems to have his eye on this change when he talks of transferring the chain business to Niagara; but I don't understand what he means by his talk of buying out W.C. If he means division of the Community, I do not see how it can be done without my consent, and he never has said anything to me about it. I hope you will be able to stop the crowding and accusations. A quarrel would be worse than not to sell or almost any other failure. I supposed that Myron was sick with ague and was as anxious to sell out as George or anybody else. If I had known he wanted to hold on there, I would have hesitated to make the proposition [and I thought] that a large part of George's object was accomplished when he wrote back that the stir against Myron was appeased. Is not this present stir a secret work of the old spirit of mischief? Myron's last letter to me was very satisfactory. He took the ground that nothing can be done in the way of moving forward and making a happy family till Towner is put down. That is my opinion exactly. That, too, is George's opinion. Why should they disagree? Can you not blow peace enough among them at W.C. to keep all side by side firm to this purpose and not anxious about selling or not selling or any other property or business movement? My instinct is, as I told George, that the original sliver got in when our side fell in with the proposition to sell our business to Wilcox, and

George and Myron with it. Is not Myron now tempted with the idea of getting away from Towner by going out, instead of fighting him out? If he is, he has not said so to me. I hope he is not, or if he is, that he will confer frankly with me and think differently. George as much as told me that he should fight it out with me, and I believe he will. Our true policy is to hold on and draw together into closer and firmer unity of heart till the unsound parts of the Community rot away.

To George JHN wrote the same day, June 21:

Since hearing about the differences between you and Myron in respect to selling, I recall the thought I had when I got your report of the vote at O.C. It struck me that possibly the Towner party saw a chance in the proposed change of capital to get in a wedge for altering the holding of the property by The Four; and I did not quite enter into your enthusiasm for selling and investing in U.S. bonds. To tell the truth, I would rather not sell without an understanding and clear previous arrangement to reinvest here or somewhere eise on the present basis of ownership.

If this or something like it is what Myron is thinking of in his hesitation, I do not think you ought to push him. My advice is to "move careful" and make sure where the money is going before you convert the real estate at W.C. into money.

I pray that you and Myron may stand shoulder to shoulder in the war with the common foe, as you have done. Please don't report what I have said in this note; but let me hear from you and Myron about it and let us three be agreed about it. Perhaps a little masterly inactivity may be the most prudent thing for the present.

"Masterly inactivity" did not suit Mr. Towner's style. The altercation over the management of the Children's House had barely died down when Mr. Towner took extreme umbrage at a report that Mr. William Kelly had circulated damaging accusations against him, to the effect that he, Mr. Towner, had been collecting evidence against Mr. Noyes of the offenses of incest and rape, and was ready to use such evidence against him whenever occasion offered.

When he accosted Mr. Kelly with having made such statements, Mr. Kelly admitted that he had made the first statement but not the second: "He denied making such statements, saying he had no positive proof of them; that what he had said was that he had heard reports of them and these reports came from so many sources that he thought they were true." Mr. Towner went on to say that reports

of the above character had been more or less rife; that they had
their origin, so far as he could learn, with M. H. Kinsley.

These accusations, as Mr. Towner wrote in a long paper addressed to the Community at large on June 18, were a baseless
fabrication. He declared that he had never collected any evidence
against Mr. Noyes, nor sought any; that he had never put anything
of the sort in writing; that he had never said he was ready with
anything of the kind to be used in criminal proceedings against him
or anybody else. He demanded that a committee of investigation be
appointed with power to summon persons to give evidence.

The inside details, before and after this challenge, were given as
usual by Harriet Skinner two days later:

> Mr. Kelly has undertaken to labor with the *betweens,* unwisely, Mr.
> Hamilton thinks. In a labor with Harriet Worden he asked her what
> made Mr. Towner take down evidence against Mr. Noyes, if he were
> not Mr. Noyes's enemy? She went to Mr. Towner with that accusation
> and he thought, I suppose, there was a fair chance of a lawsuit, which
> is his highest form of enjoyment. He came to Mr. Kelly, took down
> what he said and wrote a long defense and had it read in Council.
> William read it with great gusto and Burnham and Martin and others
> railed and blasphemed—they thought Mr. Towner was *so* abused—
> that there never was a man so innocent and so lied about. He denied
> the fact and made it out that he was the subject of dreadful persecu-
> tion. His friends were for having the paper inflicted on the Evening
> Meeting but Mr. Hamilton resisted that, said Mr. T. could make his
> denial in a few words and not say so many things calculated to stir up
> bad feelings.
>
> Our side said very little, only Theodore. He said that whether Mr.
> Towner had done what Mr. Kelly supposed or not, there certainly
> was some ground for the feeling among Mr. Noyes's friends that
> there was danger of his being accused by persons in the Community.
> He had been told that persons in the Community stood ready to ac-
> cuse him. Martin owned that he had heard something equivalent, but
> from persons that we ought not to mind. He wanted the committee of
> investigation to go into the matter deep, and that there should be a
> guarantee which should make Mr. Noyes's friends feel easy, and
> which made the other party hang their heads. They talked about the
> way we have of saying such a person has a bad spirit—is under a bad
> control, etc., talking about the Towner spirit, etc. Theodore said that
> his father had always claimed to be an inspired leader and to have
> *spiritual insight* and that he had been received as such, and the Com-
> munity had been built up and carried on, on that basis. He did not
> defend it but stated it very forcibly and it aroused an awful fury.

Mr. Burnham said that had been played out, etc. Martin said he had rather have the case go into the courts and have a smash-up than to go on any longer in this quarrel—anything to end it.

Mr. Kelly's written apology was handed to Mr. Towner the next week, on June 25: "I am willing to acknowledge to Mr. Towner that I think I should have taken pains to have made a more thorough examination as to the evidence of these reports before giving them credence or circulation. I am willing to acknowledge my fault in this, and think I can give him assurance that he will not have again similar cause of complaint from me."

This did not satisfy Mr. Towner, who replied on July 5:

> The willingness to acknowledge the fault referred to, that is, believing and circulating evil reports about another without having made sufficient examination as to their truth, is all the amends I desire, so far as that is concerned. He *thinks* he can give me assurance that I will not again have similar cause of complaint. I shall be glad to be assured and am ready to receive in a brotherly spirit any assurance that may be offered. But this is only incidental and circumstantial and has nothing to do with the main question of the origin and truth of the reports stated in my communication of June 19. Reference to that will show that my complaint was not personal to Mr. Kelly merely. I named M. H. Kinsley also and intended to make my complaint general and asked to have the truth or falsehood of the charges made known. They ought to be proved or explicitly disavowed as false by all concerned, so I must still ask the committee as before.

The Minutes of Council for July 6 reported the reading of this correspondence and noted that, after some consultation between Mr. Towner and Mr. Hinds, it was decided that instead of a committee of investigation, the letters should be read to the family in the Evening Meeting. George Campbell commented that this procedure would leave the matter in an unsatisfactory shape, since it reiterated the charges against Myron Kinsley. It was optional, he wrote, when and how Myron replied to Towner's charges: "On the whole I can't but think that the correspondence, instead of vindicating Mr. Towner, will react against him, and that Mr. Kelly's frank acknowledgment will react in his favor."

Harriet reported the occasion:

> The Kelly-Towner correspondence was read in meeting last night. John Freeman remarked that it was understood that it was not to

lead to any discussion, but two or three things were said. William
wanted it to be understood that Mr. T. *coveted investigation.* Charles
said that he was one of Mr. Noyes's friends, but it was justice to Mr.
T. to say that he, Mr. T., had said Mr. Noyes had done nothing
which exposed him to the law. Mrs. Hawley broke in two or three
times and finally got it well out that she had no ill-will to Mr. Towner,
but that some time ago he interviewed her and cross-questioned her
in reference to her experience in Brooklyn and asked her the details
about it. She did not know as he had any bad motive, she did not
accuse him of it, but the devil back of him did have a bad motive
and tried to raise a muss.

The following exchange of letters between William Hinds and
Mrs. Elizabeth Hawley is dated July 8 and 9. Mrs. Hawley may be
remembered as the eccentric and irrepressible young convert who
in 1837 sent Mr. Noyes's famous *"Battle-Axe* Letter" to Theophilus
Gates, publisher of *The Battle-Axe and Weapons of War,* a radical
journal. Gates published it and thereby, perhaps, started John Humphrey Noyes on the course which led to the later formation of the
Putney and then the Oneida Communities. With age Mrs. Hawley
had not grown more repressible.

Mr. Hinds's letter was certainly intended to pacify:

Dear Mrs. Hawley: Please try to recall the "interview" you referred
to last evening and see if you did not name the wrong person. Mr.
Towner says he had no such conversation with you.

I remember we talked that matter over some months ago and presume our conversation is the one you had in mind. I did not suppose
there would be any harm come of it and should not have referred to
it if you had not mentioned something about your past experience
that rather naturally suggested it. But if anyone is to be blamed, pray
don't blame Mr. Towner (who has more than his share of accusation
to bear) nor even "Old Nick," but

Your friend, WAH

Mrs. Hawley was not to be cozened:

Dear Mr. Hinds. Yes, Mr. Towner was the first person who spoke
with me on the subject. I remember the time, place, and the questions
he asked. True, I talked with you, C. A. Burt, and others who called
on me, on the same subject. I said I did not know as Mr. T. had any
object in asking and repeat it now. But from what has transpired
since, its effect on myself, and what is now going on, *plainly the devil*

had an object. Your excessive tenderness of Mr. Towner is super-natural. The bitterness that is going toward Mr. Noyes is super-natural. In working out such a problem as Bible Communism, what if there have been grave mistakes? Is not Mr. Noyes capable of humility? Of rectifying mistakes of his own making? These are ques-tions I ask myself. Surely I have cause to lay up things and cherish bitterness if any have, but I do not, and am grateful for benefits. Hence I recognize the supernatural in the warfare now pending, the tenderness of some toward Mr. Towner and their bitterness toward Mr. N. I, for one, have no ill-will toward Mr. Towner; yet I think he has undertaken a big job and should have counted the cost before setting himself to work to destroy Mr. N.'s influence. Now to my mind, this is going too far. I do not think Mr. Towner has any apprehen-sion of Mr. Noyes's work of life. I have not written this from any ill-will but in pure friendship, as the kindest thing I can say. Yours in friendship bound,

E. G. Hawley

There is no record whether or not Mr. Towner ever saw this correspondence, but it would appear that his mind was not at rest on the subject, for he wrote again to Mr. Kelly, requesting copies of any letters he might have which "compromised" him as a mem-ber of the Community. Mr. Kelly replied briefly that he possessed no such papers nor did he know where they were to be found. Mr. Kelly reported this to Mr. Hamilton: "He still feels uneasy—doesn't seem to feel that his case is entirely cleared up yet. I presume this late experience will teach me to be pretty careful how I give him advantage again. But I don't know as anything else would have re-vealed to me the real diabolical nature of his hatred of Mr. Noyes. I got a little taste of it."

Having been brought specifically into the controversy by Mr. Towner, Myron Kinsley made his reply to George Campbell on June 24, 1880:

Mr. Towner has never told me very much what he intended to do or how he felt, but he has told me that Mr. Noyes's course was damnable and outrageous—this with his own lips. I told W. A. Hinds some time ago that this was the worst thing I had heard Mr. Towner say, but I had heard that he had said other things. There is no use of Mr. Towner's trying to dodge the question in regard to Mr. Noyes. I have been told by some of his followers or by his best friends in person to me (and not through Russian scandal, either) I mean in earnest talk about the future of the Community when I was trying to see what could be done to conciliate the two parties when I was acting as mediator, that persons in the Community would go before the proper persons as witnesses against Mr. Noyes and that Mr. Towner had said there was no doubt but what he could be arrested. I was told by one of Mr. Towner's best friends and one that was in daily communication with him that if it became necessary they would go themselves as witnesses and gave me to understand that they had consulted Mr. Towner about it. I have not told all this to any one yet; not even Mr. Noyes, and did all I could last summer to have the family feel good to him, and as I was acting as mediator, I did not think it best or right to tell all that was said to me by either party, or to call names, nor have I now, nor shall I until I think it best. Mr. T. has commenced by calling me into it thus far. That is all I have to say at present.   Myron.

In a letter to Mr. Noyes on June 24, mainly reporting that he had been unable thus far to sell the Wallingford property, Myron mentioned the Towner letter: "I may be summoned to Oneida as witness in the case of communism vs. Townerism. I do not fear the verdict of the trial if it is before the whole Community as it ought to be."

George Miller also wrote to Mr. Noyes on June 24:

Yours of the 21st confirms the fear I had that you would not like the proposal to sell W.C. unless the money could be pledged to Niagara. But I found that not only the Townerites but Theodore and Frank were shy about making any such pledge and it appeared that to burden the plan with any such condition would kill it at the outset. It seemed to me at the time that it was a good point to secure unanimity and to appease the special fury just then raging against Myron and which, if not diverted, must have ended in his deposition and the occupation of Wallingford by Townerites. Indeed Mr. Towner hinted to me that he could find men to fill the places here and named J. N. Norton as one of them. Theodore also was much inflamed against what he called Myron's independent course of action and said publicly that he "ought to come to O.C. and be put through the mill."

At this time, June 21, Mr. Noyes wrote to Myron, not mentioning the Towner affair but reassuring him about the sale of Wallingford:

As you are the agent appointed to sell the W.C. property, I will say to you what I thought at the time I received George's report of the vote at O.C. The easy way the Townerites took the proposition to sell struck me as suspicious. At the same time they entirely ignored the principal part of my message which proposed the reinvestment of the W.C. capital at Niagara. Putting these things together I thought there was reason to suspect that they were moving for some purpose connected with their old project of changing ownership.

I see no good reason to sell without a clear previous arrangement to invest the proceeds in land and business for a new Community. I am not willing to put the capital into government bonds to be controlled by Towner and "town meetings." Please let me know your mind about this, and in the meantime keep the business in your own hands and "move careful."

He also sent word in a note by Mr. Pitt: "Mr. Noyes says however it may be with his friends at O.C., he is not one who believes in trying to make things worse in the Community in order to force a division and get rid of the malcontents. He does not believe in that policy and never has had any sympathy with it. On the contrary, he believes in working for good order and *the things that make for peace:* and he will work heartily, even with his enemies, to secure these things."

This note, Mrs. Skinner reported to JHN on June 25, pleased the opposition party very much, especially Mr. Burnham: "There was a great change in their spiritual state. What the operation was, I don't exactly know, but the social relations between the two parties are very much improved. I suppose in some way there was a loosening up of the evil power and then this wonderful Providence of that note slinging in peace."

The "wonderful Providence" may have been something like remorse, since the meeting that morning had been extraordinarily violent. As Mrs. Skinner described it: "Theodore ran out in the midst of it and rallied Augusta and Arthur and twenty more perhaps of that set and they hissed from the gallery and said ugly things. Arthur showed he was ready to lead a mob; he kept calling out, 'This shall go in the papers!' " Two men of the less radical wing of the Townerites, having been shown Mr. Noyes's note by Mr. Hamilton, were "thoroughly frightened by the element which was raised in that meeting. The conservatives of that party were as much distressed as we were. They told Mr. H. they could not control the bad spirits. Mr. Hamilton told me it was like this: we were living in a glass palace but the Townerites in a shanty, and they had nothing to lose in a fight with stones, and we had, and we must not go into a fight with them with their own weapons, and voting was one of their weapons."

This seemed miraculous enough but it may be that the real quietus was made by a resolution offered by Mr. Hinds on June 25, "for consideration at some future time":

> Whereas the differences heretofore existing in the Community have been increased rather than diminished for the past few months, and there is little prospect of securing upon our present basis the internal harmony essential to the peace and prosperity of the Community; and whereas it is imperative for the sake of our aged members, our invalids, our children, and all classes who might be thrown upon the world without adequate means of support, that at least our productive businesses should be effectively prosecuted—
>
> Therefore, resolved that the Council recommend to the Community the appointment of a commission consisting of two representatives of the three principal parties of the Community, selected by the parties themselves (Mr. Noyes to be a member of the Commission and to serve personally or by proxy, as he may choose), to consider and report what changes, if any, in our present arrangement are, in their judgment, necessary to enable us to continue our communal organization in peace and good order and with a reasonable prospect of prosperity; or, if this is seen to be impracticable, then to further consider and report upon what basis, other than communism, our relations as a business organization can, in their judgment, be best conducted.

There was no immediate report of how this document was received by the Council, or whether it was at this time divulged to the Community family. In the Council on Monday there was a slight tilt between Mr. Burnham and Theodore in which Mr. Burnham reminded the members that Theodore had used the expression *Holy Horror* in describing certain of Mr. Burnham's pious utterances. This, he thought, was scoffing at religion. Theodore remained unregenerate. Mrs. Skinner made only a brief reference to the most important matter on June 29: "I was quite surprised at William's resolution. I should think John ought to see it."

21

The Commission Meets

The Administrative Council meeting on July 2, 1880, was reported by Mrs. Skinner to Mr. Hamilton, who was visiting Mr. Noyes at Niagara:

> Theodore introduced the subject of our financial prospects; he thought we were drifting toward bankruptcy—that we must do something soon or the Community would have to break up. His remedy was to make a rule that every able-bodied person should work for the Community four hours a day and have wages for what they did more. He spoke of the children—the school of wastefulness and idleness they would come into when they left the Children's House; was astonished to see their ignorance of the value of money and time. Martin was in favor of Theodore's plan, if they could no better; we couldn't fold our hands much longer. William and Mr. Burnham opposed Theodore's plan; thought it would make an end of communism. William asked if Mr. Noyes knew about the state of things here and if his own late resolution had been reported to him. He said Mr. Noyes was a wise man and had had great experience and he hoped he would have some advice to give. It is evident that William depends on Mr. Noyes after all, to save the Community.
>
> William's resolution was referred to in the Council and it was thought it should take precedence of Theodore's in the discussion.

It was understandable that Harriet should close wistfully. "It has been a hard day here for me spiritually."

Not all of Theodore's friends—nor his father's—agreed with his proposal. Alfred Barron wrote Mr. Hamilton on July 5 that he did not want to pay a cent of wages to Community people but was willing to sink $100,000 in the work of "rotting off the parasite element." He had a plan of his own which involved the framing of a new covenant for all the young people to sign as they became of age, binding them to industry and obedience if they wished to stay in the Community, although he admitted that it would be a painful thing to require a son or daughter to step up and sign such a thing—

or to secede. George Campbell wrote that he would not be willing to assent to such a scheme unless Father Noyes advocated it and he, too, questioned the effect of such an innovation upon the Community covenant. Mr. Kellogg had not been present when Dr. Noyes's scheme was presented but judged from what he heard that the discussion got quite warm and eloquent, but he was personally against it. Mr. Freeman voiced no opinion but wrote Mr. Hamilton that Theodore had no idea that his proposal would be passed but merely wanted to "keep things stirred up." If that was his intention, he evidently succeeded. The motion was not passed, but people talked.

In the next Business Board meeting, July 4, Mr. Hinds started another hare. Why had the committee on terms and sale of the Wallingford property taken no action? The minutes of that meeting recorded that "some remarks were made upon the delay in its action, its cause, and occasion, during which it was stated that some of the committee and some of the family at W.C. were not in favor of selling, while some were, and it was thought that this division of feeling hindered the action."

On this same day Myron Kinsley wrote to Mr. Noyes on the same subject: "I have been approached several times by Mr. Wallace with a view of buying us out and starting a rolling mill here with our water-power. Mr. Wilcox of Meriden Britannia Co. also has spoken to me about it and I would like your mind about it before I say anything to O.C. about it. Suppose that we offer our Shop, Power and Farm for $175,000, they to pay us $100,000 cash and we to take $75,000 stock in the rolling mill. It would give us a chance to put some money into a Community at the Falls and a business there, too." His idea was to move the chain business to the American side of the river which would save both tariff and freight costs: "I look at the chain business as my business to a great extent and I would like to give up the spoon business."

At the next meeting of the Business Board a week later, Myron had apparently changed his mind:

As at the previous meeting of the Board E. S. Burnham and M. H. Kinsley were named as not being in favor of selling the W.C. property, that statement was denied, by the former in a note and by the latter orally, he being present. From the committee on sale, M. H. Kinsley reported that nothing definite had yet been done as to fixing prices on the property; that he had been waiting action on the part of those of the committee here; that he had told some persons who might buy that our property was for sale; that he thought it could not be sold in one lot. Some discussion followed of an informal nature, principally on the point as to selling the business and going out of it, or transferring it elsewhere. That evening the selling committee met and in unanimous agreement recommended to the Business Board the following proposition:

"Resolved, 1st. That we recommend to the Community to move the Spoon business to Niagara Falls as soon as cash for the purpose can be obtained from the $100,000 capital now in the business, or from the sale of real estate at Wallingford not included in the Spoon Business—not including Cozicot." Four other recommendations regarding this transfer were cited, and that evening, in place of the usual family meeting, the hour was devoted to considering this proposition. It had a mixed reception.

All seemed convinced of the great desirability of securing the Niagara power, looking simply at it in its financial aspects, but viewing it politically, some stoutly opposed it. Dr. Noyes explained that financially considered, he voted for it, but still, he should oppose the measure until the politics of the family were in a more harmonious condition. So with M. E. Kinsley, W. A. Hinds, and others. Mr. Hinds emphasized as objectionable the fact that the Niagara location was in the vicinity of the "grand King Bee," though he decidedly favored it, looking at it financially.

The account of this meeting, as reported in the *O.C. Journal,* did not please Mr. Hinds who concluded that "the Journalist failed to get his idea and, on invitation, furnished the following correction, so far as allusion to himself is concerned. 'What I consider objectionable is the establishment of another Community under conditions that would induce rapid growth by selecting material from the O.C.; thereby rendering her less able than now to cope with her increasing difficulties; and I named among these conditions a flourishing and profitable business, a specially healthy climate and the attractions of the grand King Bee; not as objectionable in any sense except as they would necessarily contribute to the growth of the new institution at the expense of O.C. in members that it is doubtful whether she can spare and live?"

Mrs. Skinner gave her account of the occasion:

Theodore was the best advocate of the Niagara plan, so far as its financial aspect is concerned. Mr. Towner spoke bitterly (and it was the only bitter speech made) about a new plan being sprung on us before the first one was carried out. Theodore's idea is, after making up our minds that it is desirable to go on with this enterprise, to make it conditional on a change of our political basis. It was amusing to hear William talk about the danger of a settlement so near the King Bee—as it would draw off all his friends—that is, the most enterprising and best part of the Community, leaving a very unsatisfactory family behind. He did not try to conceal that he knew that Mr. N.'s friends were the salt and backbone of the Community. What a piece of John's luck this is. I should think everybody would see it and jump into the boat.

Arising from a seemingly small and unimportant difficulty at Oneida—the fact that a number of the young men had for the past year been buying horses in defiance of the Community's rule forbidding individual ownership—the large and fundamental matter of the legal ownership of the Community itself came into question.

Some ten years before, when a seceding member attempted a form of extortion from the Community, Noyes and the Central Members realized that they needed legal protection against this kind of attack. In this quandary they applied to a Utica attorney who changed their original constitution and substituted a "Constitution of the Four" by which, as explained earlier, all Community property was transferred to a committee of four "property owners." Although it was well understood that all members really had equal ownership of the Community assets, this appointment of the Four served to defend the Community from blackmail and extortion.

At a meeting of the committee on legal liabilities on June 22 it was recommended that in order to protect itself from the possible extravagances of the young men, the Community should publish a notice refusing responsibility for unauthorized purchases made by individuals claiming to be members. This motion was not pressed since it was thought that it might affect the credit of the Community unfavorably. Instead they passed a resolution condemning "the private ownership of horses and other such outside property."

However, as Mr. Pitt wrote to Mr. Woolworth: "The prominence which this matter has assumed and its intrinsic importance to the business welfare and character of the Community has led Mr. Noyes to think that the Four, who *legally* own all the real and personal property of the Community and who are responsible for its debts and business reputation, ought to take some definite and decided action to protect themselves and the real Community from such disorderly and irresponsible individual action, to protect the credit of the Community abroad and to save it from perhaps ultimate bankruptcy."

Mr. Noyes's solution, outlined in a letter of June 22 to Mr. Hamilton, suggested that, for the safety of the Community credit, the Four, as the legal owners of the Oneida Community, give public notice over their signatures that they would not be responsible for the debts and contracts of individual members of the Community made without consultation and without written authority from the Community Four. This notice should state explicitly that from the time of its issue all previous authorizations to individuals to do business for the Community—to buy or sell or make contracts or incur obligations of any sort—were *withdrawn* and only those who had new and written authorization, signed by the Four, would be recognized as Community agents.

Since the other three members of the Four were in favor of this action, Mr. Woolworth, who was then in California, was asked to send his power of attorney authorizing the others to sign his name to such a notice, "to be used whenever an emergency should occur which seriously demands such action." From Oneida Mr. Hamilton wrote immediately that in his opinion, at the *present time,* a majority of the Community would choose to have their interests in the hands of the Four, and he thought that feeling would increase. Alfred Barron wrote that he liked the idea:

I have always supposed that we made a deposit of reserved power in the Four for some such emergency as this and that that deposit of sovereign power was sufficient to save our home and business. When we come to it, I want to see the Four exercise its proper legal power in some sovereign act; that is, do it right in the teeth of the democratic assumption that the Business Board is sovereign in all matters pertaining to business. The fight will be on the point whether there *is* any sovereign power in "the Four" which the whole Community is bound to respect. Towner and his crowd are trying, it seems to me, to hold the terrors of the law over us. I have had it in my heart all the time that something would yet come from Mr. Noyes to extricate us from our disagreeable situation and his plan looks like the true thing.

Before any action was taken on this proposition, on July 13 the Council took up Mr. Hinds's resolution of June 25, and after considerable discussion it was agreed that "the following persons be suggested to Mr. Noyes and Mr. Hamilton, as the commission provided for in the resolution, with the understanding that they were to be free to propose any changes or additions to it, viz.: Messrs. J. H. Noyes, E. H. Hamilton, M. H. Kinsley, T. R. Noyes, M. E. Kinsley, W. A. Hinds and H. W. Burnham."

On July 16 the Council again discussed the matter of the commission and heard a message from Mr. Noyes saying that he would prefer not to serve on the commission on account of his health—difficulty of hearing etc.—but that he had many thoughts on the situation which he would present at the proper time. Mr. Hamilton also wished to be excused on account of his health and at the suggestion of the two men, Mr. Albert Kinsley and Otis Kellogg were to be named in their places.

The Business Board's debate on July 14 over the sale of the Wallingford property and the removal of the spoon business to Niagara had been effectually blocked by Martin's amendment that no such removal or investment could be made until existing difficulties in the Community were removed, and another amendment by Myron that the project be abandoned for the present and the committee be discharged. No vote was taken. After these maneuvers the Townerites reckoned Martin as one with Theodore and the Third party, and Mr. Burnham objected to his being a member of the commission as giving too much weight to that party. Thereupon Martin said frankly that he objected to having Mr. Burnham a member because he held on to old ideas and things which had passed away and could never be restored.

The membership of the commission hung fire for several meetings. Mr. Towner objected to Myron Kinsley on the ground that it would save expense to have someone else take his place who would live at Oneida. He also was in favor of having the question of who should constitute the Commission referred back to the Administrative Council for decision, and in addition to this, complained that the original terms of the resolution had not been carried out in respect to the selection of members, according to which the three parties were to select their own members. Harriet Skinner commented that "this was probably his own fear instead of William's —with a view to his own membership. William saw at once that that would not go and did not push it—though he said that personally he should like to have Mr. Towner on, but supposed it would do no good to propose it."

On July 18 the resolution on the commission was considered by the family in Evening Meeting and adopted, with the addition of Frank Wayland-Smith as a member. The commission held its first meeting that afternoon, all members present except M. H. Kinsley. The commission was organized by the selection of T. R. Noyes as chairman and W. A. Hinds as secretary. The *O.C. Journal,* July 18, 1880, recorded that "it was voted to invite all persons to freely express their ideas to the commission on such subjects as properly came before it," preferably in writing or, for such as desired to appear before them, of making short addresses of not more than fifteen minutes. The next meeting of the commission was to take place three weeks from that day. T. R. Noyes was asked to invite his father to communicate any thoughts and suggestions which occurred to him respecting the subjects before the commission.

The preamble to the original resolution had undergone some changes:

Whereas great differences exist in the Community and many think there is little prospect of securing upon our present basis the internal harmony essential to the peace and prosperity of the Community; and whereas the continuance of the existing condition of things will seriously imperil the financial condition of the Community: and whereas it is imperative for the sake of our aged members, our invalids, our children, and all classes who might be thrown upon the world without adequate means of support, that at least our productive businesses should be efficiently prosecuted:

Therefore resolved that the Council recommend to the Community the appointment of a commission consisting of Albert Kinsley, Geo. Campbell, W. A. Hinds, T. R. Noyes, M. H. Kinsley, M. E. Kinsley, F. Wayland-Smith, and H. W. Burnham to consider and report what changes, if any, in our present arrangement are in their judgment necessary to enable us to continue our communal organization in peace and good order and with a reasonable prospect of perpetuity. Or, if, in their opinion, this is impractical, then to further consider and report upon what basis other than communism our relations as a business organization can, in their judgment, be best conducted.

It was mentioned in the meeting this evening as very desirable that matters to be discussed by this Commission should not be a subject of gossip in the diningroom or talked about in any way in presence of nonmembers of the Community.

The commission project was accepted by the family in meeting the next evening, but it would have been too much to expect that Mr. Towner would miss a chance to object. There were three Kinsleys on the commission; it would be better to have some other of the old families represented, especially since it was uncertain whether Myron could come to the meetings. This was immediately understood by the Noyesites as an attempt to get rid of Myron, who was Mr. Towner's *bête noir,* and a possible chance for himself to be nominated. George Campbell, who reported this affair, wrote that they insisted on their program and Mr. Towner had to withdraw. He also said that in case Myron or Mr. Albert Kinsley, who was old and deaf, could not be counted on, Alfred Barron would do in their place. He also reported that he had concluded that the "true inwardness of the commission business was another attempt—by the Townerites—to change the property tenure."

This referred to an encounter of some months back between Mr. Towner and the young lawyers of the Community in the matter of a new deed drawn up and recommended by Mr. Towner relating to the Wallingford property. Frank Wayland-Smith wrote Mr. Noyes that in this new instrument Mr. Towner had inserted words which would create a trust estate instead of the previous tenure of the Four. Although it had been tacitly understood by the members of the Community that the property had been held in trust for them, this trust had never been expressed, and its expression in Towner's new deed would alter the tenure of the property. Charles Joslyn confronted Mr. Towner with this opinion who said flatly that he wanted the trust expressed. Charles disagreed and assumed the business himself, dismissing Mr. Towner from further responsibility in the matter.

It was known that both Mr. Hinds and Mr. Towner had urged that an entry be made in the Property Register to the effect that the whole of the Community property was given for communism and would belong to those who remained in communism even if they were a small minority; this to be signed by the Four as an acknowledgment. A committee was appointed to investigate this suggestion but did not pass it. Later a committee, possibly this same one, was appointed to investigate the expediency of getting special legislation in respect to the Community's method of holding property. Mr. Noyes was understandably disturbed by this and expostulated: "It is, in my opinion, a very unfair thing that, in a Community divided into two parties, a man who belongs to one party, and is even the leader of it, should be the working lawyer of both parties and have the making and changing of the legal papers of the Community in his hands."

Four months later, on May 4, 1880, in response to an inquiry from Mr. Hamilton, Mr. Noyes wrote:

I see that the prelude of the revolution, creating a committee for investigating the expediency of getting special legislation in respect to our method of holding property as you report it, say that *I suggested the idea some years ago.* I do not think this is true. I *know* that my prevailing thought has always been that Ward Hunt's plan was good and sufficient, and being the plan of a thoroughly impartial man, was more satisfactory to the Community *as a whole* than anything that we could get up among ourselves; and I do not think I have ever said anything to the contrary. I mention this to you for the benefit of whom it may concern and that I may not be held responsible for a move which seems to me specially unwise at the present time.

Mr. Hamilton was relieved by this disclaimer: "I am glad that you could deny the report that you had favored the plan of getting special legislation on our method of holding property. I did not remember that you ever had. Mr. Kinsley said he did not believe the report when he first heard it. Mr. Kinsley and CSJ both say they do not think anything farther will be done in the matter. That Mr. Towner had said that he did not see that any change could be made. But Towner is not to be trusted. I hear reports of his party not being satisfied with the present covenant, or something of the kind. That is a matter, however, that they cannot change."

The newly appointed commission met for the first time on July 18, elected Dr. Noyes for chairman and William A. Hinds for secretary, and adjourned until August 8.

Whether Mr. Hinds's Resolution of June 25, 1880, which gave rise to the commission eventuating the dissolution of the Oneida Community six months later, was solely his inspiration, or whether it was a combined effort of Mr. Hinds and Mr. Towner, cannot be determined. No letters or diaries by either man for this period are known to be extant. Both men had opposed the investment at Niagara until some satisfactory settlement of the political differences at Oneida was made. Mr. Towner had lodged a vociferous protest against what he claimed were slanderous attacks by certain members of the other party. Mr. Hinds had said, in the Administrative Council of June 25, that he had lost all hope of their ever achieving agreement under this present government. His resolution proposing the appointment of a commission was made and laid on the table until July 13.

Frank Wayland-Smith recorded its next appearance:

Martin Kinsley was on the commission as a representative of the "Third party," whereas he belonged to the Hinds-Towner party. I objected to this arrangement when the matter was presented to the Community in Evening Meeting, July 17, and Dr. Noyes stoutly supported my view. He also nominated me as a member of the commission. Thus amended the commission stood: Church party—Albert Kinsley, George Campbell, M. H. Kinsley; Hinds-Towner party—W. A. Hinds, H. W. Burnham, Martin E. Kinsley; Third party—Dr. Theo. R. Noyes, F. Wayland-Smith.

This commission was approved by the Committee July 17 and had its first meeting July 18, at 3 P.M. in the Council Room. The commission met for the second time August 5 instead of August 8, as first intended, as there was a decided feeling in the Community that it should act promptly.

In this second meeting we all spoke on the difficulties and dangers of the present situation. The principal of these are:

1. *In regard to leadership and government.* We have now no government worthy of the name. The Council is a failure. The young people do just as they like.

2. *We have now no religious unity,* which is the cornerstone of communistic success. The Community was founded on a belief in Mr. Noyes's practical inspiration. Now, not more than one-half the people

believe in that. The others have lost their confidence in him to a degree that destroys his control of affairs.

3. *Our business credit is threatened by our divisions and internal dissensions.* Our businesses are so expanded that we have been obliged to borrow about $60,000 of the banks, besides some $30,000 of "deposit loans" from our neighbors and work people. If these loans should be called in it would pinch us badly. We would be obliged to mortgage or sell our real estate.

4. *Our own members are, many of them, no longer industrious.* They see no object in toiling while the earnings and profits are controlled by others, they getting merely a comfortable living.

5. *We are no longer so economical as formerly* and the present government is powerless to prevent waste and extravagance.

6. *The young people are no longer under proper control.* They are nominally under the authority of the Youth's Committee, a body of their own choosing, and they do just as they please. Some of the young men have begun to smoke, drink, and swear, and the children will soon catch the habits from them.

At the second meeting of the commission, these were the difficulties which, we were all agreed, rendered it practically impossible for us to remain in our present situation. Some changes must be made. What shall they be? At subsequent meetings of the commission various plans were proposed and discussed.

The official "Report of the Commission" was as follows:

The next question in order was whether anyone had a plan which promised to bring the Community as a body back to the conditions of the past, and at the same time remove the present difficulties. No plan was offered, and no one saw any present probability of a return of the whole Community to their former status.

Opportunity was then given for the presentation of modified Communism. Two plans under this head were offered: The first mentioned was by Wm. A. Hinds, which, however, he did not present as wholly his own. It proposed to keep the present accumulated property intact, carry it on together as at present, but allow wages to such as preferred to work for wages, they being paid only for what they chose to labor more than a fair proportion of hours; at the end of the year, after deducting from the Community income all common expenses, all wages to members and a certain agreed sum to reduce our debt, to divide the remainder equally amongst the adult members.

It was urged against this plan that it did not remove some of the greatest difficulties the Community was now facing and suggested no means whereby the different parties could separate if they wanted to.

The second plan of modified communism was presented by Mr. Albert Kinsley. It proposed to divide the Community into two classes —the class of pure Communists who should hold the property and manage the businesses and government of the Community, assuming all responsibility for the payment of its debts and guaranteeing to both classes a permanent home and support, the second class to enjoy all the common benefits of the society but to receive wages and have no vote in the management of affairs. It further proposed to pay all members who might choose to withdraw from the Community a liberal sum.

The plan was pronounced liberal but met with serious objections; it was feared that the introduction of class distinctions among those who had previously lived on an equality would prove an endless cause of evil-speaking and contention.

Mr. Burnham offered not a plan but rather a suggestion by which he believed it possible to reach a state of agreement. This suggestion was to revive Bible Communism in the Community by inviting the services of some outside reputable Evangelist who should turn their hearts to the spirit of the Bible—and there leave them.

The last plan offered was that for resolving the Community into a cooperative or joint-stock company; this sponsored by Dr. Noyes and F. Wayland-Smith. The latter described it thus: "This plan did not meet with much favor because both the large parties in the O.C. are afraid to declare in favor of anything anti-Communistic. They meant to keep their records all right."

After we had discussed and argued four hours a day for several days without coming to any agreement, it was proposed that Myron Kinsley and I should go to Niagara Falls to report to Mr. Noyes and ask him for his plan of settlement. Mr. Noyes was at first not inclined to go into the matter but after a little urging, he consented to hear what we had to say. Then I laid before him all the principal difficulties of our situation and the plans proposed to remedy them. After this talk, Mr. Noyes retired to his room and went to work on the subject. The next morning [August 10, 1880] he produced the following paper:

"To The Community"

"Your commission, after some discussion of opinion and plans among themselves, sent to me for an expression of my views. I respond briefly and frankly, as follows:

"My theory that Communism, in order to be successful, must have for its basis a sincere religious faith, is well known to you all. The history of the Community to which I have given the labor of my life, is an embodiment of that theory.

"It is hardly necessary to say that I still believe in this theory and no other. After thus making my own record clear, without urging or expecting its acceptance, I now proceed to give my views of what seems to me to be the proper practical course for the Community to take in the present attempt to reach a harmonious settlement of our difficulties. My scheme is one which Myron and Frank have received with approval and even enthusiasm, and this encourages me to present it to the commission and to the Community. They say it is entirely new.

"I assume that we all earnestly wish to settle with each other peaceably—that we hate lawsuits as we hate war—that we are ambitious to set an example which is perhaps unprecedented, viz., that of a Community breaking up without rapine or injustice or mutual abuse of any kind.

"I think we can do this by simply putting our affairs into the hands of an *outside arbitration*. Hitherto we have always found when differences of opinion divided us into parties, that after a long debate, the only way to come to any practical conclusion was to choose an arbiter, that is, to call in the one-man power *pro tem,* and this is so because it is comparatively easy to be unanimous in choosing an arbiter when it is utterly impossible to attain unanimity by jangling.

"In disputes hitherto the Community has found arbiters within itself. In the present greater emergency, all the possible arbiters within our own body belong to one or another of the various parties in the conflict of opinion. Hence the necessity now for seeking arbitration outside. I propose that the present commission, instead of wasting time in discussing various plans of its own members, should go into the world around us and find a man or, if it is preferred, *three men* of probity and skill, to whom it can safely intrust the settlement of our affairs. I would have the business conducted as far as possible in a confidential manner. I would have the arbiters well paid for their services and free to take any length of time that they find necessary. Above all, I would have every member of the Community sign an agreement beforehand, to abide by the decision of the arbiters, without appeal. This should be done the next thing after an agreement to adopt the plan of arbitration.

"In order to make the settlement complete and final, the subjects intrusted to the arbitration should be the question of the change of tenure, of joint stock, of communism new and old, of wages and how to apportion them, of account-keeping with individuals, and of all the other financial questions about which we are now wrangling. In a word, I propose to let in upon our present business-status the eye of an impartial tribunal, and I am ready to abide by its decisions as to what we ought to do.

"In the interest of peace and decency, I think the matter presented to the arbiters should be strictly connected with our present business status, and that all going back to the social relations which have passed away should be avoided.

"I wish this presentation of my scheme to be regarded as only an outline which I hope the commission will be able to fill up without much debate among themselves or in the Community. One great blessing which I hope for in this disposal of the matter is relief for myself and for the body of the Community. Yes, immediate relief from further doubt, anxiety or responsibility. It seems to me that a single vote now may end the trouble for all of us, at least until the decision is rendered; and afterward, if we take the decision peaceably, as coming from God.

"J. H. Noyes"

This proposal was generally approved by the commission, all but one member voting for it. But while they were working out the questions to be asked of the arbiters, Mr. Hinds asked leave to present a new plan, which was to have the Community set off to himself, Martin Kinsley, and as many others as agreed to the plan, the hardware business at Willow Place. Under this plan, the new group were to organize as a joint-stock company of, as Hinds calculated, from sixty to a hundred persons, former Community members.

At the next commission meeting Mr. Hinds presented a list of followers he estimated as one-fourth of the Community, counting in children and invalids. In the discussion that followed it was discovered that the hardware business which he wished to take over had brought in during the past six years more than all the other businesses put together; therefore if they acceded to Mr. Hinds's plan, they would be giving one-half the productive business to one-fourth of the members, or double their fair share. The plan, naturally, was not accepted.

At this point, August 15, having rejected all previous suggestions, the commission returned to a more favorable consideration of the joint-stock plan and decided to send Myron once more to consult with Mr. Noyes.

On the evening of August 18 Myron journeyed once again to Niagara with a paper containing "T. R. Noyes's, F. Wayland-Smith's, and C. S. Joslyn's plan of settling our difficulties, with the claim of M. H. Kinsley for the Niagara family, written out for Mr. Noyes by M. H. Kinsley *as he understands them":*

1. Divide all our property at O.C., W.C., Cozicot, and Joppa, including in fact all property into shares of preferred stock, and leave it out to arbiters (if we cannot agree ourselves) how this property can or shall be divided.

2. Shall it be divided equally among members? Shall such persons as Homer Smith and Arthur Towner (who have been here but a short time) have as much as Otis Kellogg and G. D. Allen who have been here and worked all their lives for the Community and helped accumulate the property? And shall those who put their all in (perhaps thousands of dollars) leaving their homes of comfort and casting it all in for a Community home, and a Community religion as taught by Mr. Noyes, who still believe as they did then, and still wish to have it devoted to communism (which clearly no one not in the Community helped to accumulate) is this to be taken out and devoted to other purposes against their wishes? Or are they to have a chance to take it out and say how it shall be used, and then divide the remaining property?

3. Not divide up our businesses to this and that party, but keep them together, make the most of them, move the W.C. property to Niagara as fast as it can well be done.

4. Choose each (by a majority of votes of all the shareholders, each share having one vote) a president, vice-president, treasurer, secretary, and from six to twelve directors (as is thought best) who shall carry on the businesses in the very best manner, other members of the family having no power to interfere with them during their term of office. This would do away with the Business Board, Financial Committee, Council, and the Legal Committee. The president and other officers having charge of all outgoes and incomes on the preferred stock and no other stock (except it is returned to the businesses of the cooperation company).

5. At the end of each year the non-preferred stock or the profit of all the businesses (after paying the expenses of the businesses and seeing that the old and young are cared for) to be divided among the members according to the shares they hold. Which money is a member's (be they he or she) to do with just as they please. They may give it to you if they choose, to be used in publishing, starting a new Community, or put into a business here or anywhere on Community principles, and they may each year add their non-preferred stock or their share of the profits to a previous gift, if they please, as well as their wages as they come from time to time to them, but each one has the right to put into the businesses each

year all of his non-preferred stock, thereby increasing his shares and his votes, as each share constitutes one vote. Should the arbiters decide that you could take out what you put in, say, from $15,000 to $20,000, you would have three or four votes to use in choosing a president and other officers, and three or four times as much money coming to you as a man like E. D. Smith who put in no money, for instance, and just so with others who put in their money.

6. All the debts of the Community (or the Four holding the property) are to be assumed by the cooperative co., releasing the Four now holding it, of liabilities, and all the property of the cooperative co. will be holden for these debts.

7. All members to have a chance to work in the different departments and are to be paid for it, but they are to work where and at what price the president and officers may choose to agree upon. And their time is to be kept by persons appointed by the president and officers to take time for the company. The wages are to be paid at such time as the president and treasurer decide upon (after deducting cost and board and other expenses) which money can be used as the person receiving it may think best. The money of minors is to be received and looked after by parents and guardians.

8. The family at Niagara to be arranged as per TRN's notes, brought by me.

9. The old who do not wish to work are to be cared for as per TRN's notes referred to above, also the children that are now in the Community.

10. No stock or shares to be sold to anyone outside of the present Community until it has been offered in a public way, so that all now in the Community may know that it is for sale, at least six months and perhaps one year, and if they do not choose to take it at its value, it can be sold outside. This was put in so that you or any others might withdraw your money and put it into a Community, or use it for publishing, or any other purpose, in a word, compelling no one to live for any length of time in a cooperative co., that does not choose to do so.

Respectfully submitted, M. H. Kinsley

This remarkable document, in its simplicity, gives some idea of the unsophisticated mind, not only of the faithful Myron but undoubtedly of many of the Community members. For years—in many cases, for all their lives—they had lived apart from the business or commercial world; they had worked in the various businesses, but they had had little or nothing to do with money. For them the Community had been an enclave wherein they lived protected, encapsulated, in a womb of safety. It is doubtful that even those who, in the recent internecine struggle, had demanded the destruction of the communal nest, had any realistic idea of what awaited them outside or how to deal with it.

John Humphrey Noyes had lived in "the World," as they called it, both before the existence of the Community and afterward, since he had left it, knew what they faced, and had warned them against it. Now he could only adjure them to move slowly and to hope for "a breeze of unanimity." Myron carried back his answer on August 19, 1880:

> To the commission and the Community: My reflections and, I trust, my inspirations, lead me to accept the plans which Myron has laid before me as being the best that we can agree upon amongst ourselves and probably better than any we could expect from an outside arbitration. I proposed arbitration only because agreement amongst ourselves seemed impossible. But if the liberal and fair spirit which seems to pervade the new plan can preside over the carrying out of it in all its details, we shall achieve a victory more splendid than any that I dared to hope for. Of course the recommendation of the commission must be followed by free thought and discussion on the part of the whole Community, and the proposed change ought not to be pushed through against the wishes of a considerable minority; but I hope for a breeze of unanimity in favor of this financial revolution like that which carried us through the social revolution of a year ago.
>
> J. H. Noyes

This communication was read and considered by the commission which voted to make a report to the Community the next day, August 20, with the following recommendations:

> 1. That the general plan which has been outlined and will follow these recommendations, be adopted, the details to be subject to such modifications as may hereafter be determined upon.
> 2. That the question of the division of the common property and determining what each one's share shall be, if it cannot be settled by discussion among ourselves, be left for three intelligent, fair-minded, and disinterested arbiters, to be selected by a commission authorized by the Community.
> 3. That as preliminary to all settlement, every member of the Community, as Mr. Noyes suggests, sign an agreement beforehand

to abide by the decision of the arbiters or such decision as may be reached among ourselves, without appeal.

4. Until the first of January next, if the settlement be not sooner effected, the control of our businesses and internal affairs be committed to "the Four" and such persons as they may associate with them—said persons to be acceptable to the commission—and the Four and their associates to have supervision of all existing boards and committees, with power to suspend any or all of them. If the settlement should not be fully effected by the first of January, the power of the Four and their associates could be prolonged by a vote of the Community.

The "Outline of the Joint Stock Plan of Settlement," as presented to the Community, contained substantially the same points which Myron's paper had made. Specific provision was made for the children, the elderly, and the invalids, as well as the offer of a guarantee of support for life to those who preferred it to the ownership of stock. It also underlined the idea that any member who preferred to live in communism under Mr. Noyes or any other leader, might do so by combining their shares and forming a Community "free from discordant elements."

It is our loss that at this time Harriet Noyes Skinner was visiting the Noyes household at Niagara, thus depriving us of her pungent comment upon the situation. Her sister-in-law, Harriet Holton Noyes, the wife of JHN, in a letter to Mr. Pitt, did give a glimpse of the Niagara scene:

After Myron had been here two days and Mr. Noyes had no light on the subject, Myron wrote him what I inclose—and Mr. Noyes virtually gave in to it. Mr. Noyes feels in very good spirits, said he felt an influx of life from the time he consented to Theodore's plan and thinks it will lead to a gathering in Canada, and he will have more freedom for missionary purposes than he has had for some years past. Myron brought a list of 110 names of adults who would be willing (should no better way be found) to leave O.C. and go somewhere with the businesses of the Trap, Hardware, Tableware, and Chain, including the Wallingford property and their share of the real and personal property, leaving the Silk, Fruit, Farm, and Horticulture to those who prefer going into cooperation or some modified form of communism at O.C. or where they may choose. W. A. Hinds got the names of sixty, including children, who would form a family at Willow Place or the Villa.

Whether "Theodore's plan" which she referred to was the grand general plan which Theodore and Frank Wayland-Smith had worked out for the change from communism to joint-stock, and which Myron had done his best to describe, or if it referred to a paper evidently brought to Niagara by Myron at this time from Theodore, and concerned only with whatever form of "family" or community his father might set up in Niagara after a breakup of the Oneida group, it is fairly certain that this paper on the status of the Niagara branch was never made public to the Oneida family nor, very possibly, ever even discussed by the Adminstrative Council or the new commission. Mr. Noyes's "influx of life" at this time is quite understandable in view of Theodore's paper and Myron's list of willing followers. Theodore's notes follow:

T. R. Noyes Notes, brought to Niagara by Myron. August 18: The following points as to the status of the Niagara branch stand broadly in my mind thus:
1. The family can consist of as many as the present family invite to join them from O.C., W.C., and no other.
2. The family to retain the right to choose its members; and to send those who become disagreeable to O.C.
3. The family to choose its own mode of life as to communism, and to administer its own internal affairs.
4. The company at O.C. to have no right of inspection except as to the manufacturing business and the safe maintenance of houses belonging to the association.
5. The association would agree to maintain business as fast as possible to give employment to all members who wish to make the Niagara branch their home for a year at a time and pay their wages in block to the Community family.
Here, the association would guarantee maintenance without work to all persons over sixty or otherwise disabled, for life, with some stated sum per year for personal expenses, and secure the payment by mortgage on all the real estate of the association. Some provision might also be included for the children now born in the Community.
Also, the liberty would be given by all who wish, to associate themselves as a Community in some part of their home buildings.

The *O.C. Journal* of August 20 reported no meeting of the Council but described the first reading of the report of the Commission: "The secretary of the commission read at some length from the minutes of its various long sessions to show the successive steps by which the conclusion was reached." The next several meetings were devoted to further readings and explanations of the text. On August 22 a recommendation for the settlement of existing differences was proposed and amended by Dr. Noyes: "Moved that the Community adopt as the first step toward the settlement of existing difficulties a reorganization in such form that the property of the Community shall be held in shares of stock."

The next evening a desire was expressed to hear, before proceeding to vote on this motion, an explanation of the other plans which had been considered by the commission. This was begun but could not be completed in one session and was put over to the next night, after which Dr. Noyes's motion was unanimously voted. This was an informal vote and

> attention was diverted to the question what salaries and wages shall obtain in the new joint-stock organization? The discussion of this question was prolonged and animated, and terminated with the almost unanimous acceptance of the following motion by W. A. Hinds:
> Resolved that in adopting a new plan of organization involving wages and dividends, it shall be with the understanding that the wages of all officials, superintendents, managers, salesmen etc., shall be moderate. Two or three only voted in the negative, and they not because they favored high wages but uniformity of wages. It was suggested and approved that outside employees shall not be paid higher wages than Community members, when the latter are willing to take their places and the directors are satisfied that the general interests of the company will not suffer by the change.

On August 24 it was settled by informal vote that if the question of the division of Community property could not be settled among the members, it be left to three arbiters to be selected by the Community. Mr. Hinds and others were unwilling to vote for the third recommendation "unless it was understood that some provision should be made by which it would be impossible for a mere majority of stockholders or directors to decide questions involving large amounts of capital, like starting a new business, building a house or factory, etc." A resolution, "some not voting on either side," resolved "that it is our wish, if it can be done legally, to have a provision requiring a three-fourths vote of the stockholders to decide questions of great importance." The third recommendation was then passed informally, without any negative votes: "That, as preliminary to all settlement, every member of the Community, as Mr. Noyes suggests, sign an agreement beforehand to abide by the decision of the arbiters, or such decisions as may be reached among ourselves, without appeal."

On the evening of August 25 the final recommendation of the commission was taken up. A substitute was offered by Mr. Hinds which provided for an "executive Committee" instead of "the Four," but this was, after some discussion, withdrawn. The recommendation, as originally offered, was passed informally without amendment.

By parliamentary rule, the commission now became defunct on making its report and a motion was then made to revive and continue it as a standing body until finally discharged. This motion was carried and it was further moved that the commission be empowered to nominate persons to act as substitutes for absentees and additional members if desirable. By general consent it was understood that a decisive vote should be taken on August 27 on the first recommendation.

22

The Agreement to Divide and Reorganize

On August 31, 1880, Mr. Hamilton both wrote and wired Mr. Noyes. The wire merely suggested Frank Wayland-Smith, Martin, and Homer as assistants to the Four during the interim; the letter amplified and explained. It also advised that both Mr. Noyes and Mr. Woolworth, who was then in Niagara, give power of attorney to someone at Oneida to act for them. Mr. Hamilton further described what was one of the last Towner attempts to direct the course of the Oneida Community. The question of the legality of organizing under the Joint Stock Act came before the meeting, and Mr. Towner, having from the beginning opposed the change, declared it to be impossible. Thereupon he went to Syracuse to confirm his opinion.

It happened that the same morning as he was returning by train from Syracuse, the party of Community men—Frank, Myron, and William Hinds—were about to board that same train en route to Utica. Mr. Towner had time to advise them that he had confirmed his opinion that the organization could not legally be done. The three committeemen nevertheless boarded the train, went to Utica and consulted Senator Kernan, who was, as Mr. Hamilton wrote Mr. Noyes, "one of the best lawyers in the state—the peer to Roscoe Conklin and a friend of Lawyer Chapman of Oneida, who had heretofore advised them." Senator Kernan satisfied the committee—including Mr. Hinds—that it *could* be done—no difficulty about it. "After this," Mr. Hamilton wrote with satisfaction, "Towner's legal opinion in the Community will not be worth much."

The following day, after the session with Kernan, three working sessions of the commission followed, in which they perfected a substitute for the four recommendations informally voted for, and in the Evening Meeting the whole was submitted to the family for its final decision. The *O.C. Journal,* August 31, 1880, only remarked further that the attendance in meeting was full, the session over two

301

hours long, the "breeze of unanimity" triumphant, and the final paper unanimously approved by the family—"it being understood that the few not voting on either side did not object."

AGREEMENT TO DIVIDE AND REORGANIZE

We, the undersigned, members of the Oneida Community, hereby covenant and agree with each other to abide by the following terms of division of ownership of property, real and personal, and of re-organization of our business and domestic affairs, whether such property be held in joint tenancy by the four Property Holders or in any other manner, except personal property acquired by individuals legitimately by means of the personal appropriations authorized by the Community, to wit:

1. A change of tenure of our property such that each adult member of the Community shall hold, in shares of stock of a Joint Stock Company to be organized under the law of New York State, passed June 21, 1875, for the formation of business corporations, that portion which shall be given or awarded to him or her.

And it is understood to be part of this plan and agreement that the manufacturing business at Wallingford, Conn., now owned by us, shall be moved to Niagara Falls as fast as it can be done by the sale, rental, or lease of the Wallingford property, which sale, rental, or lease are hereby authorized, excepting one-half acre of land and the new cottage at Cozicot. And it is agreed that a sufficient waterpower at Niagara Falls shall be secured at once, for which and other expenses involved in starting the business there, the Community is to make an advance of cash, to an amount not to exceed two thousand dollars ($2,000). (*Carried in Evening Meeting, August 31, 1880. O. H. Miller dissenting.*)

2. That now and until the first of January next, if the division and reorganization are not sooner effected, the control of our business and internal affairs be and hereby is committed to the four present property holders of the Community, and such persons as they may associate with them, said persons to be acceptable to the commission— and the four and their associates are to have supervision of all existing boards and committees, with power to suspend any or all of them. If the reorganization should not be fully completed by the first of January next, the power of the four and their associates can be prolonged by a vote of the Community. (*Carried unanimously in Evening Meeting, August 31, 1880.*)

3. To divide the present property according to some plan to be agreed upon among ourselves if, after due and earnest effort, this is found possible. For that purpose we agree that if any plan shall re-

ceive the votes of nine-tenths of the members, we will adopt it without appeal, and make the vote unanimous. If, after such effort, it is found impossible to agree upon a plan of division among ourselves, the question shall then be referred to arbiters outside the Community. These arbiters are to be chosen by the commission. (*Carried unanimously in Evening Meeting, August 31, 1880.*)

4. In order to make the dividends of the new company as large as possible, we agree to do all we can, both as stockholders and (if elected) as directors, to keep the wages paid to officers of the company and to superintendents, agents, and other employees as low as is found consistent with the most efficient management. (*Carried, August 31, 1880.*)

5. We will do all we can to secure to the present members of the Community and their children now living in the Community, wherever located in homes established by the company, certain privileges and immunities to be conferred by the company, e.g.:

1. The right to employment by the Company in preference to others not members of the Oneida Community, other things being equal.
2. The right to inhabit the dwellings belonging to the Company, at a rent no higher than will, in the total, cover their maintenance, superintendence, insurance, taxes and general care.
3. The right to purchase goods for their own individual or family consumption through the Company at wholesale rates, paying only actual cost, including transportation and legitimate expenses in buying and distribution.
4. The right to the use of a common kitchen, diningroom, laundry, library, the use and enjoyment of the lawns and common grounds, together with such common immunities and privileges as it may be found expedient to retain. (*Carried unanimously, August 31, 1880.*)

6. Opportunity will be given at the time of reorganization for certain aged and invalid members of the Community to secure, instead of stock, a guaranty from the new company binding it, under suitable conditions, to support them and give them a home for life, including care in sickness, in one or another of the homes of the company, together with a reasonable sum for clothing and incidental expenses: the said guaranty to be secured by bond and mortgage on so much of the real estate of the company as may be necessary for this purpose, or in some other satisfactory manner, until such time as the company can establish a fund which shall furnish equal security. Or, if these persons desire to live elsewhere on a guaranty, they shall be entitled

to receive in quarterly installments a sum equal to the annual cost of their living in the homes of the Company. (*Carried unanimously in Evening Meeting, August 31, 1880.*)

7. The new Company shall make a suitable annual appropriation for the support and education of every child now born and belonging to members of the Community until they become sixteen (16) years of age; said appropriations to be paid in advance in equal quarterly installments and to be expended by the parents or guardians. In case of death under sixteen, the appropriation shall cease. (*Carried unanimously.*)

8. All members of the Community who are or may be absent from O.C. during the course of this reorganization may empower others to vote for them as substitutes or proxies; but no minor has the right to vote on the terms of this reorganization. (*Carried unanimously in Evening Meeting, August 31, 1880.*)

It falls oddly—and yet nostalgically—on the eye to find in the *Journal,* September 1, 1880, after a notice that the commission was readying the foregoing paper to receive signatures, the account of a "Big family Bee at the Arcade these days, to do peaches, plums, pears etc.—mushrooms plenty in the pastures."

From Niagara Harriet Skinner wrote to Mr. Hamilton that her brother "keeps himself quite ignorant of what is going on there. I realize that you and others stand and shelter him, and that you will enter into his joy. I am sure it is the best thing he can do for you there—to keep himself in this serenity. It is continence of the highest kind. I have been very much interested to hear how Mr. Kinsley is upholden. It is certainly miraculous. Give him my love, and tell him it encourages my faith in the power of the resurrection. Myron's case, too, is wonderful. It seems as if the devil meant to kill him, but missed and only made him smarter for his work."

On September 1, 1880, 203 members signed the "Agreement to Divide and Reorganize": "In witness whereof we have hereunto set our hands on the days and months of the year 1880 indicated below: Signed, September 1, 1880."

For the next fifteen days the commission toiled away at the enormously difficult and complicated problem of implementing the agreement they had labored so long to achieve. Frank Wayland-Smith, a member of the commission, appealed on September 14 for help to Mr. Noyes:

The ticklish part of the whole business is, of course, the determining what each one's share shall be in the division. Seven plans have thus far been presented. According to the terms of the paper we have all signed, if any plan receives the votes of nine-tenths of the adult members, it shall be adopted as unanimous. In order to present clearly the point on which I wish your opinion, I will briefly sketch the seven plans of division we have before us.

The general conditions of the problem, on which all the plans are based, are these:

The Community consists of adult members	213
Between 10 and 21	13
Under 10 years	64
Total	290

Total value of property brought in by members	$144,161.44
Total years of membership, including children over 16 years	5,987 years
Total years of membership over 16 years	4,727¼ years
The capital stock of the Company is to be	$600,000

PLAN NO. 1. (BY ALFRED BARRON)

1. Each one who brought in property to first have the full value of it returned in shares of stock.

2. A sum of $20,000 to be set aside as an "equalization" or "relief" fund, to relieve a little those whom this plan nips.

3. The seventy-seven children to have each $500, on arriving at majority, in stock of the company. This calls for setting aside $38,500 in stock to be held for them until they reach their majority.

4. After restoring the original deposits and setting aside these other sums, the total amount withdrawn will be $202,661.74. Subtracting this from the capital stock, or $600,000, we have left $397,338.26. This remainder to be divided among all who are over sixteen years old, according to their term of membership after sixteen.

5. All children under sixteen to be supported and educated at the expense of the company.

PLAN NO. 2. (BY A. KINSLEY)

1. Depositors to draw out in stock all they put in.

2. The remainder to be divided according to duration of membership after sixteen years old.

3. Each child to be supported until sixteen, and then be given $100 in cash from the annual earnings of the company, as a start in life.

PLAN No. 3. (BY T. R. NOYES AND F. WAYLAND-SMITH)
(Called by everybody the "Compromise Plan")

1. One-half the property brought in by members to be returned in stock of the company.

2. The remainder to be divided according to duration of membership over sixteen years of age.

3. Each child to be supported as above and have $100 at sixteenth birthday.

PLAN No. 4. (BY J. W. TOWNER)

1. Each adult to share equally in the whole $600,000, no part of the deposits being returned to those who brought it in except as contained in their equal share. Each adult's share would be $2,446.48.

2. Each child is to take as many 1/21's of an adult's share as his years are proportioned to twenty-one.

PLAN No. 5. (BY W. A. HINDS)

1. The total property to be divided according to duration of membership without regard to age, sex, or color. This proportion explains it: As 5,987 years: the individual's years of membership, : : $600,000: the individual share.

2. Any deficiency for necessary support under sixteen, to be taken by the Company.

PLAN No. 6. (BY C. S. JOSLYN)

1. The total property to be divided according to duration of membership over sixteen. Children under sixteen to be supported by the company.

PLAN No. 7. (HANDED IN BY A. KINSLEY AND AUTHORSHIP UNKNOWN)

1. To restore *three-fourths* of the property brought in by those who brought it in.

2. The remainder to be divided and the children treated as in his Plan No. 2.

Now, the point on which I wish your opinion is in regard to the property brought in. Those who brought it seem to be quite hearty in desiring to get as much of it back as possible. This is perfectly natural, and I wish we were rich enough to do it. But unfortunately, we are not, and under Plans 1 and 2, a goodly number came out so slim that they naturally look with favor on some of the other Plans, as 4, 5, and 6. At this moment it looks as if the tussle would occur over the plan No. 3 as a "Compromise." I think that part of the Community which brought in nothing would be brought to consent to restore one-half to depositors, but many of them emphatically say that they will not go a fraction over one-half because these early depositors have the longest record of membership and draw on the remainder accordingly. They will, therefore, be the rich class, even if they get only one-half what they brought in. But Uncle Albert Kinsley says in commission that his party will never come down to one-half. He finally said he thought they ought to have at least ⅝ of what they put in, and that he, personally, would come to that but not one-half. So at present we are stuck on this ⅛ difference, and the matter will be put before the family this evening.

I must add that I think it desirable to not let in an acknowledged legal claim for the whole property put in, because of the claims of heirs of deceased depositors, outside and inside the O.C. It would surprise you to know how rapidly claims of one sort or another are developing outside. Our proposed action seems to be perfectly well known among all seceders. This is why I hope we can agree promptly among ourselves, without arbitration which would probably consume many months and some thousands of dollars and lay us open to all conceivable claims.

No written reply to this communication appears in the records. Frank Wayland-Smith commented in his journal: "It took some days to even approach agreement. Those who had joined Mr. Noyes in the early days of the Community and had put in considerable property did not at all relish the idea of dividing with a lot of impecunious newcomers equally. To help on an agreement, Dr. Noyes and I drew up a large sheet with eight long columns, showing how much each one's share would be under each plan of division. That was a work of heavy labor, but it did much to settle the matter."

The "Commission Record" for September 15, 1880, reported the outcome:

The various plans of division had been explained and discussed in general assembly of the members of the Community during several evenings previous to September 15 and two long sessions were held in the "Council Room" on the fifteenth, at which all the plans were explained to those who were present by Dr. Noyes and F. Wayland-Smith. The sheets were also exhibited so that everyone could get an idea of about how they were coming out in the division. In these ways everyone became informed, and the general leaning toward the Compromise Plan made it tolerably certain that was the only one we could agree upon amongst ourselves without putting the matter out to arbitration. Up to the 15th of September the commission had not been able to agree unanimously upon any one plan; but on that day they did, as already mentioned. When this was announced to the family at the opening of the Evening Meeting on the 15th, it did much to confirm the hesitations and procure substantial unanimity. The feeling of agreement on the "Compromise Plan" of division seemed so general that a trial vote was called for. The Question was put thus:

Voted that the "Compromise Plan" of division be adopted, its provisions being as follows, and its results substantially as in the 7th column of the sheets drawn up:

1. One-half of the value of the property brought in to be returned, in shares of stock, to those who brought it.

2. All persons who have passed their sixteenth birthday since joining the Community to have a bonus of $200, and all children now born to have a bonus of $200 each when they become sixteen years old; these sums to be issued *in stock* to all who have reached the age of sixteen years on or before January 1, 1882—after that *in cash*— to parents or guardians, from the earnings of the company.

3. The remainder of the capital stock, after satisfying the above provisions, to be divided amongst all the members over sixteen years of age according to time of membership over sixteen.

4. All children now born to be supported and educated at the expense of the company until they arrive at the age of sixteen.

5. Aged persons and invalids to have the option of a guaranty of support for life in lieu of stock, as previously agreed.

6. Widowers to have two-thirds and widows one third of the amounts brought in by themselves and their deceased partners as a credit, subject to the same rule of division as other property brought in.

The informal trial vote on the above, on the Evening Meeting of September 15, was by rising. Wm. A. Hinds and F. Wayland-Smith were appointed tellers to count heads. Absent members were quite fully represented by proxies. The feeling was so unanimus and settled in favor of the plan that a formal and binding vote was called for. Mr. J. W. Towner protested with some warmth against pushing the matter through so hastily, but as he had been absent some days on a visit to Vineland, N. J., he was less prepared than the rest of the family. It seemed desirable that final action in so important a matter should be taken while we were so well agreed, that the vote was proceeded with. The result was as follows:

VOTE ON THE COMPROMISE PLAN BY "YEA AND NAY"
EVENING MEETING, SEPT. 15, 1880

Yea	Nay	Absent	Not Voting
166	1	37	7

Supplementary Vote, Evening Meeting, Sept. 16 and 17

Yea	Nay	Absent	Not Voting
33		7	5

Summary

Persons voting Yea	199
Persons voting Nay	1
Persons not voting	5
Persons absent	7
Total number of adult members	212

The number of votes necessary to the adoption of a plan of division under clause 3 of the "Agreement to Divide and Reorganize" was 192, that being nine-tenths of the number of adults. Therefore when the number was overrun as recorded above, no further effort was made to secure the formal vote of the absentees. The announcement being publicly made that the "Compromise Plan" was adopted, the commission continued its labors with renewed courage.

Frank Wayland-Smith commented:

Only a few stood out against this plan. Sewall Newhouse, the old trapper, would not sign any paper or agree to any plan. James W. Towner objected strenuously to adopting the plan until more time had been given to study it, but he was disregarded. Only two persons chose the guaranty of support for life to shares of stock. These were Mr. H. W. Warne and Miss Henrietta Sweet, an ancient and acidulated maiden.

It was decided to organize as a "limited liability" company, under the style, "Oneida Community, Limited." The capital stock was put at $600,000. We worked away for a long time at the details of the new system. One point that required much attention was to so arrange matters that no one should be allowed to subscribe until he or she had signed a release to the four property holders of the Community, and an agreement to let all bygones be bygones, cutting off all legal claims based on the past, and assenting to certain conditions as to the control of the stock. On these points there was much disagreement, and it looked at one time as if the whole reorganization would fall through. A few of the most bitter and selfish persons took counsel of James W. Towner how they might stay the proceedings. Towner himself did not like the proposed form of release. He openly said in Evening Meeting that he wanted to be left free to institute a libel suit after the settlement.

But a large majority were for pushing ahead, so, after taking careful counsel of Hon. Francis Kernan of Utica, it was voted that the following paper should be signed by every adult before he or she was allowed to subscribe. The form of receipt and release was drawn by Mr. Kernan.

"Received of John H. Noyes, Erastus Hamilton, William H. Woolworth, and Charles Otis Kellogg, a co-partnership doing business under the firm name of the Oneida Community, the several sums set opposite our respective names being ten per cent of the value of the share or part of the property of the said Community awarded to the subscribers respectively in the plan of division of property adopted and accepted on or about September 15th, 1880, which said share or part the subscribers severally agree to accept in full settlement and satisfaction of all claims demands or causes of action of every nature whatsoever either in law or equity against the members of the said co-partnership and each or any of them and against such members of the Community or Association known as the Oneida Community of which the said co-partnership is the business representative, who have signed this instrument. And for a valuable consideration by each received from the others, the parties hereto mutually release and discharge each other of and from all claims, demands and causes of action whatever concerning or touching property or rights of property or personal injuries or torts, which either or any of them may have against the others or any of the other subscribers hereto.

Dated and sealed, November   1880."

The second paper required to be signed by everyone before subscribing for stock was the

AGREEMENT AS TO CONTROL OF STOCK

"We, the subscribers, proposing to organize a business corporation to be called 'Oneida Community, Limited,' do hereby covenant and agree one with another and each for himself as future stockholders of said company, as follows:

First. That any of the shares of stock owned and held by us, or either of us, may be sold, given or otherwise conveyed to any other stockholder of said corporation, or to any person, either minor or adult, who is, at the time of the organization of said corporation a member of the society known as the Oneida Community, at any time after said stock shall have been fully paid for, without notice, at the pleasure of the owner or holder.

Second. That for the purpose of guarding against such transfers and conveyances of stock as might embarrass or injure the said Corporation, we will not sell, give, pledge, or otherwise convey, or offer for sale or pledge, or make a contract to sell, give, pledge, or otherwise convey any of our stock in said corporation which we hold or own or have any control of, to any person outside of, or who does not own any stock in the said Corporation and who was not at the time of the organization of said corporation, a member of the society known as Oneida Community, for a period of three years from the first subscription for said stock, without the consent of two-thirds of the Board of Directors of said corporation.

Third. That if, at any time after the said period of three years shall have expired we desire to sell, give, pledge or otherwise convey our stock or any part of the same, we will give to the President or Secretary of said corporation—who is to notify all the stockholders by suitable written or printed notice—at least sixty days notice in writing of our intention to sell, or otherwise convey the same and we will sell or transfer the same to any of the stockholders on payment to us or offering payment to us of real value of said stock within the period of sixty days.

Fourth. That in case of disagreement between contracting parties as to the real value of the stock, of the said Oneida Community, Limited, then the decision shall be left to three arbiters, one of whom may be chosen by the person wishing to sell, another by the Board of Directors of said corporation, and the third by these two: and their decision or that of a majority of them shall be conclusive as to the real value of said stock."

A final comment by Frank Wayland-Smith concludes the story: "Although a few gave out that they would never sign these documents, yet when the time came to subscribe for stock and they saw that there was no such thing as getting the stock without signing the documents, they wilted and signed, all but the old trapper Sewell Newhouse who was too foxy to sign anything. So he did not draw his share of stock, but C. O. Kellogg, one of the Four, took it to hold until Newhouse was more tractable. The business of subscribing passed off without the least disturbance and the new company was soon fully organized."

At the meeting for the election of Directors, held in November 1880, the following nine persons were chosen to serve for the next year: Theodore R. Noyes, Erastus Hamilton, Alfred Barron, Martin Kinsley, Charles Otis Kellogg, Myron H. Kinsley, George Campbell, James W. Towner, and George D. Allen.

After getting the final certificate of incorporation from the Secretary of State at Albany, on November 20, 1880, the Directors proceeded to elect officers, as follows: E. H. Hamilton, President; George Campbell, treasurer; Alfred Barron, Secretary.

So ended the Oneida Community.

> Time present and time past
> Are both perhaps present in time future,
> And time future contained in time past.
>
> T. S. ELIOT, *Burnt Norton*

Epilogue

"Time past," one might say, came to an end on January 1, 1881, and "time future," which had been contained in "time past," began its new life on that day as "time present." A new life, a new way of being, Community no longer but separation and each individual for himself.

Tiny Aunt Julia Ackley who had come with her husband in 1847 to join Jonathan Burt in the little group on Oneida Creek which grew into the Oneida Community, wrote in her diary on January 1, 1881: "We are all joint stock today but I don't see but I can be just as thankful as I ever was." Two days later she wrote: "A good many have gone to work today that haven't done but precious little for months and months." She also recorded a strange new experience: "Bought the first spool of thread today that I have bought in the Community thirty-three years."

Jessie Kinsley, so young and so delightful, moved to Niagara with her new husband, Myron, and her new baby, and, as she wrote many years later: "I was most unsophisticated and green. Our hired girl, Maggie, was often imagined by strangers to be the mistress because she wore fine clothes and had assurance. I would always forget to use money which I then handled for the *first time*."

Harriet Worden wrote in her diary: "The New Year has begun and we now bid adieu to communism and Monday we will enter 'O.C. Limited' with all its terrors. I have no pleasure in the contemplated change—instead, my outlook is not especially cheering."

It is not surprising that for some, especially women like Harriet who were left with no husband and several small children, the prospect did hold terrors. The new company had actually made provision for them, but it was certainly not lavish. There were hard days ahead for many of them—and even, as it happened, hard days

312

for the new company which was launched with such high hopes. The new officers and directors were honest, intelligent, and devoted men, but their only business experience had been in the management of a Communistic organization. Now, in the cold world of individualistic modern enterprise, they found problems never before encountered.

A thousand questions must be answered, problems solved. What dividends could the company pay its stockholders? What salaries should employees be paid? One-and-a-half percent on the capital stock was voted for the first quarter of 1881, and the salaries of the three officers were: president, $1,000; secretary, $800; treasurer, $800. The first plan was to pay all superintendents $3.00 per day; second and third assistants, $2.50 and $2.25 respectively; but this was later changed to a salary basis of $900, $750, and $650 per annum.

H. V. Noyes, in "A History of the Oneida Community, Limited," recorded that "this first year was a strenuous one so far as the Board [of Directors] was concerned. The new financial responsibility to stockholders and the whole business of organizing both the profit departments and the tag ends left over from the old Community kept the Directors feverishly busy. It is safe to say that more Board meetings were held in 1881 than in any other year in the history of the O.C.L. Daily meetings at 4 P.M. were the rule during the first few months." Of the next year he wrote: "Directors' Meetings were held much less frequently in 1882 and discussions were less prolonged. It would appear that by this time the O.C.L. had become fairly well organized and all details were left to the various departments, the Board concerning itself only with major general problems." He also added that "net earnings before dividends during this ten year period 1881–1891 averaged about 7½ percent and dividends paid averaged slightly less than 6 percent. Apparently no real business progress was made in the first ten or twelve years of the Oneida Community, Limited."

1883 and 1884 were depression years, business slow to bad. In this year Mr. Hamilton retired. The H. V. Noyes manuscript remarked that "there is a tradition that Mr. Hamilton was advised by J. H. Noyes to withdraw voluntarily. Mr. Noyes was still leader in control, and he probably thought the best interests of the O.C.L.

would be served by a change at this time. It was apparently agreed that Mr. Hamilton should step out and Mr. Campbell, who had been treasurer, should take his place."

At this time the trap business was the principal breadwinner in the company, with the silk business next and the tableware business, located in Niagara Falls, just beginning to be a good earner. The fruit-canning business at Kenwood was a steady if small enterprise, and it is amusing to note that, as though their present diversity of manufactures was not enough, during these years the O.C.L. toyed with other lines as foreign to them as the making of lace-paper doilies, nickel trimmings for Pullman cars, and a patent lamp, none of which enterprises came to fruition. There were also a number of small departments left as heritage from the old Community; the farm with a large dairy of purebred cows, the carpentry shop, a livery stable, and, of course, the upkeep of the Community buildings.

In 1886 John Humphrey Noyes died, and his death, as his son Holton Noyes wrote, "left his spiritually minded followers leaderless —his flock without a shepherd, as Business management had been combined with spiritual considerations during the entire history of the Oneida Community and the O.C.L. up to this time. It was, perhaps, only natural and to be expected that the termination of so long and so personal a leadership should result in a chaotic period."

Specifically, there was a new contentiousness in the election of each year's Board members. In 1887, a "hot contest"; in 1888, a number of ballots were first thrown out as defective, then admitted and counted. Although business that year was 14 percent behind the year before, the usual dividend was declared, and it was voted to begin the manufacture of chain in Canada. The election of 1889 was really a stormy one, with the Inspectors of Election counting the votes *"behind closed doors."* Mr. John R. Lord was elected president, and at the directors' meeting which followed, the secretary recorded that "a purpose to recognize God in our business was expressed and cordially endorsed by all." The village name "Community" was formally changed to "Kenwood."

The H. V. Noyes manuscript described the difficult situation then existing:

A peculiar political situation had arisen at this time, one which would be difficult perhaps for businessmen of the present day to conceive of. Since the death of J. H. Noyes in 1886, the people of the Oneida Community Limited who, it must be remembered, were formerly members of the Oneida Community and to whom religious considerations had always been of greater importance than business matters, had been floundering around in a leaderless maze of religious experience. Many had taken up ordinary church religion and some had taken up spiritualism with its possibilities of communication with the dead. These spiritualists, through their "mediums" actually claimed to have daily messages from J. H. Noyes and other departed Communists. Many very worthy people took up with this spiritualistic movement, and spiritualism, like all other religious cults, is intolerant of disagreement, so that in 1890, O.C.L. politics had very little to do with business matters. There were two parties—the spiritualists and the anti-spiritualists.

Suffice it to say that the situation did exist and that the so-called spiritualists were in control of the company's affairs for a few years. Only a few years later, the coming of the new generation with its virile leadership changed the Oneida Community, Ltd., and entirely released it from its religious background, substituting a social theory of business.

Probably never before in the history of the company had there been so sharp a political battle as this election. During the year 1894, Pierrepont Noyes (a son of John Noyes) had made a very complete study of O.C.L. affairs, both political and commercial. He became convinced that the business provided a foundation for unlimited development and earning power. He exercised his director's prerogative (or duty) and personally investigated each department in detail. In the course of these investigations he came upon certain conditions which convinced him that a complete political change was necessary and also possible. He therefore set about a campaign for proxies in the course of which he personally interviewed nearly every stockholder, going in many cases considerable distances and visiting out-of-the-way corners. In the campaign he had the support and active assistance of many others, but he, himself, engineered it, and provided the necessary ammunition and follow-through. The result was so much a personal victory that he immediately came to be regarded as the leader of the new party. This party had no religious entanglements; it stood only for the business advancement of the O.C.L. and the preservation of Home and Society at Kenwood.

When the Board organized, Dr. Theodore Noyes was elected president by a strict party vote of five to four. Within a very short time, practically all members of both of the old parties became enthusiastic supporters of the new management and political parties entirely disappeared. The spirit of compromise and internal harmony became a fixed and basic pillar in the O.C.L. structure. Older members of both political parties, after fourteen years of turmoil, settled down with relief to peaceful enjoyment of the new harmony.

Since this book cannot be a history of the new Oneida Community, Limited, it will be enough to say here that the new company grew and thrived through good times and bad, for the next seventy-five years. New generations succeeded old, old businesses were discarded, new ones were introduced. From a corporation of $600,000 in 1895 it grew to the astonishing figure of $71,000,000 in 1972. Factories multiplied, employees multiplied by ten. Foreign branches were established, the name was changed to Oneida Limited, Silversmiths.

What has remained of the old, after nearly a hundred years since the breakup? Some buildings; the Mansion House, looking from the outside very much as it did in 1880; the lovely lawns and gardens where a hundred years ago excursionists descended from the Midland Railroad (now defunct) to wander under the trees and eat strawberry shortcake in the diningroom or attend an entertainment in the Big Hall. There is a Historical Society Museum where many of the artifacts of the old Community may be seen, along with some of the short dresses worn by the women of the Community. There are photographs. There are books and bound periodicals from an early date.

More than all this, I hope and believe, there is a something different, a trace of the old Community spirit which believed not only in Salvation from Sin but in equality and fraternity, which believed that it was possible to create a family of three hundred— or nowadays, of three thousand—who would share equitably and stand together. That, which is our heritage whether or not we claim it, is our most valuable legacy from those earnest men and women who lived together happily for a quarter of a century and, when that was no longer possible, agreed to return to what they had learned to call "the World." The breaking of those intimate and cherished ties makes a sad story to at least one of their descendants, but leaves her, nevertheless, proud of her heritage.

Bibliography

BOOKS

Abolition of Death. A chapter in John Humphrey Noyes's *The Berean,* which was printed at the office of the *Spiritual Magazine* in Putney, Vt., in 1847. The section of the chapter printed is titled "Hints to Philanthropists." Privately printed by Jack T. Ericson, 1970.

American Communities: Brief Sketches of Economy, Zoar, Bethel, Aurora, Icaria, the Shakers, Oneida, Wallingford, and the Brotherhood of the New Life, by William Alfred Hinds. Oneida: Office of the *American Socialist,* 1878; 2nd rev. ed., 1908.

First Annual Report of the Oneida Association: Exhibiting its History, Principles, and Transactions to January 1, 1849. Published by order of the Association. Oneida Reserve: Leonard and Co., printers, 1849.

Second Annual Report of the Oneida Association: Exhibiting its Progress to February 20, 1850. Published by order of the Association. Oneida Reserve: Leonard and Co., printers, 1850.

Third Annual Report of the Oneida Association: Exhibiting its Progress to February 20, 1851. Published by order of the Association. Oneida Reserve: Leonard and Co., printers, 1851.

The Berean: A Manual for the Help of Those Who Seek the Faith of the Primitive Church, by John Humphrey Noyes. Putney, Vt.: Office of *The Spiritual Magazine,* 1847.

The Bible Argument: Defining the Role of the Sexes in the Kingdom of Heaven, by John Humphrey Noyes. Reprinted from the *First Annual Report of the Oneida Association,* 1849.

Bible Communism, a compilation from the annual reports and other publications of the Oneida Association and its branches. Brooklyn: Office of the *Circular,* 1853.

The Burned-Over District: The Social and Intellectual History of Enthusiastic Religion in Western New York, 1800–1880, by Whitney R. Cross. New York: Harper Torch Books, 1950.

Communistic Societies of the United States. The Classic Eye-Witness Report of the Economists, Zoarites, Shakers, Amana, Oneida, Bethel, Aurora, Icarian, and Other Utopian Communities that Flourished in 19th-Century America, by Charles Nordhoff. New York: originally published 1875; republished by Hillary House, 1961.

Confessions of John H. Noyes, by John Humphrey Noyes. Oneida Reserve: Leonard and Co., printers, 1849.

317

The Days of My Youth, by Corinna Ackley Noyes. Oneida: privately published, 1960.

Dixon and His Copyists, by John Humphrey Noyes. Oneida: Oneida Community, 1871–74.

Essay on Scientific Propagation, by John Humphrey Noyes. Oneida: Oneida Community, n.d.

The First Hundred Years, 1848–1948, by Walter D. Edmunds, with photographs by Samuel Chamberlain. Oneida: privately published by Oneida Ltd., 1948.

Heavens on Earth: Utopian Communities in America, 1680–1880, by Mark Holloway. New York: Dover Publications, 1966.

A Goodly Heritage, by Pierrepont Burt Noyes. New York: Rinehart, 1958.

A History of American Socialisms, by John Humphrey Noyes. Philadelphia: Lippincott, 1870.

Home Talks, by John Humphrey Noyes. Alfred Barron and George Noyes Miller, eds. Oneida: Oneida Community, 1875.

John Humphrey Noyes: The Putney Community, George Wallingford Noyes, ed. Oneida, 1931.

Male Continence, by John Humphrey Noyes. Office of the *American Socialist.*

My Father's House: An Oneida Boyhood, by Pierrepont Burt Noyes. New York: Farrar and Rinehart, 1937.

Old Mansion House Memories, by One Brought Up in It, by Harriet M. Worden. Oneida: privately published, 1950; a reprint from articles in the *Circular,* 1871–72.

Oneida: Utopian Community to Modern Corporation, by Maren Lockwood Carden. Baltimore: The Johns Hopkins Press, 1969.

The Oneida Community: A Record of an Attempt to Carry Out the Principles of Christian Unselfishness and Scientific Race-Improvement, by Allan Eastlake. London, 1900.

Paul's Prize, report of a Home-Talk, by John Humphrey Noyes, n.d.

The Religious Experience of John Humphrey Noyes, George Wallingford Noyes, ed. New York: Macmillan, 1923.

Salvation from Sin: The End of Christian Faith, by John Humphrey Noyes. Oneida: Oneida Community, 1876.

A Yankee Saint: John Humphrey Noyes and the Oneida Community, by Robert Allerton Parker. New York: Putnam's, 1935.

PAMPHLETS

"Christ Came As Promised," by John H. Cragin. Kenwood, N.Y., copyright 1895.

"Did Jesus Teach That It Is Right To Be Rich?" A Critical Enquiry by John

H. Freeman, lifelong member of the world-famous Oneida Community, and now Assistant-Treasurer of the Oneida Community, Limited, n.d.

"Faith Facts: Or A Confession of the Kingdom of God and the Age of Miracles," George Cragin, ed. Oneida Reserve: Leonard and Co., printers, 1850.

"A Gynecological Study of the Oneida Community," by Ely Van de Warker. *American Journal of Obstetrics and Diseases of Women and Children,* Vol. XVII (1881).

"Health Report of Oneida Community Children," by T. R. Noyes. Oneida Community, August 1878.

"Mutual Criticisms." Oneida: Office of the *American Socialist,* 1876.

"The Oneida Community," by Constance Noyes Robertson. Reprinted from *New York History,* April 1949.

"The Oneida Community," by Constance Robertson. Privately printed, n.d.

"Oneida Community As It Was and Is," by Felix Shay. Reprinted from *Roycroft.* Melbourne: The Specialty Press Pty. Ltd.

"The Oneida Community, A Dialogue," by Henry J. Seymour, one of the original members, n.d.

"The Oneida Community Experiment in Stirpiculture," by Hilda Herrick Noyes, M.D., and George Wallingford Noyes, A.B. Reprinted from *Eugenics, Genetics, and the Family,* Vol. I (1923).

"The Origin of the Oneida Community or the Corporation of Bible Perfectionists at Putney, Vt." n.d.

"Outline of Bible Theology." Extracted from a letter by a lady to the New York *World,* June 2, 1889, leaflet 30A.

"Seventeen Reasons for Believing that the Second Coming of Christ is Past," n.d.

PERIODICALS

The *American Socialist.* Oneida, March 30, 1876–December 25, 1879.

The *Circular,* J. H. Noyes, ed. Brooklyn, November 6, 1851–October 12, 1854.

The *Circular.* Oneida, January 25, 1855–February 2, 1864.

The *Circular,* by Oneida and Wallingford Communities, March 12, 1864–March 9, 1868.

The *Circular,* by Oneida Community, March 23, 1868–March 9, 1876.

Free Church Circular. Oneida Reserve, February 20, 1851–July 15, 1851.

The Perfectionist and Theocratic Watchman, J. H. Noyes and J. L. Skinner, eds. Putney, Vt., March 22, 1845–February 14, 1846.

The Spiritual Magazine. Putney, Vt., March 15, 1847–November 23, 1847.

The Spiritual Magazine. Oneida Reserve, August 5, 1848–January 17, 1850.

The Spiritual Moralist, J. H. Noyes and G. Cragin, eds. Putney, Vt., June 13, 1843 (one number bound with the *Witness*).

The Witness, by John H. Noyes. Ithaca, N.Y., August 20, 1837–September 23, 1837.

The Witness. Putney, Vt., November 21, 1838–January 18, 1843.

Index

Abbott, Daniel: on women and children, 230; 251

Ackley family, 4

Ackley, Harriet, and Children's House, 263

Ackley, Julia C.: notebooks of, *xiv;* 312

Administrative Council (1879): members, 122; Myron Kinsley's report on, 133–34; on social etiquette, 166

Administrative Council (1880): criticizes *Pinafore,* 228; on the Four, 285; on home for JHN, 225; substitutions, for, 260–61; *see also* Chapters 14 and 15

Agnosticism, 19, 37

Allen, George D.: Administrative Council (1879), 122; Administrative Council (1880), 210

Allen, Harriet E.: Administrative Council (1879), 122; Administrative Council (1880), 210; on children, 255; on Complex Marriage, 156

Allen, Henry G., donates Wallingford property, 8

American Communities, 71

American Socialist: end of, 186–87; first appearance of, 12, 44; on end of Complex Marriage, 161, 165; rebuttal to New York *Times,* 71–73

Andover, 1

Anthony, Nora, *xv*

Atwell, Charles B., 80

Bailey, Ann Sophronia Hobart: accuses Theodore Noyes, 57; accuses FW-S, 57; and Joseph Skinner, 52, 67–68, 93; and TRN, 8, 37–38; confession of, 62–63; criticized by JHN, 58–63; description of, 52; O.C. dissatisfaction with, 57; *see also* Chapter 3

Bailey, Daniel: leaves O.C., 52; 24–26, 37, 62

Barron, Alfred: Noyesite, 13, 148–49; on Complex Marriage, 212; on the Four, 284–85; on joint stock, 203; plan for division, 305

Barron, Helen Miller: Administrative Council (1879), 122; Administrative Council (1880), 210; 13

Barron, Homer, Noyesite, 13

The Battle-Axe and Weapons of War, 2–3, 275

Beard, A. F., 78, 85

"Bee," 8

Berlin Heights, Ohio, free-love community, 19, 141

Berry, Assemblyman, 98–99, 104

Bible Communists, 1, 14, 291

Bloom, Clarence, 263

Bolles Mary: Administrative Council (1879), 122; Administrative Council (1880), 210

"Boston influence," 24

Breakup, reasons for, 14–21

Brooklyn Commune, 8, 10

Burnham, A. S., Administrative Council (1880), 210

Burnham, Edwin S.: on propagation, 214; Third party member, 13, 207; 101

Burnham, Henry W.: Administrative Council (1879), 122; Administrative Council (1880), 210; leads Bible classes, 46, 67; on Complex Marriage, 157; on William Woolworth, 40; Townerite, 12, 107

Burt, Charles: O.C. salesman, 257; 94, 131

Burt, Jonathan: on personal appropriations, 231; 4, 312

Bushnell, Candace, leads Bible classes, 46

321